MASTERS OF THE TURF

MASTERS OF THE TURF

TEN TRAINERS WHO DOMINATED
HORSE RACING'S GOLDEN AGE

BY EDWARD L. BOWEN

EP
ECLIPSE
PRESS

Lexington, Kentucky

Library of Congress Cataloging-in-Publication Data

Bowen, Edward L.
    Masters of the turf : ten trainers who dominated horse racing's golden age / by Edward L. Bowen. -- 1st ed.
        p. cm.
    ISBN-13: 978-1-58150-149-0 (hardcover)
    ISBN-10: 1-58150-149-8 (hardcover)
    1. Racehorse trainers--United States--Biography. 2. Horsemen and horse-women--United States--Biography. 3. Horse racing--United States. I. Title.
    SF336.A2B694 2007
    798.40092'2--dc22
    [B]

                                                                2006029728

Printed in the United States.
First Edition: 2007

Distributed to the trade by
National Book Network
4501 Forbes Blvd., Suite 200, Lanham, MD 20706
1.800.462.6420

A Division of
Blood-Horse Publications
Publishers Since 1916

TABLE OF CONTENTS

INTRODUCTION

~~~~~~◦~~~~~~

This volume focuses on trainers of Thoroughbred racehorses. In selective narrowing of that focus, the author and the staff of Eclipse Press concentrated on great horsemen of the early decades of the twentieth century.

The longevity of horsemen is evidence that the backstretch has certain salubrious aspects. The combination of required outdoor presence, physical activity, and the pulse-exciting gamut of victory and defeat seems to promote long lives. While there are sad exceptions, most of the subjects herein had lengthy lives, regardless of whether concepts of healthy living guided their lifestyles away from the barn.

Each of the trainers celebrated in this volume was active during the 1920s. In several cases that decade represented the conclusion of a career, while in the case of, say, Hirsch Jacobs, the 1920s was a roaring beginning. Thus, we have here a collection of horsemen whose lives crossed paths within that one decade but whose careers on American racetracks spanned a century, from the 1870s to the 1970s.

Part of the justification for longevity's being seen as a measure of greatness is that the sport of racing requires adjustment to different situations. Give a sport a century, and changes will occur. As racing changes, so must its star horsemen if they are to remain on top. The corollary is that, as in most endeavors, the word "great" is equated with the phrase "to stand the test of time." Brief success, however spectacular, rates the B word (brilliant) and not the G word (great).

Certainly, the great trainers in this volume stood the test of time and also answered the challenge of change. Sometimes the change resulted from altering their own place within the structure; sometimes it was a change in structure itself.

Consider:

• The four-mile heats, testing mature runners of James Rowe's days as a stripling jockey contrasted with the two-year-old sprinting futurities of Rowe's later days as a trainer. Similarly, the status of the Futurity itself illustrates the phenomenon of change. The Futurity's status as the ultimate among American two-year-old races was altered by a richer middle distance race. In 1953 the mile and one-sixteenth Garden State Stakes, for two-year-olds, became the richest Thoroughbred race for any age group or at any distance in the world. The best stables jumped to it, as they had when the Futurity was created in 1888, and the juvenile scene suddenly was altered.

• Ben Jones (with his son Jimmy), whose early success had depended on quick-maturing sprinters, won that Garden State Stakes with Barbizon. However, the Joneses eventually would place their greatest stamp on the mile and a quarter Kentucky Derby.

• Hirsch Jacobs and Guy Bedwell graduated from managing stables of a great number of winners to managing stables of a number of great winners.

• Jacobs and John E. Madden took change another step by creating fashionable breeding operations as outgrowths from their days when workaday wins were the expedient just to pay the feed man.

• Sam Hildreth and Preston Burch were uprooted from America to train in France and got along rather well in what surely were bizarre circumstances from their points of view.

• The ten chapters (Jones father and son are combined in one chapter) in this volume address horsemen of common excellence built upon divergent backgrounds. To some of them, a life around horses was the most natural of concepts. Others were led to the horse by happenstance — and the financial necessity to succeed at something.

As youths, Hildreth and Bedwell were Western cowboys of sorts, and Preston Burch was the son of a trainer. Rowe and Sunny Jim Fitzsimmons broke in as Eastern jockeys while Max Hirsch was a runaway Texan who also became an Eastern jockey. Madden was a scuffler who broke into racing with trotters, as did Derby Dick Thompson. Ben Jones was a cattle rancher's son, longing to deal with horses. In contrast, Hirsch Jacobs was the Brooklyn-born son of an occasional racegoer.

Each one learned, or honed, the arcane specialty of training glorious animals to create glorious moments. Such moments thrill afternoon crowds, who can appreciate the glory and marvel at the achievement. What enthralls these crowds are masters, man and horse — Masters of the Turf.

CHAPTER 1

JAMES ROWE SR.

In fifty years James Rowe trained thirty-two champions. Nobody else in the history of the American Turf can make such a claim or have it made on their behalf. True, what constitutes a champion is a concept requiring considerable explanation and interpretation, but even given the changing standards of the term, Rowe stands tall indeed.

In 1936 *Daily Racing Form* began a formal vote to designate champions in various age/sex divisions. In 1950 the Thoroughbred Racing Associations began conducting a vote on its own, and from time to time American Thoroughbred racing might have duplicate champions. Among examples, Bold Ruler and Dedicate split the honor of Horse of the Year in 1957, as did Moccasin and Roman Brother in 1965 and Fort Marcy and Personality in 1970.

Beginning in 1971, the Eclipse Award format unified the *Racing Form* and TRA polls and also incorporated the National Turf Writers Association. Since then, there has been one Horse of the Year per season, and jimmying of procedures has more or less eliminated ties in the various divisions.

Well, starting with 1936 as the dawn of "official" championships meant that a great deal of American Turf history existed in a sort of limbo. Not long before the advent of the Eclipse Awards, Kent Hollingsworth, then editor of *The Blood-Horse*, pored over the history of racing as passed down by such stalwart journalists/historians as John Hervey, Walter Vosburgh, Joseph A. Estes, and Joe Palmer. Based on his conclusions relative to their opinions, Hollingsworth published in *The Great Ones* a list of division and overall champions (Horse of the Year) starting with 1870.

The Blood-Horse from time to time has published this list, which in many circles had taken on the imprimatur of officialdom. There are individuals within the racing press today who will actually use the phrase "voted Horse of the Year" about some long ago beast who predated by many years anything that could be reasonably called a vote. The late Hollingsworth would be pleased by the credibility assigned his efforts, while at the same time aggrieved by the sloppiness of reporting and general lack of understanding that everything prior to 1936 should be looked upon as different from votes commencing in that year.

To put Rowe's thirty-two champion racehorses into perspective, perhaps it is useful to point out that, through 2005, the prolific modern trainer D. Wayne Lukas had trained twenty-four Eclipse Award winners. Further driving home the point, consider that if all the Calumet Farm champions in the era of the Jones boys had been credited to the father, Ben A. Jones, rather than split between him and son Jimmy, the old man's total for Calumet would have been an even dozen champions — slightly more than one-third of Rowe's total. (Jones also had an earlier champion, Inscoelda.)

Less than a decade before he trained his first champions, Rowe was riding horses of equal merit. He was the leading rider in America from 1871 to 1873, and his mounts included illustrious heroes such as Harry Bassett, Joe Daniels, and Abd-El-Kooree. Rowe lived until 1929, active to the last, so that it truly could be said that he was associated with top Thoroughbreds for nearly sixty years.

What changes in the racing game he saw! The young stripling who excelled in heat racing and four-mile "dashes" had, by the end of his career as a trainer, won ten editions of a contrasting phenomenon, the Futurity, a six and a half-furlong race for two-year-olds, which was at one time the richest of all races. He also lived to see, and help create, the enormous national prestige of the Kentucky Derby, a race that did not exist when he was first involved on the Turf.

CIGARS AND PEPPERMINTS

Rowe was born in the environs of Richmond, Virginia, in 1857. As a small child, he might have been vaguely aware of the start of the Civil War four years later but likely had some inkling about current events by its conclusion (1865). What may well have escaped him was that the impetus of the sport of horse racing was shifting from the South to the North. In 1866, Jerome Park opened in New York, ushering in an era of opulence at Eastern racetracks. The pride of place of New York racing within the overall shape of the American Turf has been challenged from time to time since then, but the aura of New York as the "Big Apple" has continually bobbed to the top.

The often-repeated story line is that Rowe was working for a newsstand, selling cigars and whatnots, at the Exchange Hotel in Richmond when Colonel David McDaniel spotted the lad as the right size to be an apprentice rider and took him into his stable. Rowe would have been about ten at the time.

New York Times columnist Red Smith once stated as fact that Rowe's reward for his first winning ride was "peppermint candy and permission to stay up until 9 o'clock in the evening."

In *The Great Ones* Hollingsworth describes McDaniel as "the most noted horseman of the East. He owned the racetrack at Secaucus, N.J., and maintained a stud farm nearby. His stable topped the owners' list from 1870 through 1874." McDaniel's stable, and its attendant action in the betting rings, generated frequent use of the phrase the "McDaniel Confederacy" — surely a touchy phrase in that era.

When McDaniel recruited young James Rowe, cigar and newspaper peddler, several permutations of the Turf were at play. As stated above, Rowe would become a leading jockey and then a consummate trainer. Frank McCabe would have second call in McDaniel's stable and in later years would be the assistant to Rowe the trainer; he would then succeed Rowe as trainer for the Dwyer brothers. In the meantime, growing up under McDaniel's roof was the son to be known eventually as "Uncle Henry" McDaniel. This member of the family was trainer of Rey El Santa Anita when he beat Domino in the 1894 American Derby and trainer of Exterminator when he won the 1918 Kentucky Derby.

By the time Rowe was about fourteen he had been astride his first great horse, illustrating his great fortune at being taken under McDaniel's wing rather than almost any other Turfman. The horse was Harry Bassett, the champion three-year-old when he won all his nine races in 1871. Among Rowe's wins on him that year were his victories in the Jerome, Kenner, and Dixie. Harry Bassett eventually extended his winning streak to fourteen. He was a son of the great stallion Lexington, sixteen times America's leading sire.

Highlights of Rowe's role in Harry Bassett's racing glories at four included his victory in the two and one-quarter-mile Saratoga Cup in 1872. Harry Bassett defeated John Harper's Longfellow, whom Turf historian Vosburgh wrote of as "beyond question the most celebrated horse of the 1870s." Longfellow struck himself on the left fore hoof going to the post, and the bent shoe crimped under the hoof, partially crippling him by the time his valiant efforts were finished. Harper retired him. The thought that Harry Bassett's victory was thus a hollow one is tempered by the fact that his and young Rowe's time for the race, 3:59, was the fastest then on record for the distance. Harry Bassett and Longfellow are listed as co-champion handicap horses for the year.

Rowe won the Travers at Saratoga the same year as well as the Belmont Stakes, aboard Joe Daniels. Rowe won his second consecutive Belmont Stakes, with Springbok, but his pair of victories as a jockey was to pale in comparison to the record eight he would win as a trainer.

Details of another victory by Rowe the jockey are preserved in a lengthy reminiscence in the old *Live Stock Record* of 1895. Therein, the author — unidentified — muses:

> I can see now in my mind's eye Col. McDaniel, short of stature, his gray locks conspicuous, as he stumped along with his inevitable cane, giving little "Jimmie" Rowe his orders. The old Colonel would always take his jockey (when) at Jerome Park over to the grass by the water jump under the big tree between the bluff track and the home-stretch. Here he would lay out the plans to be followed, emphasizing and directing the boy's attention with his cane, which he would wield so vigorously in his earnestness that most of his boys would watch the stick more than the old Colonel, as if he might make a mistake and bring it down on their backs. And little "Jimmy" Rowe, a small lad even for his age, would look up at the old Colonel and nod assent to each and every direction and wave of that famous stick.

Central memory of this article was of "Little Jimmy's" victory on Abd-El-Koree in a four-mile race at Jerome in 1871. Rowe moved quickly enough to get the jump on the renowned Billy Hayward, aboard Helmbold. The latter came back to challenge. Rowe could ride at ninety-five pounds, which the three-year-old carried that day, getting nineteen pounds from the older Helmbold.

"With Rowe holding Koree together with the skill of a veteran," the Mc-Daniel horse held off Helmbold to win by a neck. The time of 7:33 was a world record for a three-year-old.

The race stamped Abd-El-Koree as top class, but "little Rowe came in for even greater credit than the horse, one of the first to commend the lad being Bill Hayward, his opponent. It was a great race, won by a gallant colt and a clever lad."

BARNUM AND THE DWYERS

Despite his diminutive stature, the "maturity" of later teen years' weight speedily brought Rowe's days as a jockey to a close. Leaving the influence of one of the characters of the Turf, Rowe fell in with another character, known in other circles. This was P.T. Barnum. The connection occurred before Barnum's name (posthumously) became associated with the lasting title in the circus world, to wit, Ringling Brothers & Barnum and Bailey. However, Barnum had employed the hyperbole "The Greatest Show on Earth" for his spectacular productions as early as 1872. At the time Jimmy Rowe was forced out of the saddle as a Thoroughbred jockey, Barnum had opened P.T. Barnum's Great Roman Hippodrome, which occupied five acres in New York City and hosted crowds of 10,000. Rowe was a rider in races and probably other equestrian displays in the Hippodrome.

Various accounts place Rowe's return to the racetrack in 1876, when he was said to be asked to take over the training of a horse for Hugh Gafney. Rowe was also said to be associated with the stable of Dick Shea but soon moved on to train for T.B. and W.R. Davis of Keyser, West Virginia.

About 1878 Rowe succeeded Eph Snedecker as trainer for Phil and Mike Dwyer. This put him squarely in the big time, although not on the blue side of racing blood. The Dwyer brothers' entrance into the sport came at a time when, ironically, the top echelon had been casting around for someone to compete against Pierre and George Lorillard, who had divvied up a major portion of the East's prizes through the early 1870s.

As recorded by Hollingsworth in *The Great Ones*:

> Some owners felt the Lorillard dominance was crushing New York racing; William Bathgate urged millionaire James R. Keene to enter racing with the purchase of Dan Swigert's good 2-year-old, Spendthrift, to challenge the Lorillard horses. Nobody asked the Dwyer Brothers … They just moved in and took over. They were poor boys, operating a butcher shop at the corner of Atlantic Avenue and Court Street in Brooklyn. They worked hard and opened another shop, then another, and eventually established a wholesale butcher business in Washington Market. A bank went up at Atlantic and Court, which says something. Mike liked to play the horses; Phil was more conservative, but he liked to turn a profit.

The Dwyers' first horse, Rhadamanthus, was purchased in August 1876 and won four of his first five races. Mike made a bundle. The Dwyers took a strong liking to the game from that point.

For the Dwyer brothers, Rowe began his unprecedented streak as a trainer of thirty-two champions for five owners.

Rowe's seven champions for the Dwyer brothers:
Bramble, 1879 handicap male and overall best;
Luke Blackburn, 1880 three-year-old male and overall best;
Onondaga, 1881 two-year-old male;
Hindoo, 1881 three-year-old male and overall best; 1882 handicap male and overall best;
George Kinney, 1882 two-year-old male, 1883 three-year-old male;
Runnymede, 1882 three-year-old male;
Miss Woodford, 1883 three-year-old filly and overall best, 1884 handicap filly/mare and overall best, 1885 handicap filly/mare and overall best;
Rowe's two champions for August Belmont I:
Potomac, 1890 two-year-old male;
La Tosca, 1890 two-year-old filly.

Rowe's champion for L.S. and W.P. Thompson:
L'Alouette, 1897 two-year-old filly.
Rowe's eleven champions for James R. Keene:
Chacornac, 1899 two-year-old male;
Voter, 1899 older male;
Commando, 1900 two-year-old male and overall best, 1901 three-year-old male and overall best;
Sysonby, 1904 two-year-old male, 1905 three-year-old male and overall best;
Delhi, 1904 three-year-old, 1905 handicap champion;
Court Dress, 1906 two-year-old filly, 1907 three-year-old filly;
Colin, 1907 two-year-old and overall best, 1908 three-year-old and overall best;
Peter Pan, 1907 three-year-old male;
Maskette, 1908 two-year-old filly, 1909 three-year-old filly;
Ballot, 1908 handicap horse, 1910 handicap horse;
Sweep, 1909 two-year-old male, 1910 three-year-old male.
Rowe's eleven champions for Harry Payne Whitney:
Whisk Broom II, 1913 handicap horse and overall best;
Regret, 1914 two-year-old filly, 1915 three-year-old filly and overall best, 1917 handicap female;
Borrow, 1914 handicap horse;
Dominant, 1915 two-year-old;
Rosie O'Grady, 1917 two-year-old filly;
Johren, 1918 three-year-old male;
Vexatious, 1919 3-year-old filly;
Tryster, 1920 two-year-old male;
Prudery, 1920 two-year-old filly, 1921 three-year-old filly;
Mother Goose, 1924 two-year-old filly;
Maud Muller, 1924 two-year-old filly.

Of these, the following ten are in the National Museum of Racing's Hall of Fame in Saratoga Springs, New York: Luke Blackburn, Hindoo, Miss Woodford, Commando, Sysonby, Colin, Peter Pan, Maskette, Whisk Broom II, and Regret. Here, the Jones boys would have been competitive if their records were combined, for together they accounted for nine Hall of Famers of their own. Rowe, himself, was in the first class of trainers elected in the initial year of the Hall of Fame, 1955.

Various descriptions remain to give insight into the type of horseman and boss Rowe became. While he perhaps changed over the years, by the time he had been well established for many seasons, he was described as following a rigid daily routine. Bill Finnegan — a trainer of note who conditioned Hill Rise when he finished second to Northern Dancer in the 1964

Kentucky Derby — reminisced about Rowe as follows:

> Back when I came around, James Rowe was the best trainer there was. He did everything by a whistle — everything about the stable was organized, systemized. They put the tubs in, did up, got their horses out, all by the whistle. He only got out two sets in a morning, have maybe 20 to 25 horses in a set. Had a man and a boy for every horse. All the horses would be lined up in the shed row and he'd go down and look over each one, feel their knees and ankles and look at their feet.
>
> Then they'd all go out to the track, line up and stand next to the outside rail. They'd all be galloped maybe a mile and a quarter, then come back and stand. He'd have Marshall Lilly [Rowe's renowned African-American exercise rider and assistant] and maybe a jockey, and those two would work all the horses he wanted worked. Well, sometimes he might have three boys. While Lilly and the jockey were working two horses, the others would be washed down and cooled out, right there on the track. The men would bring their buckets and rub rags with them to the track and it was all done right there on the outside rail. Today, of course, you couldn't do that — you'd get run over and killed standing there on the rail trying to wash down and cool out 20 horses.
>
> Now, Sam Hildreth was an entirely different kind of trainer, having maybe one man for three horses. Hildreth was awful strong on feed, and bedding — his horses would stand in high bedding. They were both good men with horses, but I always thought Rowe was the better.

Mose Goldblatt, who for many years handled a secondary division of Harry Payne Whitney's racehorses, offered another description of Rowe as a professional soon after the trainer's death:

> Rowe was a rough taskmaster. He neither spared himself nor his helpers. Up before light every day of the year, no matter what the weather might be, he always had his help up and doing. When an ailing horse required his personal attention, he would stay with it indefinitely. He got used to sleeping in box stalls when he was a stable boy and budding jockey back in the '70s ... He found it just as easy to make himself comfortable in a box stall after he turned 70, when there was need of his presence at the stable, as he had when he was a kid. But exacting as he was, his help all loved and respected him. No man ever got more willing service out of hands of all sorts. And no man ever had about him men of more intelligence. He employed no dumbbells. Once a man won a place in his organization

he kept it because he deserved it. [Rowe] never permitted shirking or overlooked carelessness. He made it plain to all that handling high-spirited Thoroughbreds was a delicate matter that required diligent as well as intelligent attention.

The first champion Rowe had for the Dwyers was Bramble (Bonnie Scot-land—Ivy Leaf, by Australian), with whom he showed he could condition a horse for distance races as cleverly as he had ridden them. The trainer was in his early twenties at the time. At four, Bramble won the Saratoga Cup, which Rowe had won as a jockey, and the Monmouth, Brighton, Westches-ter, and Baltimore cups. Bramble was the Dwyers' first champion, and with him they set the tone of their enterprise, which was to get all they could out of a racehorse and then sell him or her, for they had no interest in breeding. Bramble was able to make only a single start at both five and six and was sold for $8,000 to General W.H. Jackson of Tennessee.

The year after Bramble's championship distinction came Luke Blackburn. In 1918, Hall of Fame (to be) jockey Jimmy McLaughlin looked back over a star-studded career and opined that Luke Blackburn was "the best horse I ever saw." He went into specifics and detailed that the colt was better than Tremont, Roamer, Firenze, Hindoo, Kingston, Hanover, and Miss Woodford.

Luke Blackburn (Bonnie Scotland—Nevada, by Lexington) was a thick, powerful colt, only about 15 hands tall. At two he won only twice in thir-teen starts but was competitive in stakes. The Dwyers noticed him and noted that he was by the sire of Bramble, so they wired an offer of $2,500 to owners S.L. Wartzfelder and Captain Jimmy Williams. Thus the colt was brought under Rowe's tutelage.

At three in 1880, Luke Blackburn had an experience typical of a good Dwyer horse. If you were winning and sound, you kept on racing. If you were winning and not so sound, you might keep on racing anyway. Luke Blackburn won twenty-two of twenty-four races, including fifteen in a row. At one point, he made seven starts in nineteen days. Just as it appeared that the only way he could lose was to fall down, he fell down, getting his legs crossed and tumbling in a purse race.

Duke of Montrose raced past the fallen horse to end his winning streak. Fortunately, Luke Blackburn arose unhurt from what was to be his only loss in twenty-four races over two seasons.

Luke Blackburn's victories included the Grand Union Hotel Prize, Ken-ner Stakes, Monmouth Champion Stakes, and Great Challenge Stakes. Along the way, Luke Blackburn was beating Lorillard horses, and the Dw-yers challenged Pierre Lorillard to bring out his best for a match race at Gravesend — a New York racetrack the Dwyers by then owned. Lorillard countered with Uncas, but Luke Blackburn beat him at one and three-eighths miles by a margin described as about fifty yards.

With the East well conquered, Luke Blackburn ventured westward to win the Kentucky St. Leger and Great American Stallion Stakes, but he suffered a fractured coffin bone in the latter race. The Dwyers had Rowe attempt to bring Luke Blackburn back at four, anyway, and he actually won his first start, but then broke down. He was quickly sold off to go to stud. He sired only three stakes winners, but one was Proctor Knott, winner of the first running of a race destined to be important to Rowe — the Futurity.

The year after Luke Blackburn's championship streak, Rowe had at hand a horse that outstripped the fifteen-race winning streak, by three races. This was none other than Hindoo, a horse whose name would be brought up over the years whenever horsemen were enthralled by a new star. To certain generations of horsemen, the comment that any horse might be seen as potentially "the second coming of Hindoo" was as strong a compliment as could be given.

Hindoo (Virgil—Florence, by Lexington) won seven of nine races at two in 1880, but his victories came in the "West" and he lost his two starts in the East. The Dwyers thought him a good enough prospect, however, and bought him for $15,000 from prominent Kentucky breeder Daniel Swigert. Sent to Rowe, Hindoo immediately commenced the winning streak of eighteen races. Among American runners on major circuits, this still ranks among the best, i.e., beneath Leviathan's twenty-three, Fashion's and Kentucky's twenty, and Boston's nineteen, but ahead of Beeswing's, Boston's (another streak), and Hanover's seventeen, and Cigar's, Citation's, and Miss Woodford's sixteen. (Source: *Thoroughbred Times Racing Almanac*.)

It may be taken as evidence as to the stable's approach that three of these (Hindoo, Hanover, and Miss Woodford) were Dwyer Brothers runners. Rowe was around for Hindoo's and Miss Woodford's streaks, and much later would direct another distinguished streak in Colin's unbeaten career of fifteen races.

Hindoo's streak began with the mile and a half Blue Ribbon Stakes in the spring in Lexington and was followed by Rowe's first victory in the then young Kentucky Derby. Hindoo also won the Clark Handicap at Churchill Downs before leaving Kentucky. In New York the colt went merrily on his way, winning two purses at Jerome Park and then the Tidal Stakes at Sheepshead Bay. The Tidal found him handling a tough field, for Crickmore had beaten him at two and had only one earlier loss in six races, and the year's Belmont Stakes winner, Saunterer, was also a challenger. Hindoo won in a gallop and the next week added the Coney Island Derby by ten lengths.

Hindoo was taken to Monmouth Park to win two more races, including one over older horses. The ease with which he was handling such assignments convinced other owners that a chance to test him for $4,000 was a poor proposition, so he got a walkover for that amount.

At Saratoga, the Travers was then run at one and three-quarters miles. Hindoo duly won it and took three other races at the track. Two days after the last of these, the two-mile Kenner, Hindoo was back at Monmouth Park, where he beat the Lorillard brothers' Monitor and Parole (then eight) in the Champion Stakes. With three days' rest, he added the Jersey St. Leger, a race for which the bookmakers offered no action.

Races with no betting went against Mike Dwyer's grain. The solution was to submit Hindoo to a match of heats against George Lorillard's Sir Hugh. Dwyer accepted severe odds of 1-12 in the first and 1-15 in the second heat and won both bets. Two days later, the eighteenth victory came when Hindoo again beat Sir Hugh, in a single-race affair. (This might reasonably be called his nineteenth win, but success in heat races is traditionally counted as one victory.)

Hindoo was finally worn down enough that when asked to give Crickmore twelve pounds in the one and three-quarters-mile September Handicap at Sheepshead Bay, he faded. Crickmore won by ten lengths, and Hindoo was third. Mike Dwyer had not seen it coming, for he bet $8,000 to win $1,000. Ten days later, Crickmore defeated Hindoo again, and even the Dwyers got it into their heads that the horse could use a rest.

At four, Hindoo's losing streak hit three, but he finished his career with a flourish of five more victories, including the two and a half-mile Louisville Cup. He won the fifth and last of that victory string in the two and one-quarter-mile Coney Island Cup but came out of the race with a tendon sheath problem that made Rowe unwilling even to gallop him. The Dwyers had no further use for Hindoo, except as a bargaining chip in a deal with Ezekiel Clay and Catesby Woodford. The owners of Runnymede Farm in Kentucky gave the Dwyers $9,000 in cash and a two-year-old filly in return for Hindoo as a stallion prospect and two Dwyer fillies. The value placed on the package was $15,000, exactly what Hindoo had cost them.

Hindoo had a career record of thirty wins in thirty-five starts and earnings of $71,875. That figure briefly stood as the all-time record for an American horse, but the previous record holder, Parole, reclaimed the status of leader soon afterward.

From 1879 to 1881, Rowe and the Dwyers had four championships, with Onondaga slipping in among the stable's giants as a more or less "regular" champion, at two in 1881. The year 1882 was highly satisfying, for in addition to Hindoo at four the stable included champion juvenile George Kinney and champion three-year-old Runnymede.

Illustrative of just how happily things were aligning for the Dwyers, the high mark of Hindoo's successful stud career was the siring of the great

Hanover, whom the Dwyers bought from Clay and Woodford for a bargain $1,350. Moreover, champion Miss Woodford was the filly they got in the Hindoo deal. She was destined to be another of the Dwyers' Hall of Famers and earned renown as the first American Thoroughbred of either gender to earn $100,000. Miss Woodford also would cause Rowe's connection with the Dwyers to end.

MISS WOODFORD

Officially George W. Bowen is recorded as the breeder of Miss Woodford, an 1880 filly by Billet—Fancy Jane, by Neil Robinson. Lore has it that Bowen had traded Fancy Jane to Clay and Woodford for a barrel of whiskey prior to the foaling but had been delinquent in documenting the transaction.

Before Rowe took over Miss Woodford, she had already established high form. The Dwyers had seen her run against their own George Kinney, who beat her in the Flash Stakes. The filly earned championship status at two that year under trainer J. Hannigan, winning five of eight starts.

The following June, she won the Ladies Handicap in her debut for Rowe and the Dwyers, launching a season of ten victories in twelve starts — numerically a modest campaign by Dwyer standards. Highlights included her eight-length win in the Monmouth Oaks and four-length score in the Alabama. During the summer she was entered with her stablemate George Kinney in a unique international race at Monmouth. George Lorillard's Epsom Derby winner Iroquois had been returned from England, and although he was far from the horse he once had been, the special Monmouth Stakes was an intriguing spectacle. Other good ones Eole and Monitor also took part. Miss Woodford set the pace but faded to last as George Kinney came along to take the honors for the Dwyers' stable. George Kinney had also won the Belmont Stakes, becoming Rowe's first winner of that event. (The following year, in 1884, Rowe won the Belmont again, with Panique.)

Miss Woodford would not face defeat again for sixteen races spread over three seasons. This streak began with the Great Eastern Handicap, which she won by eight lengths with a high-class male, Drake Carter, trailing. She was not only winning, but doing so by daylight margins, and she concluded the season by winning the Pimlico Stakes, that time setting the pace again but withstanding the challenge of stablemate George Kinney.

At four Miss Woodford's card was exceedingly light for a Dwyer runner, only nine races, but they included some stern concentrations of action. She won them all, including a match with the Lorillard star Drake Carter. Miss Woodford won by ten lengths on that occasion. Heat racing had not completely disappeared, and two days after she beat Drake Carter they met again in a contest of two-mile heats. This was the Great Long Island

Stakes. The vaunted Midwestern distaffer Modesty, winner of the Kentucky Oaks and American Derby, was also on hand. Miss Woodford won the first heat by three lengths, the second by four. The combined times of 7:04 1/4 established an American record. Miss Woodford is regarded as Horse of the Year for the second consecutive year. No other filly or mare has two such distinctions, either in the pre-voting or voting era.

Rowe brought Miss Woodford out at five to win a purse race before she gave nineteen pounds to the champion Lorillard filly Wanda in the Coney Island Stakes. Miss Woodford won by a length for her sixteenth consecutive triumph. She then bid farewell to the winning streak, in the Farewell Stakes, failing to give nine pounds successfully to the Lorillard Brothers' good horse Thackeray. She rebounded to win the Ocean Stakes, Monmouth Cup, and Freehold Stakes, so that she had won nineteen of her last twenty.

Winning was not so frequent thereafter, although Miss Woodford was competitive against the best. She lost her third race in succession, when Freeland beat her a head, but came back to beat Freeland in a match race in another grim battle.

Around this time came the split of Rowe and the Dwyers. In considering the hard campaigns of some of the Dwyer horses, one is tempted to wonder how often Rowe felt uncomfortable with what the stable was doing. As a young man given a superb opportunity, he understandably might have been unwilling to risk his position by challenging his bosses. At the time Miss Woodford was five, in 1885, Rowe was still a couple of years from his thirtieth birthday, but he had the gumption to stand firm on behalf of the horse.

It has been commonly reported that after the match-race victory over Freeland, Rowe announced Miss Woodford needed to rest the remainder of the season. The Dwyers refused, and Rowe resigned. Slightly more detailed versions also have been published. Ed Heffner, who claimed a long association with Rowe, and the Turf writer using the name of Roamer recalled the circumstances similarly many years later:

> Miss Woodford had developed a leg problem, and Rowe had decided she should not fulfill an engagement — one said for a match race, the other said it was the Great Long Island Stakes of two-mile heats. Instead of drawing her (denying her feed) as he would on a race day, Rowe fed her as per the usual schedule. Phil Dwyer noticed this and inquired of the reason. Advised that Rowe had decided to scratch Miss Woodford, he demanded that she run. "If she starts, I'm through," said Rowe in this recollection. "I still say run her," countered Dwyer. It was Mike Dwyer — the brother usually attributed the more aggressive image — who tried to make peace, stating

that an apology would straighten things out, but Rowe would not apologize because he thought he was in the right.

Whatever the exact details, Rowe's assistant, Frank McCabe, was promoted and thus was on track to complete Miss Woodford's career and later would be a part of such campaigns as Hanover's twenty for twenty-seven season of 1887. Phil Dwyer might have felt vindicated initially, for Miss Woodford won again that year, but she did little more before a rest was finally provided. Miss Woodford was the champion handicap distaffer that year and came back to repeat yet again at six, retiring with thirty-seven wins in forty-eight starts and earnings of $118,270. (She was lame after her last race and was sold to James Ben Ali Haggin but was a failure as a broodmare.)

STARTS AND STOPS

Various accounts hold that after his departure from the Dwyer post, Rowe trained for a number of owners, including Ed Heffner, H.O. Bernard, and A.F. Walcott. Four years passed before he emerged again with another of the top jobs.

If the Dwyer brothers were major horsemen without the badge of social prominence, Rowe's next boss was another sort. August Belmont had started at the bottom, too, in one sense, but he was the son of a Jewish banker in Prussia, so young August's time in the trenches involved sweeping floors for the banker Rothschilds in Europe. By the time he came to America in 1837, Belmont had other posts with Rothschilds on his resumé, and he took it from there. One can be in meats or monies in New York City, rise similarly to the top of his profession, and be perceived rather differently. The Dwyers owned a butcher shop that was replaced by a bank. Belmont owned a bank.

Belmont's status in New York society was such that he was invited to be president of Jerome Park before he ever owned a racehorse. Leonard Jerome's track used his name when it launched the Belmont Stakes in 1867. Once August Belmont got involved, he did so in a high-class manner, and it was fellow mogul William Collins Whitney — although sometimes a rival of the Belmonts in industry — who suggested a new track be named posthumously in his honor. Hence, Belmont Park, which celebrated its centennial in 2005.

Belmont developed Nursery Stud on Long Island and had considerable success, but when his trainer, Jacob Pincus, left to take on the Pierre Lorillard stable, Belmont's racing fortunes declined. In 1882 he began selling his yearlings and dropped out as an owner of a racing stable. Then, in 1885, Belmont leased Kentucky property, to which he gave the established name Nursery Stud, and he bought the 1883 English Derby winner, St. Blaise. By the time his St. Blaise foals were ready for the races, Belmont had taken Rowe aboard as his trainer.

Starting in 1888 with Belmont, Rowe sent out the 1889 stars Fides and Raceland, and then in 1890 the stable had two St. Blaise juveniles who established themselves as champion juveniles. Potomac, as the top two-year-old male, gave Rowe the first of his ten Futurity winners. Launched in 1888, the Futurity was the antithesis of the stayers' Cup races that Rowe had known as both jockey and trainer. A two-year-old race of six and a half furlongs, the Futurity imposed a sequence of nomination and eligibility fees that swelled its purse to gaudy heights for the day. The first running had been worth $40,900 to winner Proctor Knott, as compared to, for example, the Belmont Stakes' $3,400 first-place purse and the Suburban Handicap's $6,812 that year. (A racing leader of the late twentieth century, former New York Racing Association chairman Tom Bancroft, once quipped that the Futurity was racing's version of a "Ponzie scheme." Nevertheless, the Futurity quickly was accepted as a virtual grail for American two-year-olds, and from one era to the next its winner was frequently anointed as the top two-year-old and implicit leading contender for the following spring's classics.)

When Rowe sent out Belmont's Potomac to win it in 1890, the Futurity was only three years old, and its victor's purse was $67,675. To further implant the race in Rowe's sentiments, the runner-up that day was Potomac's stablemate Masher. No other owner-trainer ran one-two in the Futurity until Bert Mitchell sent out the John D. Hertz stable's pair of Anita Peabody and Reigh Count to dominate in 1927.

Belmont's and Rowe's other juvenile champion of 1890 was the St. Blaise filly La Tosca. Two young champions by the home stallion boded well for the future, but Belmont died that November, and the dispersal at auction of the racing stable was hastily accomplished before the year was out.

Once again but in different circumstances Rowe was bereft of one of the plum jobs in racing. This prompted a sea change in career, although he remained in racing. After Belmont's death, Rowe served as a racing official in California and was a starter back East. This was in the days before mechanical starting gates, of course, and the physical action of starting a race prompted the *Live Stock Record* reference to him as a "burly flag dropper." He was said to weigh about 190 pounds, having doubled himself since his early riding days.

Training racehorses was the ticket for James G. Rowe, however, and he went to work for brothers W.P. Thompson Jr. and L.S. Thompson at Brookdale, a farm and training center in New Jersey. D.D. Withers had established Brookdale, and it was to be a key part of Rowe's career, generating a strong sense of loyalty to New Jersey in his heart. Rowe's final run as trainer of a great stable was to be for Harry Payne Whitney, who for some years leased Brookdale and bred and wintered his horses there.

The Thompson connection was not long lasting. The brothers' father, Colonel W.P. Thompson, died in 1893, and although the property was retained, the family decided to sell the horses and leave the game in 1899. Before their departure, Rowe sent out the Thompson brothers' filly L'Alouette to win the Futurity and earn recognition as the best juvenile filly of 1897. Rowe acquired from the Thompson operation at least two horses, The Huguenot and Chacornac, champion two-year-old of 1899.

RETURN TO THE TOP

Success and timing are often intertwined, and the next key event in Rowe's career found him on the upside of life's seesaw. James R. Keene hired him as trainer. One man's opportunity can hinge on the opposite scenario for his fellow man, and in this case, Keene's stable had experienced a downturn in 1898. As recalled by Keene's son, Foxhall Keene in his memoirs *Full Tilt*, "Frank Brown had trained the horses for the two years following the withdrawal of Billy Lakeland, but now we acquired the services of James Rowe, [who was to be] an associate until my father gave up racing in America … 1898 was dark, but in '99 came the dawn."

James R. Keene understood life's ups and downs just as poignantly as would a lad who outgrew a successful riding career, trained champions for major owners who either died or fired him, and took odd jobs in the game to tide him over. The young Keene had gone through a litany of jobs before dealing in mining shares in Nevada launched him toward his first fortune. The West could not contain him forever, and he traveled to New York in a private train car, liked what he saw, and dug deeply into the treasures and travails of Wall Street. It was he who answered racing's call that the Lorillard brothers were tearing up the game, and he purchased Spendthrift to launch his racing enterprise. The horse won the Belmont Stakes, Jersey Derby, Champion Stakes, and — for good measure — the Lorillard Stakes.

By a gambling nature might a man rise and by a gambling nature sometimes he might fall. Keene did both. "How many men would have survived the descent from millions to pennies?" asked one who was familiar with Keene's collapse and rise from the ashes. "He bent his head when the storm raged and pushed onward, and twenty years later he was the admired and envied and feared king of Wall Street."

Rowe caught him at a good time, for Keene would have more than a dozen years to live — exceptional job security compared to Rowe's earlier stints — and with Castleton Stud in Kentucky he had the bloodstock and bankroll to provide champion after champion. (Years earlier, during his first foray into racing, Keene had bred Runnymede, who was acquired by the Dwyers and trained by Rowe to three-year-old championship distinction in 1882.)

In accepting the job, Rowe offered the bonus of having Chacornac at hand to sell his new boss, and he saddled the colt to become another winner of the Futurity and champion two-year-old, in 1899. The *Thoroughbred Record* of September 2, 1899, reported that Keene had purchased the horse only two days before the Futurity. That year, Keene also had the top handicapper in Voter, something of a rarity in championship designation in that he specialized in sprints that season.

Before Rowe's arrival, Voter (Friar's Balsam—Mavourneen, by Barcaldine) had become the first three-year-old to win the young Metropolitan Handicap, in 1897. Keene then sent him to England, but Voter failed to win in seven races and was returned to America. He was a major part of Keene's surge of success as recalled by son Foxhall: "When Rowe took our horses in charge, things began to change ... Even old Voter came to life, and his recovery was a nice piece of veterinary work on Rowe's part."

Keene continued that Voter had been so difficult to control in England that "he had been trained with pulleys on his bridle. This rough treatment had ricked his back." Referring to Rowe's strategy in terms of veterinary science might have been something of a stretch, but it apparently worked. What Rowe did was sacrifice a sheep. This was not done in a Biblical spirit, but as therapy. Foxhall Keene suggested that the technique of placing the bloody skin over Voter's back acted "as a sort of poultice."

After that therapy, Voter won five of six races at five in 1899, including the six-furlong Test and seven-furlong Coney Island Stakes. Historian Vosburgh wrote of Voter that he "had immense propelling power in his quarters, but ran too fast to stay far. Besides, his temper was so bad he often wore himself out before a race." Still, it seems likely the horse's earlier prominence influenced his status at five. (Voter was to sire a fellow champion, named Ballot. Nobody thought of the name Hanging Chad for a voting-theme sequence of names in those days.)

When Rowe arrived, Keene already had purchased and raced into stardom the seminal horse Domino, and although Domino left few foals before his early death, the best of them, Commando, was waiting in the wings.

Commando (Domino—Emma C., by Darebin) was a big, coarse sort whom Keene declined to include in the early fee payments for the Futurity. Nevertheless, he came to hand quickly and won five of six races to earn recognition as the best two-year-old of a new century, in 1900. He won his first five races, including two major purses for the day, the $10,000 Brighton Junior Stakes and the $15,000 Junior Champion. Commando then lost the $20,000 Second Matron when his jockey, Spencer, was so careless in not noticing the onrushing Beau Gallant that he was set down by stewards for a week.

In 1901 Rowe used Commando's debut to win his own third Belmont Stakes. The colt then won the Carlton but broke down during the Lawrence Realization (then run on the Fourth of July) and was retired with seven wins in nine career starts and earnings of $58,196. Like his sire, Commando died young, but he got ten stakes winners of which Colin and Peter Pan were Hall of Famers and Celt, a leading sire. Even an unraced son of Commando, Ultimus, would be an influential stallion.

In 1904 Rowe brought to the races a colt who had so impressed him in early trials that the trainer resorted to dishonesty to keep him in the stable. At the time, Keene was sending some horses to England, and Sysonby seemed a reasonable candidate as he had an English pedigree and was intended to be an English colt from conception. Marcus Daly, who owned the Bitter Root Stud in Montana, also acquired a farm in England, and there he bred his Orme mare Optime to the stallion Melton in 1901. Daly died that year, and his English stock was imported to be sold in this country, where Keene bought Optime for $6,600.

The foal she thus bore at Castleton Stud was named Sysonby. The name was suggested by that of the sire, Melton, as Keene's son Foxhall leased a lodge named Sysonby in the English village of Melton Mowbray. When time came to select which of Keene's young horses would go abroad, Rowe swaddled Sysonby in blankets and bandages and convinced his master that the youngster was too ill to make the voyage.

Sysonby started impressively, winning by ten lengths in his debut, a margin he duplicated in both the Flash Stakes and Saratoga Special. In between, he won the Brighton Junior by a more modest four lengths. The effect of such brilliance meant his subsequent defeat by the filly Artful in the Futurity was met with shock and suspicion. It was thought something was amiss, and two days later, Rowe and Keene accosted Sysonby's groom when they noticed an uncommon roll of cash on his person. They wrested the confession that he had administered a tranquilizer to the horse.

Between the race and this discovery, Rowe almost found himself dismissed again by an aggrieved owner. In this case, Keene was outraged because the trainer had left the barn on the evening of the Futurity. "I will not have a man who would leave Sysonby at a time like that," Keene declared. Son Foxhall interceded on Rowe's behalf, assuring his father that the trainer had not left Sysonby's side until assured the horse was all right. "He could do nothing by staying there and looking at him," Foxhall pointed out. "He probably felt too badly to be able to remain at the stable." The son wrote later that, "Mr. Keene finally saw reason, and the storm died away in distant mumblings." Sysonby was adjudged sufficiently recovered that he was sent out for more action three weeks later, and he won the Junior Champion Stakes.

At three, Sysonby went nine for nine and cemented a status in the minds of horsemen of several generations that he should rank with Man o' War, Citation, and Colin as the best four horses of the century then in progress. Only Keene could claim two in this foursome, for he also was to breed and race Colin.

Sysonby's first start at three was in the Metropolitan Handicap, which was the feature race on the grand occasion of the opening of Belmont Park. Despite giving thirteen pounds to the older Race King as early at three as May 4, Sysonby escaped with a dead heat for the win. His later performances brought wins in the Tidal Stakes by four lengths, the Commonwealth Handicap by four, the Lawrence Realization by six, the Iroquois by two, Brighton Derby by four, Great Republic Stakes by three, Century Stakes by three, and Annual Champion by four. His richest race was the $50,000 Great Republic, in which he was turned sideways at the break and bolted far to the outside before righting himself and defeating Diamond Jim Brady's nice runner Oiseau.

A great horse, but ill starred, Sysonby was discovered to have blood seeping from a pimple on an ankle following a workout the next spring. Within a week, his body was covered with such sores, and veterinarians told Rowe the horse had a liver disease and blood affliction known as variola. Treatments failed, and Sysonby died in his stall at Sheepshead Bay. A crowd of four thousand was said to have turned out for his funeral. Such was his public fame that his body later was exhumed and the skeleton placed in the American Museum of Natural History in New York City. His record was fourteen wins in fifteen starts and earnings of $184,438.

At the time of Sysonby's death, Keene was cloistered in a suite at the old Waldorf-Astoria hotel, his health so delicate that the uplift of spirit from his horses' successes was regarded as important to his survival. Conversely, the shock of sudden bad news was to be avoided, and his staff attempted to protect him from learning of Sysonby's death from outside, informing him as gently as possible. Rowe probably thought that, as in the case of Belmont, his stint with this giant among sportsmen was to be short-lived, but Keene survived for eight more years.

Delhi (Ben Brush—Veva, by Mortemer), a homebred foaled the year before Sysonby, was a companion champion to the great horse. He gave Rowe his fourth Belmont Stakes in 1904, and Keene his third, as co-champion three-year-old. He was co-champion handicap male in 1905, in both cases sharing the honors with Ort Wells.

In 1906, Court Dress (Disguise—Hampton Belle, by Hampton) was adjudged the best two-year-old filly, and she repeated as best three-year-old filly of 1907. The year 1907 also saw the emergence of the horse that Keene regarded as his best. This was Colin.

THE UNBEATEN

For Rowe there were champions and great horses, and then there was Colin. Rowe went so far as to remark that his epitaph should be restricted to the single phrase that he had trained the wonderful colt.

With the Dwyer brothers' technique of buying and not breeding, and with his time training for Belmont being short, Rowe had never had the experience of training a champion that was the offspring of another champion he had trained. Colin was his first of this pattern, being a son of Commando. The dam was Pastorella, by Springfield.

As was true in the case of Sysonby, Rowe's keen eye discerned quality in Colin early. This was a good thing, for Keene was unimpressed because of an unsightly blemish on a hock of an otherwise lovely colt.

As if taking a page from the Dwyers' book of equine management, Rowe sent out Colin three times from May 29 to June 5. The colt won all three races, including the National Stallion Stakes and Eclipse Stakes. He bucked his shins in his third start and secured for himself a rest of three and a half weeks, after which he reappeared to win one of the rich races of the day, the $25,000 Great Trial Stakes. Colin proceeded to win his remaining races, never by less than one length and by as much as six. They were the Brighton Junior, Saratoga Special, Grand Union Hotel, Futurity, Flatbush, Produce, Matron, and Champagne. In two of the last three, his runner-up was Fair Play, a dashing colt carrying the old Belmont colors, which had been adopted by August Belmont II, son of Rowe's former patron.

With twelve wins in twelve starts as a two-year-old, Colin set a numerical standard that was not matched until the filly La Prevoyante's duplicate dozen-of-a-dozen campaign at two in 1972. Clearly, Colin was the top two-year-old of 1907.

Rowe brought Colin out of winter quarters to enter the Withers Stakes on May 23, 1908. He defeated Fair Play again that day, but press reports had him coming out of the race with a leg problem. He was reported to have been declared out of the Belmont Stakes, with a tendon injury, perhaps even a bowed tendon. (What that phrase inferred at the time might have been less severe than in today's parlance, for Domino was said to have raced through his entire career with two "bowed" tendons.) The rules of the day allowed for late entries, and Colin showed up on a rainy, foggy Belmont Stakes day, after all, to traverse one and three-eighths miles against Fair Play and King James.

Poor visibility precluded fractional details in the race chart until the stretch call. Jockey Joe Notter had Colin in front with a bit of daylight over Fair Play. Notter spent a good part of his remaining days saying that, No, he did not fail to recognize that Fair Play was coming at him; it was just that Colin was tired enough of the long muddy trip that his hanging on to win by a head was the best the rider could get the colt to do.

Colin's last race, three weeks later, was prompted by politics. Keene, who had once been urged to enter racing to create some competition for a dominant stable, now contrived to race Colin to prove that, even without betting, a great racehorse could fill the stands. The Percy-Gray Law against gambling had been passed by the New York Assembly. Colin won the Tidal Stakes in a betless exhibition, which perhaps suggests some exaggeration in tales of his lameness for the Belmont. Alas, the stands at Sheepshead Bay were only half-filled.

Colin was retired with fifteen wins in fifteen starts and earnings of $180,912. Because La Prevoyante did not follow her twelve-for-twelve juvenile campaign with an unblemished record thereafter, the reality of a major American horse going through an entire career unbeaten did not come into play for eighty years after Colin's retirement. When Personal Ensign got up just in time to nip Kentucky Derby winner Winning Colors in the 1988 Breeders' Cup Distaff, she preserved her three-season career status of being unbeaten, at thirteen for thirteen.

Although political maneuvering forestalled the cessation of New York racing until 1911, at the time of Colin's last race at three, the prospects at home seemed so unsettled that Keene sent the horse to trainer Sam Darling in England. Colin won in a private trial that Darling arranged but could not be kept sound enough to contest an official race, and he was retired to stud. Colin was a shy foal getter, but of his eighty-one foals twelve were stakes winners, and a tendril of the Domino line has survived. Modern horses tracing in the tail-male line to Colin include Ack Ack, Youth, Teenoso, Broad Brush, and Concern.

The *American Racing Manual* lists leading owners starting in 1902. Keene topped the list for the first time in Sysonby's day, 1905, and led every year through three more years, or through Colin's final season of 1908. Trainer statistics for leaders by wins began with 1907, and Rowe was first that year with seventy wins. He did not top that list again, but insofar as money earned, he was the national leader in 1908 ($284,335), 1913 ($45,936), and 1915 ($75,596).

PETER PAN AND MASKETTE

Colin might have been the best of the best, but he was no island insofar as quality horses to carry the Keene silks of white, with blue polka dots. In 1907, when Court Dress was the top three-year-old filly and Colin the top two-year-old colt, they were joined by Peter Pan as best three-year-old colt — duplicating Rowe's 1882 distinction of having three champions for the Dwyers in one year. A threesome was around again in Colin's second championship year, for he was joined by Maskette as champion two-year-old filly and Ballot as top handicap male. After Colin's retirement, the Keene stable still held sway with Maskette having a second championship at three, joined by Sweep as top two-year-old colt. The next year, 1910, saw the last of the Keene championships with Ballot again as handicap horse and Sweep as three-year-old male.

It is difficult to imagine a Hall of Fame horse getting lost in the shuffle for attention, but with the likes of Colin around, Peter Pan was perhaps less of a public star than he deserved to be. He was the second-leading earner of 1907, but such was the power of the Keene stable that the first and third — Colin and Ballot — were also in the barn, while other Keene stakes winners that year included Superman, Celt, Frizette, Court Dress, and Transvaal. It needs be pointed out that this was not an era of weak stables, not with Harry Payne Whitney, August Belmont II, John E. Madden, and Sam Hildreth, churning the same waters.

Like Colin, Peter Pan was a champion son of champion Commando. A foal of 1904, he was out of Cinderella, by Hermit. Peter Pan won ten of seventeen races for Keene and Rowe at two and three in 1906 and 1907, earning $115,450. He was near the top at two, although he failed in the Futurity. At three he won the Belmont Stakes, giving Rowe his fifth winner of the classic and enabling him to pass R.W. Walden as most prolific winner of the race to that time. (When he won his fourth, with Delhi, Rowe moved out of a tie for second in number of Belmont winners; he had been tied at three with his former mentor, Colonel McDaniel, and his former assistant, Frank McCabe.)

After the Belmont, Peter Pan's winning races included the Royal Standard Stakes, Brooklyn Derby, Tidal Stakes, and Brighton Handicap. He was retired to stud at Castleton and became Commando's best son at stud. He was to figure in Rowe's future, for after Keene's death Peter Pan was purchased as a stallion by Harry Payne Whitney.

Maskette was another Hall of Famer, although she did not receive the honor until 2001. She was by the Domino stallion Disguise—Biturica, by Hamburg. At two in 1908, she won her first four races, a quartet comprising an overnight race, the Spinaway, the Futurity, and Great Filly Stakes. In the revered Futurity, Maskette defeated Sir Martin, the champion two-year-old colt, but she could not repeat that win when they met again in the Flatbush Stakes. She bounced back from her only defeat to win the Matron in her final start at two.

The Matron launched a winning streak that Maskette took up the following year, and it reached six races as she won the Ladies, Gazelle, Alabama, and two other stakes. Then in the Aqueduct Handicap, she finally met defeat again when she just failed to last against Firestone after leading from the start. She was giving thirteen pounds to the runner-up and seven pounds to the high-class colt Olambala.

Rowe put Maskette up for the year, and when she came back at four she was only to win two handicap races and no stakes. However, in the first of her victories, she defeated the champion colt Dalmatian, and in the Sheepshead Bay Handicap she finished within a half-length of King James. She was retired with twelve wins from seventeen starts and earnings of $77,090.

Maskette was the last of the Hall of Fame horses Rowe had with Keene, but not the final champion. In addition to two-time handicap leader Ballot (Voter—Cerito, by Lowland Chief), Sweep came along to be champion at two and again at three in 1910, the last year before anti-gambling legislation finally shut down New York racing.

Sweep (Ben Brush—Pink Domino, by Domino) won two of Rowe's favorite races, the Futurity and Belmont stakes. After winning the Belmont with Peter Pan in 1907 and Colin in 1908, Rowe had missed in 1909, but Sweep's 1910 victory gave him three out of four. Sweep also won the Lawrence Realization and had a career record of nine wins in thirteen starts with earnings of $63,948. He was later a two-time leading sire.

The New York Turf fell silent in 1911, and Keene shipped a large stable to England, but Rowe did not go over to train. Near the end of the year, Keene sold Castleton Stud to David Look for $250,000, and the next year he sold his entire yearling crop. Keene died in 1913, and the remaining horses were dispersed. (During the sequence of breaking up the stable, Keene at one point had given Rowe the classy runner Iron Mask in lieu of some of the training expenses. Rowe sold Iron Mask to his future patron, Harry Payne Whitney, for whom the horse was a major winner here and abroad.)

UNCERTAINTY, THEN REGRET

Rowe moved quickly to start another chapter of his career. In the January 21, 1911, issue of the weekly *Thoroughbred Record*, considerable space was devoted to the deal whereby Rowe would move to France to train and manage the stable of American Herman Duryea. Commentary included the observation that the transition from America, where many horsemen trained by the stopwatch, would be easy for Rowe, because he was not a proponent of that approach. He was quoted to have said, "I think that timing is not the essential feature when trying horses, especially yearlings, and I would be satisfied to make a selection out of a set of untried colts by watching them gallop on the lawn." The article opined that "his ability to judge a horse's speed while galloping or when let down for a high trial is second to none."

A month after that article was published, however, the same periodical carried news of Rowe having been hired instead to take charge of the breeding operation of Harry Payne Whitney. Despite the cessation of racing in New York, Whitney was planning to expand his acreage at Brookdale in New Jersey, an operation established by D.D. Withers and at that time under lease to Whitney. Not only would Whitney campaign a substantial stable in England, but he harbored the hope that racing would eventually be restored to New York. He would be ready. Rowe was to manage Brookdale and ship out for a race from time to time.

The Whitneys and Duryea had an association. Following the custom of taking down one's name in times of grief, the Whitney stable for a time was raced in Duryea's name after the founder, William Collins Whitney, died in 1904.

Harry Payne Whitney had become involved in racing during the short but dynamic years of his father's participation in the Turf. The family fortune had originated with the father, who abandoned a career in politics to establish himself as a businessman in New York. (Marrying the sister of oil tycoon Oliver Payne, of course, did nothing to impede William Collins Whitney's rise in status.)

Rowe was familiar with Brookdale, having trained for the Thompsons. Further, there were some years when at his suggestion Keene leased part of it for his yearlings to be broken and conditioned. Sysonby had been among those broken there.

Now, Rowe was set in a post that would carry him through the final eighteen years of his life. In his strong affection for New Jersey and Brookdale, he once boasted to a visitor that "more Futurity winners were bred within a radius of twenty miles from where we sit than in the whole state of Kentucky." (Harry Payne Whitney began relocating his breeding enterprise to Kentucky in 1916, so presumably Rowe had to take a different tack in at least some of his conversations thereafter.)

Brookdale became the locus of Rowe's operations. He established a strict routine of bringing the horses wintering there out from the shed row on March 1, regardless of weather.

The racing hiatus in New York lasted only two years. In 1913 among Whitney horses returned from England and handed over to Rowe was Whisk Broom II. Bred by Captain Samuel S. Brown, Whisk Broom II had been purchased as a yearling by trainer A.J. Joyner, who later sold him to his American patron, Harry Payne Whitney for $2,500, the same price Joyner had paid. Joyner might not have made much of a deal there, but he did have the opportunity to train the horse, for he was among American trainers who repaired to England when New York went dark. Whisk Broom II (Broomstick—Audience, by Sir Dixon) won seven of twenty-three races for Whitney and Joyner in England. He captured several nice stakes and placed in the classic Two Thousand Guineas. His real scores, though, also slipped through Joyner's grasp.

Rowe had him ready for New York racing's first day back, May 30, 1913.

The horse was assigned 126 pounds for the Metropolitan Handicap. This race was run at a mile, which was seen as Whisk Broom II's best distance in England, where the handicapping system had him carrying as much as 138 pounds. Whisk Broom II won the Met by one and a half lengths, giving twenty-six pounds to the lightly weighted runner-up G. M. Miller. The weights were adjusted to 130 on Whisk Broom II and 106 on G. M. Miller for the mile and a quarter Brooklyn Handicap, and — despite Whisk Broom II's perceived fondness for a shorter route — the result was the same as the Whitney horse won by a length and a half. Next came the Suburban Handicap, also at a mile and a quarter, and Whisk Broom II must have felt he was back in England, save for the dirt rather than grass underfoot. He was assigned 139 pounds and was fully extended to get home by a half-length over Lahore, to whom he gave twenty-seven pounds. Meridian, considered America's best among what racing there was in 1911, finished third under 119 pounds.

Whisk Broom II's recorded time for the Suburban was 2:00, which was so sensational that its accuracy was widely doubted, but it stood for nearly fifty years as officially the fastest ten furlongs ever run in New York. Kelso matched the time in the 1961 Woodward, and Gun Bow (1:59 3/5) eventually broke it in the 1964 Brooklyn.

Whisk Broom II, then, had swept what came to be known as the New York Handicap Triple Crown, a series that for many years (but no longer) was more or less the assumed target for the best three-year-olds when they graduated to the handicap ranks. Only three other horses have won all three in one year, Tom Fool (1953), Kelso (1961), and Fit to Fight (1984).

Rowe was aiming Whisk Broom II for the Saratoga Handicap when the horse was injured and retired to stud. His get was to include John P. Grier, Man o' War's sternest challenger.

The spring of 1913 also brought another victory for Rowe in the Belmont Stakes, as he saddled Whitney's Prince Eugene (Hamburg—Eugenia Burch, by Ben Strome) to win the classic. It was Rowe's eighth Belmont and would be his last, but that number was enough to stave off Sam Hildreth (seven) and remained in 2006 a record not only for the Belmont but also for any of the individual American Triple Crown races.

Whitney certainly revered classic races, but by and large the Whitney bloodstock might be said to slant slightly more toward speed than, say, the August Belmont II operation. The Belmont Stakes was then run at a mile and three-eighths. Too much should not be made of this pattern, but, as matters transpired, there would be more Futurity winners for Whitney but no more Belmont Stakes winners. This is admittedly splitting hairs, for there were to be a pair of Kentucky Derby winners, not to mention Johren's victory in the mile and five-eighths Lawrence Realization.

Also during 1913, Rowe won another Futurity, with Pennant (Peter Pan—Royal Rose, by Royal Hampton), whom he had purchased for Whitney for only $1,700 from a segment of the Keene stock's break-up. The victory was worth $15,060, the least in its history.

So, New York racing was back, but purses were not up to what they had been, or would be again, and Whitney's purse total of $55,056 was enough to make him the leading owner for the first time.

The year after the distinctions of Whisk Broom II, Prince Eugene, and Pennant, Rowe brought out the filly Regret, destined for a unique fame in the history of the Kentucky Derby. Regret was a lovely chestnut by Broomstick—Jersey Lightning, by Hamburg. Her two-year-old campaign was compressed into two weeks at Saratoga, where she won the Saratoga Special in her debut, then continued facing males to win the Sanford Memorial and Hopeful Stakes. Regret carried 127 pounds in both her second and third starts. She was then put away with the status as best two-year-old in the country.

Far away, Colonel Matt Winn, manager of Churchill Downs, coveted the thought of luring her to his Kentucky Derby. The headline grabbing 91-1 victory of Donerail's 1913 Derby victory and the quality of its next winner, Old Rosebud, in 1914, had given some welcome vigor to the national image of what had been a regional event. A champion from one of the very elite Eastern stables would be another rose in the Derby's wreath. Winn wrote to Algernon Daingerfield of The Jockey Club, asking for his assistance in imploring Whitney to send Regret to Kentucky.

In the end, that is exactly what Whitney did, and Rowe prepared her to go a mile and a quarter off no racing, the Derby being her first race in nearly nine months. The preparation faced last-minute obstacles, for a late snowstorm had created large drifts near the Churchill Downs training track, and workmen had to be hired to attend to the problem. Then, too, Regret was in season and eating daintily, and a downpour during Derby week had Rowe wondering if he should really run the filly. The day of the race was bright and the track fast, however, and Regret led from the start under jockey Notter to defeat Pebbles by two lengths.

Whitney famously announced that she had now won the "greatest race in America," and he did not care if she ever won another race. The fact that, for the first time, a filly had won the Derby — and in a time of suffragette efforts here and there — added to the emotions of the moment. With some fortuitous circumstances, the Kentucky Derby had become a major league national sporting event.

Despite the jovial goings on in Kentucky, tragedy had befallen America, and the Whitney family in particular, for Mrs. Whitney's brother, Alfred G. Vanderbilt, had been lost when the *Lusitania* was sunk the day before.

Guided by prevailing custom, the Whitney name was withdrawn from view, and the stable for the rest of the year ran in the name of old associate L.S. Thompson. It was Thompson who was nominally the leading owner in America that year, with $104,106.

It was also in Thompson's name that Regret made her one remaining start that year in the Saranac Handicap, back at Saratoga, after another break of three months. The interval between races was likely a result of the stresses of the Derby trip. Walter Vosburgh wrote that Regret came out of the Kentucky adventure with a slight breathing defect, which, though not serious enough for her to be labeled a "roarer," meant she was never fully 100 percent again. Nevertheless, Regret won the Saranac, in which the beaten field included The Finn, winner of the Withers, Belmont Stakes, and Manhattan Handicap. With only two starts, Regret was anointed the best racehorse of either gender in America for 1915.

Regret's subsequent schedule is consistent with the handling of a horse with some troubles, although persevering with her if she were less than herself seems at odds with the special affection Whitney was said to have for her. Nearly a year went by before Regret returned to action at four. She lost her unbeaten status with a thud. After she raced away to lead at a fast pace in the Saratoga Handicap, Regret weakened quickly and finished last behind the high-class Stromboli. A month later, she won an allowance race, but that was it for her four-year-old season.

Still carrying on with the former champion, Whitney and Rowe brought Regret back at five. On May 31, 1917, she won an allowance race, and three and a half weeks later came out for the Brooklyn Handicap at a mile and an eighth. She carried 122 pounds, giving five pounds to stablemate Borrow. The 1914 Kentucky Derby winner, Old Rosebud, and the current Derby winner, Omar Khayyam, were also entered, marking the first time three Derby winners had met. The stalwart Roamer, Boots, and Stromboli also were in the exceptional field.

Regret led from the start and almost went wire to wire in front, but her own stablemate, Borrow, got up to win by a nose, setting an American record of 1:49 2/5. Whitney had said euphorically two years earlier that he did not care if Regret ever won another race, but he surely seemed to have wanted her to win that Brooklyn, for he was said to be in tears after the race — while leading in the winner! One explanation was that Borrow's jockey, Willie Knapp, ignored instructions to let Regret win if she could, but others defended Knapp by pointing out that Old Rosebud was making such a menacing bid that it was no certainty Regret could hold off that contender. As it turned out, Regret did hold off Old Rosebud to be the first home among the Derby winners.

Borrow (Hamburg—Forget, by Exile) was a well-traveled old fellow. He was nine years old at the time, presumed to be past his prime, but Knapp had advised Rowe before the race that Borrow was as sharp as ever. Borrow had been one of those sent to England, where he won the Middle Park Plate at two. In 1914, when Regret was two, Borrow was back in America, where he won the Saratoga Handicap, Yonkers Handicap, and other races, and was reckoned the champion male handicapper of the season.

The Brooklyn Handicap was not the end for Regret, for she won her two remaining races at five, the Gazelle and a handicap purse, taking her career record to nine wins in eleven starts. For the third year in four campaigns she was given championship status, as handicap female. Regret reigned in splendid isolation as the only filly to win the Derby for sixty-five years, finally being joined in that tiny club by Genuine Risk in 1980 and Winning Colors in 1988.

Regret's career also coincided with that of Dominant, the champion two-year-old of 1915. Dominant was bred by James R. Keene and was purchased from his estate by Whitney for $2,200 as a weanling. Dominant was a huge colt by Delhi, with whom Rowe had won a Belmont for Keene, and was out of Dominoes, by Domino. Dominant swept through a series of Saratoga juvenile races of 1915, winning the Special, United States Hotel, and Hopeful. He carried 130 pounds in the Hopeful. His bulk and fragile limbs meant his early retirement was not surprising. (The colt who had passed from one great stable to another would have his impact on a yet another, for Dominant was to beget Dice, a brilliant two-year-old who was an early star in the budding Wheatley Stable of Mrs. Henry Carnegie Phipps.)

Amazingly, the year Dominant was the champion two-year-old, Rowe and Whitney won another Futurity but with another of their juveniles, Regret's full brother, Thunderer.

Whitney would have no further great horses during Rowe's lifetime, but a succession of champions and other major winners continued. Rosie O'Grady (Hamburg—Cherokee Rose II, by Peter Pan) won the Fashion Stakes and Clover Stakes to be champion juvenile filly of a moderate crop in 1917.

In as lengthy a career as he assayed, even a trainer as astute as James Rowe Sr. could make a mistake. One was his evaluation of Johren. A son of Spearmint—Mineola, by Meddler, the colt was bred by Whitney in England, foaled in 1915, and sent to this country. *The Giants of the Turf* (by Dan M. Bowmar III, The Blood-Horse) quotes Rowe's disdainful evaluation of Johren at two: "He can neither gallop, canter, nor walk."

The colt was relegated to a division of Whitney horses whose efforts were credited in race charts to Albert Simons as trainer. Johren made ten starts at three in 1918 before he broke his maiden. Going into the Suburban Handicap, Johren had won only two of thirteen races, but he won that handicap under 110 pounds, with the older star Cudgel fourth under 133.

Having hit his stride, Johren won the Belmont Stakes, which, presumably, could have been Rowe's for the asking — giving him nine wins in the classic, instead of eight.

Johren next defeated Kentucky Derby winner Exterminator in the Latonia Derby and added another win in a handicap race before suffering two losses. Rowe manfully stepped up to be Johren's trainer of record when he won the August 27 Huron Handicap, and the head trainer's role was cited in Johren's victories in his remaining races, the Saratoga Cup and Lawrence Realization. The latter, accomplished over a single opponent, Whippoorwill, occurred in Johren's twenty-second race of the year.

Rowe did not get credit for Johren's Belmont, but the horse's championship designation of 1918 is ascribed here to Rowe for his late-season status as trainer of record. We openly confess that an alternative posture would be as legitimate as ours.

In 1919 Vexatious shared three-year-old filly championship status with J.K.L. Ross' Milkmaid. Vexatious was by Rowe's old star for Keene, Peter Pan, whom Whitney had purchased from the dispersal for $38,000. The price was the highest of the Keene dispersal, for E.R. Bradley was also keenly interested in Peter Pan and was difficult to outbid. Vexatious was out of Contrary, by Hamburg. She won the Alabama Stakes from Milkmaid and Coaching Club American Oaks winner Polka Dot. Her victory over males in the Lawrence Realization was a matter of good luck, for she got the nod when Over There was disqualified for interference. Vexatious was in the right place — second — at the right time, for the foul had been interference with two other runners rather than the filly.

For the Whitney stable, however, the moment of 1919 consigned most emphatically to the pages of history was the triumph of Upset (Whisk Broom II—Pankhurst, by Voter) in the Sanford Memorial. Benefiting from traffic that impeded a budding superstar — Samuel D. Riddle's Man o' War — Upset held on to win by a half-length. He was getting fifteen pounds (130 to 115). It was the only loss of Man o' War's career and gave birth to the myth that the meaning of the word "upset" in the sense of a surprising sporting result was originated by the incident. This is amusing but, unfortunately, not true.

A New York stable as strong as Whitney's would be expected to continue taking its best shots at a rival champion. So it was. Upset was second to Man o' War in the Grand Union Hotel Stakes, and John P. Grier stepped up to try in the Futurity, also finishing second. Rowe would bash his head against the stone wall that was Man o' War with increasing frustration through the following year.

That year, 1920, found Tryster and Prudery adding to the Rowe–Whitney champion total, as juvenile colt and juvenile filly respectively. Both were by Peter Pan. Tryster (Peter Pan—Tryst, by St. Amant) was unbeaten at two when he won his debut, then reeled off wins in the Juvenile, Keene Memorial, and Youthful. He had already carried 130 pounds before being freshened for Saratoga, where he beat his female counterpart Prudery by a head in a memorable Saratoga Special. Tryster was not out again until the fall, when he shipped to Kentucky and defeated Grey Lag and Behave Yourself in the Kentucky Jockey Club Stakes for his sixth win.

Prudery (Peter Pan—Polly Flinders, by Burgomaster) won the Fashion early and then the Rosedale, beating Careful, with whom she shared championship designation. Prudery later added the Grand Union Hotel Stakes and beat Careful again in the Spinaway.

Again, however, it was a moment with Man o' War that rings down from the Whitney stable of 1920. The Sanford Memorial of 1919 had demonstrated how circumstances might beat a great horse, but the closest anyone ever got to beating Man o' War on merit was in the Dwyer Stakes of 1920. Rowe had John P. Grier at his absolute peak, and the Whitney colt was in receipt of eighteen pounds. John P. Grier (Whisk Broom II—Wonder, by Disguise) raced with Big Red from the start, even getting his nose in front in the stretch. Rowe had consigned many other horsemen to foot-stomping, cigar-crushing reality over the years with the likes of Colin, Sysonby, and Hindoo. This time, he was the one who had to suffer through the inevitable. Man o' War surged ahead to win by one and a half lengths.

Upset also took his shots at three and was the well-beaten runner-up to Man o' War in the Preakness and the Travers. Another Whitney horse, Wildair, was Man o' War's runner-up in the Withers Stakes and Potomac Handicap (getting thirty pounds). In two seasons, Rowe ran against Man o' War ten times and wound up one and nine. Still, the qualities of his colts gained a measure of success while further underscoring the greatness of Man o' War. John P. Grier that year won the Aqueduct, Edgemere, and Annapolis handicaps, while Upset was second in the Kentucky Derby, as well as the Travers and Preakness, and scored a major triumph in the Latonia Derby.

In 1921, Prudery repeated as a champion when she won the Alabama and Miller stakes. The experience with Regret had whetted Whitney's appetite for more Kentucky Derbys and he, among all owners, was unlikely to be hesitant about running a filly. Prudery was no Regret, but she did finish third in the Derby.

That year brought another Futurity score, Rowe getting his ninth win in the race, with Bunting (Pennant—Frillery, by Broomstick). The year 1921 also was the year that Rowe and Whitney won the Preakness with Pillory. Thus, Rowe had at least one win in each of the races later to be linked as the Triple Crown.

THE FINAL YEARS

In 1924 two fillies shared honors in the juvenile division, and they were both Whitney fillies. Mother Goose (Chicle—Flying Witch, by Broomstick) rounded out Rowe's ten wins in the Futurity. She beat Stimulus in the big event, whose winning purse had rebounded to $65,730. She had jousted with stablemate Maud Muller, losing to her and another stablemate, Swinging, in the Rosedale, but beating Maud Muller in the Fashion. Maud Muller got the better of Mother Goose again in the Astoria, and Mother Goose needed the prestige of the Futurity to gain equal status.

Maud Muller (Pennant—Truly Rural, by Broomstick) won three other stakes, including the Clover and Demoiselle. Yet another Whitney juvenile filly, Elf, won the Youthful and Hudson and ranked third behind her stablemates in the division.

That year, 1924, marked Harry Payne Whitney's return to the top of the owners' list. He would land on top again in 1926 and 1927. The comparable statistics for breeders in money earned became available in 1923, and Whitney stepped up the next year to lead in that category, too. He returned to the top in 1926 and held the title for the rest of his life — and beyond. This status at that phase of his career was testimony to the breadth of quality of his breeding and racing operation, for there would be no more great horses, and only two more year-end champions, until the year Whitney died.

As for Rowe, he was involved enough in the development of the Whitney horses up to the final months of his life that he was quoted on the quality of the top juveniles of 1929, but he could not be active enough to be the trainer of record. In addition to the realities of age, Rowe was grieved by the death of one of his sons two years before his own death.

Those final seasons of both Whitney's and Rowe's lives saw a continuation of success in coveted races.

Since winning the Derby with Regret in his first try, Whitney had thrown sixteen other horses at the race, once (1920) starting three in the same running, but without success. Then, in 1927, Whiskery secured his second Derby. This gave Whitney a record of two wins from nineteen Derby entrants. Young Fred Hopkins had been assigned enough responsibility that he was trainer of record for Whiskery's Derby, just as he had been that spring for the Preakness victory of Whitney's Bostonian — quite a start to a young man's career. Hopkins had Whiskery from the summer of his two-year-old form, so, unlike some compilations, we do not ascribe the colt's championship status to Rowe.

In 1928 the Whitney stable won the Preakness again, with Victorian (Whisk Broom II—Prudery, by Peter Pan), but by then race charts credited such victories to one of Rowe's sons, James Rowe Jr., as trainer.

During the last months of his life, James Rowe Sr. was aware of the potential of a pair of two-year-olds, Whichone and Boojum, and he presumably took pride in the fact that — in his own diminished role — their successes were to be credited to James Jr. Boojum beat Whichone in the Hopeful, but Whichone won the Futurity and the juvenile title.

Ah, the Hopeful and Futurity — what lilting names, what comforting memories.

James Rowe Sr. died at seventy-two, on August 2, 1929. He had been battling what was described as an aggravated neuritis condition for several months, although he was in Saratoga for the races and attended to the stable every morning until about two weeks before. When taken by car to the hospital, he said mournfully to fellow trainers and friends Tom Healey and A.J. Joyner, "This is my last ride. I've fought it as long as I can and I know I'll never come back." Friends had been somewhat confident that a short rest would improve Rowe's condition, but Rowe reportedly suffered a heart attack in the hospital and passed away quickly.

Marshall Lilly, long a key employee, said, "I felt he was gone when he left the house. He came down the steps with his eyes on the ground and then halted for a minute, raising his head for a last look about the stables, shaking his head sadly as if saying good-bye. Not a word did he speak before dropping his head and walking off to the car. It was his farewell to the stable and the employees who served him faithfully for so many years."

Rowe was the first of three major trainers — towering figures — to die within three months, being followed by Sam Hildreth and John E. Madden. To put this into a modern perspective, one might ponder the impact if Woody Stephens, Charlie Whittingham, and Laz Barrera all had died within such a short span.

Published accounts from the time invite the thought that Rowe was the most beloved of the three contemporaries lost so rapidly, and he was referred to as "Uncle Jimmy" in some of the retrospectives. R.T. Wilson, president of the Saratoga Racing Association, said, "It is with the deepest regret that I learned of the death of Mr. Rowe. What we of the organization think of him may be judged from the half-masting of our flags, something we have never done for another trainer." (Regardless of whether this rankled the families of other trainers who had died during the Saratoga season, it was a rather indelicate statement.)

Madden, who would survive Rowe by only months, was gracious, likening Rowe's record to that of a great English trainer, John Porter.

To recapitulate, Rowe won the Belmont Stakes with eight horses: Colin, Commando, Delhi, George Kinney, Panique, Peter Pan, Prince Eugene, and Sweep. Rowe won the Futurity with ten horses: Bunting, Chacornac, Colin, L'Alouette, Maskette, Mother Goose, Pennant, Potomac, Sweep, and Thunderer.

EPILOGUE

Rowe had been married twice. He was survived by his second wife, Eliza, and by four children. Eliza was appointed administrator of an estate valued at $600,000.

As noted above, one of the sons, James Rowe Jr., was an assistant and then trainer of record. Nevertheless, Harry Payne Whitney opted for a more experienced hand to head the stable and named T.J. Healey to that post, with the younger Rowe to be an assistant.

The following year was sad and tumultuous for the Whitney clan, but the horses were spectacular. Harry Payne Whitney died in the autumn of 1930, just as his Equipoise was emerging as another of those champions who achieve greatness. At the same time, Whitney's sister-in-law, Helen Hay Whitney, campaigned one of Equipoise's chief rivals, Twenty Grand, in her Greentree Stable.

After Harry Payne Whitney died, his son, C.V. Whitney, took over the stable, inheriting not only Equipoise but also future champion Top Flight. The *American Racing Manual* assigns leading breeder status to Harry Payne Whitney from 1926 through 1931, gives that status to Harry Payne Whitney Estate for 1932, and combines Harry Payne and C.V. Whitney as leading breeder(s) in 1933, 1934, and 1938. Thus, Harry Payne Whitney was still making his mark eight years after his death.

Over at Greentree, Twenty Grand's trainer, Tom Murphy, took a swing at even larger status than he enjoyed as a result of the 1930 racing campaign. He resigned from his post and offered $125,000 for Twenty Grand on behalf of a syndicate. By the summoning of his own version of Murphy's Law, he found himself with neither the job nor the horse to train. Mrs. Whitney looked to James Rowe Jr., who stepped in to guide Twenty Grand to his victories in the 1931 Kentucky Derby, Belmont, Dwyer, Saratoga Cup, Lawrence Realization, and Jockey Club Gold Cup. Twenty Grand was the 1931 champion, destined for the Hall of Fame.

Young Rowe's taste of the honey so long enjoyed by his father was stunningly brief, however. He died of a heart attack on October 21, 1931, barely a month after Twenty Grand's last race at three.

CHAPTER 2

SAM
HILDRETH

S am Hildreth was a paradox, or perhaps several paradoxes. He was born to a vagabond horseman who would uproot his family guiltlessly to travel the Southwest for a race and a wager here and there. Sam later migrated east as a toiling serviceman of the racetrack — a blacksmith — until he took the plunge to become an owner and trainer.

Thereafter, Sam Hildreth was, at one time or another, a budding success; an outcast banned from the upper-crust tracks; a trainer for the uppermost of all upper-crust owners; the leading racehorse owner in America; the worldly owner of a French chateau while plying his trade abroad; a reformed drinker who re-established himself although his patron served time in jail; and a grand old man revered in some quarters for his kindness but also smeared with the remark that "he had as much skill and as little class as any trainer that ever saddled a horse." In the end — whatever percentage of his personal yearnings might have been scuttled or fulfilled — he died a millionaire.

WANDERLUST AND HORSES

"The craving I've always had for race horses, I reckon my father passed along to me in his blood," began *The Spell of the Turf*, the autobiography Hildreth produced with James R. Crowell in 1926 (J.P. Lippincott Company). Hildreth was born in Independence, Missouri, on May 16, 1866. His father was described in the *New York Telegram* as a tobacco planter who owned a stable of racehorses. It was the horse aspect of Vincent Hildreth that his son recalled most vividly from his youth.

Hildreth wrote that he and his five brothers and four sisters "grew up in a race horse atmosphere … When you don't see much else besides a racing barn, and when all the talk you hear is about Thoroughbreds, it just naturally gets into every fibre of you." The image of a "racing barn" and

"Thoroughbreds" is misleading in this description, for it suggests a fixed locus and pedigreed stock. Vincent Hildreth, however, was a roamer, and his racers were apt to be what were loosely described as "quarter horses" before the actual breed was named. His son recalled his father's motto: "You can't settle down and be a racing man, too; it's one or the other. And, as for me, I'm a racing man. That's me all over."

For the Hildreth family of that time, horse racing meant picking up lock, stock, and barrel and heading for where the action was said to be. "If you had a good horse and somebody came along and said he had a better one, you matched them, and that was the end of it," as Sam put it years later. "Next to his family, my father loved two things best — his horses and his rovings." As for other aspects of education, Sam recalled that as a young-ster he just assumed the whole world was made up of people immersed in the horse, and he had no notion, or counseling, that there were millions of children in big cities whose lives revolved around other matters.

Actually, his father did have some other activities. Growing tobacco was something that was tolerated to help with expenses, but even that could feed a man's gambling heart. Once when the family was living in Cunning-ham, Missouri, Vincent's casual approach about money caused him to lose $5,000 on a bet about a local election. The season's tobacco crop went to pay off the bet, although Vincent had not included the portion of the crop that Sam and a sister had been toiling over. He gave them each $5 for their shares.

Sam claimed to be about five years old when he first started dealing in horses. The tale went that he took a horse one of his brothers gave him, swapped it for a pony, and then swapped the pony for a gelded horse. Vin-cent approved of this last beast, figuring it was a Thoroughbred that had been stolen and then passed from one owner to the next. Sam entered him at the Nevada, Missouri, state fair, where the gelding won a couple of races and was sold for $750. "I'd made a neat profit on my first horse transac-tion," he wrote years later. "The only sad part of it was that father was a little harder up than usual and kept the money."

The tale of a mare named Red Morocco illustrated Hildreth's memories of his upbringing. As recounted in *The Spell of the Turf*, Vince Hildreth was "down at the general store" one night when he got wind of a fellow named Jim Brown down in Texas who had a lot of speedy runners and a passion for betting on them. This offhand knowledge sang to the wanderlust in Vince Hildreth's make-up. Hildreth figured that this Mr. Brown surely had nothing at hand that Red Morocco could not handle.

This paragon of family support hustled home and told his wife to start packing. The Hildreths were headed to Texas. Mrs. Hildreth apparently shared a bit of her husband's soul, for Sam wrote, "It didn't phase mother any, she was a Thoroughbred all the way through — came from the Crawfords of Virginia — and I reckon she got so used to roving with father that she liked it."

The fellow they were looking for, Jim Brown, was something of a legend for aspects other than racing horses. He was credited with helping clean up the notoriously lawless Lee County, Texas, by taking on the role of sheriff and capturing the famed bandit and killer Wes Hardin and his gang. As might be expected of such a local hero, Brown could organize a bit of advantage in any horse race, especially one against an outsider. Mindless of such nuances, Hildreth went for a $5,000 match against the best Brown could offer, which was a mare named Gray Alice.

Although the Hildreth family lived in Kentucky from time to time, they were identified at that moment as being from Missouri, so the crowds that were summoned via the mysterious sportsman's communications systems of a pre-telephone community saw the match as Missouri versus Texas. The locals took a hold by giving Hildreth's first jockey choice $100 simply to leave town. Some of the more sporting citizens considered this too underhanded even for Brown's crowd, so they told Vince about an equally adept rider in another town, and he was duly sent an invitation.

Brown's track — two strips of dirt separated by a grassy lane — was typical of the place and time. The dirt strips, Hildreth wrote, were created by the high-tech method of the day, i.e., a large iron cauldron turned on its side and dragged by a team of horses.

Red Morocco took an early lead in the two-furlong dash, but locals had gotten to the new jockey, too, and convinced him to make her veer onto the hard grass lane. "She wasn't plated for that kind of racing," Hildreth recalled, and Gray Alice closed in time to beat her by a nose:

"From the day we set foot in that Texas town we'd never had a chance to win that match race with Jim Brown's horse. And in later years old John Huggins, who was well known around the New York and Chicago tracks in the 1880s and early 1890s, and who had once been Brown's racing partner, told me that it would have been like pulling teeth to have got that five thousand if we'd won … Our five thousand was gone; all our hopes blown up; all those days of travelling down to Texas wasted."

Brown, though, took pity on Vince Hildreth when he saw how down and out he was. He gave him $5,000 and some cattle and other horses, for Red Morocco. Hildreth had no choice but to accept the deal, although his son knew "it nearly broke my father's heart to leave that grand old mare in strange hands."

Given Vince Hildreth's way of conducting his affairs, it is not a surprise that his son's memoirs refer to him training for other owners from time to time. During one of these phases, Sam had reached the age when he started to ride in races, and he whimsically claimed to have contested 248 races and to have won them all — confident that while he could show no proof of the claim no one could provide proof otherwise, either. He wrote that his last race riding took place in Dallas "along about 1882," at which time he was gaining weight too rapidly for that career to continue.

Hildreth set out on his own, taking a job at the Belmont Hotel in Parsons, Kansas, because the owner of the place also had a racing stable and the job included training the horses as well as clerking and bartending.

FARTHER AFIELD

The wanderlust virtually inherent in Sam's life gave rise to thoughts of the East. His father had told him that in 1866 two great things had occurred — the birth of Sam Hildreth and the inauguration of racing at Jerome Park. Whether Vince Hildreth really had an eye to the East or not, it is true that Jerome Park, launched by Leonard Jerome, was a key cog in the development of New York racing on a grander scale than the pre-Civil War Turf. Horse racing was a national sport, and in New York, especially, it was a vehicle for the expression of wealth and social prominence for owners of both old and newly minted fortunes.

After four years of the racetrack/hotel gambit, Hildreth had saved enough money to launch a blacksmithing business with a partner, Louis Long. He noted that "there was more money in plating race horses than training them."

Their skill at this craft was the two lads' ticket to the Eastern tracks, to which they set out in 1887. Sam Hildreth was twenty-one at the time. Their success also allowed Hildreth some modest investments in bloodstock, and nearly forty years later he recalled the pride in being "an owner of Thoroughbred race horses, just as my father had been. But we didn't let it go to our heads because we'd climbed to a new station in life — Louis and I just kept plugging away at blacksmithing and trying to do a good job for the Eastern horsemen ... I saw that it would lead to the target I was shooting for, horses and more horses in my own barn, and I was content to play along until that day came."

Having grown up watching the likes of Red Morocco on makeshift straightaways, Hildreth now marveled at the exploits of such nationally acclaimed Thoroughbreds as Hanover, Kingston, Salvator, and Miss Woodford on the great oval tracks of a bustling era. He was taken aback, however, by the place racing played in the people's lives:

"It was even new to me the way Northerners talked about racing as a sport. A sport? Here they were talking about horse racing as a sport — the thing Vincent Hildreth and his whole family had been doing all their lives and thinking about it all the time as though it was just as much a part of a human's life as going to sleep at night. And the money they would spend for a horse made me pop-eyed — remember I wasn't much removed from six dollars a month for riding and forty dollars a month for training."

That a successful owner had to be ready to unbelt generously was under-scored by Mike Dwyer, who with his brother Phil had parlayed a successful butcher-shop business into one of the dominant racing stables in history. Hildreth was shoeing horses for the Dwyers, and Mike counseled him, "If you ever want to build up a good racing stable, the only thing to do is to get the best horses the market offers. Get plenty of horses, but get fast ones. Then you'll make lots of money."

Well, paying big money requires having big money, and it was some time before Sam Hildreth was in that situation. When the day did come, he must have harked back to Mr. Dwyer's admonition, for Neil Newman wrote of Hildreth after the end of the trainer's life that "he never hesitated to spend his own money for what he deemed to be high-class horses." Nor was Hil-dreth reticent when it came to spending on behalf of others. In his mem-oirs, he summed up his idea when operating on his own behalf as, "My motto has always been to go a little slow when things were not running just right, and then let out the wraps when you know the turn has come." As for his approach when buying for someone else, he left the following recollection of a transaction on behalf of owner William Collins Whitney. Hildreth had spotted the young Ballyhoo Bey in Eugene Leigh's barn and told Whitney about him. Whitney said to buy him, and "there was no men-tion of price." Hildreth proceeded with the deal and led the colt back to the Whitney barn the very same day.

" 'He's certainly a good looker,' Mr. Whitney said when he saw him for the first time. Then he asked, as an afterthought, 'How much did you pay for him?'

"Upon learning the price was $12,000, Whitney remarked, 'My hat's off to you, Mr. Hildreth. You're certainly no piker.' "

When Hildreth was in his early twenties, though, he was dealing in cheaper stock. One day during that time Mike Dwyer remarked that he had not seen any of Hildreth's horses in action lately. The young man la-mented that his horses belonged in selling races (similar to modern claim-ing races), but he was afraid of losing them. The old gentleman said he could solve that by pledging to top any bids and so would salvage the horse for Hildreth. The young fellow's options were thusly enhanced.

The urge to own a racehorse had been fulfilled while the blacksmith firm was still in business, but Hildreth wanted more. He wanted owning and training to be what he did, not just something else he did while making a living as a smithy. Long continued with his workaday tasks, but Hildreth launched out on his own.

The change in career meant dropping down to the New Jersey circuit, which, aside from Monmouth Park, was a cut below the glamorous New York scene. Hildreth wrote fondly of such tracks as Guttenburg, Gloucester, Clifton, Linden, and Elizabeth, defending them against a general reputation as "black spots on the record of the Turf." He averred that "they were conducted on the square and the racing was clean." This was supported by the reminiscences of another great trainer, Sunny Jim Fitzsimmons (a jockey at that time), who also graduated from the lesser tracks to the best ones and who years later recalled very few instances of chicanery on the lower rung.

Admittedly, as a counter argument, it must be said that Hildreth's early career might bring into question his standing as an apt judge of such matters. That horse racing was a vehicle for betting had been drilled into him as a young man, and he had certainly seen men rewarded for taking an edge — sometimes to the disadvantage of his own family.

During his days at those winter tracks in New Jersey, Sam proved adept at taking unsound horses and turning their form around. This was the groundwork for landing big odds, but the struggle to pay for his horses, and expenses, left little discretionary coinage to bet on them. At Clifton, Hildreth spotted an opportunity and convinced one Charles Primrose — who worked for the track's owner, George Engeman — to have his boss bet $200 to win and $200 to place on one of the Hildreth horses. Engeman obliged, the horse won, and Hildreth's cut constituted a step up the ladder. Press accounts years later suggested that Primrose appreciated the fact that Hildreth was ever grateful.

A story of about this time suggests a lack of prudence on Sam Hildreth's part in terms of his associates. Hildreth was training a filly named Dixie, who was owned by a well-known gambler named Bert Webster. Having been charged with the murder of an actress, Evelyn Granville, in a Broadway hotel, Webster was in jail and in need of some ready cash to hire an attorney. Hildreth produced Dixie ready to win without attracting notice in advance. Webster scraped up his last $3,000 and, at 10-1, this was turned into a sum sufficient to cover the situation. The upshot was that Webster — innocent or not — received only a minor sentence.

One lesson learned from seeing great horses was that lesser animals might be sacrificed, in a manner of speaking, as their foils in training. During those developmental days Hildreth won a slew of races with Toano, who earlier had toiled as a workmate for James Ben Ali Haggin's champion Salvator.

Suggesting that Hildreth balanced the art of winning races with the art of winning bets was his own story of having paid $10,000 on the spot for a house near the Guttenburg track, where he recalled living for three years

— in the Toano era. The problem of his success was that he could not get decent odds on his horses with the bookmakers, who were the conduits of betting at the time. Hildreth's memoirs address this with a tale of a fellow who approached him with an understanding of Hildreth's situation and volunteered to become his betting commissioner. He would make nightly visits to the Hildreth home to be told on whom to bet, but without the bookmakers suspecting the connection. Hildreth bragged that "for a year and a half we worked this system before anybody got wise to it." (Over a number of years, Hildreth looked to William "Billy" Allen Pinkerton to handle his out-of-town bets. Pinkerton and his brother ran the family detective agency, which had been founded by their father. Hildreth and Pinkerton were also very good friends.)

The commissioner who had come to Hildreth and worked so well with him was none other than Frank James, brother — and a former cohort — of the notorious outlaw Jesse James. Hildreth must have taken much pleasure in writing or explaining to his autobiographical collaborator:

"Scrupulous honesty! That's what they'd call it in business ... When Frank James quit being a desperado he washed the slate clean. He was going straight as a string when I knew him, and there were plenty of chances for him to cheat me ... You'd never have suspected Frank James of being one of the notorious brothers who held up trains and caused a reign of terror through the Middle West in the early days. He looked more like a country storekeeper or farmer."

Not everyone was so comfortable with Frank James' past. Many years after Hildreth's death, his widow quipped to columnist Red Smith that Frank and Billy Pinkerton "never really cared for each other."

RACING FORTUNES

Hildreth wrote of meeting a Miss Mary E. Cook at Saratoga in 1892, of how she had an adverse impression of racing men, but how quickly he realized he was "running for the most valuable stake I'd ever gone after. And I knew it wasn't going to be any walkover, either." For all the Cook family's harsh assessment of "racing men" in the aggregate, the family was friendly with one of them, Fred Burlew (later the trainer of 1922 Kentucky Derby winner Morvich), who spoke up for the young Hildreth. Sam and Mary were married on August 4, 1892, having known each other a month.

The way Hildreth pursued the sport/life of horse racing produced rapid changes in fortunes. He wrote that he had $50,000 when he was married and a few months later, "I was so flat they could have placed a water-level on me and found a perfect plane." He had watched his father approach his own form of racing similarly, and he wrote matter-of-factly that being up one day and down the next was just part of the game. He apparently had the sort of attitude that was not panicked by the down times, always assuming that a win was around the corner. It was not just an attitude but also an ethic:

"It makes little difference what else there is in your make-up as long as you can bound back with a smile when things are breaking the worst possible way ... Take your winnings with a smile and tell yourself what a lucky fellow you are. Take your losses with a smile and forget them. But whatever comes or goes, smile. If you don't you're gone — on the race track."

On one occasion in these days of wandering, Hildreth was struggling at the Ingleside track in San Francisco when he was injured in a trolley car accident. He received a $500 settlement from the adjuster and promptly bet it on a horse named for his friend, W.A. Pinkerton. We have only his word on this and find it somewhat difficult to accept that even a man of such spirit as described would have done so rash a thing, but, according to his telling, that is exactly what he did and the horse won at 3-1. Hildreth kept on playing horses until "he had a regular-size bankroll again. I was back in my stride."

The natural thing was to buy up some horses, and one of them, St. Lee, won the Baldwin Hotel Handicap at 4-1: "This gave the Hildreth account at the local bank another good boost." In the trolley car accident Hildreth had slid half a car length on his hands and knees. Looking back, he linked his new success to the moment and looked to the sport of baseball for a simile likening it to "sliding home with the winning run."

If he had ever heard of putting aside part of one's wealth and investing only what he could "afford" to lose, at this stage of his life, he apparently gave the idea no heed. Setting anything aside "for a rainy day" was hardly a lesson from his formative years.

As we have said, Hildreth escaped such sad straits in the long term but seemingly was more than willing to flirt with the possibility through much of his life. The San Francisco episode of A Streetcar Named Inspire is made more dramatic by the realization that it came after Hildreth's first big welcome into the big time. His retelling dismissed it airily: "I was down until the street-car jumped the track, spilled me, and I tumbled into a winning streak. And only the year before, I had been sitting pretty as the trainer for the stable of E. J. Baldwin, or Lucky Baldwin, as everybody knew him the country over."

The deal with Baldwin put Hildreth into contact with one of the more memorable characters of his life, and he devoted a page or two to the massive landowner in his memoirs:

Santa Anita Ranch was the great property Lucky Baldwin laid out in Arcadia, near Pasadena (California), after he had grown prosperous. There was every imaginable kind of fruit and vegetable growing on its fifty thousand acres — grapes, lemons, oranges, and even great fields of wheat. The wheat was one of the things he took most pleasure in. When we used to go horseback riding together over the ranch, the most beautiful place of its kind I've ever seen, we would come to an elevation and he would sit there on his horse, straight as an arrow and reminding you of a general surveying the field of battle. "Look at that wheat, Sam, just look at all these acres of the finest wheat in the world." ... Santa Anita Ranch was the biggest thing in his life. He loved it even better than he loved the horses, and he wouldn't part with a foot of it.

(The present day Santa Anita racetrack occupies a part of that acreage and is bordered on one side by Baldwin Avenue.)

At the time Hildreth hooked up with Baldwin, the trainer had a brother-in-law, Frank Taylor, associated with the stable, and Hildreth sent his own string to California with Taylor while attending Baldwin's division in the East. Apparently, Baldwin was in a reduction mode, for in addition to winning about $65,000 in purses by Hildreth's telling, they sold off more than $100,000 worth of horses in six months. Hildreth had neglected to get the most possible out of this deal, for his arrangement with Baldwin was $500 a month in salary and 10 percent of race winnings. He had not thought to negotiate 10 percent of the sales!

Hildreth was back in Chicago as the end of the nineteenth century neared. He recalled that Ed Corrigan was again the boss of Midwestern racing and had developed a stable of his own. The two crossed swords when Corrigan bid up and bought Lucky Dog out of a selling race. Since Lucky Dog was a remaining horse from the string Hildreth had purchased after his fortuitous streetcar accident, he took offense at losing him, especially to one of the people he had trained for a few years earlier. He took his revenge by buying Hurley Burley off Corrigan after she, too, had won a selling race. Not only did Hurley Burley land a number of races for Hildreth, but the name came to the attention of a pair of stage-show producers, and they used the phrase Hurley Burley for a successful production. Hildreth said he sold Hurley Burley to William C. Whitney for $10,000.

BIG TIME FOR A SHORT TIME

It was with Whitney that Hildreth made a major climb up the ladder. Whitney was a highly prosperous transportation tycoon by the final years of the 1890s and went into racing in a big way. In 1899:

I was back on the Eastern tracks when Mr. Whitney sent a messenger and asked me to see him in the clubhouse.

"Mr. Hildreth, how would you like to train my horses?" he asked.

The question dropped out of a clear sky. There were no preliminaries.

"Who recommended me?" I asked.

"Nobody. It's my own idea. I'd like to have you manage my horses."

"When would you like an answer?"

"Now."

"All right, it's agreeable to me."

"Then it's agreed that you are to handle my horses."

There had been no talk of wages or commissions ... He had made up his mind he wanted me as trainer and was willing to pay any reasonable sum I might ask. It was just the same with him as though he were picking somebody to manage the transportation lines in New York.

Hildreth recalled training for Whitney for two winters and one summer. This was in the early days of the Whitney family dynasty, which was to breed and race an ongoing sequence of distinguished horses through the few remaining years of W.C. Whitney's life and the careers of his son, Harry Payne Whitney, and grandson, C.V. Whitney. The likes of Regret, Equipoise, Top Flight, First Flight, Phalanx, Counterpoint, Career Boy, and Silver Buck in turn wore the Eton blue and brown colors of the Whitney dynasty. (Late in the twentieth century, Marylou Whitney, C.V. Whitney's widow, bought back into the old Whitney broodmare families, and she and later husband John Hendrickson have added to the legacy with such moments as Birdstone's Belmont and Travers stakes and Bird Town's three-year-old filly championship.)

In the days of Hildreth and the founder of the dynasty, the Whitney stable was a fresh force on the scene. Not only did W.C. Whitney undertake to buy, breed, and race a major stable, but he also was instrumental in the renovation of the old Saratoga racetrack and in the establishment of Aiken, South Carolina, as a fashionable and salubrious winter headquarters for elite Thoroughbred stables.

Hildreth's choice of what event to highlight in his writing of those days is an amusing reminder that, at heart, he never got over the lure of match races. In later years columnists did retrospectives on more than a half-dozen match races Hildreth was involved in, and most were on the major tracks, many miles and years since his wandering days with his father. In the case of his Whitney stable tenure, Hildreth delighted in recalling how he had trained Admiration to defeat May Hempstead in a match of mares at Sheepshead Bay on July 1, 1899.

The tale gave him a chance to recall a deal with John E. Madden, another self-made man of the Eastern turf and at various times a friendly rival, physical combatant, and begrudging friend. Madden's modus operandi was to breed or buy horses, train them to show high potential, and sell them at a big number. As we have said, Hildreth loved to buy — harking back to Mike Dwyer's ministrations.

In the case of Admiration, Madden underestimated her when he agreed to sell her to Hildreth (for Whitney) for $4,000 if she worked a mile in 1:42 or better, with Hildreth's rider, Dick Clawson, in the irons. Admiration set sail so quickly that, well before the mile was completed, Madden suggested that $4,000 was not a sufficient price for such a flyer. Hildreth enjoyed his position. Madden held that Admiration was worth $10,000, and Hildreth privately agreed but reminded him that she was, after all, a maiden and that "a bargain is a bargain." Nevertheless, he caved. He went with Madden to confer with Whitney, who already had been told the price would be $4,000 if the filly passed muster. Whitney paid the $4,000 for Admiration but also paid $3,000 each for a couple of broodmares. Thus, Madden could say he got his adjusted price, and Whitney could say he paid what was agreed to and just happened to buy a couple of mares in an adjunct deal.

Admiration had been of little account at two, but when Hildreth got her he used liniment and steaming to cure her back's tendency to cord up. She had won five straight races, including the Spring Special over Ethelbert, when the camp of May Hempstead came looking for a match.

Before Madden bought Admiration, Eugene Leigh had trained her and May Hempstead. Leigh was sufficiently convinced that May Hempstead was the superior that he gave Hildreth a friendly warning not to "get in too deep" in backing Admiration. May Hempstead had started her campaign in Tennessee, winning the Derby and Oaks at Memphis, and had continued on her winning ways. Hildreth recalled that "the Southerners were crazy about her."

Hildreth told Clawson, "There's yellow in that May Hempstead. Just let out from the start and stick close to her." He took occasion to recall with pleasure that Whitney was not on the scene, being represented by his son, Harry Payne Whitney, and the latter had confessed to Hildreth that the excitement was too much for him and he would wander off somewhere during the race.

As matters turned out, Hildreth had the laugh, for Admiration stalked the pace and rolled home an easy winner, getting a mile in 1:40 1/5. The young Whitney, having steeled his nerves after all, slapped Hildreth on the back and shouted, "Well, we did it, didn't we, Sam old boy?"

Hildreth's enjoyment was enhanced by the fact that Admiration was a daughter of Kingston. Back in the Dwyer days when Kingston ran, he was regarded as second fiddle to stablemate Hanover, but Hildreth developed a preference for him. Later, he bragged that he had trained most of the best offspring of Kingston, and Admiration was one of them. She was reckoned the champion three-year-old filly of 1899.

Although Admiration had a strong place in Hildreth's memory, Jean Bereaud was probably the best horse he trained in his time with Whitney. (The spelling of Jean Bereaud's name has vexed proofreaders over the years. The French Impressionist painter for whom he was named was Jean Beraud, but the *American Stud Book* places an extra letter "e" in the horse's name; hence Jean Bereaud.)

At two in 1898, Jean Bereaud won four juvenile stakes for owners David Gideon and John Daly. The fourth was the Great American Stakes on June 11, and that same day, Whitney — probably with stable agent Madden striking the deal — bought the colt for $40,000. Whitney was to receive whatever purse money he won that day. The $9,750 prize accounted for some reports placing the purchase price at $30,000. For Hildreth and Whitney, Jean Bereaud added the Tremont, Great Trial, and Double Event before tailing off and losing his last two races that year. He is regarded as the champion two-year-old of 1898. (Technically, the Whitney stable was raced in the name of the owner's son-in-law, Sydney Paget, in 1898 and 1899).

The following spring, Jean Bereaud (His Highness—Carrie C., by Sensation), won the Withers in his return and next out gave Hildreth his first victory as trainer of a Belmont Stakes winner. The Belmont had not yet been linked with the Kentucky Derby and Preakness as part of the American Triple Crown, but since its inception in 1867 it had been a bellwether event on the New York Turf. Leg problems kept Jean Bereaud from further racing at three. It was also in 1899, the year Jean Bereaud won the Belmont, that Hildreth purchased the Kingston yearling colt Ballyhoo Bey from Eugene Leigh's barn. That was the deal that elicited from Whitney the curious compliment that Hildreth was "certainly no piker," although it was Whitney money, rather than his own, that the trainer was doling out.

This would prove an astute purchase and yet led to cessation of Hildreth's occupying arguably the most plum spot for a trainer at that time. On May 22, the colt made his debut and was favored, but he finished third in a field of five going five furlongs at Morris Park. The *Daily Racing Form* chart caller made a routine observation for such a circumstance, to wit, that Ballyhoo Bey "was probably a bit short, and the race will do him good." In this case, things were not that simple, however. Hildreth wrote that the colt came out of the race with a temperature of 103. Ballyhoo Bey had been fit and healthy going in, but Hildreth recalled after the fact that the youngster had been stabled earlier in a barn where a coughing outbreak occurred. "It was a peculiar case of the illness developing suddenly while the race was being run," he recalled. This was not actually so peculiar, for the stress of a race on a horse with incipient illness summons such results more often than perhaps was recognized at the time.

By Hildreth's telling, certain parties circulated the idea that the defeat was caused by poor feeding that showed Hildreth did not know how to look after a horse properly. This concept was passed along to Whitney. Whether influenced by innuendo or his own disappointment, Whitney made a financial settlement upon Hildreth and dismissed him as trainer. Madden took over the stable on an interim basis and then arranged for John W. Rogers to have the permanent post, but not before Madden brought Ballyhoo Bey back to win the rich Futurity on August 25. Tod Sloan returned from England to ride the colt in the top juvenile race of the time.

At the age of sixty, Hildreth waxed philosophical on the matter in his memoirs: "I know to this day who it was that did the knocking, but it is not bothering me. A thing like that is just part of the game."

In 1900, however, the Ballyhoo Bey incident touched off a story so sensational that it gave rise to numerous versions. Even as meticulous a Turf historian as Kent Hollingsworth wound up giving two slightly different versions in one volume, *The Great Ones*. Hollingsworth quoted the October 2, 1900, edition of the *Morning Telegraph* to the effect that Hildreth, having brooded over the matter for several months, was moved to action when he encountered Madden one evening in a restaurant near Morris Park. Hildreth grabbed a walking stick from a gentleman who was otherwise a nonplayer in the proceedings. Hildreth rearranged the place settings of a few tables with the crooked end of the weapon as he advanced upon Madden's table, and then felled the supposed villain with so strong a blow over the right eye that the stick broke. Madden had been a boxer as a youth and was meticulous, perhaps to the point of vanity, about his physical condition, and he jumped up, knocked his assailant floorward, and leapt upon him with such energy as to summon a speedy apology.

Elsewhere in *The Great Ones*, Hollingsworth's details are slightly different, although the gist, or nub, of the matter remains the same. Here, Hildreth had gotten drunk earlier in the evening, slugged a waiter, and wandered off firing a pistol. Later that night, still in rambunctious spirit, he spied Madden and whacked him with a walking stick behind an ear — left or right, not recorded. In this version, too, Madden showed extraordinary resilience and smote Hildreth with such a telling blow that the assailant "landed cold sober."

This incident involved too much high-speed action to be told consistently. Columnist Joe Vila's specifics in 1929 took the incident back to within a few days of Hildreth's parting with Whitney (perhaps there was more than one incident) and suggested that Hildreth made a motion consistent with the drawing of a firearm, right there in the Morris Park clubhouse. He reported that The Jockey Club stewards issued a fine and a warning. The prolific Neil Newman published a rendition very much at odds with the apparent consensus. By his account, the dust-up at Morris Park preceded — and prompted — Hildreth's firing from the Whitney post. Still another version, under the nom de plume of Spur, had Hildreth taking a gun into a washroom, where "a battle royal ensued. It was battle of big, powerful men — a titanic struggle." How the guy with the gun relinquished the advantage is not elaborated upon in this version.

Further complicating one's comfort in accepting of the published accounts are Hildreth's own blithe claim to a continuing friendship with Whitney and Newman's account that, at the time of the troubles, Whitney gave Hildreth the promising two-year-old colt Gold Heels, "feeling he owned the conditioner something."

Although Gold Heels was allegedly a gift horse, Hildreth took the worst of that deal, too. The trainer had been set down by stewards following his extracurricular ruckus, so he could not, of course, openly train and campaign Gold Heels on the local circuit. He assigned him to Dave Sloan as a ploy, but when Sloan ran the colt in a selling race, Mike Clancy figured out the ruse and bought the horse. When Hildreth went to Sloan for payment, Sloan responded that, under the circumstances, the transfer to himself obviously had been a gift, and he refused to pay. Hildreth, having contrived to deceive the authorities, could hardly go to them for redress. Moreover, Gold Heels, who changed hands several times, developed into the best older horse of 1902, when he won the Suburban and Brighton handicaps and Brighton Cup for owner F.C. McLewee.

Back in 1900, on the day before the stewards could respond to Hildreth's shenanigans and suspend him, he had gotten in a good score. Hildreth saddled a horse of his own, Beau Gallant, to deliver Commando his only defeat as a two-year-old. The event was the $20,000 Second Matron at Morris Park, run on October 2, and the outcome evinced from *Turf, Field, and Farm* the disgusted statement that Commando's jockey, Henry Spencer, "literally threw away the race" with his "stupid carelessness." This account claimed that while enjoying a two-length lead with about a furlong to run, Spencer looked to his right but not to his left. Beau Gallant sped past on the latter side.

The result was questionable enough that the stewards called in bookmakers' betting sheets to see if they suggested more than "stupid carelessness." Apparently nobody was thought to deserve being set down, save Spencer himself and, of course, Hildreth, but that was for nothing connected to the race, per se.

Regardless of which specific story of Hildreth's wild night (or day) out appeals most to the taste of the reader, it appears safe to say that The Jockey Club denied Hildreth a license when renewal time came up, and he was missing from the Metropolitan scene for four years. Newman opined that

Hildreth never would have received a renewal as long as Whitney lived. W.C. Whitney died in 1904, and in due course Hildreth was reinstated.

BIG MAC ATTACKS AND OTHER STARS

In the meantime, Hildreth had set out on more of the wandering that must have spoken to his soul. Thanks in part to Beau Gallant, he apparently was flush at the time he left New York. The *New York Times'* estimate of his activities between May and October had him winning $250,000 in bets and race earnings, and his thirty-horse string was said to be worth another $100,000.

During the next four years Hildreth's fields of battle included Chicago (again), New Orleans, and Memphis. By December 1904 Hildreth had apparently found a solution to one of those down times that he expected, and accepted. The *Thoroughbred Record* placed him as operating out of a glass-covered barn at Montgomery Park in Memphis and being "absolutely horseless." He was in charge of fifty-six horses, of which thirty-nine were "well-bred and highly tried yearlings," but his only personal interest in any of the animals stemmed from the fact that his wife owned two of them. All the others Hildreth had sold to E.E. Smathers, who was making a sea change of direction by moving over from the Standardbred segment of the racing order.

"I am not going out of the business," Hildreth assured the trade weekly. "I will continue to train the horses for Mr. Smathers and I hope to do better for him than I would myself."

Hildreth added a comment that seems stunning as it came from the lips of a horseman who already had trained — and would again — for a pillar of the sporting aspects of the Turf: "All I want horses for is to bet on them, anyhow, and I may as well bet on any other man's horses as my own. Mr. Smathers pays the feed bills and I haven't to worry about that."

Smathers was to be included, with Whitney, August Belmont II, and a few others, in a stratus of owners who garnered from Hildreth posthumous praise. The trainer, or his co-author, summarized much about the Turf with enviable succinctness:

"It is at the race track more than any place I know that you are able to get the measure of your man. You see him as he is at play and again you see the serious side of him as he is in his work, for horse racing is a constant changing from one to the other. You see the good winner and the bad loser and the bad winner and the good loser. The sport of racing brings out one side of a fellow's character."

The best horse Hildreth trained for Smathers was McChesney, who Hila wrote cost $40,000. Hildreth went into some detail over McChesney's appearance in the Harlem National Handicap (Chicago), his account being highly complimentary to his own wife as well as to his owner. He lamented to Smathers that he was unable to find a really top jockey for the race. Mrs. Hildreth, whose horse Favonius was due to be ridden by Charley Gray, volunteered to release the rider to ride McChesney. Smathers protested, but, as Hildreth testified, "There's one thing I've never tried to buck in this life. That is a woman with her mind made up. I told Smathers we'd lost that particular argument. "

With Gray aboard, McChesney rambled home through the mud and "E.E. Smathers bubbled over with happiness." Hildreth later learned that Smathers had won $100,000 betting in a future book. Smathers giddily forced a $1,000 bill-of-thanks upon Mrs. Hildreth, assigned the winning purse ($7,865) to the trainer, gave jockey Gray $2,500, paid the stable foreman and exercise rider $500 each, and remembered the groom with $250. In the tradition of the day, there was an actual silk "purse" hung on the wire over the finish line for the winning connections to receive ceremoniously. Hildreth enjoyed telling that the actress Blanche Bates joined the group, having "rooted hard for McChesney."

McChesney was sent east, but since Hildreth was still persona non grata in New York, brother-in-law Frank Taylor's name was invoked as official trainer. McChesney won several races, including the Twin City Handicap, First Special, and Second Special.

In *Racing in America (1866–1922)*, Walter Vosburgh described McChesney (Macduff—Manola Mason, by Top Gallant) as "about the most noted race horse in training in 1902 and 1903." Another racing historian, John Hervey, touched on the rumors that Hildreth "hopped" horses (some suggested it was a combination of strychnine and arsenic) and pointed out that several of Hildreth's best colts wound up with fertility problems. "Big Mac" — yes, Hervey actually called McChesney that — sired very few foals in his years at Elmendorf Farm before being shipped off to Argentina. Hervey made no specific declaration as to whether Big Mac received any special sauce from Hildreth, for he pointed out that the horse had several trainers. Moreover, the small number of foals might have been a matter of limited opportunity, for in that time Elmendorf owner James Ben Ali Haggin "collected stallions as freely as Caruso did fancy waistcoats." Haggin bought McChesney after his racing days.

Hildreth helped Smathers to some big days, but after two years the owner was said to have given orders that all the horses be sold. Smathers was quoted by columnist Vila that, "It has cost me a quarter of a million dollars to find out that conducting a racing stable of runners is far more difficult than owning and driving trotting horses."

Smathers was not so disgruntled as to quit frequenting New York racing as a fan and bettor, but his sporting interest later focused more on following the New York Giants and Yankees in baseball. (Therein lay a development that would lead to the final great chapter of Sam Hildreth's career.)

Getting a bead on just whether this Sam Hildreth was a sportsman, rogue, or rogue sportsman is complicated. In 1906 the *Thoroughbred Record* published a brief note that, "Samuel C. Hildreth, one of the prominent owners on the American Turf, has quit the bookmaking business after one year's trial, which cost him $41,800. He found the track followers were wiser than the bookies, and he will try to retrieve his losses by running his horses and backing them to win when he thinks his chances are the best."

NEW YORK, AGAIN

Contrast this to the fact that he was reinstated in New York and by 1909 emerged as America's leader in earnings, not only as a trainer, but also as an owner. The *American Racing Manual* had begun publishing the owners' figures as of 1902 and the trainers' figures as of 1909. Hildreth led both columns in earnings for three years, 1909–11:

Leading Owner By Earnings (no win totals given)

1909 $159,112
1910 $152,645
1911 $ 47,473 (no racing in New York, 1911–12; Hildreth headquartered in Canada in 1911)

Leading Trainer By Earnings

He was to lead the trainers by earnings no fewer than nine times and by wins twice, as set down here:

Year	Wins	Earnings
1909	73	$123,942
1910	84	$148,010
1911	67	$ 49,018
1916	39	$ 70,950
1917	23	$ 61,698
1921	85	$262,768
1922	74	$247,014
1923	75	$392,124
1924	77	$225,608

Leading Trainer By Wins

Year	Wins	Earnings
1921	85	$262,768
1927	72	$161,569

Hildreth's emergence as the leader via horses in his own silks of black, white sash, and blue sleeves, was launched in part by Fitz Herbert. A son of Ethelbert—Morganatic, by Emperor, Fitz Herbert was bred by Perry Belmont and transferred to trainer Andrew Jackson Joyner in lieu of payment of a training bill. The colt was a foal of 1906.

Although himself a noted trainer, Joyner raced Fitz Herbert in his own name but turned him over to Johnny Schlosser to train. After early defeats convinced Joyner that Fitz Herbert was a morning glory, the two-year-old was sold to Herman R. Brandt for $2,500. A few wins prompted Joyner to offer Brandt a handsome profit, as he tried to buy back Fitz Herbert for $10,000. Brandt refused, but then passage of the Hart-Agnew Law cast doubt on the future of New York racing by its anti-gambling stance. Brandt hastily looked up Joyner and said $10,000 would be just fine for the colt, but Joyner by then had been assigned to take a division of Harry Payne Whitney's stable to England. He was in no position to purchase the colt, regardless of whatever opinion he might have held about the future in New York. In another example of Hildreth's lifelong heed to old Mike Dwyer's advice to buy plenty of fast horses, it was he who stepped in and bought the colt on his own behalf, reportedly for the $10,000 asking price.

Fitz Herbert ran ten times through the rest of the year for Hildreth, winning three. Hildreth wound up the year in California, where Fitz Herbert won the Garvanza Handicap in 1:37 3/5. In modern times, California tracks have had the reputation of being faster than those in the East and Midwest; perhaps that insinuation was already developing, for Fitz Herbert's time was the fastest then on record for a two-year-old at a mile.

At three in 1909, Fitz Herbert turned in a stunning campaign, winning fourteen of fifteen, and he is regarded retrospectively as the overall champion racehorse that year. One race he did not win was the Belmont Stakes, but Hildreth won that classic anyway, with the colt Joe Madden. (Joe Madden was the leading earner of 1909, with $44,905, but money is not everything in championship decision making.)

The Suburban Handicap had been inaugurated in 1884 and was regarded as one of the most important races in America, perhaps the single most important. Fitz Herbert followed Africander (1903) as the second horse to win the handicap as a three-year-old. He got in with 105 pounds but was giving a pound to the runner-up, Alfred Noble, a four-year-old.

Looking back nearly four decades later, Neil Newman wrote in *The Blood-Horse*, "Fitz Herbert was actually never menaced until the Lawrence Realization in July." In addition to the Suburban, he had won the Pocantico, Broadway, and Advance stakes and had walked over in the Coney Island Jockey Club Stakes. Then Olambala came to challenge in the Lawrence Realization, off a victory in the Latonia Derby two starts back. Each carried 122 pounds. Fitz Herbert led from the start, but Olambala rumbled up from fourth and got to within a length of the leader in the stretch. Fitz Herbert would not allow him to take the lead and got home by a length in 2:45, a record for a mile and five-eighths at Sheepshead Bay. Fitz Herbert was ridden that day by Vince Powers, who would carve a unique niche for himself as the only rider to lead the nation's jockeys on the flat and later do the same in the jumping division.

Hildreth was not averse to hard campaigns, but he was no butcher. He let up on Fitz Herbert until the autumn when the grand colt continued winning, taking four more victories. Then came his only defeat of the year, when the filly Affliction came across the field from the outside so recklessly that she ruined the Occidental Handicap from the start. Fitz Herbert went to his knees and could not recover in the race.

Within a week he took up 130 pounds and won the Jerome Handicap, again beating Olambala (120) by a length, this time at a mile and five-sixteenths. Giving an additional five pounds to Olambala, he beat him again, at a mile and one-eighth, in the Election Day Handicap, before heading down to Maryland to conclude his East Coast season. There he won the Hall Stakes under 131 pounds, setting a track record of 2:08 at Pimlico. Only two days later he was back for the Bowie Stakes, the conditions of which let him in with only 106 pounds. Fitz Herbert set a new American record of 3:25 4/5 for two miles.

In addition to racing the top three-year-old in 1909, Hildreth also had under his shed row the champion older horse. This was King James. Bred by Madden, he was by Plaudit, one of the five Kentucky Derby winners that master horseman bred. A foal of 1905, King James was out of the Purse-bearer mare Unsightly. He was destined to become the first $100,000-earn-er Madden bred, and that he accomplished most of this in Hildreth's colors indicates the two wheeler-dealers would not let the occasional physical assault preclude them from doing business in the arena they shared. It was said they eventually became friends. (The aforementioned Belmont Stakes winner Joe Madden, named for one of Madden's sons, was another who went from Madden to Hildreth.)

Historian Newman wrote that in King James' first two seasons the colt won only five of twenty-nine races, but Hildreth was emboldened to pay a good price to buy him. He reported it as $8,000 while other sources placed the price at that rather popular figure of the day, $10,000. "After Hildreth purchased him, he displayed marked improvement," Newman noted. Improving on the efforts of one so renowned as John E. Madden would do nothing to assuage rumors that Hildreth had some secrets of the sort that would not be mentioned in his memoirs.

Traveling from the East to Canada and to the West, King James won ten of twelve at age four, including the Metropolitan and Brooklyn handicaps, the Toronto Cup, and the California Handicap. (In winning the Metropolitan and Brooklyn with King James and the Suburban with Fitz Herbert, Hildreth got a sweep of the three races for many years revered as the New York Handicap Triple Crown.)

Various observers held the view that Hildreth was a cold, calculating fellow to whom horses were instruments of either betting or racing and nothing more. Others suggested a more animal-friendly attitude. Hildreth himself belied some sentiment in his tendency to call King James "King Jimmy," and he indicated admiration in writing of him as "stout and strong, possessed of a lion's courage." King James was unusually voracious at the feed tub, and Hildreth "had to almost kill him to get him ready for a race."

Even at that, King James' heavy eating was perhaps less bothersome to Hildreth than it might have been to other trainers. In a profile on Hildreth in the sprightly young magazine the *New Yorker*, not long before the horseman's death in 1929, author Nevin Busch Jr. wrote:

> One funny part of his system is the way he keeps his stable fat. When the horses are led down to the track to be exercised early in the morning, he looks them over and sends some back to the barn; these are the ones he thinks look in racing condition. Most other trainers exercise even the horses that are ready to do their best; in fact, if any other trainer sent an entry to the post as fat as some of Hildreth's horses are, no one would believe that it was fit. Because he keeps flesh on them, his horses last longer, and are able to retain top form with only short layoffs during an entire season.

At five in 1910, King James carried 129 pounds to the champion filly Maskette's 123 and got up to beat her by a half-length at a mile in the Sheepshead Bay Handicap. Newman regarded that as one of King James' best races of the year, along with the Brighton Mile, in which he closed with a rush to defeat Hilarious. Part of the great stable raced by James R. Keene, Hilarious had been second only to Fitz Herbert among the three-year-olds of the previous year.

King James was retired to stud, having won or placed in forty-eight of fifty-seven races and earning $107,546. He had won at distances from five and a half furlongs to one and a quarter miles and while carrying up to 142 pounds. (He was not generally a success at stud and was moved from farm to farm during his breeding career, but one thread comes down to present time through his son Spur. Winner of the Travers Stakes, Spur begot Sting, sire of Questionnaire, and the male-line sequence of importance thereafter went through Questionnaire and Free For All to Rough'n Tumble. Rough'n Tumble sired 1968 Horse of the Year Dr. Fager, a factor in twenty-first century pedigrees, but it was a lesser son of Rough'n Tumble, Minnesota Mac, whose branch of the sire line brought us Holy Bull and his 2005 Kentucky Derby-winning son Giacomo, etc.)

The year King James was five, 1910, Hildreth repeated as leading owner, as noted above. Fitz Herbert was back in action that year but limited in his campaign. He had begun to show soundness problems by the end of his three-year-old season and was never completely sound again. At four, Fitz Herbert ran only twice but won both times, taking the Jockey Club Weight-for-Age at a mile and one-eighth and then defeating old rival Olambala (116) under 130 pounds in the mile and a quarter Brooklyn Handicap. Despite the brevity of that campaign, he is recorded by historians as, again, America's best racehorse for 1910.

The wealth of talent Hildreth orchestrated during that year also included Novelty, whom he tabbed late in his career as the best two-year-old he had ever trained. In 1910 Novelty won eleven of sixteen races and earned $72,630. He carried as much as 135 pounds victoriously, and his major triumphs included the Saratoga Special, Hopeful Stakes, and Rensselaer Handicap. Hildreth still loved match races, and Novelty defeated Textile in such a two-horse battle at Saratoga. The Futurity, the juvenile's major dash at six furlongs, had been moved temporarily to Saratoga from Sheepshead Bay. One of Hildreth's stable jockeys, Carroll Shilling, brought Novelty home under 127 pounds over Bashti (118). The winner's purse was $25,360, well under the $67,675 the Futurity was worth to Potomac as far back as 1890 but still a handsome contribution to the leading owner's total.

Novelty was another sired by Hildreth's old favorite, Kingston. His dam was Curiosity, by Voter. For one who trolled others' fishing grounds, Hildreth must have found satisfaction in acquiring Novelty from the stable of another of the giants of the day, James R. Keene.

Historians settled on seven champions or co-champions of divisions for racing in 1910. Hildreth owned three of them. In addition to older male Fitz Herbert and juvenile colt Novelty, the stable included Dalmatian, who is ranked with Keene's Sweep atop the three-year-old males in the unofficial chart of champions compiled by Kent Hollingsworth as editor of *The Blood-Horse*.

Dalmatian, like Fitz Herbert, was an Ethelbert colt bred by Perry Belmont. He was out of Ionis, by Magnetizer. Although the racing establishment had been successful to that time in its delaying tactics against anti-gambling reform, New York Turfmen were nervous about the future. Hildreth got the two-year-old colt in 1909 for only $400 after Belmont told his trainer, Doc Carter, to sell everything on the farm that he had recently launched in Kentucky. While noting that "I've never had a liking for professional reformers," Hildreth conceded that, if not for their activities, he would not have gotten Dalmatian for such a modest figure.

Dalmatian won the Travers, Coney Island, Brooklyn Derby, and Empire City Handicap. Hildreth placed his earnings at $39,000 and recalled selling him for $40,000 afterward to Louis Winans of Baltimore. (Fitz Herbert was to be sold to Winans at the same time, but he had been pin-fired as a yearling, and Winans did not want any horses that showed the scars of having been fired, regardless of their success.) Dalmatian was sent to England, where he won the Manchester November Handicap.

In 1911 the hammer fell. All ruses were exhausted, and New York racing was shut down. Several top stables scurried to England; others dispersed to states that still allowed racing, but those states did not prosper at New York's expense. The market for Thoroughbreds presaged the stock market crash eighteen years later. Hildreth repaired to Canada for much of 1911 before swinging down to Maryland in the fall. His earnings as trainer and owner were less than one-third of what they had been in 1910, but he led North America in both categories.

Distraught, Hildreth put up his whole stable for auction on September 7, 1911, but he was too sharp a self-protectionist to fall victim to his own despair. The first horse had barely gone through the ring before Hildreth thought back to what Perry Belmont had done and realized he did not have the stomach for a similar fire sale. "I could picture them bidding a few dollars for Fitz Herbert or King James or Novelty, and I'd rather have given the whole lot away than to take the prices I knew were far, far below what they should be. It was a mistake to offer them at auction." The sale was off.

Hildreth's recollection of how he handled the situation next is similar to logic teachers' phrase "decision-by-indecision." He would wait in the thought that "a better solution would come out of a bad muddle. Yes, that was the thing to do."

Well, as so often happened, Hildreth got this one right. A few days later, he was sitting in the library of the home he had by then purchased in Sheepshead Bay when, not for the first nor the last time, a major industrialist came calling. In this instance, the telephone call came from Charles E. Kohler, whose last name was affixed to the pianos he manufactured and sold. Kohler invited Hildreth to his Ramapo Farm the next day, and in the subsequent meeting, Hildreth agreed to sell him all that was left in his stable, for $150,000, and to take the lot to Europe and train them for racing there.

Hildreth paused in his memoirs to suggest that puffing a cigar or two over this deal was far superior to the disillusion of watching his stable of stars be sundered into many, underpriced divisions. He accepted, forthwith.

Here Hildreth's and Crowell's version of events bumps up against rumor. The Hildreths took jockey Carroll Shilling (destined to a sad and alcoholic end) with them to England, where A.J. Joyner (briefly owner of Fitz Herbert) showed them around. Hildreth's rendition was that he did not feel comfortable with the English pattern of racing, which would require horses being moved from course to course for individual races or split among different locales at the same time. He concluded that sending the stable to France was preferable, and Kohler consented.

Other sources suggested that the preference for France stemmed from the fact that Hildreth learned he would not receive a license to train in England.

Whatever the real case in England, Hildreth encountered problems with officialdom in France. He cited August Belmont II and Baron Maurice de Rothschild as major figures in racing, internationally, and they sent letters on his behalf. Five months passed before Hildreth received a license.

It might be plausible to think that a visitor would choose France over England because stabling outside Paris would involve less tedious, day-to-day travel than setting up at a central yard in England. Against this must be stacked the fact that, in those days, very few flat races in France were open to horses from abroad. Thus, if Kohler agreed for Hildreth to set up shop in France, the likes of Futurity winner Novelty and champion Fitz Herbert would be trained to become steeplechasers. Another ameliorating aspect to this, however, was that Kohler, in his enthusiasm for the Turf, leased a breeding farm in France.

To have a stable of high-class New York horses of last year struggling to adjust to steeplechasing this year is something as foreign to modern sensibilities as can be imagined. There were, however, a share of victories, and Hildreth's book includes a photo of Futurity winner Novelty clearing a jump in the Prix de Monte Carlo in Nice in 1913 — surely a singular moment in the history of Futurity winners.

During one special international week of racing at Maison-Laffitte, non-French horses were allowed on the flat, and Novelty crammed two victories into the meeting. Fitz Herbert had stepped on a stone and had to be retired. To keep some semblance of regular action, Hildreth acquired some French platers to campaign.

Hildreth was more vexed by officialdom than rewarded by his charges. He picked up on the fact that a veterinary official had targeted American horses for drug testing, and indeed Hildreth was accused of doping after heroin allegedly was found on the tongue of one of his runners. Eugene Leigh, another international horsemen whom Hildreth had known for years, suffered a similar accusation. At length, Hildreth recalled, that particular veterinary official was determined to be a "rank faker" and had been merely "craving to be in the public eye."

Whether due to a new sense of financial responsibility or success, Hildreth wrote that he was able to transfer $100,000 from his New York account when he moved to France. He and Mrs. Hildreth frequently passed a handsome chateau and kept telling each other that it was totally impractical to purchase it, but, eventually, they gave in and did just that. Hildreth had to wire to New York for another $30,000 or so to pay for the necessary repairs and improvements. How far he had come from Red Morocco!

The lack of opportunities for their horses would eventually be solved, as Kohler and Hildreth planned it, by Kohler's acquisition of the farm in France and the eventuality of Fitz Herbert, Novelty, Uncle, and others siring French-bred colts and fillies. This plan was ended abruptly, and sadly. In June 1913, Kohler traveled from America to France. He died suddenly, only five days later — "cut down at the time he expected to get the most out of life," lamented Hildreth.

Hasty arrangements were made for the horses to be dispersed at Deauville. Fitz Herbert and Novelty were among those sold for stud duty. Novelty was sent to Brazil, where he preserved some importance as the Kingston male line progenitor for several generations.

Hildreth recalled that August Belmont II, perhaps the most important figure in American racing, was in Paris at the time of Kohler's death. Racing had returned to New York, as some creative interpretations of the law had been invoked, and, by Hildreth's telling, Belmont asked him to come home and train his stable.

Hildreth wrote of his homesickness and noted that he and Mrs. Hildreth were able to sell their chateau to fellow American John Sanford and almost get out on the price and renovation costs.

"The stay in Paris had been fine, and we had had our share of success with the Kohler horses," Hildreth recalled, "but after all there's no place like home. I was anxious to see the old familiar faces again in the paddocks. I was itching for somebody to come along and give me a hard slap on the back and shoot a few American cuss words in my direction … It wasn't because I didn't like France especially, but because I do like America particularly."

YOU CAN GO HOME AGAIN

So it was that Vince Hildreth's son Sam, chased out of New York less than fifteen years before, was invited back and hired to train for the chairman of The Jockey Club and head of the racing commission, in sum, given perhaps the most prestigious training job of all.

Hildreth reveled in his return after fifteen months but not out of arrogance:

> In all my years of racing I never got a finer kick out of anything than the one I received when I again set foot on an American race course. Back in the old haunts, among my old friends, and the old scenes just as they were before we'd gone to Europe. It was a beau-

tiful summer day, the day of our return, and the fragrance of the flowers and the soft beauty of the green shrubbery lining the walks of the Saratoga race course, and the flags flying and the band up there in the grandstand … all of it gave me a thrill that comes once in a lifetime. Maybe my friends will not say I'm a demonstrative fellow, but I was so tickled by it all that I could have danced around and given three rousing cheers, all by myself. I went around shaking hands with everybody … I felt like shaking hands and I did. I was almost sorry I'd gone on the water wagon while we were in France.

This was but one of several references Hildreth and co-author Crowell slipped in to *The Spell of the Turf* about drinking. It is not specified that the alleged assault on Madden created any change of habits. Instead, Hildreth places the change in France. In another reference, he states that memory of a run of luck that prompted much convivial celebration by others was enough to "make my mouth water, even now that champagne is no more for me." He asserts, looking back from the book's origins of 1926, "I have been a teetotaler now going on fifteen years."

Hildreth would write in admiration that the sportsman Belmont could be more friendly and kind when he was losing than when he won. The early days of their arrangement brought less success than Hildreth yearned for, but Belmont consoled him that, "We're both doing everything we can to make our horses win, and that's the most anybody can do. Forget that I own the horses and look upon them as yours. Then we'll both be happy." Belmont changed trainers several times in his career, and he might have intended his added comment as a reminder: "And just keep this fact in mind: If the time ever comes that I think the horses aren't being handled to the best advantage, I'll let you know."

To suggest that he was unhappy with the early results would indicate Hildreth's exceptional expectations. Belmont's Stromboli (Fair Play—Saint Priscilla, by Rayon d'Or) won eight races in 1914, recalled William H.P. Robertson in *The History of Thoroughbred Racing in America*. Robertson put the year into perspective: "Like a patient returned from the hospital, by 1914 American racing, although by no means recovered, began to show signs of getting back its strength."

In 1913 Harry Payne Whitney's Whisk Broom II provided the Turf a highlight by sweeping the Metropolitan, Suburban, and Brooklyn handicaps. The old races had been picked up, prestige intact. Two years later Stromboli won two of the three, the Metropolitan and Suburban, for owner Belmont and trainer Hildreth. Nevertheless, Hildreth wanted more. Then, in 1916 and 1917 Hildreth had the sort of combination he had become accustomed to in the years immediately before his French excursion. In

Belmont homebreds Friar Rock and Hourless, the stable had back-to-back three-year-old champions.

Friar Rock was by the English Triple Crown winner, Rock Sand, whom Belmont had imported, and he was out of Fairy Gold, the dam of Fair Play. It was a pedigree that turned around the combination that would produce Man o' War, who was by Fair Play and out of a Rock Sand mare.

Hildreth wrote that Friar Rock was "not only the best horse I have ever trained over a distance of ground, but the best I have ever seen." He was given to superlatives and from time to time changed his mind about the best horse he had trained, but Friar Rock did have a credible claim on such distinction. After winning a pair of stakes at two, he started his three-year-old season in 1916 losing the Metropolitan, then matched Fitz Herbert's feat of defeating older horses in the Suburban Handicap. He lost the Withers but snapped back to run away from his field in the Belmont Stakes. He scored two notable victories under light weights against older horses, in the Suburban and Brooklyn handicaps. He remains the only horse to win both those handicaps at three.

Through the rest of the 1916 season, Friar Rock won some and lost some, but he capped his season with an impressive win in the mile and three-quarters Saratoga Cup. There he faced only two horses, but they were cracks, The Finn and Roamer. The Finn was 4-5, but Friar Rock ran him down and then held off Roamer to win by two lengths. Friar Rock is reckoned the best horse of any age in 1916. Belmont then sold him to Madden for $50,000.

The following year, 1917, brought Hourless onto the stage among the three-year-olds. Hourless was by Negofol—Hour Glass II, by Rock Sand. The son of a French Derby winner, he was foaled at Southcourt Stud in England and imported by Belmont as a yearling.

At two Hourless had won the Juvenile early on, then after several defeats won the Grand Union Hotel Stakes and late in the season added the Eastern Shore and Annapolis Stakes. Hildreth recalled that he had "dazzling speed" and that trainer and owner sensed that "we had a horse of exceptional qualities, one that would leave his mark on Turf records in the second year of his running."

As a three-year-old, Hourless started with a win in the Withers Stakes. This was followed by a ten-length victory in the Belmont Stakes, in track-record time of 2:17 4/5 for the mile and three-eighths. It was Hildreth's fourth win in the Belmont and the third for owner Belmont, as both a breeder and owner. After adding the Southampton Handicap under 130 pounds, Hourless encountered Omar Khayyam, an English-bred who that spring had become the first foreign-bred winner of the Kentucky Derby. The two English-breds hooked up for the first time in the Brooklyn Derby (renamed the Dwyer Stakes the following year). Hourless was a big, long-striding horse who could not handle wet going, and he was unable or un-willing to extend himself so was last of four starters as Omar Khayyam won. Hildreth used Hourless as an example to debunk the often-stated opinion that a good horse is supposed to be able to run in any footing.

Omar Khayyam proceeded to sweep the Kenner, Travers, and Saratoga Cup before he met Hourless again in the Lawrence Realization, at level weights. The race had a field of only three, but Hildreth recalled that his rider, Jimmy Butwell, managed to get shut off at one point and to drop his whip. In a prolonged duel Omar Khayyam defeated Hourless by a nose. Hildreth confessed he could not stand to see a horse lose such a race when he was convinced he should win, and he unleashed a stream of curse words that prompted Belmont's observation, "Mr. Hildreth, I didn't know you had it in you to get as mad as that."

Before a series of anti-climactic, or worse, match races from 1941 through 1975 dampened American racing's enthusiasm for the *mano a mano* style of racing, matching two stars was a more common reaction to rivalries. Hildreth, of course, had been weaned on just such a concept. With Belmont's complicity, he approached Colonel Matt Winn, then manager of Laurel, and asked if he would put on a special race between Hourless and Omar Khayyam. Winn could sense it was prompted by pique over the Realization, and he knew how to turn this to his advantage. Winn in due time announced that Omar Khayyam's owner, Wilfrid Viau, and trainer, Dick Carman, were agreeable. The race would be known as the American Champion Stakes and would be run at a mile and a quarter, $10,000 a side. The only caveat was that the track must be fast. Belmont decreed that if Hourless won, the money would go to the Red Cross for war relief, for World War I had become a grim reality of the time. Belmont, in fact, was crossing the Atlantic when the race was run. At age sixty-five he had accepted a commission and an overseas assignment.

Rain postponed the race for a week. When it was run, on October 18, many horsemen expressed their agreement with Hildreth about Hourless' superiority, and he was 3-4 against the other colt's odds of 13-10. Ever-ett Haynes was Omar Khayyam's jockey, and Hildreth had done nothing to discourage the presumption that Butwell would be back on Hourless. About ten minutes before it was time to saddle, Hildreth told his assis-tant to report to the jockey room and bring out Frankie Robinson for the mount! Hildreth explained that he was "a cool-headed youngster with a fine pair of hands and good judgment of pace." Robinson was good enough to be under contract to the Whitney stable.

Hildreth wrote of the match race as "the most remarkable horse race I have ever seen," again hinting at a taste for hyperbole. Another who wrote glowingly of the event in his memoirs was J.K.M. Ross, whose father, J.K.L. Ross, was establishing a major stable around that time and in two years would win the first Triple Crown with Sir Barton. The Ross memoir, *Boots and Saddles* (written with Van Varner some forty years later), tells of the younger Ross' boyhood memories of those and other thrilling horses:

"I prattled about hairline finishes and dead heats to such an extent that my father … attempted to put a damper on my enthusiasm. 'Match races are wonderful in prospect — that's why they're run — but … they are often terrible duds.' "

The Hourless–Omar Khayyam race was anything but a dud. As would be the case in other match races, it was the supposed closer whose connections set out to dominate the race. Thus, Omar Khayyam sped the first half-mile in :47 4/5, although the Laurel track was never known to be particularly fast. Hourless stalked him. Haynes realized how fast they were going and slowed to a :25 1/5 third quarter-mile, then finished a mile in 1:38 2/5.

Robinson brought Hourless up gradually, and he reached even terms by the furlong pole. For a time, "Neither gave an inch," Ross recalled, "but in that final sixteenth of a mile, Hourless gradually and inexorably drew away, an inch or two only with each stride. Omar Khayyam fought on, and gamely, but … Hourless, refusing to be denied, crossed the finish line a length in advance of the stouthearted Omar Khayyam … "

The time of 2:02 was a track record.

Hildreth and Crowell wrote with the same passion of Ross and Varner, to wit, "the most remarkable part of the performance was the way he had done it. The last quarter was run in :23 3/5, a speed that you will usually find in the early part of sprint races instead of the last two furlongs of a distance contest … Hourless' speed was the kind that will test the heart and running qualities of any race horse. None except one that has the fibre of a champion can accomplish it."

Hourless raced no more at three while Omar Khayyam had one more important victory and was well ahead in earnings. The list of champions compiled by *The Blood-Horse* lists the colts as co-champions as three-year-olds for 1917, with the older Old Rosebud the Horse of the Year in retrospect.

MORE BARGAINS

August Belmont II was undergoing a difficult time in his life. Not only was he in Europe for the war effort, but his dogged investment in the Cape Cod Canal project had crimped his finances. Worse, the death of son August III grieved him. He did not lose interest in his horses but made the decision to sell most of his yearlings during several seasons. Most famously, he sold Man o' War as a yearling at Saratoga in 1918, the great future champion landing with Sam Riddle for $5,000.

Of the horses on the racetrack that Belmont disposed of, several were acquired (some reports indicate leased) by Hildreth himself, and they helped sustain the momentum of success as the trainer moved into his fifties.

One of these was Lucullite (Trap Rock—Lucky Lass, by Ormondale), who won the Colorado, Juvenile, and Youthful stakes in 1917 while racing for Belmont. Then, prior to the Hopeful, Debadou kicked him near the start and injured his leg so severely that he did not regain his best form until he was a four-year-old. That year, for Hildreth, Lucullite won nine of seventeen races, his five stakes wins including the Manhattan, Aqueduct, and Edgemere handicaps. In another stakes, the Mt. Vernon, he carried 127 pounds and defeated champions Old Rosebud (126) and Sun Briar (128). Nevertheless, historian Vosburgh regarded Lucullite's best performance to have come in the Toboggan Handicap, in which he gave eleven pounds to the crack sprinter Billy Kelly and was beaten only a neck despite being "crowded several times."

Another major winner Hildreth acquired from Belmont was Mad Hatter (Fair Play—Madcap, by Rock Sand). Mad Hatter was a contemporary of 1919 Triple Crown winner Sir Barton, and he defeated the Ross stable champion in the Pimlico Autumn Handicap (getting twenty-one pounds) at three that year. This race was central to a dust-up described by Dorothy Ours in her 2006 book *Man o' War: A Legend Like Lightning* (St. Martin's Press). Author Ours describes accusations by Sir Barton's trainer Bedwell that Hildreth had "influenced" John Loftus, jockey of Sir Barton, to blow the race. Whether this accusation was taken seriously or not, Hildreth was not disciplined.

Mad Hatter also won the Latonia Championship by eight lengths, earning $44,090, an enormous purse at the time. Even so, he was not rated second best three-year-old to Sir Barton. That runner-up status was assigned to Purchase, yet another horse whom Hildreth had, well, purchased. Named for a town in Westchester County, New York, Purchase was owned by George Smith, for whom he broke his maiden at Saratoga and subsequently ran third behind Dunboyne in the Futurity. But for swerving severely early in the race, Purchase might well have won the Futurity. Sir Barton, although still a maiden, ran second in a hint of what was to come.

Purchase was by Ormondale, a Futurity winner and among the few good horses sired by the English wonder horse Ormonde. (The 1886 English Triple Crown winner had impaired fertility.) Purchase was out of Cherryola, by Tanzmeister. Hildreth was familiar with both the sire and dam and, impressed by the colt's glorious appearance, made an offer, and Smith accepted it.

To Hildreth, Purchase was "a great, massive horse, for a 2-year-old, with a rich chestnut coat that sparkled, a broad noble head that is the mark of a fine race horse, and a smooth action that told of a world of speed and power yet to be developed." Eventually, Purchase was one who earned the encomium of "the best horse I ever trained, and I say that without any strings to it."

Purchase was injured late in his two-year-old year, and the next spring when Hildreth was eyeing the Kentucky Derby, the big colt reared in his stall and injured himself by hanging his feet in his hayrack. As Sir Barton raced through the first Triple Crown, with the Withers Stakes thrown in for good measure, Hildreth stewed in the thought that he had a horse that could have been doing such things.

Given the hand he was dealt, Hildreth by and large kept Purchase away from Sir Barton after he got him back to the races. When he did challenge the Triple Crown winner, he picked his spot adroitly. The challenge came in the Dwyer, Sir Barton's first race after the Belmont. Ross recalled it as one of trainer Guy Bedwell's few mistakes, for he felt he had let up on Sir Barton and then not tightened him enough to face Purchase while giving away nine pounds. Sir Barton led most of the way, but Purchase came along and beat him by three lengths.

Purchase won nine of eleven races at three that year. His other winning races included the Stuyvesant Handicap (129) over Eternal, the Saranac (133), Huron (134), and Saratoga Handicap. The year saw the inauguration of the Jockey Club Stakes (later Jockey Club Gold Cup). While this race was destined for a high rank among America's coveted prizes, the first running was disappointing, for Purchase was the lone entrant to arrive at the start for a walkover.

Neither of the two races Purchase lost diminished his status. In the Brooklyn Handicap, he carried 117 pounds, a high weight for a three-year-old in an open handicap during the summer, and was second to another three-year-old, Eternal (103). The other loss came at the hands of the great old campaigner Exterminator in the Saratoga Cup, one of those races that left Hildreth steaming in the thought that he should have won.

Hildreth recalled turning down an offer of $300,000 for Purchase that autumn. The agent carrying the offer never identified his client, but Hildreth conjectured it was J.K.L. Ross trying to add to his already burgeoning team. A few weeks later the colt struck some obstacle on the track while working at Laurel and tore ligaments in his right foreleg. The injuries at both two and three prompted Hildreth to regard the Adonis of the Turf as a hard-luck customer. Hildreth got Purchase back to the races at five, when he won two sprints downstate, carrying 140 pounds in the latter, before wrenching an ankle on the train to Saratoga. Purchase was then retired, having won fourteen of twenty-three races, to earn more than $39,000.

The next year, 1920, saw Sam Riddle's Man o' War parade through his three-year-old season unbeaten. In his memoirs, Hildreth paused to pay homage to the horse, although he neither owned nor trained him. The chapter recalling the career of Purchase is titled "The Horse of the Century", and generously describes Man o' War as "the greatest race horse the American Turf has ever seen." Without apparent gnashing of teeth, Hildreth recalled that he had handled Man o' War's full sister, Masda, and, given her morning speed, he might have bid on Man o' War himself had he not been concentrating on horses in training instead of yearlings. (Hildreth chose not to mention that it had been he who advised Belmont to get rid of Masda.)

During Man o' War's domination, Hildreth slipped in some highlights of his own in 1920. One was the Brooklyn Handicap, in which horses he owned and trained ran first and third, with champion Exterminator finishing fourth. Hildreth's Cirrus (Tracery—Morningside, by Meddler) defeated Ross' Boniface while Hildreth's Mad Hatter was third. Cirrus had been bred by Harry Payne Whitney from the portion of his broodmare band that he quartered in England and was purchased by Hildreth for $25,000. After his retirement, Cirrus died in a fire at Rancocas Stud, a conflagration that also took the young sire prospect Inchcape.

Also in 1920, the four-year-old Mad Hatter won nine races, including the Pimlico Serial No. 2, in which he not only beat Sir Barton again but also the latter's vaunted stablemate Billy Kelly. Mad Hatter's victory in the Bowie Handicap found him defeating an exceptional field including Exterminator, Paul Jones, The Porter, and Boniface.

The biggest moment for Hildreth in 1920, however, might have been his introduction to Harry F. Sinclair.

ONE FINAL, SPECTACULAR FLOURISH

Hildreth had been leading trainer in earnings in 1916 and 1917, and then the Sir Barton and Man o' War connections, Bedwell and Louis Feustel, had taken over for the next three years. In 1921 Hildreth was to be back on top, and he had another illustrious character in tow.

Hildreth wrote that one afternoon at the races late in 1920, the caterer Harry M. Stevens introduced him to Sinclair. Not long afterward, Hildreth's former patron, E.E. Smathers, introduced him to the same individual, explaining that this Sinclair fellow was big on baseball and that he, Smathers, was trying to convince him that horse racing was a better sport. Sinclair and Hildreth enjoyed a laugh about the fact that forces were throwing them together. Before the brief meeting ended, Smathers had Hildreth mark his and Sinclair's cards, and Hildreth put them onto several winners.

This sequence of circling several productive numbers was repeated several times and piqued Sinclair's interest to the extent that he and Hildreth started a pool arrangement to use Sinclair's money to bet on Hildreth's picks. This led Sinclair to ask Hildreth to sell him a share in one of his horses — a suggestion quickly accepted.

Sinclair and Hildreth had an essential spirit in common, but with different facades. The young Hildreth had seen the world of horse racing and accepted it as the true life, and his changes of course had been only to climb to a different level of the same essential. The young Sinclair had had similar leanings toward upward striving, but having started as a pharmacist, he found it necessary to seek an entirely different milieu. He found himself in the oil business and presently became head of Sinclair Consolidated Oil Corporation, a holding company with a billion dollars in assets. Hildreth had to like such a fellow.

In 1920, the year he met Hildreth, Sinclair had lost millions in attempting to have his Federal Baseball League establish parity with the National League and American League, but it did not dent his spirit. This horse racing looked good to Sinclair, and he moved quickly. By 1921 he had purchased the former Turf kingpin Pierre Lorillard's handsome farm, Rancocas, in New Jersey, and he and Hildreth had become partners in the operation and in the horses Hildreth had owned solely a few months before.

At the start, Sinclair saw Rancocas as a partnership with Hildreth. He was perhaps forgetting that as successful as his trainer friend was, there were a number of serious zeroes separating a man who reveled in having $100,000 and himself, who dealt at the $1,000,000,000 mark. Hildreth fairly soon had to come to the man with the thought that the splendid farm, its upkeep, and the drive to purchase top-class horses put the venture above his capacity. No matter. Hildreth would stay on as trainer and manager, and the farm and horses would belong to Sinclair. Hildreth always loved the independence of owning his own stable, but once again a patron had come calling with a deal that brooked no denial.

In 1921 the fledgling Rancocas was the leading owner in America, with $263,500, and Sam Hildreth returned to the top of the trainers' list. The pattern would be repeated the next two years.

Mad Hatter was the mainstay among the older horses, having joined the Rancocas fold to carry the green-and-white silks at five. He was regarded, along with grand old Exterminator, as best of his age division, and he got in a victory over the co-champion in the Kings County Handicap. Mad Hatter also won the Metropolitan Handicap and a second Jockey Club Gold Cup among his eight victories.

However, the star of Rancocas, and, indeed the horse rated best in America in 1921, was Grey Lag. John E. Madden bred Grey Lag and came to rank him as the best horse he had ever bred. This put Grey Lag above Sir Barton and four other Kentucky Derby winners. Grey Lag was by Madden's five-time leading stallion Star Shoot and out of Miss Minnie, by Meddler.

Madden sold Grey Lag as a yearling along with a filly, to an up-and-coming trainer, Max Hirsch; the price was a Madden favorite, $10,000. Grey Lag (named for a northern European species of goose) showed promise at two in 1920, and a number of onlookers thought him unlucky not to win the Futurity. Hildreth, trolling for himself and Sinclair at the time, asked Hirsch to price the colt and got the answer of $40,000. This did not end the negotiations, but closer inspection did. Hildreth noted an odd patch of gray hair on Grey Lag's back, and it spoke to some superstition he harbored, and he demurred.

After Grey Lag won the Champagne Stakes, however, Sinclair himself asked Hirsch what it would take to buy the horse. He brushed aside Hirsch's conscientious reminder that Sinclair's trainer had already turned down Grey Lag. Hirsch quickly added $20,000 to the former price, and Sinclair declared the deal done, at $60,000. Hildreth may have had a number of superstitions — he would never ship a horse to another track on a Friday — but a countering principle was not to offend an owner throwing money at horses.

Through the rest of the year, Grey Lag won the Remsen and Autumn Day stakes for his new owner and trainer, although Tryster was reckoned the best two-year-old of the crop.

The next year Grey Lag was the best thing around, winning nine of thirteen races and earning $62,596. He got off to a shaky start, though. A stone bruise caused his withdrawal from the Kentucky Derby two days before the race, but he won one of his first two starts after his recovery. Then came eight consecutive victories, the highlights of which included Hildreth's fifth Belmont Stakes, followed by a score in the Brooklyn Handicap over a remarkable field presenting Exterminator, Mad Hatter, Derby winner Paul Jones, John P. Grier, and Eternal.

Grey Lag added the Dwyer on July 7, and Hildreth, or Sinclair, must have gotten carried away. By the end of the month, he had won five more races. That got to the bottom of Grey Lag, and he finished the season with three consecutive defeats, although noble on each occasion.

At four in 1922, Grey Lag won five of six races. His lone defeat was a memorable occasion when he tried for a repeat over Exterminator in the Brooklyn Handicap. This time Exterminator (135) got up to beat Grey Lag (126) by a head. Historians, splitting hairs, place Exterminator as Horse of the Year, although he shared rank in the handicap division with Grey Lag.

Sinclair and Hildreth also had the champion two-year-old colt in the barn in 1922. This was Zev, yet another champion bred and sold by John E. Madden. Sinclair named him for one of his attorneys, William Zeveley, and, as matters transpired, he would one day need attorneys more vitally than racehorses.

Zev was by The Finn—Miss Kearney, by Planudes. At two he did not break his maiden until his sixth start, but thereafter Zev won four more races in succession, including the Grand Union Hotel Stakes and Albany Handicap. He was third behind Dunlin in the Hopeful and second to Sally's Alley in the Futurity. He was not the best of the two-year-olds but was regarded as best of the two-year-old colts. Sally's Alley was a filly. Had there been an Experimental Free Handicap in 1922, she surely would have topped all others, regardless of gender.

In 1923 the Rancocas express rolled on, and Zev moved to the fore. Overall, he was regarded as the best horse of any age, although sharing three-year-old male honors with In Memoriam. Grey Lag ran only five times at five but won four of them and stood alone among older males.

That winter Sinclair was at the Beach Club of fellow Turfman Colonel E.R. Bradley in Palm Beach when Bradley offered 5-1 odds to anyone present who could name a horse that would eventually start in that year's Kentucky Derby. Sinclair signed up to bet $5,000 that Zev would answer the call to the post. Joshua Cosden similarly spoke up on behalf of his horse, Martingale.

Zev began the season by winning the Paumonok Handicap but ten days later threw in a dismal performance in the Preakness, finishing twelfth. This was many years before Woody Allen's quip that "80 percent of success is showing up," but Sinclair had a nice bundle riding on Zev's simply "showing up" for the Kentucky Derby, so show up he did. The race was run one week after the Preakness. In a 1964 article for *The Blood-Horse*, the gifted journalist George F.T. Ryall recalled that "Hildreth and [assistant] Dave Leary made no secret of the reason that Zev was running in the Derby — it was [the] bet Sinclair made months before."

Neither Sinclair nor Hildreth troubled themselves with a trip to Louisville, leaving that duty to Leary. Zev went off at 19-1, but led from the start and cruised home by a length and a half. Ryall's recollection was that when Sinclair and Hildreth, who were racing at Jamaica in New York that day, were told the result, they were speechless. (Bradley had a tough day, for, in addition to Zev fulfilling Sinclair's bet, Cosden's Martingale joined the Rancocas colt in the Derby field, and, in fact, ran second, at 19-1.)

Like many good stories, this one probably is not so simple as it was often told. Between the May 12 Preakness and May 19 Derby, Hildreth popped Zev into the six-furlong Rainbow Handicap on May 15. He duly won, proving he was none the worse for his troubles in the Preakness. Hildreth's memoirs note that paramount among those troubles was that Zev had been kicked at the post a few moments before the start of the Preakness. Moreover, Earl Sande, the previous year's leading rider, was sent south to ride Zev at Churchill Downs although Rancocas had a busy afternoon scheduled at Jamaica. Grey Lag that day finished second in the Long Branch Handicap while Lady Diana, Tester, and Flying Cloud all won for the stable on the same card.

It was, nonetheless, assistant Leary who was handed the trophy by Kentucky's governor, E.P. Morrow, as reported in the *Thoroughbred Record*. Morrow assured him in the oratorical style of the day that, "the struggle, the triumph, and the glory and success of your great horse is complete. His place is safe, for he is now a part of Kentucky's history. No conquering Caesar returning to Rome was ever more joyously acclaimed."

Zev's place in Kentucky Derby history is clear, but Leary's and Hildreth's are subject to different interpretations. *The Blood-Horse* tabular histories of the Derby have credited Leary as being the trainer, and the Churchill Downs annual media guides continue to list him as such. We are aware that a great deal of diligence has gone into preparing and maintaining the Kentucky Derby media guides throughout the years and are not casual about suggesting changes. However, evidence seems weighted toward Hildreth deserving credit for winning the Derby with Zev.

First, there seems no doubt that Leary was Hildreth's assistant. The *Thoroughbred Record*'s contemporary report identifies him as such after noting that neither Sinclair "nor the man who prepared Zev for the spring campaign" was in attendance. That careful wording would have been consistent with a late change in trainer for Rancocas, but *Daily Racing Form* charts designate Hildreth as trainer for Zev's race on the Tuesday before the Derby as well as for his next races afterward, i.e, the Withers, Belmont stakes, etc.

So, in addition to his seven Belmont Stakes victories, we believe Hildreth is due recognition as winning trainer in one Kentucky Derby. (An amusing aside is that Hildreth's memory, or an editor's misunderstanding of intent, let him down during preparation of his memoirs. In the chapter detailing the Hourless–Omar Khayyam match race in 1917, Hildreth makes reference to Frank S. Hackett as "my chief assistant since the death of Dave Leary." If that were true, then Leary's "showing up" in the Derby winner's circle in 1923 was much more than 80 percent of success; it was a bonafide miracle! Presumably, Hackett was already working for the stable in 1917 and *was to become* Hildreth's chief assistant after Leary's death some years later.)

Zev defeated Martingale by a half-length in the Withers, then toured through a continuing sequence of victories in the Belmont Stakes, Queen's County Handicap, an overnight race, and the Lawrence Realization. He must be accorded a place beside other horses that can be thought of as capable of winning the Triple Crown but for one form of misfortune or another.

In October 1923, the sportsmanship and vision of various parties contrived to bring about a remarkable event for the time. A bit of boastfulness was also part of the mix. That summer, on a return voyage from a trip to England, Sinclair had fallen into a discussion with some fellow passengers about American owner A.K. Macomber's recent purchase of English colt Parth. The horse (destined to win the Prix de l'Arc de Triomphe) was only classic-placed, but Sinclair expressed his willingness to match Zev against him for $100,000 a side. The press was informed of this boast and out of it began the cogitations that eventually led to a more appealing match, Benjamin Irish's Papyrus, the winner of the great Epsom Derby, to be brought across the Atlantic to meet the best American three-year-old in a match race. It was not automatic that Zev would be the choice of a committee formed to decide, but eventually he was selected after Hildreth gave sufficient testimony that the horse had overcome a slight problem with the frog of one foot.

Hildreth recalled that the situation summoned "one of the most pleasing things that have ever happened to me … Mr. Belmont turned to the other members of the committee and spoke to them in a serious tone: 'I've known Mr. Hildreth for a great many years, and I've had him with me as a trainer of my horses. If he gives me his word he will send Zev to the post in fit condition, it's plenty good enough for me.'" If true, that must have been a sweet moment to one who had once been banished by The Jockey Club!

Despite such bonhomie, Hildreth challenged the good will of the organizers when, true to one of his superstitions, he insisted on saddling Zev at his regular "lucky" spot in the Belmont Park paddock, instead of in the special location that was provided to give the spectators a better view of the historic proceedings.

Hildreth, nevertheless, was fascinated with the adventure of Papyrus, who had three weeks at Belmont Park to prepare after a six-day voyage on the high seas. He was aware that one professional, no matter how successful, could learn from another, and he was said to have observed every move made by Papyrus' trainer, Basil Jarvis. Hildreth befriended his rival and gave him a hand up into the box in which Hildreth himself was standing, to watch the race. Ironically, Jarvis has come down through the years as either somewhat arrogant or stubborn. He did not heed the advice of trainer Joyner — who had experience in England as well as America — to shoe Papyrus with plates that provided traction after overnight rain turned the track muddy. Zev, whose plates were changed, galloped home by five lengths in a race whose running was not as exciting as its place in history.

The Zev–Papyrus match was disappointing, but racing men saw through the fact that it was a muddy track that made it noncompetitive. They recognized that a European horse could cross over and challenge. Indeed, the very next year the grand French colt Epinard appeared on this side of the Atlantic for three international specials. He won none of them but ran so well that he underscored the practicality of such an adventure and showed that a horse could maintain his form over a period of time. It would be almost three decades before the Washington, D.C., International began to make such transatlantic voyages routine. Today, of course, the Breeders' Cup, Dubai World Cup, Japan Cup, etc., regularly bring together fields from around the racing world. Papyrus and his team deserve a bit of the credit.

After the great international special, Zev won the Autumn Championship at Pimlico, then headed west for the rich ($50,000-plus) Latonia Special. This brought him up against Admiral Cary Grayson's My Own, who had had some support as the American that should have represented his country against Papyrus. Zev, at 2-5, had no trouble with My Own, but both went down to the standout performance of In Memoriam, who won by six lengths.

Defeat one of Hildreth's pets, and it was likely the idea of a rematch in the form of a two-horse race would be mentioned. Sinclair was of a similar constitution, and without much delay the Zev–In Memoriam match was arranged for two weeks later at Churchill Downs, $10,000 a side with the Kentucky Jockey Club to add another $10,000. For the Saturday between, Hildreth sent Zev back to Pimlico, where he won the Fall Serial No. 3. At Churchill Downs, Zev had a daylight lead in the stretch, but In Memoriam closed relentlessly, and they hit the wire together. The judges' verdict was Zev, the winner by a nose, but a Pathe Films' motion picture of the event later gave strong indication that Carl Weidemann's colt was the actual winner. The use of photo finishes was more than a decade away, so In Memoriam's jockey, Mack Garner, could only fume and ask in frustration, "How far do you have to win by around here?"

(Neil Newman summarized Hildreth's record for match races at recognized American tracks as six wins out of seven. The victories were Admiration over May Hempstead, Novelty over Textile, and Zev over Papyrus in New York; Hourless over Omar Khayyam in Maryland; Zev over In Memoriam in Kentucky; and, more obscure in history, Witful over Claude at Memphis. Hildreth's lone defeat in a match race was when he tried unsuccessfully to defeat Dick Welles with Grand Opera in Chicago, back in 1903.)

Aided by the $100,000 from the match with Papyrus, Rancocas Stable earned $438,849 in 1923. This figure not only meant that Rancocas topped the owners' list for the third time, but it also established a record that would stand until Whirlaway helped Calumet Farm earn $475,091 in 1941. Hildreth accounted for most of the total, of course, $392,124, and was again the leading trainer.

In 1924 Hildreth led the trainers' list for the last time, but Rancocas would never again top the owners' list. Zev, as champion three-year-old and Horse of the Year, was the tenth and last champion Hildreth trained (joining Jean Bereaud, Fitz Herbert, King James, Novelty, Dalmatian, Friar Rock, Hourless, Mad Hatter, and Grey Lag.) At four Zev won six races, but only two of them were stakes, the Kings County and Fall Serial No. 1 (under 130 pounds). The latter marked the conclusion of a five-race winning streak, the other four victories coming in overnight races. All in all, 1924 was an anticlimactic year for Zev although he became the first horse in history to earn as much as $300,000. In three seasons he had twenty-three victories in forty-three starts and earned $313,639.

Also in 1924, good old Mad Hatter won the Suburban Handicap as an eight-year-old. Thus, Hildreth, who had won the great race with two of its youngest winners (Fitz Herbert and Friar Rock) won with the oldest horse ever to have scored in the Suburban. Mad Hatter also won the Queens County Handicap that year. More of a star of 1924, however, was Mad Hatter's younger full brother, Mad Play, another Belmont-bred. Mad Play was three that year and became Hildreth's seventh and last Belmont Stakes winner. (The others were Jean Bereaud, Joe Madden, Friar Rock, Hourless, Grey Lag, and Zev. As of 2006 seven Belmont wins still rank him second, only to James Rowe Sr., who had eight.) Mad Play also won four other races from a total of seventeen starts, the wins including the Brookdale, Continental, and Yorktown handicaps.

Not every purchase turned out successfully, even for Sinclair. The approximately $100,000 he paid for Man o' War's full brother, Playfellow, was retrieved after prolonged court action because the horse was a cribber. Playfellow was eventually turned back to Quincy Stable and trainer Sunny Jim Fitzsimmons. There was some comment in the press that it must have been Sinclair who pushed the issue, for the thought was that Hildreth's approach would have been more likely to take his licks and make the best of the situation.

Prior to the 1925 season Hildreth warned Sinclair of dismal prospects. A cough had swept the stables, and efforts to get Zev and Grey Lag back to their best form failed. Sinclair took it in stride, and, as matters transpired, it was a better year than Hildreth expected.

Mad Play provided one of the highlights by defeating the top ranked older horse, Sting, in the Brooklyn Handicap. He also won the Saratoga Cup, Long Beach, Queens County, and Empire City Handicap among the seven races he captured that year. Sam Riddle's Man o' War colt American Flag prevailed among three-year-olds, but Rancocas had a colt in the second rung of that division in the imported Silver Fox. The English-bred Silver Fox won the Empire City Derby, Shevlin, Saratoga Sales Stakes, and

Carter Handicap (over champion Sarazen) in New York, and shipped out to win the Cincinnati Derby. Hildreth wrote of his surprise when assistant Frank Hackett pointed out during the summer that the stable was on top in earnings. By the end of the year, Riddle led the statistics with $199,143, a figure that underscored how spectacular Rancocas' total had been the year before. Sinclair's stable stood a competitive second with $175,840. Hildreth's four-year hold on first among trainers was ended; he was third, with $136,240. In 1926, both Rancocas and Hildreth dropped out of the top ten in earnings although the trainer ranked third in wins, with sixty-nine. In 1927 he was the leader in wins, with seventy-two, but illness reduced his activity in 1928, when he was credited with thirty-five wins. In 1929, the last year of his life, Hildreth won twenty-six races.

WHAT SORT OF FELLOW?

Sam Hildreth's health had begun to break by his early sixties. He spent the winter of 1928–29 in the warmth of San Diego. New York journalist Ed Curley took it upon himself to suggest that Hildreth had had a lifelong habit of suppressing emotions and that contributed to his failing health. The stable languished, but assistant Hackett soldiered on to the best of his ability.

Curley tossed out phrases such as "master mind" and "magician of the horse," and "wonderful character of the Turf." Hackett thought it insufficient: "Wonderful does not express it. There has been only one man on the Turf for me, and that is Sam Hildreth."

Hildreth got back to work, and the *New Yorker* piece remarked that, "He is still trainer for Rancocas and continues to race the stable while his employer is in jail."

Hildreth was taken to Fifth Avenue Hospital in September 1929, where he underwent delicate abdominal surgery. He died on September 24, with Mrs. Hildreth and his surgeon, Dr. Benjamin Tilton, at his bedside. Hildreth was sixty-three. Mass was held at St. Patrick's Cathedral in New York, and burial was in a Catholic cemetery in Saratoga, where the Hildreths had a home in addition to a place in Jobstown, New Jersey. The estate was valued at more than $1 million, including Liberty Bonds, U.S. Steel shares, and $100,000 in cash split between two banks.

Mrs. Hildreth survived him by many years before her death in 1961. Despite her years in New York and the time as mistress of a French chateau, she perhaps retained a sense of affection for the wilder, earlier days. In her 1952 interview with Red Smith, she was quick to show Smith a gold nugget that "Wyatt Earp gave me. He picked it up in the Klondike."

Retrospectives of Hildreth's career stressed his distinction of having trained four horses that earned more than $100,000, a major milestone at that time: Zev ($313,630), Mad Hatter ($194,525), Grey Lag ($136,675), and

Mad Play ($136,432). For much of his career, records of trainers were not kept, but various publications confidently estimated that Hildreth had sent out horses to earn more than $5 million. In addition to his seven Belmont winners, he had a particularly distinguished record in the New York Handicap Triple Crown. Although he never trained a horse that swept all three in one year, he won seven runnings of the Brooklyn Handicap (King James, Fitz Herbert, Friar Rock, Cirrus, Grey Lag, Little Chief, and Mad Play), five each of the two other handicaps: Suburban (Fitz Herbert, Stromboli, Friar Rock, Grey Lag, and Mad Hatter); Metropolitan (King James, Stromboli, Grey Lag, and Mad Hatter, twice).

When an individual leaves a 286-page autobiography, published within three years of his death, one would hope to have a strong feeling for his character. Hildreth was cagey about how much of himself, and any negatives, he gave his readers. He made no comment on the frequently reported belief that he was part Indian.

Outside observers' evaluations range between disdain and idolatry.

The death of fellow great trainer James G. Rowe less than two months earlier made comparisons inevitable. Neil Newman's take on the pair was expressed as follows in the *National Turf Digest*: "Both were masters in their professions, but otherwise had little in common. It is true both were reserved, but there was a gentility about Rowe that was utterly lacking in Hildreth. The former was beloved by the rank and file of racegoers, the latter was merely respected."

Later in the article, Newman got tougher: "In Hildreth's long career I only heard of two instances which proved he was not utterly devoid of the finer feelings." He details these as Hildreth keeping Fitz Herbert's former owner, Herman Brandt, on his payroll for life because of the latter's financial woes, and the other was acquiring Stromboli after his racing days ended and keeping the horse on his own farm. Hildreth, in fact, named his own two hundred acres near Rancocas, Stromboli Farm.

It was Newman who, in another article, really took off the gloves. Having conjectured that Hildreth's fellow trainers were probably glad to hear the news of his demise, Newman expressed "doubt if he ever believed in God, feared the Devil, or respected anyone. It has been said of Samuel Hildreth that he had as much skill and as little class as any trainer that ever saddled a horse."

Others observed that Hildreth had little feeling for horses, or people, and used them only for the financial good they could do him. Conversely, Nelson Dunstan once wrote: "The late Sam Hildreth had a genuine affection for horses. Not necessarily race horses, but all horses regardless of breeding."

Certainly, Hildreth's writing of Stromboli would indicate considerable affection, or a good feel for revisionist public relations. Stromboli had been a major horse who was forced into retirement by injury. Two years later Hildreth brought him back, enjoyed how stunned the racing world was to see the old fellow's name in the entries, and gloried in his winning two out of three at ten before being retired permanently:

> Of all the things a fellow training horses is called upon to do there is none that has ever interested me more than to take a cripple and make a new race horse of him … My friends give me credit for having restored a lot of famous cripples, and if I've had more than my share of success in this line I reckon it's because I let nature help do the mending. I don't like firing irons any more than the horses themselves. Plenty of rest, liniments, patient handling, and the proper amount of work are a pretty good cure in themselves. Of all these I recommend patience. You can't make horses recover any quicker than nature will permit. But you can form a partnership with nature.

J.K.M. Ross's version of the Stromboli example, from the memory of his own youth, was that "I think he managed this feat through the power of love. That was his way."

Ross continued that Hildreth's patience was "monumental." To young Ross, Hildreth was nothing like Newman's version. Ross recalled him as a kindly teacher, who always welcomed him to the barn and showed another form of patience, that of an older man barraged with questions by a youngster:

"His heart and manner were gentle; courtesy was his hallmark. Both he and his gracious wife loved horses and dogs and young people — in what order it would be difficult to say, though their tolerance toward me makes me think the latter came first. They had no children of their own, but they always had dogs, generally little white ones, and they were treated like rich uncles."

Hildreth himself wrote of imagined "conversations" he had had with Stromboli — "Stromey, old-timer" — and laced his memoirs with affectionate tales of his and Mrs. Hildreth's favorite dogs. A photo of Hildreth with Stromboli on the farm shows him looking the way the *New Yorker* profile described:

> He is a broad-shouldered, white-haired gentleman, with glossy, nervous brown eyes, and a clear, tough-looking skin that is sunburned all the year-round. Everything about him seems to have been made to last — his knob-like cheekbones make his face look square, and the rest of his body is warmly covered, even in summer, with various thick, protective layers of clothing. His overcoats are squarely cut, and have exceptionally big buttons; his shoes are heavy; he always wears a waistcoat and a big watch chain, and his

short, white mustache covers his mouth like a flap over a pocket. That mustache is symbolic in a way, for he is very close-mouthed.

Indicative of the difficulty of getting a bead on just what sort of fellow Sam Hildreth was is an interview Horace Wade did with Frank Catrone in 1968, three years after Catrone had hit the big time and won the Kentucky Derby with Lucky Debonair. Catrone had ridden for Hildreth as a youngster.

Said he early in the article:

"Racing with him was a cold dollars-and-cents proposition, and this hardheaded business-like approach to the sport may have had much to do with his success. He never permitted sentiment to sway his judgment or his heart, and horses and men were only tools of the trade to be used and then cast aside when their value was done ..."

Wade then read for Catrone some of the more eloquent and philosophical passages from *The Spell of the Turf*, after which the former jockey did a sort of about face:

"Hildreth loved horses — and animals. No Thoroughbred in his care ever was mistreated, and he poured out the same lavish attention on other members of a backstretch menagerie that cluttered up his stable aisles."

One fellow, one interview, two different insights: Which better captured the real Hildreth?

As he closed his memoirs, Hildreth once more harked back to his father: "Fifty years ago that was, and in all this long journey down the stretch of time I've never forgotten that the thing uppermost in Vincent Hildreth was his love for horses and a gentleness of character that lay behind an unpolished exterior."

Upon taking leave of the subject of Sam Hildreth, however, we prefer not a paean to Vince Hildreth, but a passage from *The Spell of the Turf*, which — either through the talents of the man or his collaborator — reaches across many decades to touch seminal feelings within us today:

If you have ever felt the spell of the race track and know what it means to hear the song of the bugle and to see the field go parading to the post in single file past the judges' stand, with the smell of the stable and the fragrance of the flowers tingling in your veins; if the call of the Thoroughbred is so strong that your world would be less than half a world without him in it to make you laugh and cry and pray and curse, then you understand the thrill that comes with the memory of Turf gladiators of the past, prancing idols of bygone days with their hearts of iron and muscles of steel and skins of satin. It is so with me.

CHAPTER 3

H. GUY
BEDWELL

The career of H. Guy Bedwell presents some discordance when placed beside those of most of the venerated trainers. His association with the very highest class of runners lasted only three years whereas his lengthy stint as a statistical leader was based on number of wins in lower-rung races. Still, he once managed to win so many races with his own nondescript runners that he was the leading owner in money won — and that in an era when almost invariably such ranking was the domain of stables redolent of quality and fashion.

Controversy seemed to court Bedwell, or he it. Within months of his greatest triumphs, he and his jockey were shouting accusations of crookedness at each other, and Bedwell was ruled off New York tracks for about six times longer than he was famed on them. Nearly three decades after he trained America's first Triple Crown winner, he saw his stable virtually wiped out by swamp fever. Bedwell could not even experience tragedy without it equating to a blot on his character. More than half a century after he collected insurance on his dead horses, a recent book suggests that he had accidentally spread the disease himself, by using contaminated needles.

Conversely, Bedwell lived long enough for photos in racing publications to progress from showing him as a wiry looking, prematurely wrinkled mien of intensity to the countenance of a rather corpulent and jovial old adopted Marylander. By the time of his death, he was hailed by well-respected peers and appreciated for having fought for the benefits of his fellow horsemen, and he even had been credited at one point for helping convince Maryland's legislature not to ban racing in the state.

IN THE IMAGE OF SEABISCUIT'S TRAINER

Harvey Guy Bedwell journeyed through a youth that made him a kindred spirit with numerous other Thoroughbred trainers of note. Their scenarios involve early connection to horses in the hinterland, learning about the animal on such an intimate level that later handling of horses seemed deceptively to spring from instinct rather than absorbed experience. In the early twenty-first century, the public has been tutored on this sort most effectively by scenes in the movie and book about Seabiscuit, in which Tom Smith camps out under the stars while nursing a gravely injured horse back to health.

Well, in addressing Thoroughbred racing, the Hollywood boys have it easy. There is not much need to embellish the tales of such men. "Hard Guy" Bedwell — for that is what he liked to say his initials declaimed — fits right in with Smith, Sam Hildreth, and others who came from plain and prairie to reign over post and paddock.

Bedwell was born on June 22, 1876, in the tiny town of Roseburg, Oregon. His family had followed the scent of gold to the West and by then had wandered on northward. Bedwell's father died when the lad was only eighteen months old, leaving his mother to raise four children on her own. In the book *Boots and Saddles*, J.K.M. Ross, whose father employed Bedwell during his glory days, observes that Bedwell was barely into his teen years when he took a job as a cowpuncher in the remote areas of Oregon. (The book bears Ross' name as author but was co-written with Van Varner, who later became editor of *Guideposts*. In 2006, a half-century after the book was published, Varner remains an avid racing fan.)

"The life in that isolated area, miles from the nearest railroad, was rugged, but it was good preparation for a horse trainer," Ross mused. " ... Part of [such horsemen's] magic obviously came from their early, practical, day-to-day existence with horses in an era when the horse was a staple of the culture and indispensable to their own livelihoods."

Bedwell had an eye on bettering himself, and after drifting as far eastward as Grand Junction, Colorado, he accepted the job of county clerk. He fooled himself if he thought this desk job was meant for him, or perhaps he was simply saving up to move to something else. At any rate, he later opened a livery stable in the same town and was back working with horses. "After that," Ross recounted, "it was a natural step for him to promote the building of a race course for the local fair grounds and, that accomplished, to take part in the events run on it. He often told me proudly how he rode in four running races and drove in six harness heats on a single afternoon."

Various tales of Bedwell's youth hold that he befriended Tom Smith and Sam Hildreth. This is plausible, for Smith also got to Grand Junction and worked for twenty years on a Colorado ranch while Hildreth's early days of race riding took him to many locales. One of Bedwell's explanations about his early days at the racetrack indicates an association with owner and Wild West show promoter Charlie Irwin, for whom Smith once worked, but by the time Smith hooked up with Irwin, Bedwell had hit, and then receded, from the big time.

(Many years later, in 1942, Bedwell told a journalist that he had, indeed, known Smith, and he delighted in telling how upset his friend got whenever confronted with the tale of how Smith as a lark once had ridden with Frank Starr's gang; Smith allegedly claimed that the gang was waylaid from a bank robbery because some "rat" had "squealed" and they landed briefly in jail.)

Bedwell as a youth is said to have ridden against Hildreth and also against a Charles Curtis. This fellow Curtis later became vice president of the United States whereas Hildreth really made something of himself. Hildreth eventually went east and became the leading owner of racehorses in America three years running.

Regardless of where fact melded with fiction in such tales, Bedwell in those days was putting down the foundations for the future, whether he realized it or not. He learned to be his own veterinarian by necessity, but in doing so he was clever enough to tap the knowledge of a local medical doctor. Many years later, his son, Lester Guy "Buster" Bedwell, also a trainer, told *Daily Racing Form* that the closest veterinarian to Grand Junction in his father's youth was in Denver, "many miles away. When one of Dad's horses was taken ill, he had to serve as his own vet. Often when he was puzzled, he went to the family physician for advice, and they'd usually come up with the usual treatment for humans, only they would multiply the dose eight times. He came to the race track knowing more about horses than most veterinarians, and it wasn't difficult for him to switch to Thoroughbreds."

Bedwell was to become known for his emphasis on keeping horses' feet healthy. Presumably, even a frontier doctor of humans had only limited knowledge of hoof walls, nail placement, frogs, etc., so in the matter of feet Bedwell let himself be taught by the horses themselves.

"During the days he operated the livery stable, he had, by chance, two stalls with mud and water in them," Ross recalled.

"Whenever he turned his horses out to water, they fought to get to these stalls. Believing that Nature was man's best teacher, he reasoned that the horses sought out the goo for the benefit of their hooves. It struck him at the same time that the wild horses he had seen on the range had perfect feet. Why? Because they had to mush around in wet soil every time they took a drink from a river or stream."

Through his long career Bedwell applied that lesson by frequently standing his horses in pails of mud, for he was determined the frog of the foot should never be allowed to become hard and brittle.

Bedwell had married in 1894, but family responsibility did not rivet him to security. He and Lotta Bedwell accepted a more vagabond life in the next decade, when Bedwell ventured into racing to the degree that he journeyed to New Orleans. By separate tellings, Bedwell indicated to journalists he had been working for a stable whose trainer became ill, and a steward thrust a trainer's application Bedwell's way; another version was that Bedwell had taken some horses to New Orleans after they were purchased from Charlie Irwin.

An early winner who boosted Bedwell into headlines as a trainer was Los Angeleno, "a real tough stayer by the American Derby winner, Rey El Santa Anita," Bedwell told a Florida track publicist years later.

"Bought him from Lucky Baldwin for $700. [Los Angeleno was the son of two of Baldwin's stars, for his dam was the champion Los Angeles, winner of forty-eight races.] He won the two mile Ascot Cup at the old Ascot Park [California] and the Thornton Stakes at four miles over the Oakland track."

In the Thornton, Los Angeleno beat Mamie Algol, who had been shipped in from New Orleans. Mamie's supporters did not accept the result at face value, and still claimed she was the better racer, so Tom Williams, who ran the track, came up with a race of duplicate conditions. Los Angeleno won again. Willie Knapp rode him both times.

If stories linking Smith, Hildreth, and Bedwell seem to have the scent of legend, the connection of Bedwell to Knapp is a more documented phenomenon. It would not be many years before both would be plying their respective trades at fashionable Saratoga, Bedwell handling America's first Triple Crown winner while Knapp delivered the only defeat in the career of the nonpareil Man o' War.

When Knapp won the Thornton Stakes for Bedwell on Los Angeleno, it marked the rider's third consecutive victory in the event. Bedwell also had multiple wins in the race, which he took two years later with Nadzu.

THE LEADING OWNER

Bedwell was in his early thirties when he decided to take the plunge of heading to the lucrative circuits of the East, a geographical reversal of the dreams of his long-deceased father. Still, H. Guy Bedwell would be a horse owner and trainer year-round. This meant that, in addition to the seasonal racing in New York and Maryland, he would ply his trade somewhere at all phases of the calendar.

As stated in that long-ago press release, in relation to various eras of Bedwell's career: "It is questionable if any man of any time in Turf history ever raced horses over more tracks than Bedwell. He ran them from the Pacific to the Atlantic and at such stops as Butte, Coeur d'Alene, and Juarez, being, in his own words, the first man on the grounds in the Mexican track, across the Rio Grande from El Paso, when it opened in 1908."

Trainer statistics were becoming available through the *American Racing Manual*, and they point to Bedwell winning thirty-four races in 1907 at recognized tracks. He started his Eastern career in high style, winning sixteen races in fourteen days at New York's Empire City. By 1909 he had risen to the point of winning 122 races during the year, to become the leading trainer in North America in number of wins. His earnings as trainer were $64,943.

The next year, however, Bedwell ran afoul of authorities. Dorothy Ours' 2006 volume *Man o' War: A Legend Like Lightning* (St. Martin's Press) describes a series of drugging incidents at the Latonia track in Kentucky that caused officials there to "decree that doping horses was a punishable offense." Bedwell was on the Kentucky scene, but after his entrant Nadzu appeared in the paddock in an agitated state that caused suspicion, he was ruled off. Officials even sought to restrain him from selling his horses, the implication being that they, too, were tainted.

There were no scientific tests for medication for many years afterward, and a long tradition of "helping" horses is presumed in addressing the history of racing as it stood at the time. Nevertheless, many sportsmen had expended considerable energy toward making the Turf a clean endeavor.

Ours states: "Bedwell couldn't overcome the raw truth that Nadzu had been hopped. He claimed that one of his grooms had taken a gambler's bribe to dose Nadzu with cocaine," and adds that Bedwell "presented telegrams of support from several of racing's most prestigious men, including Jockey Club chairman August Belmont Jr." In what way Belmont cared about the case, or Bedwell at that time, is difficult to assimilate. A local racing official adamant about Bedwell's violation was the paddock judge, a veterinarian, Dr. William Keogh. As Ours concludes the incident, Keogh died before the year was out, so Bedwell agitated for reinstatement, which he won, and happily resumed his career.

In those days Bedwell by and large was racing his own horses. His record was eye-catching. He returned to the top in number of wins in 1912 with eighty-four. This launched him on a streak of six consecutive years (1912–17) as North America's leading trainer in number of wins, and he was also leading owner in number of wins in each of those years. His peak year produced 123 victories in 1916. He thus had seven years, total, as leading trainer in wins, and this stood as a record for trainers until Hirsch Jacobs went seven in a row (1933–39) en route to a career total of eleven years as the leader.

The statistics for 1916 are all the more remarkable, for it was in that year that Bedwell also led owners in earnings. His distinction was testimony to his concept that horse racing was an activity for the full calendar. An enthusiastic horseman-turned-writer, Bob Moore, relished in retelling the story for an article in the *Horsemen's Journal* in 1971:

Quite a feat, when the type of horses he (Bedwell) raced is considered. He established this record in a manner typical of the man — persistence. When the sun rose on December 31, 1916, the leading money-winning owner was R.T. Wilson, whose Campfire had accounted for $49,735 of his total of $71,036. The leading horse in Bedwell's barn was Manokin, who had contributed $8,330, the rest coming from platers who had averaged $500 or less for each win. But Bedwell was still in the game, still sending horses to the post at Cuba's Oriental Park. That afternoon, one of his horses (Mr. Sniggs) finished third to add $25 to the pot, and in the very last race of the year, his King Tuscany got down on top to earn $400, and Bedwell was the leading money winner by $64.

LIFE AT THE TOP

The 1916 ascent of H. Guy Bedwell as leading owner came only a year after a dashing young Canadian had begun to put into play his own ambitions on the Turf. Commander J.K.L. Ross was the son of the founder of the Canadian Pacific Railway, and his personal interests included sailing and fishing. When his country became involved in World War I, Ross was in the unique position of being able to donate to Canada's war effort three large yachts, to be converted into vessels of warfare, while he himself served on submarine patrol and convoy duty.

He also had been thinking of launching a racing stable. Thoroughbred racing was not abrogated in North America immediately, so Ross did not have to put those ambitions on hold. By 1915 he had arranged for a friend, Captain William Presgrave, to train his fledgling stable, which began with the purchase of a dozen horses. Presgrave, however, died in the autumn of 1916.

Forced to ponder the rapidly changing situation with his new stable, Ross concluded he had entered the sport on too tentative a footing. He then purchased a large tract of land at Vercheres, near his home city of Montreal, with the intent of breeding horses there. This decision to some extent reflected the sense of competition between residents of Montreal and those of Toronto, which by then had the more prestigious circuit. He also followed the recent lead of major New York stables by sending agents to purchase stock in England.

Although fueled with horses, land, ambition, and a personal fortune, Ross still needed a new trainer. He wanted the best. Bedwell's leading status of 1916 could be interpreted as an elite achievement or a workmanlike accumulation of unimportant victories. Either through fairness, wisdom, or naiveté, Ross apparently was unperturbed by questions over whether churning out wins with cheap horses indicated a like ability to turn out major wins with top horses.

As recalled by the younger Ross, Bedwell found himself in a position similar to that of many a sports figure toying with discarding what is good for what might beckon as even better: "Now, loathe as Bedwell was to dispose of his own horses to concentrate on another's, he could not resist the adventurous prospect of creating a truly smashing stable any more than he could refuse the tantalizing sum my father offered him for his services." The deal was struck, and Bedwell became trainer for the older Ross in the autumn of 1917, selling off most of his own horses while convincing his new boss to incorporate a few of the better ones into the new arrangement. Nevertheless, the sell-off began late enough that Bedwell completed his series of years as the leading trainer in wins, with sixty-six.

Bedwell was not a native Marylander but had found the horsemanship and racing of the state attractive enough that he by then owned a small farm, Yarrow Brae, not far from the Laurel racetrack. At Bedwell's urging, Ross purchased neighboring Bolingbrook Farm, a large property, although he already had the vast acreage in Quebec. By that time, the political realities of racing had changed, and the purchase made good sense. While wartime racing in the United States continued, Canada's government had halted the sport earlier in the year.

"Racing had been on uncertain footing, too, since the entrance of the United States into the war," the younger Ross commented years later. "There was much discussion about its being stopped altogether, but this, of course, never came to pass. Still, it was obvious, if there were to be any racing at all, it would be in America, and this convinced my father that he should have a base in that country."

Bedwell also used the uncertainty to finagle the purchase of a developing champion for his new boss.

Moore's account credited trainer Bedwell with confidence that racing was safe in the United States. This was based on the knowledge that Admiral Cary Grayson, the personal physician to President Woodrow Wilson, had a Thoroughbred farm and racing stable of his own: "Bedwell believed that nobody was going to stop racing as long as Grayson had Wilson's ear."

Years later Bedwell looked back on those days and described a more complicated spin on the situation. World War I days produced rampant rumors that oats were to become scarce, or nonexistent, for a nonessential activity such as horse racing. In the colorful conversational style of his later years, Bedwell recalled for *The Blood-Horse* in 1942:

This fellow [Herbert] Hoover wasn't the president back in 1917, but he was the food administrator, or something. Everybody had heard the rumor that he was going to 'freeze' oats, or whatever you call it when the government wouldn't let you buy something you needed and had the money to pay for.

Well, I'd had my eye on Cudgel a long time. He was a three-year-old then. Old Pop [John] Schorr had him, and he was a tough man in a horse deal. When all the horsemen, including Pop, got the jitters about Hoover and his oats, I got a price on the horse. I knew a fellow who knew a fellow who knew Adm. Grayson. He told me the admiral said they weren't going to stop letting us have oats. So, I wired Cmdr. Ross, "Send me a fast 25 thousand and I'll buy you a good horse." I got a draft right away and no questions asked. I closed the deal with Pop that night. When he had the money signed over, he said "Well, Guy, you bought yourself a horse. I hope you can find something to feed him," and he laughed because he thought he had got the best of me.

Next day it was in all the papers that you could buy all the oats you wanted. Well, Pop came to me, and he was crying. He begged me not to tell my owner that the deal had been made, to take back the draft plus a thousand for myself. I said no. Then he told me Mom Schorr would kill him. That almost moved me, because Mom could be a terror when she was roused up. But I wouldn't give in.

Ross got a star, and, in fact, the situation was also sunny in the Schorr household. When Bedwell encountered Mrs. Schorr and told her of her husband's fears, she scoffed at the notion that she would ever "kill him" for making a quick $25,000: " 'Listen, Mr. Guy Bedwell, $25,000 can never break a leg. A horse can.' "

Ross' son's recollection of Cudgel's purchase was different, but Bedwell looked fine in that version, too. That account dated the sequence to the afternoon Ross, his son, and Bedwell had watched Hourless defeat Omar Khayyam in a match race in the autumn of 1917. Ross had no ownership of either horse, and he mused aloud, "I'd give a fortune to own a horse like Hourless or Omar Khayyam."

"I know of such a horse," Bedwell put in, "and I think I could get him for you ... I saw him in Kentucky this summer ... and if I had him I'm sure he could beat both your Hourless and Omar Khayyam." This version concludes with Bedwell traveling to Kentucky and closing the deal with Schorr for $30,000.

Cudgel, a son of Broomstick—Eugenia Burch, by Ben Strome, had been bred by the powerful Harry Payne Whitney breeding operation but had cost Schorr only $1,500 as a yearling.

Cudgel was part of the powerhouse stable that Ross and Bedwell gathered and campaigned as the 1918 season played out. Another was Billy Kelly, and Bedwell here again gave himself credit for craftiness. In Moore's article, he recounted that Ross was anxious to buy Billy Kelly as soon as he saw the two-year-old win the Flash Stakes that summer at Saratoga. Bedwell urged patience: "He'll probably win the Grand Union, too. They'll try a handicap and the weight will stop him. Then we make the offer." The younger Ross concurred, step by step, in this case, aside from the second win being in the United States Hotel Stakes rather than the Grand Union Hotel Stakes. "Weight will bring him to us," he recalled Bedwell predicting.

Billy Kelly's next step was attempting to win the Albany Handicap under 133 pounds, and, as Bedwell had foreseen, he lost. He was beaten a length by Star Hampton, to whom he gave eighteen pounds.

Billy Kelly had cost W.F. Polson only $1,500 as a yearling. After winning a series of stakes in Kentucky that spring, and then winning at Saratoga, Billy Kelly, a gelding, was worth more than Polson could afford to turn down. Ross bought him for $27,500. Mrs. Polson wept at the sight of the horse being led from her husband's barn to another, and she cared enough about the horse to make sure Billy Kelly's favorite cat went with him.

By year's end Billy Kelly was ranked co-champion two-year-old, and Cudgel was a champion older male for the first of two years.

Cudgel had already made headlines before Billy Kelly was taken into the Ross stable. That spring, when the Maryland season began at Havre de Grace, Cudgel had three overnight preps before winning the Pimlico Spring Handicap. This victory represented an early fulfillment of Ross' dream and Bedwell's prediction, for Cudgel defeated none other than Omar Khayyam.

The first time Ross got away from his duties in Ottawa to see Cudgel race was when the colt appeared for the King's County Handicap at New York's Jamaica racetrack. Under 130 pounds, Cudgel came along to win by three-quarters of a length from Spur. Cudgel continued to scrimmage with the best of a good handicap division, which included the high-class Roamer, while the three-year-olds Johren and Exterminator also challenged the older horses. Cudgel won some and lost some, and Bedwell returned him to the West at one point to win the Kentucky Handicap.

Cudgel's best race came in the historic Brooklyn Handicap, in which he carried top weight of 129 pounds and defeated Roamer, Westy Hogan, Borrow, and 1916 Kentucky Derby winner George Smith.

After ten races in eleven weeks, he was rested briefly then brought back at Saratoga, where he ran well, although overshadowed somewhat by Roamer. Continuing into the fall, Cudgel in his last race of the year ratified his status with another victory over Omar Khayyam, while giving him six pounds in the Dixie Handicap. Cudgel is regarded as the champion handicap male of 1918.

Through that spring and summer of 1918, other winners carried Ross' colors, including the steeplechaser Dramaturge. Ross had a share of poor luck, too, however. He was game to go for the best, but when he bought an English colt of extremely good, classic breeding, he was destined for disappointment. Wigstone was by Bayardo and showed high speed in his trials. He seemed to have his debut won, but when stable jockey Lawrence Lyke flourished his whip in premature celebration, it caused the horse to shy and bang into the rail. He finished the race but lost by a half-length. Wigstone injured his shoulder in the incident and was away from racing a long time. He later bowed a tendon and was retired. Another import who failed was Fitzwilliam, who, Ross decried, "could not master the intricacies of the starting barrier" and "didn't choose to run with the rest of the field." Fitzwilliam redeemed himself somewhat by siring Ross' Hallucination, who in those days was regarded as the best horse ever bred in Canada.

Lyke did not last long with Bedwell, whose intense manner was hardly compatible with frivolity of any sort. Young Earl Sande then came to the stable, en route to a Hall of Fame career.

When Billy Kelly was transferred to Bedwell, there was time for him to run twice more at venerated Saratoga. The gelding, who aroused comments of being as small as a polo pony and ugly as a mule, had great action in a race, and he carried Sande and 130 pounds to an eight-length victory in the Sanford. Handicapper Walter Vosburgh upped the weight to 135 pounds for the Grab Bag Handicap. Had any buyers been waiting for him to fail in a handicap that day, they did not get their wish. Vosburgh next assigned him 140 pounds for the Adirondack, and Ross declined although Bedwell thought the horse could win it.

With a new man spending money for top prospects, it was inevitable in those times he would attract the attention of master horseman John E. Madden. Among Madden's two-year-olds was a well-bred colt named Sir Barton (Star Shoot—Lady Sterling, by Hanover), a half brother to champion Sir Martin.

Sir Barton was a handsome chestnut but had tender feet. Madden campaigned him as if he were a good horse, running him in a series of stakes, but the colt did not earn a penny from his first four starts. Nevertheless, there was a hint of quality, and Madden convinced Ross to buy him for $10,000. In his first start for Bedwell, Sir Barton ran sixteenth of twenty in the Hopeful Stakes.

Two weeks later in the Futurity, however, Sir Barton sprang to life, and he ran a fine race to be second to Dunboyne, with Purchase third. Sir Barton was in traffic for part of the race and then closed well enough to give his supporters license to think he might have won it with a clear trip. It was the hint that Bedwell and Ross had hoped to see.

Billy Kelly, though, remained the chief standard-bearer for Ross in the juvenile male division. After his break following the Saratoga meeting, the gelding resumed his campaign in Maryland, where he beat older horses in a prep before taking the Eastern Shore under 135 pounds and several other races.

A year after being set to daydreaming by the Hourless–Omar Khayyam match race at Laurel, Ross found himself back at the same track as a participating owner in just such a high-profile, two-horse race. The other two-year-old to emerge most notably that year was J.W. McClelland's Eternal. He was an impressive winner of the Hopeful and then added two more races, including the Oakdale Handicap under 130 pounds. As Billy Kelly was a gelding, he was not eligible for the Futurity, and Eternal had not been nominated anyway, so the showdown could not come in what would have been the logical vehicle otherwise. A match race was arranged for late October in Maryland and given the name the McLean Cup.

The race was played out during a dramatic time, when glory on the narrow world of the Turf was tempered by human concerns on and off it. Several nations so recently confronted with "the Great War" now had another international tragedy visited upon them. A deadly influenza epidemic swept Europe and America. Thousands died. Earl Sande and the young Ross each contracted the disease but had only mild cases.

Meanwhile, Bedwell was finishing up his job for the year with a flourish. On the Saturday before Billy Kelly's match race (Monday), Ross and Bedwell won the Chevy Chase Steeplechase with Dramaturge, the Dixie with Cudgel, and another race with the promising filly Milkmaid.

In the six-furlong match race, however, the young Sande was outridden by the veteran Andy Schuttinger. Both riders were tentative early, resulting in a slow initial pace, and it was Schuttinger who took advantage and got the drop on Sande. He gunned Eternal to a three-length lead, and although Billy Kelly made a courageous run, the McClelland colt held on by a short head. Billy Kelly came out of the race with a cut ankle.

Ross responded kindly to Sande after the match, but Bedwell upbraided the young rider. Not only had Sande let the other jockey get the jump on him, but he had been beguiled by Schuttinger's trick of seeming to leave room on the rail in the upper stretch only to close the hole and force Sande to steady briefly. Sande was brilliant, but young, and the incident was to echo two years later, in an even more dramatic context.

Billy Kelly, who had won fourteen of seventeen starts, was accorded equal billing with Eternal as champion two-year-olds, retrospectively.

At the end of the year, Ross had risen from relative obscurity to be the leading owner in America. His stable total of $99,179 was about $4,000 more than that of A.K. Macomber, who had led the previous year. Most of the Ross stable's earnings were attributed to the main division, and Bedwell was the leading trainer in earnings, with $80,296. Thus, Bedwell had completed a grand slam: He had, at one time or another, been the leading owner in earnings, leading owner in wins, leading trainer in earnings, and leading trainer in wins. In 1918, however, he was bettered in the trainer-wins category by Kay Spence (who also had been suspended briefly during that troubled time at Latonia back in 1909).

Before 1918 closed, Ross made a dramatic move toward even greater success in the coming year. He purchased War Pennant, War Marvel, and Motor Cop from Macomber for $75,000.

Before Bedwell could anticipate 1919 very much, however, he faced a serious illness, but not the flu. The bright and promising Sir Barton became ill "with a case of blood poisoning so severe and so alarming that for days everyone expected him to succumb," as young Ross recalled. "Night and day, an anxious Bedwell nursed the colt, seldom leaving his stall until, finally, the crisis was past." Perhaps the old days of veterinary field expedients in Grand Junction were put to use again.

Bedwell was in those days a highly strung sort. Photos in paddock or winner's circle show the prematurely wrinkled, weathered, withered-looking face of a small man actually in some of the prime years of life. An often repeated incident had him kicking a young employee in the backside, and when the lad asked what he was doing to deserve it, Bedwell said that was the problem, "You're not doing anything."

Young Ross provided a searing image of Bedwell:

> There seemed little sentiment in his make-up, either for horses or for people, though I remember well his touching devotion to his jolly wife, Lotta, and their young son and daughter … The only horse I think Bedwell truly loved was our ewe-necked Billy Kelly; all others were expected to win, or he had no use for them. To Bedwell, at all times, the win was the important thing.

> Though he was high strung and seemed to be seething inside, Bedwell's outward display was normally taciturn. Before races he became jittery, however, and he lived constantly on the border of irascibility. He was easily provoked and could erupt violently. He had a bad stomach, which was either the cause for or the consequence of his small appetite. I never seem to recall his eating at all. He was a teetotaler, but he smoked cigars voraciously, and when he wasn't smoking, he was chewing gum. To the stable hands he was a martinet, and they were all afraid of him. Jockeys, too, knew him as a stern disciplinarian … although he openly admired his assis-

tant trainer, the ex-great jockey Cal Shilling. Bedwell was cold and tough, but he was a wizard at his profession and as such gained the respect of the racing world.

Another description spoke of Bedwell's nervous habit of fiddling with three silver dollars he held in his hands, and it was said that he would never utter two words when one was sufficient.

Nevertheless, Bedwell was not entirely aloof. In September 1918 the *Thoroughbred Record* published a lengthy piece in which Bedwell is quoted extensively. He was asked "if he had any patent right on the art of training." He smiled as he replied:

> Hardly. I use common sense, that's all. Of course the fact that no two horses are alike calls for the exercise of judgment. I try to give my horses the same sort of attention that a physician gives his patients. If you keep a horse normal and well, he is bound to respond to training.
>
> There is no secret about my methods [although] I use perhaps more cooked feed than most trainers. Every night, unless they are to race the next day, every member of my stable has a supply of cooked oats with a little corn. This is mixed with bran. I am a believer in hay, and keep three kinds before my horses all the time. I like California hay, alfalfa, and mixed clover and timothy. A good hay eater is usually a good race horse, just as most men who are big eaters of bread are healthy and able to do a good day's work. All animals must have a certain amount of roughage if perfect health is to be maintained. Always there is water where a horse may have as much as he wants.
>
> Another thing which I think has contributed to the condition of my horses is the fact that winter and summer there are no doors on the stables. I want all the air I can get to reach my horses. They are clothed, of course. I use three or four light blankets in preference to one heavy one, and these are put on and off according to the temperature.

Bedwell then moved on to speak of the importance of feet, as described elsewhere. The article singled out Cudgel as an example of Bedwell's mastery: "Perhaps the best piece of training that Mr. Bedwell has ever done under the eyes of New Yorkers was the bringing back of Cudgel after his hard campaign last spring. Those who had not seen the big four-year-old between Aqueduct and Saratoga were amazed at the condition he displayed when stripped for his engagements at the Spa. The horse had put on at least one hundred pounds of flesh, and it was as firm as marble. The bloom on his coat had the lustre of satin and his eye was like a jewel."

Bedwell put it down to, "Physic [a physic ball], following with light work alongside a pony. He came back like a rubber ball. He was galloped with the pony until he showed me he wanted to run, and the rest was the usual routine."

Bedwell's way with words presaged a time when he would be regarded as a jovial storyteller!

THE FIRST TRIPLE CROWN

Billy Kelly and Eternal were the co-favorites in the winter books for the Kentucky Derby, which had become a nationally acclaimed race in recent years and was the obvious first major target for both. Billy Kelly ran twice at Havre de Grace, and his victories over older horses while giving some of them weight in the Harford and Philadelphia handicaps were testimony to his quality and to Bedwell's ability to get a horse fighting fit off training. Meanwhile, Sir Barton had recovered from his illness, and assistant trainer Shilling had begun to speak up on behalf of his potential. Sir Barton, too, was sent to Louisville.

The trip illustrated Bedwell's attention to detail. In addition to tack and enough feed and hay for the trip, Bedwell insisted that water from Maryland be sent along, too, because that was what the two horses were accustomed to drinking.

Many a horse has been undone by the scrutiny and helter-skelter aspect of the lead-up to the Kentucky Derby. Although in 1919 the hubbub was moderate compared to what it would become in the days of television camera crews and multiple media arrivals, it was already enough to get to the bottom of Bedwell's tolerance.

"This happy hysteria was not designed for Bedwell," was how the younger Ross styled the situation. "The responsibility of a Derby favorite did not rest easily on him. He became almost impossibly irascible, kept his mouth plugged with cigars, or chewing gum, his face screwed in frowns. He lost weight almost visibly and by Derby Day was a walking wraith."

The young Ross probably was not privy to all that was going on prior to the race. Bedwell on several occasions years later recalled he was not sure which of his horses was better as the race approached. Billy Kelly had all the accomplishments on his side, but Shilling had been a great rider and was still a great judge. Sir Barton had once been 100-1 in the winter book and was still regarded as a 25-1 chance.

"I determined to find out" who was the better, Bedwell was quoted years later by Oscar Otis in *Daily Racing Form*. In such a situation, it was essential that even the riders not know exactly what was happening. "I put [Johnny] Loftus on Sir Barton and Sande on Billy Kelly. I told them to go a mile and a furlong. Sande was instructed not to let Sir Barton pass him. Loftus was told to beat Billy Kelly if he could. Well, Sir Barton beat him rather easily. The few persons looking on then and there agreed that the maiden, Sir Barton, would be the Derby winner."

Knowledge is generally a wonderful thing to share, but on the racetrack this sort of knowledge becomes less useful the more it is shared, for the price drops. In another interview three decades or so later, Bedwell elaborated on the tale to suggest that Sir Barton had outworked Billy Kelly several times but "nobody knew that but me and Cmdr. Ross and the two exercising boys and the clocker. I staked the clocker and he didn't talk."

In Louisville, Bedwell bummed accommodations in the Galt House Hotel, sharing a suite with a friend, whom he advised quietly to back Sir Barton. He loved recalling that his "host" still got 10-1 and won $5,000, appending that "it pays to be hospitable."

Bedwell also recalled conferring with Ross on what the owner's personal action would be. As a reminder that the purse was not the only thing sporting owners were trying to win, he recalled that Ross outlined a plan in three $100,000 increments. The first $100,000 would be bet on the stable entry, to win; the second was for a bet with prominent horseman Ed Simms that Billy Kelly would beat Eternal, regardless of where they finished; and the third was for an audacious bet of $100,000 against Simms' $300,000 that Eternal would not finish in the money.

When they returned to the train depot and Ross' private car, Mrs. Ross was frantic. Word had come that her father had suffered a stroke. Despite the proximity of the Kentucky Derby, the owner of two contestants rushed back to Canada. On the way, he managed to get down only the $100,000 straight bet. The entry went off at 2.60-1.

Stable jockey Sande was on Billy Kelly, which invites all sorts of speculation. Were the stories of the trials showing Sir Barton the better actually exaggerated over the years? Did the fact that both owner and trainer were betting cause them to keep the stable jockey on Billy Kelly so as to hide the fact that they had concluded Sir Barton was the better? Did Sande side with Billy Kelly despite knowing Bedwell's opinion?

At any rate, the rider of Sir Barton was Johnny Loftus. As is true so often in the fraternity of the Turf, there was some history in that. Back in 1912, as noted in Dorothy Ours' book on Man o' War, the vagabond Bedwell had tried out a new track in Charleston, South Carolina, when Kentucky racing shut down for the winter. For that venture, he borrowed from Kentucky trainer Rome Respess his rising teenage jockey, Johnny Loftus.

There was no declaration to win posted for the Ross entry as Billy Kelly joined his maiden stablemate — unraced since the Futurity eight months earlier — in the 1919 Kentucky Derby field of twelve for a mile and a quarter over a heavy track. Young Ross believed that the idea was for Sir Barton to set the pace, which would help Billy Kelly, but that in the event he could win the race himself, Loftus was to keep going on Sir Barton rather than try to pull him back in favor of the other horse.

Sir Barton set the pace, all right, establishing a two-length lead early, and he never was headed. Eternal tracked him early before falling back to finish tenth. The chart shows Billy Kelly staying in close attendance in third and then getting to within a half-length of Sir Barton in the stretch, but the maiden then scooted away to win by five lengths. The purse was $20,825, considerably less than Ross won betting and a great deal less than he would have won had he gotten his entire pre-race portfolio in play. Bedwell admitted to getting "kind of rich myself that afternoon." (Ross had been pushed into a $50,000 bet well in advance by the shady character Arnold Rothstein, and in due course Rothstein's check arrived as well.)

Ross had done what no other owner had done to that time in having two horses in the same colors (orange and black) come home one-two in the Kentucky Derby.

In those days the Derby, Preakness, and Belmont had not been connected mentally and emotionally by the Turf as the "Triple Crown." Still, the Preakness was an important race on its own, the Ross stable had taken on a Maryland base, and one of Ross' earlier nice winners, Damrosch, had won the race in 1916 before Bedwell came on board. So, even though the Preakness was set for Wednesday, only four days after the Derby, Sir Barton was soon on a railroad car headed back to Maryland.

Eternal was back for another try, and the twelve-horse field also included the Futurity winner, Dunboyne, as well as Sweep On. Moreover, Harry Payne Whitney's Vindex, although last in the Derby, had such a stunning trial between the two races that he, too, was considered a threat.

The Preakness showed another bit of shrewdness on the part of H. Guy Bedwell. In the days before mechanical gates, starts were far more precarious than they are today. It was not unknown for a horse to be entered for the sole purpose of having its rider watch his stablemate and to cause commotions that would delay the start until the favored runner was balanced and set for the break. Bedwell made a late decision to run the filly Milkmaid as an entry, for he knew that Dunboyne and Vindex were erratic and he was afraid one of them would wrest a "flying start" despite the starter's best intentions.

Milkmaid had quality and, indeed, would end the year as a champion in her own right, but that day Sande's instructions were to wheel his own filly to delay the start should he see Sir Barton in a compromised situation. (This could not be done ostentatiously, for a rider could be fined or suspended if such action was obvious.)

As things transpired, the roguish behavior of Dunboyne prior to the start hurt only himself, for he was more or less left at the post, while Loftus got Sir Barton away cleanly. The race of nine furlongs was something of a repeat of the Derby, and Loftus brought the Ross colt home four lengths on top. Eternal finished second. Milkmaid was in season and so, perhaps, perfectly placed to be troublesome, but her efforts were not needed.

Sir Barton and Billy Kelly (who did not contest the Preakness) were sent on to New York. Sir Barton was the new hero upon the stage, but Billy Kelly was still beloved and received an emotional ovation for winning the Toboggan Handicap at Belmont Park.

The Preakness had been run on May 14, and ten days later Sir Barton came out for the one-mile Withers Stakes. Eternal was once again in the fray, although the field was down to six. Sir Barton was about 1-3 at even weights. This time, a few minutes before the race, Bedwell told Loftus to reverse tactics and let Eternal set the early pace. The crowd and movie cameras surrounding Sir Barton in the paddock unnerved the usually stolid colt enough that Bedwell had to take the bridle and lead him away to help Loftus restrain him from bursting through, or into, the crowd.

Eternal teased his fans, and worried the Ross stable with his early three-length lead, but Sir Barton came to him and drew off to win by two and a half lengths.

On June 11, Sir Barton appeared for the Belmont Stakes. It was then run at a mile and three-eighths, rather than the mile and a half of today, but was the longest race the colt had tried. Sir Barton was a horse that needed company to work his best, and Bedwell freely used such as Cudgel or Milkmaid in this context, along with a group of horses that enjoyed little fame themselves.

Sir Barton faced only Sweep On and the latter's pacemaker, Natural Bridge, in the Belmont. He was 7-20. Loftus got him away well and he dominated, winning by five lengths and setting an American record for the distance, 2:17 2/5.

He had thus won the three races that would be solidified as the American classics and had thrown in the old Withers Stakes as well. "Horse of the Century" was a phrase freely expressed. It was a very young century at the time, but the following year when the phrase was earned by Man o' War, it was a phrase that would stick.

Eleven years passed before any other horse won the Derby, Preakness, and Belmont, but Sir Barton's role in putting the three races into a joint context was the beginning of the benevolent mania known as the Triple Crown.

Young Ross recalled that Sir Barton had begun to "train off" and was sore for the Belmont. Bedwell persevered, though, and, in the mind of the young observer, made one of his few mistakes by not resting Sir Barton. In his first start after the Belmont, the colt was beaten in the Dwyer. He lost to Purchase, a star in his own right.

Thereafter, Sir Barton showed form that suggests the tenderness of his feet played havoc with Bedwell's ability to produce him in top fettle with any consistency. (Whatever the track condition, Bedwell routinely had strips of piano felt placed between Sir Barton's hooves and shoes.) The colt won four of his remaining nine races that year, although his overall campaign, of course, was enough to anoint him the era's equivalent as Horse of the Year.

According to Ours' book *Man o' War*, Bedwell and Loftus had a falling out when they engaged in a loud shouting match immediately after Sir Barton lost the Autumn Handicap that fall. When Loftus felt he was hopelessly beaten, he let up on Sir Barton and he finished third behind Sam Hildreth's rising star Mad Hatter. Bedwell intemperately suggested that Loftus had colluded with Hildreth. Loftus shot back that Bedwell had given him a "cold" horse to ride, the implication being clear that sometimes Bedwell's horses had been running with hop. Ours concluded that newspapermen might have heard this but most did not pursue it. Loftus went so far as to go to Ross, but the owner refused to concede the possibility that his trainer had been hopping horses. Since Loftus had been criticized for some other rides — including Man o' War's loss that year in the Sanford Memorial — it was he who took the brunt. The jockey lost his license.

Author Ross found Sir Barton an interesting study. The horse had "nerves of steel," and other admirable traits, but was a loner, one Thoroughbred who did not even like stable pets. Ross and Varner composed a succinct summation: "He remained ever disinterested and aloof, a patrician and snob."

Three other champions graced the stable rolls that year, so that Ross and Bedwell had either a clear champion or co-champion in all but one of the categories recognized for the season. Constancy was co-champion two-year-old filly; Sir Barton stood alone as champion three-year-old male and as Horse of the Year; the aforementioned Milkmaid was a co-champion three-year-old filly; and Cudgel was back as co-champion older horse. Only in the two-year-old male division were Ross and Bedwell shut out, and that division was the private preserve of none other than Man o' War.

Constancy, the two-year-old filly, had been foaled abroad but was not imported directly by Ross. Instead, he had purchased her that June from A.B. Hancock Sr., owner of Claiborne Farm. Hancock had acquired her from her breeder, M.J. Musker. She was by Ambassador IV—Simena's Daughter, and Hancock assured Ross that she had shown high speed in her trials.

Constancy was in great shape by the time she was purchased and pleased Bedwell immediately. Ross and Bedwell thought she was a perfect foil for a betting coup, for the stable's success was making it difficult to get much of a price on their winners. With several minions perched around the track with flashlights, Constancy was worked under the cover of darkness one morning, and legend has it that she got a half-mile in :44 3/5, not just good, but astounding, for the time. The conspirators repaired to breakfast, thinking they had gotten away with something, but their faces fell when Tom Murphy, a scout for bookmaker John Wallace, strolled into their midst. "Well, Commander, you nearly got away with it," he said, and it seemed clear the chance at good odds had disappeared. Murphy's next comment brought a sigh of relief, for he had mistaken the filly's identity: "It's easy to see that Milkmaid is certainly fit."

Constancy was entered for the Spinaway, which was a good stakes although not positioned as Saratoga's climactic one for the division as it is today. Bedwell put Loftus on a stablemate, further to confuse the books, giving third-stringer Tom Nolan the mount on Constancy. Ross got an average of 15-1 on his bets, although the price tumbled from 20-1 to 4-1. His son was counseled not to make his own larger-than-usual bet until the father had concluded his dealings, another insurance against the bookmakers acute sense of smell. Constancy got away cleanly and led by four turning for home, a margin she increased to five at the wire. Young Ross shared in the revelry of the staff. The chauffeur, who had realized something was up when asked to take a party to the track before dawn, won $1,000.

Constancy was then second in the Schuylerville.

Sam Riddle's Man o' War had shown himself a spectacular colt, but he had not yet convinced horsemen of his extreme greatness. After all, he had suffered a defeat when Willie Knapp (who had ridden Los Angeleno for Bedwell a dozen years before) got Upset home ahead of him in the Sanford Memorial.

Ross thought Constancy's own speed might also bring down Man o' War, so she was entered in the Hopeful. Nolan was on Constancy, for Loftus rode Man o' War. Constancy got such a large lead early that, in ordinary circumstances, she would have appeared a certain winner, but Man o' War closed with such tremendous speed and power that he beat her by eight lengths. Another filly, Cleopatra, closed to beat Constancy for second.

Constancy suffered no ill effects from her tiring effort and within three weeks had won four races, including the Eastern Shore. She was ranked with C.E. Rowe's Miss Jemima atop the two-year-old fillies.

The Ross co-champion in the three-year-old filly division of 1919 was Milkmaid, who shared the honor with Harry Payne Whitney's Vexatious. Milkmaid, by Peep O' Day, was another whom Ross had bought from Madden. She had been purchased the previous year, some weeks after Ross bought Sir Barton. Milkmaid had won a couple of races before the deal.

Young Ross, in his teenage sentiments, regarded Milkmaid as "by far the most beautiful filly I have ever seen. She was perfection ... Marvelously feminine, her eyelashes were luxuriously long, as was her tail." Her groom in the Madden stable was a fellow known as Port. He, too, had been smitten by Milkmaid, whom he called "Daisy," and when he led her over to Bedwell's stable he intended to stay with her. There was little choice for the new trainer than to put him on the payroll, and so Port remained Milkmaid's faithful groom.

Vexatious defeated Milkmaid in the Alabama, but the Ross filly achieved enough in a stern campaign to gain equal status. She won the Gazelle and beat colts going a mile and three-sixteenths in the Kenner at Saratoga. Bedwell was game to send his horses against each other, and in the Potomac Handicap, Milkmaid ran third behind Sir Barton and Billy Kelly in a Ross stable sweep.

Cudgel's highlights in his second older male championship (shared with Willis Sharpe Kilmer's Sun Briar) included the Hudson Handicap, in which he gave twenty-two pounds to Spur. In the Merchants and Citizens, Cudgel carried 132 and beat Star Master (122), the great Exterminator (126), and Sun Briar (132). That fall, in the Havre de Grace Handicap, he came from eighth to defeat Exterminator while giving him three pounds. Sir Barton was third, in another example of Ross and Bedwell not avoiding collisions of their own stars.

With the competition from his own stable, Billy Kelly had no chance to squeeze into a championship bracket but continued as a powerful winner. His key efforts included wins in the Harford, Philadelphia, Toboggan, Capital, and Pimlico Serial Weight-for-Age. These were all sprints, although little Billy had shown in the Derby that middle distances were not beyond him.

"That rousing autumn campaign of 1919 was the zenith for us," the younger Ross recalled. "Not again were we able to send forth a comparable phalanx of insistent winners ... Some of our finest races lay ahead in 1920, but they were more intermittent."

Ross and Bedwell had set a high standard, indeed, in 1919. For the second year, Ross was the leading owner in earnings, and his total of $209,303 was more than double his leading figure for 1918. Bedwell again was the leading trainer in earnings, with $208,728, but his sixty-three wins on the top stages fell thirty-three below Spence's leading figure in sheer number of winners.

THE UNRAVELLING

Early in 1920 the four-year-olds Sir Barton and Billy Kelly both had setbacks. Sir Barton seemed to be rounding into form when he and Milkmaid ran one-two in the Climax Handicap, but he soon was sore again. Likewise, Billy Kelly came out of a tough race in need of time off after losing the Paumonok to Dunboyne.

To some extent Boniface filled in for them. Boniface was a five-year-old bred by John Madden and was by Transvaal—Cerina, by Meddler. He would compile a career record of ninety-three starts, with thirty-four wins, and his earnings of $120,000 would actually place him first among all the horses Ross campaigned. Boniface had been injured as a young horse while being schooled at the start and ever after became frightened when horses were lining up around him. Starters eventually began placing him on the outside, and he became somewhat more tractable.

During 1920 Boniface came through when the stable was idling a bit otherwise. That May he won the Pimlico Spring Handicap, then was sent west to take the Clark Handicap in Kentucky. By the end of the month, he had added another stakes in another locale, for he won the Connaught Cup at Woodbine in Ross' home country.

That Boniface was not strictly second-tier was indicated by his sterling race in the Suburban Handicap, in which he went under by only a head to that year's Derby winner, Paul Jones, with redoubtable old Exterminator behind him, along with Upset. Bedwell kept him in action, and he next won the Excelsior. He also was to make his mark at the venerated Saratoga meeting, winning the Delaware Handicap, although by that time things were going better with Sir Barton.

In the meantime, the lovely Milkmaid had also done her best to keep Bedwell happy. She won several races and finished third to Motor Cop once. (Motor Cop and the two other purchases from Macomber were useful runners but not heroic.) Then in the Ladies, Milkmaid dueled another champion, Cleopatra, and barged home by three-quarters of a length.

That year, Bedwell was from time to time disgruntled by the way Ross expressed pride in his own city, province, and country. Ross had taken on the post of president of the Blue Bonnets track in Montreal and naturally wanted to help upgrade racing there and allow his countrymen to see some of his best horses. Against Bedwell's wishes, Milkmaid was sent to Montreal for the Windsor Hotel Cup and was beaten by Soldat de Verdun. Purses won by the Ross horses in Canada were credited to Fred Schelke, which perhaps accounted for at least part of Bedwell's attitude.

By the time Saratoga rolled around, the nation was caught up in Man o' War mania. He had graduated from star to superstar to icon. Although he did not run in the Derby and thus was no Triple Crown winner, his status towered over even that of Sir Barton.

Sir Barton had been given about two and a half months off and reappeared at Saratoga in good enough bloom and soundness to run two spectacular races. The first was the Saratoga Handicap, in which he carried 129 pounds and gave three pounds to Exterminator. Jockey Sande provided a colorful blow by blow, adhering to the racetrack custom of speaking in the present tense. After a half-mile, Sir Barton had put away his first challenger, The Porter, then "Mad Hatter runs up alongside and [Buddy] Ensor hollers, 'I've gotcha, boy!' And he did look like a big locomotive, but I wasn't worried. I still had a snug hold of Sir Barton and had the inside going into the turn. The last glance I get of Buddy he is terribly busy trying to keep the mad one from boring out. Then Old Bones [Exterminator's fond nickname] comes up with Andy Schuttinger. We're lapped at the quarter pole. I hit Sir Barton twice. Surprise! He pulls away, and we coast under the wire three lengths' winner with a little left."

The time was 2:01 4/5, a new track record for a mile and a quarter. "I cannot believe there was a time when my father and Bedwell — all of us — were more exultant," the younger Ross wrote nearly forty years later, the strong feelings still evident.

Sir Barton's Saratoga slate was interrupted by a quick trip to Fort Erie, Canada, where he galloped home under Sande and 134 pounds in the Dominion Handicap. (Fort Erie is just across the border into Ontario, and Bedwell was trainer of record.) Sir Barton seemed to be keeping his form better than at any other time since the Triple Crown, and back at Saratoga, he was up for another brilliant performance in the Merchants and Citizens Handicap. Going a mile and three-sixteenths, he had 133 pounds and was giving eighteen to Gnome. Again, Sande set sail from the start, and setting a strong pace throughout, Sir Barton held on to beat Gnome by a nose. This time he set not just a track record, but also a world record, 1:55 3/5.

In addition to Sir Barton's two major wins, the Saratoga meeting for Bedwell and Ross included other highlights. Milkmaid had been rested after a bleeding incident, and although Bedwell was capable of producing her dead tight, bookmakers were more liberal in her odds than usual, so the older Ross made a big score when she came back to win the Salem Handicap at seven furlongs. Milkmaid added another win at the meeting, in the Galway Handicap over the same distance.

Although Man o' War had finally been challenged in his successful duel with John P. Grier in the Dwyer Stakes, there was still a yearning within the public for the great horse to face the best that could be brought to him. Sir Barton's resurgence made him the clear choice as that horse. In the enthusiasm of hoping for such a spectacle, it was easy to forget that Sir Barton was not necessarily a horse to ask to remain at his peak form race after race.

Dorothy Ours recalled that Bedwell taunted Man o' War's trainer, Louis Feustel, about not allowing the three-year-old to meet Sir Barton. Feustel at one point became so annoyed that he blurted out that they could race them "this morning," putting up $100 or $500.

Such decisions, of course, were actually up to the owners. Man o' War's owner, Sam Riddle, and Ross, sat back to await racetracks' offers for a match race, and when the otherwise mundane Kenilworth Park came up with a $75,000 winner-take-all offer, the deal was struck. The race was to be run on October 12.

The match preoccupied the Turf from the moment the arrangement was made, and there were some prickly issues. A.M. Orpen, proprietor of Kenilworth in Windsor, Ontario, was known more as a promoter than as a sportsman, and Ross did not receive universal appreciation from his own countrymen for bringing his great colt and Man o' War to Canadian soil.

There was the point of who would ride, too. That year, Clarence Kummer had become the regular rider of Man o' War but had ridden Sir Barton several times, too. He was to ride Riddle's colt, and Bedwell still harbored concerns about Sande in a match race. The memory of Billy Kelly's loss to Eternal two years earlier stilled gnawed at him. Bedwell first convinced Ross to bring in Frank Keogh as a standby, and then he convinced the owner that Sande was highly pent up and was having some bad rides. Hours before the match race, Ross went to Sande and explained he would not be riding. This was a devastating blow to the tearful Sande. It was all the more cutting, for Keogh had been criticized for not finishing particularly strongly on Gnome when Sande and Sir Barton beat him. Now, he was to be replaced on a historic occasion by a fellow he had so recently outridden! Young Ross conjectured that the pressures of the race for once had compromised Bedwell's judgment.

The track was hard, and Sir Barton's tender feet might have bothered him. Nonetheless, neither Bedwell nor Ross claimed that he could have beaten Man o' War, although they were convinced that the best of Sir Barton could have made a better race of it. Man o' War, the overwhelming 1-20 favorite, won by seven lengths in the last race of his career.

Sir Barton made three more starts, twice with Keogh aboard and once with W.J. O'Brien. He was beaten in all three. (Loftus must have seen some gallows humor in the fact that one of the defeats was to Mad Hatter, in the Pimlico Serial #2, although in the sequel, Billy Kelly and Sir Barton ran one-two against Mad Hatter.) Billy Kelly's other scores that year had included the second of his three Harford Handicap wins and a Highweight Handicap under 136 pounds.

Sir Barton was retired with thirteen wins in thirty-one races and earnings of $116,857. He was a failure at stud and eventually was sent to a U.S. Army Remount station. There is a bit of irony there, for, back in 1918 in that *Thoroughbred Record* article, Bedwell had discussed the idea that racing should provide more stallions for the overall needs of the country, both for times of peace and times of war — for in those days such application of equines was still a factor. He went so far as to suggest that certain races be designated for the winner "to go to the government." It was under different circumstances, but, eventually, one of the champions he trained did just that.

Exterminator was named older male champion for 1920, so the Ross stable had no champions that year. Nevertheless, the stable earnings of $250,586 exceeded that of the national leading total of the previous year. In the earnings column, this was not enough to lead a third consecutive year, for the Whitney stable collected $270,675. Bedwell did help put his employer on top in terms of number of wins, however, with 118, but enough of them were credited elsewhere that Bedwell missed leadership among trainers by wins.

Sande requested, and received, cessation of his contract and went on to his own continuing greatness as a jockey. The Ross stable led in number of wins for the next two years, under trainer Henry McDaniel, but had no further champions. By the end of the decade, Ross had suffered financial setbacks and eventually had to close the stable.

As for Bedwell, his poor judgment in his discussions prior to the match race was one of several factors that would lead to suspension of his license and, therefore, the end of his days with Ross. Dorothy Ours sets out the scenario that The Jockey Club received testimony from Man o' War's camp that prior to the match race, Bedwell had made an approach that he receive some payment even if Sir Barton lost. It was probably not sinister such as, I'll make sure my horse loses, if you pay me, but more likely an old scuffler's discomfort with the concept of a $75,000 winner-take-all race! Come on, guys, surely the second horse ought to get something!

Nevertheless, it was highly inappropriate and technically was the crime of asking to be paid for losing. The Jockey Club, having had Bedwell in its sights since Loftus' implicit accusations, denied Bedwell a license in New York. The ruling was often assumed to result from Bedwell's becoming insistent in Maryland that his assistant Shilling be allowed to ride. Shilling had been ruled off after a series of infractions and fights with other jockeys. (Shilling came to a sad end, being found frozen to death at Belmont Park, after which a coroner's report referred to alcohol poisoning.)

The Jockey Club had influence in Maryland but not regulatory authority. Eventually the state racing commission in Maryland threatened to pull Pimlico's license to operate if Bedwell were not reinstated. Once again Hard Guy Bedwell was back in action.

THREE MORE DECADES

Bedwell had nearly three decades left in his life, and his career. He was not reinstated in New York until 1938 but trained in Maryland and elsewhere during the intervening years. The Jockey Club did not purposely make headlines over its rulings. Journalist and historian Neil Newman reported in 1938 that the lifting of the ban was quietly revealed in the May issue of the *Racing Calendar*, The Jockey Club's official publication.

Bedwell was something of a hero to Maryland racing. Around the time of his suspension, the state legislature seemed subject to give in to anti-racing elements. Bedwell went to a friend, Billy Norton, one of the leading senators and so effectively set him straight that Norton reversed his position and supported racing from the floor in Annapolis.

Bedwell kept Yarrow Brae and had a breeding operation, standing modest stallions in Maryland as well as in California. In addition to racing his own horses, he was hired by some of the better stables in Maryland. In 1924 he was back on familiar territory, as America's leading owner in number of wins one last time, with eighty-six victories to his credit.

Bedwell's irascibility that the young Ross had described was still noticed by those who worked for him during the 1920s. Humphrey S. Finney, who eventually rose to such status in the sales world that the auction pavilion in Saratoga is named for him, had two painful stints as Bedwell's employee.

In his book written with Raleigh Burrows, *Fair Exchange* (Charles Scribner's Sons), Finney remembers that he was forewarned before his first application to work for Bedwell but was so determined to move from other aspects of the horse world into the Thoroughbred segment that he took the plunge. "Yarrow Brae means 'land of the free,' " Finney mused years later, "and if ever there was a misnomer that was it." Bedwell worked his help seven days a week, and "no one stayed with him very long."

Bedwell apparently had his own convictions concerning rules and what to do about them. Notwithstanding his reported status as a teetotaler, during Finney's first tutorship, the young man's duties during Prohibition included driving into Washington, D.C., to pick up contraband whiskey at Union Station. Thus did Bedwell stock his liquor supply. Similarly, since he raced in Maryland part of the year and then went to Canada, Bedwell would stock his staff for the next cycle with boys smuggled down across the border. Finney recalled that Bedwell's methods included hiding lads in train cars or in the trunks of automobiles.

Finney escaped as soon as a viable alternative presented itself, but life's and unemployment's implacable road soon found him peddling a series of treasured racing volumes for the $100 that might support him for a time. Alas, this all led back to Yarrow Brae. In his second experience of doing time for Bedwell, Finney was assigned to look after stallions. Surprisingly, Bedwell employed a veterinarian at the farm, and this good man and Finney shared a stall between identical accommodations provided the stallions Fair Gain and Thunderstorm. Finney noted wryly that, "One thing you had to say about Bedwell: he treated his horses as well as his people."

Finney thanked the vet years later for helping him learn about making bathtub gin, and, on a more serious horseman's level, he lent his voice to much of the admirable qualities ascribed to Bedwell over the years:

"He knew how to train a horse for a sprint or a route, and he knew how to bring one up to a particular race. Though irascible and demanding, he was a thorough horseman. You can learn from a man like that. You respect him for what he is, even though you can't develop an affection for him. While I sometimes questioned the wisdom of being in his employ, in later years I was amply rewarded by what I had learned in my second whirl with the 'sage of Savage,' (the community of Savage, Maryland). I gained more experience in breaking yearlings, and I learned about the horse's hoof. Few men alive knew more about feet than Bedwell (that motif again), who could shoe a horse about as well as a farrier."

Even admiration had its drawbacks. Finney made Bedwell the offer that if the boss would teach Finney about the horse's foot, the young employee would volunteer to do the routine trimming. Bedwell agreed, but there was a price: "Things irked Guy that might not have bothered most employers. He especially didn't like his help 'gallivanting around on Saturday nights.' Bedwell thought a man around horses should be as fresh and alert on a Sunday morning as on a Thursday."

So, of course, whenever Bedwell suspected Finny had made minimal use of his mattress through a night, the boss would find plenty of hooves in need of work the next morning.

Eventually, Bedwell began complaining about the difficulty of keeping his operation out of the red. Finney — with his lovely command of the language — thought the comments "had the earmarks of a preamble to a salary-lopping, so I bid Bedwell a final farewell."

The Blood-Horse began tracking stakes winners for trainers in 1929. Available records show Bedwell winning stakes with fifteen horses between 1934 and 1948. He occasionally flirted with a big horse, and having perhaps become convinced of the importance of pedigree, had some of his best successes with horses acquired from top outfits.

He claimed Mad Frump from C.V. Whitney on November 15, 1934, acting for A.C. Compton, whose stable he trained. Mad Frump had won several stakes, but was of such modest standing in the Whitney stable that he intermittently was risked in claiming races. Nine days after Bedwell claimed him, Mad Frump won the Bryan and O'Hara Memorial Handicap. Mad Frump was by none other than Mad Hatter! *The Blood-Horse* ran a photo along with that report, and it invites wonder as to what had happened to the tense, wired-tight countenance of the glory days. Apparently, Bedwell was able to avoid grinding away his spirit in bitterness, and he must have finally discovered that eating was all right for humans as well as for horses. The photo shows a balding pate, wide face, and the pleasant smile of a colorful old adopted Marylander. The photo could not have been taken more than fourteen years after the days of Sir Barton and Billy Kelly, but the transformation is remarkable.

Among Bedwell's better horses in the post-Ross era was Sun Egret. This one was purchased from Exterminator's owner, Willis Sharpe Kilmer, on behalf of Compton. The colt was by Sun Briar. Bedwell went west with Sun Egret in the winter of 1938, and for a time the colt imposed himself into the classic picture when he won the San Pasqual, Santa Maria, and San Vicente. In the San Pasqual, Bedwell and Compton ran one-two, with Sun Egret and Clingendaal. In the Santa Anita Derby, Sun Egret led at the eighth pole but gave way to Stagehand and Dauber. He finished third, and stablemate Legal Light, whom Bedwell trained for Ral Parr, finished fourth. Illustrative of the ironies of the Turf, Stagehand was trained by Earl Sande, who by then had had his own troubles and was trying to find his way as a trainer after his Hall of Fame days as a rider ended. (Bedwell and Sande were said to have had a rapprochement of sorts when the trainer made a point of congratulating Sande after his victory on Zev against Papyrus in their match race in 1923.)

Sun Egret did not proceed along the Kentucky Derby trail. (Bedwell had tried the Derby with Typhoon, finishing fifteenth in 1928 and did not have any further starters.) However, he was a successful campaigner through the age of five, winning a total of eleven stakes, most of them back in Maryland.

When racing was established in New England, Bedwell made that circuit a part of his routine, and his victories there included the 1938 Rockingham Park Handicap with Gerald. In 1939 he had a good prospect when Parr's Victory Morn won the Eastern Shore Handicap and two other stakes, but Parr died, and in his estate dispersal, Victory Morn was bought by Maxwell Howard for $21,600.

Bedwell's relationship with Major Parr was amusing. Several times Parr approached Bedwell about training for him, and he finally recognized there was never any valid explanations for his being put off. Finally, he confronted Bedwell and received the reply that Bedwell generally trained for owners who did not know a great deal about racing and so they left things to him. Parr, however, as an experienced horseman, might be expected to interfere.

Parr struck a deal. Each day they were both at the races, they would meet in the bar at an appointed time and share two rounds of drinks, each buying one round. Should Bedwell have anything to ask of Parr, he would answer. Otherwise, the owner would remain silent as to matters of the stable. Bedwell admitted that over time he received various bits of good advice from this regimen. The association with Parr had its own connections to the old days, for Parr had won the Kentucky Derby with Paul Jones in 1920, and it was he, too, who purchased the old Ross farm in Maryland in 1929.

Although Parr had died late in 1939, the 1940 season was to be a good one for Bedwell. He had been hired to train some horses for Elizabeth Arden, the cosmetics queen, who then raced as Mrs. Elizabeth G. Lewis prior to campaigning under the banner of Maine Chance Farm. Mrs. Lewis' Jacomar won the Shevlin Stakes in New York with Hugh Dufford the trainer of record, and then Bedwell, having been reinstated there, took over as trainer of record for his victories in the Bay Shore and Huron handicaps. That same year Mrs. Lewis' Magnificent won the Endurance Handicap for Bedwell.

The 1940 season also took Bedwell back to Saratoga, where for a time, Nasca was seen as the leader in the juvenile filly division. She was by the obscure stallion Rosolio, but won the Spinaway and Schuylerville before she bucked her shins in the Adirondack. Bedwell trained her for her breeder, Breckinridge Long.

Bedwell almost got back into a match race scenario in 1940, two decades after Man o' War–Sir Barton. That spring, his own two-year-old Blensign, purchased from H.H. Cross, won the Dover and Ral Parr stakes. Prior to the Dover, Belmont Park had arranged a special race with Millsdale Stable's High Breeze, another early star who had won the Juvenile Stakes, contingent on Blensign winning the Dover to stay unbeaten. Blensign won but had injured a hock at the start and could not contest the match.

In 1941 Bedwell again fell afoul of authority. Drug testing had come in well in advance of that year. One of Bedwell's runners tested positive and the trainer was suspended.

Back in action in 1942, he resumed winning a few stakes here and there. He also was an outspoken leader on behalf of horsemen's interests via the Horsemen's Benevolent and Protective Association.

In 1947 misfortune again befell Bedwell. Author Ours places the blame partially on himself. During the outbreak of equine infectious anemia in New England, fourteen of Bedwell's horses died. Ours' book states as fact that Bedwell had been injecting some of his horses with testosterone. Apparently, commonly used needles spread the infection. (Known as swamp fever, or sometimes marsh fever, EIA is the deadly disease for which Dr. Leroy Coggins eventually developed a test in 1970. There is still no known cure, so control is essential. Thus, the phrase Coggins test became ubiquitous in the horse world.)

Bedwell's losses to swamp fever included perhaps the best horse of his own he had raced since Las Angeleno. Prognosis had been bred by Calumet

Farm and was by Blenheim II—Diagnosis, by Sweep. Blenheim II was a leading stallion and sire of Whirlaway, who was also out of a Sweep mare. Prognosis was a half brother to the filly Good Blood, a major stakes winner by the great Bull Lea (and she would later foal champion Barbizon).

Madden and Ross could hardly have conspired to turn over a horse of better breeding to Bedwell, but this one he bought on his own for $5,000 after Prognosis had made but one start for Calumet. At three and four in 1946–47, Prognosis won the Maryland Handicap, Bunker Hill Handicap, and Tomasello Memorial. He won fifteen of forty-two races and earned $73,225 prior to his fatal disease.

Bedwell rose from the ashes of the swamp fever debacle, for his horses were insured. He collected $125,000 with which to restock, although the IRS gave him some troublesome guidelines about replacing like with like; for example, a $10,000 settlement on a specific horse should result in a purchase of another $10,000 horse rather than two for $5,000 each.

The last two stakes winners Bedwell trained were both purchased for his own account with his insurance settlements. In the winter of 1948, he went back to California and there purchased Torchator from Walter McCarty after the colt had won a pair of three-furlong juvenile sprints. Bedwell returned to Maryland with Torchator and won the Bowie Kindergarten Stakes.

Later in 1948 Bedwell won his richest purse as an owner. He had bought Daily Dip from C.V. Whitney and presumably used up a bit of the $40,000 individual settlement from Prognosis. Daily Dip was a four-year-old with another exceptional pedigree, being by classic winner Mahmoud and out of a mare by the great Equipoise. That summer Bedwell sent him out to win the $25,000 Myrtlewood Stakes at Arlington Park, pocketing a winner's purse of $18,800.

Bedwell lived several more years. In the meantime, the transformation from his frenetic days apparently was complete. As early as 1942, after Brownie Leach had visited him, the writer remarked in his column that "Guy Bedwell enjoys nothing in the world quite as much as rearing back in a tackroom chair, with his feet on a tack trunk, and talking horses for an appreciative audience. On such occasions, his hand moves monotonously back and forth, shooing green horse flies as if such a gesture had become a reflex action with him through long custom [perhaps replacing fiddling with silver dollars?]. Bedwell is one of the few men who lives up in almost every respect to the specification for race track 'characters' laid down by such authors as Charley Van Loan and Gerald Beaumont."

It was during the rambling conversation that ensued that Bedwell told the story of buying Cudgel because John Schorr was afraid of an oats shortage, the details of Ross' betting plans for the 1919 Derby, and the tale of Tom Smith's moment as an outlaw. Bedwell also stressed that Cudgel, not Sir Barton, was "the best horse I ever trained."

As he arrived at his mid-seventies, Bedwell from time to time spoke of selling Yarrow Brae, retiring, and moving to California, where "we have a beautiful home at Santa Anita, with the track in our front yard." He never got around to that move.

Mrs. Bedwell died in July 1951. Bedwell must have liked being married, for by October he had wed the former Ann F. Brown of Boston. Bedwell himself suffered a heart attack at Yarrow Brae and died on December 31, 1951, in Prince George's County Hospital, Laurel, Maryland. He was seventy-six.

Sunny Jim Fitzsimmons, a fellow sojourner on a horse trainer's long travels, expressed his admiration: "Bedwell was as good as there ever was. Any time a man takes his own money, puts it into horses, and consistently succeeds over a long period, he's got to be good.

Bedwell's second wife and his son and daughter survived him. The son, Buster, had been his assistant at times and established his own career as a trainer. Buster took out a trainer's license at eighteen in 1921, and it was probably not a coincidence that his father was suspended at the time. Buster Bedwell was a horseman for more than forty years. He died at the age of sixty-four in 1967.

Although his own success did not approach the best times of his father's, Buster did have a chance to share in the experience of having nice horses in his stable. He won a pair of stakes with Ethel Hill's War Knight before the horse was sent west to another trainer and won the 1946 Santa Anita Handicap.

In the fall of 1939, Gus Ring was the last in a series of owners of the filly Lady Maryland. Lady Maryland had won the Carroll Handicap and three other races from eighteen starts for trainer P.D.L. Watts. She then was sent to Buster Bedwell, who ran her in five races, of which she won the last, the Ritchie Handicap at Pimlico. She was voted the champion handicap filly of the year.

The next season, Buster Bedwell kept the filly until she was moved to A.G. Robertson for her last start. That year, Bedwell won two handicaps with Lady Maryland. Those were modest victories compared to Sir Barton's glories, but H. Guy Bedwell's son could say he, too, had trained a champion.

CHAPTER 4

JOHN E. MADDEN

John E. Madden started life poor. He built up his stake as a wheeler-dealer, based partially, but not totally, on his prowess as a trainer, and then developed his own breeding enterprise to produce the raw product for the all-important sale sector. He had no partner and probably did not want one. (Well, as is so often the case with Madden, it is not that simple; he did have partners from time to time in that he on occasion retained an interest in a horse he sold.)

To sell a racehorse that goes on to greatness for another stable and to do so without a wrenching regret requires a narrow focus on the goal and an inner discipline. "Better to sell and repent than keep and repent" is one of the maxims often attributed to him. This is sometimes shortened simply to "Better to sell."

Had Madden been an inventor, he would happily have sold his idea to someone else for a large sum and been perfectly content for the next guy to establish the patent and reap his own rewards. Had Madden been a sculptor, he would have been content to sell his wax original and let the next guy deal with the foundry and subsequent sales of bronze castings.

An arch example of Madden's way of going was his involvement with the horse Hamburg. This represented a maze more than a crossroads, for Hamburg was a recurring profit center that Madden bought, won with, sold, and finally repurchased for someone else. It would be pat to append that Madden then bred his own series of champions by Hamburg, but, in fact, he never bred a stakes winner by the horse. However, the powerful Whitney outfit, for which Madden bought back Hamburg, bred the stallion to produce champion Artful and at least nineteen other stakes winners.

From the sale of Hamburg, Madden made his great leap into breeding with the purchase of a farm he named Hamburg Place, just outside Lexington. His selection of land was strategic, for a fit driving horse could get him from Lexington's Phoenix Hotel to the lush young farm before a luncheon reveler could lose interest in a horse Madden had on offer. Getting to the farm might be simple, but in his earlier strivings, much had to be achieved to allow Hamburg Place to come into Madden's life.

FEET AND FISTS

Before he began to deal by his horseman's wits, Madden used his physical gifts to pull himself out of a dreary economic stratum. For his day, he was a husky sort, standing nearly six feet and weighing 180 pounds. Many years later J.K.M. Ross, whose father bought notable horses from Madden, recalled him as "the large and jovial John E. Madden. An Irishman without question and hearty as a Celt should be, Mr. Madden was a rough-hewn gentleman, a shrewd horse trader, and he had the largest pair of hands I have ever seen."

He was born in Bethlehem, Pennsylvania, of parents who had emigrated from Roscommon County, Ireland. John E. Madden was born on December 28, 1856, the middle of three young children his mother was left to support after his father, Patrick, died in 1860.

The genesis of this American success story was the rugged coal and steel region of Pennsylvania, where Madden's father had found employment in the zinc works before his death. In later years many a tough young scrapper would find his way out of this hardscrabble life via a college football scholarship. John E. Madden came along before this avenue was open, but Madden was captain of his high school baseball team, holder of state high school records in foot racing from one hundred yards to five miles, and an amateur boxing champion.

Such were the entertainment options of working-class Americans in those days that these activities were more than diversions for youth. They were spectator attractions that drew crowds at local fields and county fairs. Tracks where young men raced were shared with trotting-horse races, and before long Madden had begun driving in these events. The fair circuit also tutored him in draft horses and road horses.

The entrepreneurial spirit took up the baton from God-given physical prowess. Madden won enough trotting races and other contests to buy his own horse, then traded it for another, and he was off on a vagabond itinerary from one county fair to another. When not behind a sulky, he could be seen in the boxing ring or racing on his own two feet, and, fortunately, he was not only brave but also very good.

Evan Shipman, an itinerant writer who would be pals with Ernest Hemingway in Paris before landing with *Daily Racing Form*, had occasion to write about the Hemingwayesque character named Madden. By Shipman's account, Madden had made enough in racing, boxing, and driving that by the time he was twenty-eight, he was owner of a gray gelding named Class Leader. Madden slept in stalls with this fellow during their rounds of the Pennsylvania half-mile tracks, but by 1887 they won a Grand Circuit trotting race in Cleveland.

Madden also took note of pedigree trends in the trotting-horse game, made some astute purchases, and at age thirty moved to Kentucky with a personal arsenal of $150,000 with which to seek even higher ground in life.

Madden was not wedded to one way to make money over another. He perceived that the world of Thoroughbred racing was more on the ascent than the trotting game, and he was horseman enough to begin a personal transition. He did not abandon one game for another any more than he gave up boxing to pursue foot racing, and he achieved enough with the trotters to make the Standardbred Hall of Fame. Gradually, however, he got involved in Thoroughbred racing and, in due time, earned his way into the Hall of Fame of that sector, too.

Madden later said he believed his first Thoroughbred purchases had come in 1888 although he was still highly active with trotters. Two years later Madden wed Ann Megrue of Cincinnati and took up residence with his bride in a suite at the Phoenix Hotel. It was a hint of establishing himself in Lexington, but any thought that it meant a stable existence missed the mark by far.

In 1890 Madden was still winning stakes with trotters, but he also won with the two-year-old Thoroughbred Dundee, who beat the future star Ida Pickwick in the Great Western Stakes in St. Louis. Ida Pickwick later was owned by Madden.

At one time Madden employed the name Gus Straus as a pseudonym in which he raced. Kent Hollingsworth explained the humor of this gambit in his book on Madden, *The Wizard of the Turf,* which recalled the horseman's admiring nickname. Hollingsworth explained that the name Gus Straus was a mirthful recognition of a Lexington landmark. The Straus building was not far from the main hotel, and the two buildings were useful when locals wished to express the slowness of any particular horse, to wit, "he couldn't beat a fat man from the Phoenix to the Straus building."

THE EAST BECKONS

Madden was still playing games with the name Straus when he took his first serious Thoroughbred east. If he named fictitious stables for humans, he also liked to give horses human names. Harry Reed was a colt he purchased from J.E. Delph for $400, prepared in Kentucky, and shipped to New York. Harry Reed won the Van Nest Stakes at Morris Park and quickly was snapped up by one of the leading figures of the day, Mike Dwyer. The purchase price was reported at $10,000.

The next season Madden had a nice pair of two-year-old fillies in Amanda V. and Myrtle Harkness, with whom he continued the tortuous masquerade as Gus Straus. Amanda V. may well have represented a knock on the door that opened into a career transition. She was by Strathmore—Lady Reel, and one can only assume her quality was in part responsible for Madden's interest in her half brother. This was a son of the champion Hanover, and when the youngster was a yearling Madden purchased him from his breeder, Con Enright. The year was 1895, the third and final year of the sensational racing career of Lady Reel's half brother Domino. Yet the price for the Hanover—Lady Reel colt has been reported through the years as only $1,200.

As if the Greek gods were wrestling overhead to determine what next was in store for this confident young Madden fellow, Hamburg proved so unruly a student that his owner was reduced to borrowing a particularly renowned exercise rider from Major Barak Thomas' outfit. Thomas was the breeder of Domino.

Hiram Steele, who was Madden's foreman for many years, later recalled the Hanover—Lady Reel yearling being breezed on six consecutive mornings, so abundant and uproarious was his energy. The colt was given the name of the city Hamburg, a word whose other connotation is evocative of his rapacious appetite. Madden himself later recalled the colt as having the appetite of two horses.

Hamburg won twelve of sixteen races at two, and James R. Keene was said to have remarked that the colt was better at that age than Keene's own idolized Domino. Hamburg came out winning for Madden, had few setbacks, and scored in the Great Trial Stakes, whose winning purse of $16,550 was one of the handsomest of the day. He was recorded as Madden's first champion as an owner, being the top two-year-old of 1897.

Naturally, a colt like that would attract some buyers, and Madden was viscerally averse to the concept of turning a deaf ear to the prophets of profit.

Having gone through his entire juvenile campaign without being lured into another stable, Hamburg now became the focus of some serious dealing. Marcus Daly, whose copper mines were productive in ways similar to the OPEC oilfields of today, was interested. He dispatched to Kentucky an agent, who struck a deal with Madden to purchase Hamburg for something more than $40,000. Indeed, the sum was rumored to be $40,001, so that Madden could say he had sold a horse for more than the accepted record of $40,000, which had stood since the horse Kentucky changed hands for that amount in 1866.

Hamburg was turned over to Billy Lakeland, who brought him out to race for Daly for the first time in the Belmont Stakes in late May 1898. In the meantime, Madden had won the Kentucky Derby earlier that month with Plaudit, whom he had purchased from the noted African-American trainer Ed Brown.

At the end of his two-year-old season, Plaudit debuted for Madden in a mile and one-sixteenth race against the champion older horse Ben Brush and won by a head. He had opened at 40-1. As Madden was a big bettor at the time, it is easy to speculate that his satisfaction in beating a four-year-old with a two-year-old was intense, indeed.

So, in the spring of 1898, Madden had a new star to replace the expensive Hamburg. When the latter finished third in the Belmont, beaten sixteen lengths by Bowling Brook, it could be suspected that Madden had put one over on Marcus Daly. More probably, Lakeland simply was struggling with how to handle Hamburg's prodigious eating habits. In time, Lakeland figured things out, for Hamburg bounced back to win his remaining four races. These included the defeat of Plaudit in the Lawrence Realization. Hamburg won four of five for Daly and earned a bit more than half his reported purchase price, or $21,785.

After purchase of his farm, Madden spent $5,000 from what was still left on a weanling he named David Garrick. He was to resell David Garrick two years later for $25,000 after the colt's victory in the Great Trial Stakes.

Madden had been breeding horses before, but with his own farm, which would grow to some two thousand acres, he set about collecting a huge broodmare band and looking for stallions to stand. A chapter in the Eclipse Press book *Legacies of the Turf*, Volume I, addressed Madden as a breeder first. The intent here is to concentrate on his career as a trainer, but the two disciplines were actually a concurrent melody and counter melody to Madden.

Beginning with records of 1898, he bred 182 stakes winners, more than anyone else until Harry Payne Whitney bred a total of 191. Madden's intent was to breed to sell — not as a yearling consignor dependent on buyers' perceptions of a horse's potential based on pedigree and conformation, but as a peddler of racing prospects already showing talent.

Racing in the major centers of the East and Midwest was not a year-round sport at the time, so Madden had late autumn, winter, and early spring months to attend to the details and pleasures of being a farmer and horse breeder. He eventually would breed about one hundred registered foals a year and would by and large dispose of them in several ways by the end of their two-year-old seasons. First, of course, were the big-ticket sales of those that flashed good form on the racetrack. Next, Madden would convince a buyer that good things might be on the horizon for those horses whose form had not yet come around.

Others he sold for modest prices, some on the cuff. The great trainer Sunny Jim Fitzsimmons once recalled from the safe enclave of prolonged success that, in the distant past, he "was training some horses at some gyp track and John E. Madden came along and gave me a couple of fillies. One of them was named Miss Angie — won a race with her at 15-1 ... Not too sure of the year. I was more worried about something to eat than I was in keeping dates." (Historian Hollingsworth took the trouble to discover that the year was 1907; the track, Gravesend. True to a horseman's priorities, Fitzsimmons had the price right, although he could not remember the year.)

One hundred foals would account for nearly 3 percent of all American Thoroughbred foals in any of the crops around the dawn of the twentieth century. Thus, Madden was supporting not only the top end of the Turf but the day-to-day, gristmill accounts of track and stable as well.

Ever willing to work an additional revenue stream, Madden had also become an adviser to William Collins Whitney when Whitney came on board as a new owner. Whitney was the sort of man of whom Madden would say: "Our rich men derive little pleasure from the pecuniary profit they realize from winning races. They have all the money they want to make life comfortable. But it is the possibility of having their equine stars defeated by nags from a poor owner's stable that gives interest to the contests of the Thoroughbred ... It is this glorious uncertainty ... that makes racing the most fascinating and exhilarating sport in all the world."

The great thing about having Madden as an adviser was that he would fill your stable not just with horses but with good horses, even when he was selling you his own. Madden sold Whitney a series of major runners including Admiration, the best three-year-old filly of 1899, for $15,000, and Kilmarnock, the best three-year-old of 1900, for $20,000. Horses Madden had not owned but bought directly for Whitney included Jean Bereaud, the best two-year-old of 1898, who cost $30,000 and won the 1899 Belmont Stakes. Madden also had influence on the breeding stock of Whitney's burgeoning operation. In 1900, Hamburg's purchaser, Marcus Daly, died, and the horse again came into Madden's realm. Acting for Whitney, Madden bought Hamburg for $60,000 from the Daly estate dispersal.

In the case of a filly named Blue Girl, Madden cleaned up on her but Whitney wound up with another champion. Madden had purchased Blue Girl for $2,550 as a yearling and won the Juvenile, Eclipse, Great American, and Great Trial with her in his own colors of cherry with white hoops on sleeves. He then sold her to Whitney for $25,000. At the end of 1901, Blue Girl was reckoned co-champion two-year-old filly. The other co-champion was Endurance by Right, whom Madden had purchased for $30,000 and the next day passed on to Whitney for a $5,000 profit.

Nasturtium was the champion two-year-old colt that same season, Madden having purchased him for Whitney the previous year for $40,000 from A.L. Aste, for whom the colt had begun his career.

In those glorious few years near the end of Whitney's life, he won back-to-back runnings of the climactic Futurity. In 1900 the winner was Ballyhoo Bey, who was the horse that caused such mayhem between Madden and Sam Hildreth that Hildreth was ruled off New York racing for several years.

Madden had arranged for Hildreth to train the Whitney horses while Madden was helping buy them. They both liked Ballyhoo Bey, and he was purchased for Whitney for $12,000. The colt lost his first start and came out of it with a fever, and rumors of Hildreth's incompetence found an audience with Whitney. Hildreth was let go, and Madden replaced him, training the colt to win the Futurity with the expatriate American Tod Sloan returning from England to ride him.

Various colorful versions of what happened some time later have been told (see chapter on Hildreth). One version was that Hildreth got into the bottle and, with his confidence thus boosted, accosted Madden with a heavy stick at dinner one night. This left Hildreth eventually a sadder but wiser fellow: sadder because he was ruled off New York tracks for a time; wiser because he had learned firsthand that former boxer John E. Madden was still a titan in a fist fight.

Most photos of those days in racetrack paddocks show men with grim, or at least intense, faces. When unaware of the camera, they usually are seen talking among themselves or down to tiny riders. When aware they were being photographed, they tend to strike poses of serious countenance as well, as if to say, "Important business is about to transpire, and I want to look important, too."

One exception appearing in *The Wizard of the Turf* shows Madden, arms folded across his chest, with a charmingly amused smile directed at Hildreth, who is apparently in mid-comment, with his own smile in return. This is illustrative of the happy situation for both men that they did not let coming to blows end for all time their mutually profitable dealings. As we shall see, after Hildreth was reinstated in New York, a number of his best horses were purchased from none other than John E. Madden.

The year after Ballyhoo Bey won the Futurity, Madden and Whitney teamed to win it again with Yankee. Madden had purchased Yankee as a yearling, risking $20,000 on his own tab. He did not let the risk hover over his own accounts for long, for he sold a half-interest in the colt and two other youngsters to Whitney for $50,000 the next spring.

Prior to the Futurity — the richest race of 1901 with a winner's purse of $36,850 — Madden is reported to have advised Whitney that he was confident Yankee could win, and that it would give more pleasure to Madden were the colt to wear the Whitney colors rather than his own. Whitney demurred: "No, John, you developed him, and you are entitled to the credit."

Madden also had the Hastings filly Gunfire in the race, which on the surface invites the suspicion that in offering to run Yankee in Whitney's colors he really wanted to avoid having an entry so as to get a better price on Yankee. Countering this unkind thought is the fact that Whitney also ran Nasturtium, so that the bookmakers presumably would have treated Yankee as part of an entry anyway.

That Futurity further illustrated Madden's pervasiveness. The field also included two other horses that Madden had sold, for $20,000 each. One was Heno, sold to telegraph millionaire Clarence Mackay, and the other was Fly Wheel, sold to Perry Belmont of the distinguished racing family.

Yankee won the Futurity, and Hollingsworth quoted the *New York World* to the effect that Whitney, not generally known for heavy betting, had put $20,000 on Yankee to place and had won $50,000. Yankee and Gunfire were both melded into the Whitney stable to run in his colors thereafter. Gunfire was the champion handicap distaffer in both 1903 and 1904. (Again, we cannot separate the trainer from the breeder, for Madden was to breed nine stakes winners sired by Yankee. The best of these was Joe Madden — named for one of Madden's sons and the Belmont Stakes winner and leading earner of 1909.)

To review, the retrospective list of champions for 1901 showed extraordinary Madden–Whitney influence: top two-year-old, Whitney's Nasturtium, purchased by Madden; top two-year-old fillies Whitney's Endurance by Right and Blue Girl, both purchased from Madden; top three-year-old filly, Madden-bred Trigger, who had been sold to Clarence Mackay. The only remaining champions that year were Mackay's Banastar and James R. Keene's Commando.

One of the interesting aspects of the way Madden went about hawking his wares was that horses became more valuable and attractive to others by winning races for him. For example, Blue Girl and Yankee won $76,000 credited to Madden before their official transfers to the Whitney stable. Madden's colors also were worn to stakes victories by five other two-year-olds that year. The end result of all the buying and selling and winning was that Whitney's stable led the nation's owners with earnings of $108,440, and Madden ranked second as owner with $103,115! On the trainers' list, Hollingsworth reported that Madden led with $127,090.

THE WIZARD'S TEACHINGS

Among John E. Madden's talents was communication. At Hamburg Place he had posted a detailed series of rules about how horses were to be handled and guests welcomed. From time to time, various periodicals published declarative accounts of his opinions. Today's world of the Thoroughbred perhaps would be appalled by Madden's practice of starting weanlings in preliminary training, ridden by lightweight boys, but his wisdom for his day is unquestionable.

Among Madden's lengthy accounts is the following, quoted in *The Wizard of the Turf*, which covers various aspects of the trainer's craft, including betting on one's own horses:

In training the Thoroughbred of today there are certain rules very essential for the success of the horse. First and foremost, I would say regular feeding, good oats and hay, bran and grass, and regular work. On work days, be sure that the horse has had ample time to digest his food.

Should the trainer be a betting man, he generally likes to wager on his horse the first time he starts. This is often followed with bad results, since to know that your horse can win the first time it must have required fast trials. One can win his first bet, but at the cost of a good horse, leaving him quite often in a nervous condition and perhaps a breakdown.

It takes a skilled trainer to handle successfully a nervous horse. A good foreman, a good nightwatchman, and a good exercise boy weighing about 110 pounds, who will adopt the balance seat [Tod] Sloan re-established [used by riders of 300 years ago], are very necessary in the training of horses. Don't overlook the necessity of having an owner with plenty of money.

If a trainer has a trial horse to be used in connection with preparing his horse, it is of greater benefit than a half-dozen workouts and gives the trainer a better line on his condition. Much depends, of course, upon the horse you are preparing for long races. You have to take into consideration the age, degree of soundness, constitution and disposition, and more especially those with extreme speed, known as sprinters, which, if easily placed, may be prepared to go a distance.

There are plenty of stayers, or horses now in training that could be stayers if they were trained to do so, but the opportunity for their development in this particular line does not exist in the same degree that it did in the past. The breed is as good, indeed better, today than when long-distance racing was an attraction. All sound horses today can stay at their own pace.

Those who decry the racehorse of today, on the ground that every [other] quality is sacrificed to speed, either entirely overlook or do not understand the term "staying." They fail to see that speed — to which they assert everything is wrongly sacrificed — is in itself the very bedrock of staying power.

Of course, in saying that staying is to a great extent a matter of training, it is not intended to be implied that a horse constitutionally a non-stayer can be made to stay by simply training him to run long distances. As a rule, when horses are really non-stayers they are so from physical conformation or lack of breeding. The natural non-stayer cannot be trained into a stayer.

Many a horse, however, judged by the running of his early days to be a non-stayer, has proved on being trained to run long distances to possess staying powers of high order. If there is an incentive to owners to look out as much for stayers as for speed milers, horses able to go a distance will soon be found in largely increased numbers. A good many horses which in these times are branded as poor stayers would have been considered good enough in that respect in the olden days, when races were certainly not run as fast as they are now.

Madden illustrated a point about the difference in horses' constitutions by describing two victories with different horses in the two and a quarter-mile Annual Champion. One was such a glutton for training that Madden had to "repeat" him, his way of saying that one morning he worked the horse one and a quarter miles and sent him back out twenty-five minutes later to work a half-mile. The other horse, not needing much work, was worked one and a half miles in his final preparation but was not "repeated."

Continuing Madden's treatise:

A horse will usually show his condition at feeding time, and if nervous, work should be postponed. Nervous horses are often subject to scouring.

Frequently you will hear of fast trials for big events. These are given, generally, by young trainers just beginning their careers, but as they grow older you will note a change in their methods, and they work instead of running trials against the watch.

The American trainer is a great caretaker, spending much money for liniments to be used on legs and body which remove soreness after a hard workout or a race. He uses grass freely, instead of the medicine ball.

Horses which are expected to take part on the prominent tracks around New York generally commence their work about Jan. 15. Many trainers do not commence until the first of February and are confined to the shed, as the weather, climate, and roads at metropolitan tracks seldom permit outdoor work at that time.

Some horses are given as much as from five to seven miles of slow jogging daily under the shed until the weather opens up. The trainer considers himself fortunate if he can get onto the course as early as St. Patrick's Day, when, after about two weeks of slow galloping, miles are made in about two minutes, and then you gradually work up to a mile in 1:45. This is the point where you can determine the soundness and constitution of your horse. A horse with a good constitution can be given more work than those to whom nature has not been so kind.

On another occasion, Madden discussed another set of details about training while, as horsemen are wont to do, reminding that each animal is an individual:

> Very few blankets are used by the American trainer. Every effort is made to keep as much flesh as possible on his horse. Lightweight Linseys are mostly used, and they take the place of the old-time woolen blanket.
>
> After a strong workout, the condition of his wind will show the condition of the horse. Generally, two days are given between work; horses are indulged in trotting and slow gallops between work. Some horses will race to their best form when given slow breezing every other day and at no time a fast trial.
>
> With a stable of 20 horses, there might be only two which require the same treatment to race successfully.

The horsemanship of John E. Madden, as we have noted, did not begin and end with the shed row of the youngster in training and/or the racehorse. Years after Madden's death James L. Donnelly offered a heartfelt testimony to Madden's complete grasp of raising as well as training horses. Employed at Hamburg Place in 1899, Donnelly spoke with Brownie Leach for an article in *The Blood-Horse* in 1943, the year of the loyal employee's retirement. Donnelly's memories illustrate the combine of breeder-farmer-trainer:

> Mr. Madden had an uncanny ability at picking good horses as well as making the right decision in problems that came up on the farm ... He used to look the yearlings over in July, and those of us who went along would watch his eye. Whenever his eyelid dropped, you could bet the yearling he was looking at right then had been picked out as a top horse. He was seldom wrong, and seldom wrong when he was confronted with a problem of farm operation, although the entire situation was something with which he [not always present] was unfamiliar.
>
> He thought fresh air was as important as anything in the raising of a good horse. We never had a stall on Hamburg Place that was without a window. In most cases ... the top of the stall was open ...

Soon after I went there to work, Mr. Madden asked, 'Donnelly, which of these barns do you think is the healthiest?' I replied that I couldn't understand why, but the coldest barn on the farm was the healthiest for horses. He told me it was because there was plenty of fresh air.

Madden also had young horses raised outdoors, with access to hay and shelter, as they chose, in three-sided sheds. These structures came to be known in Kentucky as Madden Sheds, although the master noted he had seen them used in England.

In 1902, Hollingsworth reports, Madden the trainer set a record of $150,576 in earnings by horses he saddled. Among the key contributors was Irish Lad, the champion two-year-old colt he sold to Harry Payne Whitney and Herman B. Duryea. Years later Madden noted that in Hamburg and Sir Martin he counted himself as having developed two great horses. As far as "training" Turfmen, he cited Whitney's son, Harry Payne Whitney, and Whitney's partner Duryea as two who gave him particular pride.

Harry Payne Whitney was destined to follow his father, William Collins Whitney, and build upon his foundations on the Turf. However, he did not wait for inheritance to place a stable of horses under his control. He and Duryea were game to have at it on their own.

Madden offered Irish Lad, whose form had prompted the master to mark up his price to $27,500, more than a ten-fold multiple on the $2,250 the colt had cost as a yearling. Although new on the Turf, Whitney and Duryea were wise to the ways of business. They countered with the idea of knocking $10,000 off the asking price, that amount to come from future earnings, should such sum manifest itself.

Irish Lad saw to this immediately, earning $17,460 in winning the Great Trial Stakes in his first start for Whitney–Duryea. He later added the Saratoga Special and Flatbush stakes and was regarded as the best two-year-old colt of his year. Harry Payne Whitney's father was not shut out of championship status that year, for his Blue Girl was regarded the best in the three-year-old filly division.

The elder Whitney died in 1904, and the horses that year were raced in Duryea's name. (William Collins Whitney was a giant in government and business as well as sport. Such men usually are not noted historically for their senses of humor, perhaps owing more to the limited light in which the media views them. William Collins Whitney showed such a sense on the occasion that Green B. Morris was teasing him over the price, $20,000, he had paid Madden for Kilmarnock. Morris made an issue of the fact that the price was no more than Morris had gotten years earlier for Kilmarnock's sire, Sir Dixon. Madden was standing nearby, and Whitney immediately reached into his own pockets and handed him a half-dollar and two quarters.)

A CHANGE IN PRIORITIES

The year William Collins Whitney died, 1904, was also an unfortunate milestone in the life of Madden and his family. Mrs. Madden sued for divorce, setting off protracted court battles that eventually ended in Madden's receiving custody of their sons, Edward and Joe. (The former Mrs. Madden married Louis V. Bell, who had bought some horses from Madden, and the couple moved to Switzerland.)

Madden thus devoted much of his time to his sons, which meant staying at Hamburg Place more than he had previously. Hollingsworth noted that he trained the boys "incessantly to become outstanding runners, boxers, swimmers, and riders." At thirteen Edward was adept enough at working horses to within a fifth of a second of the target that rumors floated around that he would soon become the jockey for his father. That did not transpire.

Charles T. Patterson, who had once trained the outstanding horse Ornament, had been Madden's top assistant since before Hamburg was a two-year-old. Thus, Madden had a trusted man to put in charge of general supervision of the racing stable, but he began running fewer horses in his own colors. This did not mean that the stream of major winners, and major sales, dwindled. In 1904 Madden won the Foam Stakes and the Great Trial Stakes with Flyback and then sold him for $17,500 to E.R. Thomas.

With W.C. Whitney gone and Harry Payne Whitney operating his own breeding and racing enterprise, Madden threw in with Francis and Tommy Hitchcock as his partners in several runners and some breeding stock. The name Hitchcock is perhaps primarily associated with a golden age of polo, but Francis Hitchcock was also president of Saratoga as well as a breeder and owner. From Hitchcock's 1902 crop Madden selected a son of old pal Hamburg as the best, and Hitchcock gave him a half-interest in the horse. The colt was out of Pansy, by St. Blaise, and so was given the name Dandelion.

Despite this somewhat delicate name, Madden developed Dandelion into a major winner. At two in 1904, he won the Remsen and Consolation stakes and then followed with the Travers and Saranac at three and the Suburban, Saratoga, Delaware, and Champlain handicaps at four. The Suburban was as hotly contested after the fact as it had been on the track.

As Hollingsworth recalled, the great rider Walter Miller put Dandelion in front after eight furlongs and still had a small lead in the stretch. Then, according to the chart of the race, Dandelion was "literally choked to a standstill and never let go until in the last furlong and then was unable to cope successfully with such a redoubtable stretch runner as Go Between under a very badly judged ride."

Dandelion had recently been second to Grapple in the Metropolitan and second to Tokalon in the Brooklyn. The Suburban result, following the other defeats, put Madden in a foul humor, and he spotted a way to challenge the stewards.

He protested that Alexander Shields had entered Go Between as a gelding when in fact the horse was a ridgling. The stewards ruled against Madden. He would not let it go and spent some time "studying law," as he put it. Madden then appealed to The Jockey Club, which reversed the stewards. As Hollingsworth described the conclusion, Dandelion got the first-place purse, for it was ruled that Go Between was not a qualified starter. Moreover, owner Shields was suspended and his trainer's license revoked. Nevertheless, lists of Suburban Handicap winners even today carry Go Between as the winner. Madden, presumably, would have preferred the credit and the money, but if a choice had to be made, we presume that getting his share of the purse represented the key victory he had sought.

By the end of 1906, Go Between had been transferred to E.R. Thomas, and he was regarded the champion older horse of the year.

Another horse Madden trained for the Hitchcocks was Tangle, who won the 1905 Adirondack Stakes and the 1906 Great Republic Stakes. Tangle was ranked as a co-champion three-year-old filly of 1906, along with Running Water.

Also in 1906 the stable included another champion in Salvidere, whose success required some of Madden's most careful and attentive work. Salvidere was a gelding with tender feet who finished second in his first start. Madden saw enough to buy him after that debut, for $3,700, then sold a half-interest to Tommy Hitchcock Jr.

Madden kept the son of Belvidere—Sallie of Navarre, by Henry of Navarre, unshod most of the time and had to work him gingerly. On at least one occasion, he put on plates only minutes before the horse reported to the paddock and removed them after the race. Madden shod Salvidere with aluminum plates, which were relatively uncommon at the time. In addition to his foot problems, Salvidere was nervous and had to be tricked into eating.

For all this, Salvidere was a runner, and Madden — the old "wizard" — got the best out of him. Remarkably, not only did the horse stay sound enough to race but he campaigned like a horse of rugged constitution and soundness, winning six stakes within the space of two months. These included the Saratoga Special, Brighton Junior, Adirondack, and Junior Champion. He was ranked the best two-year-old of 1906, and assistant Patterson was even quoted as saying he thought the boss regarded Salvidere as the equal to Hamburg "in his best days." It is illustrative of many things about Madden, and about horses, that this dainty gelding might be spoken of in comparable terms as the powerful, prodigious workhorse that was Hamburg.

FROM SIR MARTIN TO SIR BARTON

While results on the racetrack were highly satisfactory in 1906, activities back at the Hamburg Place breeding operation that spring would destine great things for the future. With his personal court battles ongoing, Madden took the occasion to name two foals from that crop for his sons. Edward was by Plaudit—Passan, by Hamburg, and thus had plenty of Madden horse tradition in his background. Likewise, Joe Madden was by the former Madden star Yankee but was out of an imported mare, Tarantella, by Peter. They were among the eleven stakes winners Madden bred in that foal crop — his high mark to that time. And while both were good, they yielded pride of place in the group to Sir Martin and Fayette.

Sir Martin was by one of the Hamburg Place sires, Ogden, and out of Lady Sterling, by Hanover. He won a pair of overnight races from his first three starts in 1908 and then won the National Stallion Stakes. Such was the quality of Madden's homebred juveniles that year that he let Sir Martin and another of them, Fayette (Ogden—Saratoga Belle, by Henry of Navarre), swap one-two finishes in the Great American and Tremont. Sir Martin was "assigned" the first race and then Fayette was the declared winner for the Tremont.

Next, in the first race of the Double Event, with each in at 129 pounds and presumably both being ridden to win, it was Fayette first, Sir Martin second. In the Great Trial, with the weights the same, Sir Martin won, with Fayette second, marking the fourth time they had run one-two. (It was Madden's seventh win in the past dozen runnings of that important juvenile race.)

Still pursuing their tandem act, Sir Martin and Fayette took up 130 pounds each in the Hopeful. Sir Martin won, but the spell was broken to some extent, for an interloper named Helmet squeezed in a second over Fayette.

The filly Maskette took Sir Martin's measure. Longtime Hamburg Place employee Donnelly had a story about this race, and what happened next. By Donnelly's telling, Sir Martin was knocked sideways at the start of the Futurity. After the race Madden approached Keene in defense of his horse's reputation and proposed a match at $10,000 a side. Keene was well up on the schedule of races and suggested that the Flatbush Stakes the following Saturday would suffice as a rematch. Madden agreed and presumably was happy to have done so, for Sir Martin got revenge with an easy victory over Maskette. Sir Martin had won eight of thirteen races and was the leading money-earner of the year with $78,590, as well as the champion two-year-old.

Even with Sir Martin's and Fayette's dominance, Madden found some good spots for his sons' namesakes. Edward won the Flash and Grand

Union Hotel stakes, and Joe Madden won the Juvenile Stakes and Prospect Handicap. A trio of Madden's two-year-old fillies, Lady Bedford, Obdurate, and Miss Kearney, also won stakes in their division.

The year 1908 also found Madden selling future champions King James and Fitz Herbert to his one-time nemesis, Hildreth. The master of Hamburg Place was very much in a selling mode, and even horses named for his sons were on the market. Joe Madden went to Hildreth and won the Belmont Stakes the next year. Edward was sold to Louis Winans for $15,000, considerably less than the $75,000 that Winans paid for champion Sir Martin at the same time.

Despite the quality in the Madden barn, the 1908 season was the year Colin was three and the unbeaten overall champion. James Rowe, trainer of Colin and other good ones for James R. Keene, topped Madden in the money-winning tables for trainers.

The 1909 season presented the fascinating spectacle of the American two-year-old champion of the previous year not being aimed at our own best races but sent abroad for the Epsom Derby. Sir Martin was favored for the great race but fell at Tattenham Corner. Madden is renowned as the breeder of five Kentucky Derby winners (Old Rosebud, Sir Barton, Paul Jones, Zev, Flying Ebony). But for Sir Martin's misfortune, he might have added the distinction of having bred an Epsom Derby winner as well. Sir Martin survived the mishap and negotiated Tattenham Corner successfully enough to win the Coronation Cup the following year.

(Ten years after Sir Martin's Derby try — and following the Triple Crown of his half brother, Sir Barton — Sir Martin was re-purchased as a Hamburg Place stallion. Madden bred fourteen stakes winners by him. Madden often counseled his staff against becoming sentimentally involved with a horse, but it was he who instructed that certain horses be buried beneath markers in a cemetery on the farm. In Sir Martin's case, there was also a chink in the concept of everything being for sale, inasmuch as Madden held him out of reduction sales late in his life and arranged for the horse to be cared for through the rest of the stallion's own days. Sir Martin died in 1930, the year after his owner's death, and was buried at Hamburg Place.)

With Hamburg Place's broodmare band growing to nearly 150, Madden achieved some gaudy figures in number of stakes winners bred from crop to crop. There were nineteen stakes winners in the 1914 foal crop, which was the year after the resumption of New York racing in the wake of a legislated ban in 1911 and 1912. This was a career high-water mark in number of stakes winners but not necessarily in production of elite horses.

In 1913 three of the champions were horses Madden had bred and sold. They were the champion juvenile male and filly, Old Rosebud and Southern Maid, and the champion handicap female, Flora Fina.

Flora Fina was a daughter of Ogden and raced for J.W. Johnson. That Madden stood Ogden, also sire of Sir Martin and Fayette, was a story unto itself. Ogden had won the 1896 Futurity for Marcus Daly and had stood one season at stud by the time of the Daly estate's dispersal. Madden was active at that dispersal, buying several for himself as well as Hamburg for Whitney, but Billy Lakeland got Ogden for $4,200.

Lakeland's groom was instructed to lead Ogden from Brooklyn to the Brighton Beach racetrack, according to Hollingsworth's book on Madden. The presence of a nearby saloon on a cold evening toyed with the good fellow's judgment to the extent that he tied Ogden to a fence outside and went inside for some restoration. Ogden got loose and was sightseeing in Brooklyn when a policeman caught him. Ogden was recovered by Lakeland the next day, while the groom — showing better judgment in the morning — made sure the trainer did not find him.

Lakeland returned Ogden to training and won six straight races with him. In an extraordinary sequence, Lakeland won a small race with Ogden on Futurity Day, then rested him one day and won both the second and sixth races on the next card! Madden offered $15,000 for Ogden, and Lakeland, having recouped his purchase price and a bit more, was happy with the profit. Madden was to sell nearly a million dollars worth of horses sired by Ogden and bred twenty-six stakes winners by him. One of these, The Finn, he sold twice, the second time for $115,000. By that time, The Finn had sired Zev and Flying Ebony, two of the Kentucky Derby winners Madden bred. The Finn was racing for H.C. Hallenbeck when he garnered three-year-old colt honors in 1915. This was something of a consolation prize, for the filly Regret was hailed as the best runner of any age in America that year.

Old Rosebud, the champion two-year-old male of 1913, was the gelding whose pedigree illustrated that Madden did not always sell everything. Once he owned a breeding farm, Madden kept some fillies as broodmare prospects as well as buying large numbers of mares. Hamburg Place had kept at least one daughter of Ida Pickwick, who had won forty-four races.

The first of Ida Pickwick's four stakes-winning foals was Ivory Bells, by Himyar, and it was Ivory Bells who foaled Old Rosebud. Old Rosebud was by Uncle, who was to be the best breeding son of Hamburg Place's multi-champion sire Star Shoot. Hamburg Place employee Donnelly recalled that when Madden sold Uncle at three for $25,000, he retained the right to send twelve mares to him the first year and thus bred three stakes winners by the young sire.

However, Uncle's quality was unknown at the time Old Rosebud was a yearling, for he was in the stallion's first crop. Madden sold him for only $500 as a yearling to Frank Weir.

Weir gelded the colt and sold him to Colonel Hamilton C. Applegate, for whom he trained him. Weir had the shrewd judgment to retain an interest in Old Rosebud, who was to star at two, three, and six and continue to make comebacks through the age of eleven. Old Rosebud was the first of the Madden-bred Kentucky Derby winners, and at six he was regarded the best older male and best horse overall. Old Rosebud won half of his eighty races and earned $74,729. Sadly, he was raced to death. As Old Rosebud's powers waned, Weir dropped him down into claiming company, and after Old Rosebud was injured in an allowance race at the age of eleven the trainer reluctantly had him euthanized.

The remaining Madden-bred champion of 1913, juvenile filly Southern Maid, raced in the name of R. Davis. She was by Plaudit, Madden's 1898 Derby winner.

As noted earlier, the 1914 crop bred by John E. Madden would eventually be seen to include nineteen individual stakes winners, the most he ever bred at one time. However, they had none of the panache of one of the eleven stakes winners Madden bred two crops later.

Famously, that 1916 foal crop at Hamburg Place included a half brother to Sir Martin, i.e., a Star Shoot colt named Sir Barton. Madden had a partner-by-courtesy in the official records of Sir Barton's breeding. During the winter of 1915–16, Vivian Gooch, who had trained Sir Martin in England, visited Hamburg Place. Over dinner, Madden bestowed on Gooch, in advance, an interest in Lady Sterling's next foal. After that foal was born, Madden registered him with Gooch as his co-breeder and then bought out his guest's share. Whatever the price, it was a needless expense, born out of hospitality, courtesy, and perhaps thanks for having tended to Sir Martin.

When Madden got Sir Barton to the races at two in 1918, the colt seemed to have style, dash, and attitude but was not much at winning races. Indeed, Sir Barton made five starts without earning a dollar. Madden, however, was campaigning him like a good horse, for Sir Barton ran in the Tremont, Flash, United States Hotel, and Sanford Memorial stakes. Records show that Madden was the owner for these races but had W.S. Walker down as the trainer of record.

Canadian railroad magnate Commander J.K.L. Ross was gathering an important stable, for which he had retained H. Guy Bedwell as trainer. In the book *Boots and Saddles*, Ross' son, J.K.M. Ross, years later looked back on Saratoga of 1918. Even taking into account that the author was about sixteen at the time, his memories comprise a telling hint of Madden's ability to frame a situation masterfully. For all Madden's success at getting horses ready to win right away, the impression young Ross retained was that, "It was his (Madden's) custom to proceed gently and slowly with the racing education of his juveniles … Several times I heard him say that

Thoroughbreds are merely babies at two, only partially developed at three, and not fully mature for racing until four. In consequence, Mr. Madden's horses often ran 'green' in their early races; he was carefully completing their education in actual competition, a practice frowned on but nevertheless done."

Well, how that squared with putting lightweight lads on weanlings was possibly something Madden left unmentioned to Ross as he was urging him to buy the stylish maiden. The younger Ross recalled, "In the Sanford, Sir Barton showed a flash of early speed but beyond that his record indicated no particular promise. I remember him nonetheless; he was fat as a barrel, but very handsome. Perhaps I recall him because my father and his trainer were interested in him. Or perhaps because I knew that Mr. Madden was urging my father to buy him."

Perhaps so.

Ross and Bedwell paid $10,000 for Sir Barton, apparently sensing, or accepting, Madden's descriptions of the horse's innate potential. It was a classic case of the buyer being spectacularly rewarded, the seller presumably content with his swag.

In his first start for Ross, Sir Barton caught a huge field in the Hopeful and thus was able to finish behind more horses at one time than he ever had before. He was sixteenth in a field of twenty. In his very next start, however, Sir Barton first gave an inkling of what was to come, for he finished second in the Futurity. (A bit later, Ross bought Milkmaid from Madden, waiting in that case until she actually had won. Milkmaid, bred by J. Hal Woodford and acquired by Madden to train and sell, was to be a distaff champion at three and four for Ross.)

In 1919, as is well known in racing lore, Sir Barton became the first horse to sweep the Kentucky Derby, Preakness, and Belmont Stakes. That was seen as an admirable feat in 1919, especially with the Withers Stakes thrown in, but it was not until 1930 that the term "Triple Crown" bound the Derby, Preakness, and Belmont together. In England the phrase Triple Crown was affixed to the Two Thousand Guineas, Epsom Derby, and St. Leger. (Coincidentally, Madden had bred a 1914 Star Shoot—Miss Kearney filly that was named Triple Crown.)

The year before Sir Barton's Triple Crown, Exterminator had won the Kentucky Derby. By Hollingsworth's telling, this champion represented one of the occasions when Madden perhaps had to grit his teeth and repeat, with some resolve, his mantra about not repenting a sale. Exterminator was part of a package Madden had bought into, but, according to his friend and neighbor, W. Rodes Estill, some time later Madden received a phone call after which he turned and said with a chuckle: "Just sold a gelding worth $4,000. Got $9,000 and two fillies for him." Presumably, the other party on the phone was J. Cal Milam (or his agent), who had been the purchaser of record of Exterminator for $1,500. Milam was selling off the gelding to Willis Sharpe Kilmer, who thought he was buying a workmate for his hot Derby candidate Sun Briar and got a champion instead.

DOMINATING STATISTICS

The pattern of champions bred, broken, trained, and sold off continued. Madden was also impressive in sheer numbers. The *American Racing Manual* first published statistics for leading breeders of 1917. Madden was the leader in races won that year, with 334, and he led that list for eleven consecutive years. In 1921 he was represented by 424 wins as a breeder, a record unmatched for more than a half-century; in 1978, another high-volume, high-quality breeder, E.P. Taylor, broke the mark when represented by 442 wins.

The *American Racing Manual* of 1923 blithely reported that Madden was the leading breeder both in wins and in earnings for the seventh consecutive year although no dollar figures were given prior to 1919. In the money list Madden's run was interrupted by a second place to Harry Payne Whitney in 1924, but the master of Hamburg Place led one last time in 1925.

Madden's pattern of selling during the season worked against his ever leading the owners lists, although he came close on occasion. Ironically for a man whose horsemanship was his hallmark, Madden never led the trainers' statistics, after the publication began recording them.

At the top end of Madden-breds, one of the best — perhaps the very best — was Grey Lag (Star Shoot—Miss Minnie, by Meddler), a foal of 1918. Max Hirsch got to Grey Lag as a yearling. Given Madden's penchant for the early training of young horses, however, he undoubtedly was not dealing in the dark in pricing the horse. A deal was struck at $10,000 (see chapter on Hirsch), and Grey Lag went on to earn $136,715 while racing for Hirsch and then for Harry Sinclair. He was a champion, or co-champion, from three through five and was regarded as Horse of the Year at three in 1921. Madden was said to rate Grey Lag the best horse he had ever bred.

In 1922 the year Grey Lag was co-champion older male, the champion three-year-old was Emotion, a Friar Rock filly bred by Madden and raced by R.L. Gerry. That same year one of the better three-year-olds was a Friar Rock colt, Rockminister, also bred by Madden. Rockminister raced for Montfort Jones when he won the Latonia Championship Stakes at one and three-quarters miles.

The 1920s saw two more of the best of Madden, in Zev and Princess Doreen. By this time yearlings rather than crack two-year-old prospects represented more of the sales. Zev was another dividend to Sam Hildreth for his willingness to let bygones be bygones. Zev was purchased for Harry

Sinclair and became only the second horse to that time to win the Kentucky Derby and Belmont Stakes. He was champion at two in 1922 and co-champion and Horse of the Year at three.

Princess Doreen was a rugged mare foaled in 1921 and was champion or co-champion of her gender at three, four, and five. She was by Spanish Prince II—Lady Doreen, by Ogden, and raced for B.B. and Montfort Jones' Audley Farm.

Zev and Princess Doreen gave Madden the distinction of having bred the leading money earners of their genders. Zev had earned an overall record $313,639, and Princess Doreen owned the distaff mark of $174,745.

John E. Madden's remarkable rise from scrapper in a rugged land did not stop at the racetrack or breeding farm. He eventually had an office on Wall Street. One of his Standardbred contacts, E.T. Bedford, had remained a friend and adviser. Madden had invested wisely in Bedford's company, Corn Products, and he was to leave an estate valued at $9 million.

Madden died at seventy-two, in 1929. He had contracted pneumonia a few weeks earlier but with a lifelong belief in his own physical strength, refused to enter a hospital. Madden's sons had been at his bedside, but he convinced them they need not tarry. He suffered a heart attack in his New York hotel room and died alone on November 3.

As early as 1919, he had run advertisements in trade publications that he had "retired from public breeding" and in recent years had sold off many of his horses. He was not out of the game at the time he died, however, and unfinished business included auction of nineteen juveniles in 1931, horses that were weanlings in the autumn their breeder died.

Hollingsworth noted that one of the disappointments of Madden's life was that neither of his sons took up his interest in Thoroughbred racing. In the immediate aftermath of his death, however, the brothers announced plans to continue operating Hamburg Place along the lines of its past.

Joe Madden told *The Blood-Horse* that, "Edward has been here now off and on for the past year and has a pretty good grip of matters at the farm already." Edward Madden, who had attained rank of captain while serving overseas during World War I, added, "I have a perfectly good business in Oklahoma that I have been practically running from here [Kentucky] ... If John E. Madden ran Hamburg Place spending half the year in New York, we figure his son should be able to run a less complicated business in Oklahoma from Kentucky."

These ambitions perhaps reflected respect and admiration for their father and a knee-jerk sense of responsibility to continue his legacy. The plans did not materialize, although the farm remained a lovely property as Joe took a great interest in polo. Joe Madden bought all but 100 acres of Hamburg Place after his brother's death in 1932, only three years after their father's death. Joe Madden died at forty-eight in 1943. Each son died at his own hand.

It was left to one of Joe's sons, Preston Madden, to restore Hamburg Place to another era of glory. Preston reactivated the farm and arranged for two of Man o' War's last good sons, War Admiral and War Relic, to stand there. In the meantime, John A. Bell III had leased a portion of Hamburg Place as Jonabell Farm, and it was on that part of the property that Robert Sterling Clark's Never Say Die was foaled. In 1954 Never Say Die achieved something Hamburg Place-born Sir Martin had tried to achieve, winning the Epsom Derby.

Preston Madden later made his own mark in several aspects of the Turf where his grandfather had excelled. He bought T. V. Lark and raced him to major victories before the horse became the leading sire while standing at Hamburg Place. Preston Madden bred and raced Pink Pigeon (with his brother Patrick) and other major stakes winners. Most satisfyingly perhaps, in 1987 he watched as a yearling he had bred and sold raced home in the Kentucky Derby, placing the name Alysheba beside the five Derby winners his grandfather had bred.

CHAPTER 5

MAX
HIRSCH

At the age of eighty-seven Max Hirsch composed a benediction to the Turf: "Being in this sport keeps you young," he said, in answer to a question about his own longevity, "because there's always another colt, another filly, to train ... you always look to tomorrow. There are always more races to run, and you live in hope of winning your share of them."

The long roll of Maximilian Justice Hirsch's lifetime of winning races began not many years after his birth, on July 30, 1880. He was born in a Texas town called Fredericksburg, and the Germanic aspects of the name were indicative of the town's origins and the state's cultural diversity, which belied its cowboy image. Hirsch's grandfather was a German immigrant who arrived in 1848. In the next generation, Hirsch's father, Jacob Hirsch, was of an age to be caught up in the Civil War, fighting for the Union army. He married a Texas girl and begot six children, a relatively large brood, which he supported as postmaster of the town.

Nearby was a connection to the prevailing preconception of Texas, a large ranch, but with a whiff of the faraway "up East." The Morris family, which had been associated with New York horse racing for more than two decades and owned the grand Morris Park racetrack in New York, owned the ranch, and young Max found work there. He had already begun riding in local races by the age of ten or so, and one day he was helping load yearlings at the Morris ranch onto a train bound for Baltimore.

"It was a hot day, and I was barefooted," Hirsch would recall time and again. "Suddenly, the urge hit me. I had to go with the horses. So, clad in blue jeans and without a word to my parents, I climbed aboard a freight car with the horses and was off to Baltimore."

In different versions told over the years, it was either at a snowy stop in Middleburg, Virginia, or destination Baltimore, that Hirsch was rescued — a shivering twelve-year-old far from home and in dire need of the blankets in which he was carried from the train. The Morris horses were being sent to Baltimore to R. Wyndham Walden. The noted trainer of seven Preakness winners and four Belmont Stakes winners by then was manager of the outfit while his son, Bob Walden, was the trainer of record.

Just how, or if, Hirsch communicated with his parents in that era — no cell phones, e-mail, or fax machines — to avoid a missing persons investigation was routinely skipped over in his retellings. At any rate, he apparently was allowed to remain in Wyndham's employment.

A fascination with animals was not born at the moment of his impetuous decision. An older brother, Louis, delighted years later in telling of how Max as a kid was always owner of "a squirrel or raccoon or dog." For one whose life would end only months before man landed on the moon, Hirsch was born in a day when covered wagons represented an exciting form of transportation as they carried adventurous citizens from east to west. Louis Hirsch recalled that Max would be on the lookout for dogs that had become footsore and lagged behind their masters' wagon trains. Max would take them home and bandage their paws, although he knew he had to turn them loose, hoping they would pick up the proper trail. Another illustration of the youngster's devotion to animals was his begging his grown brother — a schoolteacher at the time — to buy a horse the boy had seen in town. The deal concluded, Max immediately was kicked unconscious by the animal, but he refrained from identifying which horse had kicked him for fear the miscreant would be sold on the spot.

When Max went to work in the East for Walden, his slender build and experience at race riding allowed him his chance as a professional jockey. Hirsch made his first starts in the saddle at official racetracks in the East, and on July 9, 1895, he recorded his first victory, at Brighton Beach, aboard A.H. and D.H. Morris' Gutta Percha in a mile selling sweepstakes of $300. Hirsch later recalled that he weighed about sixty pounds and was so weak after the race he needed help carrying the saddle and lead weight pads. (The silks of all scarlet were the same that had been carried to victory by Francis Morris' Ruthless in the first Belmont Stakes, in 1867. Hirsch was to add his own distinction to the Belmont Stakes, but as trainer of four winners, not as a jockey. Descendants of Francis Morris also included John A. Morris, by whose time — the latter twentieth century — the silks were renowned as the oldest still in use in America.)

Hirsch recalled R.W. Walden as "one of the severest trainers known" and once described how the trainer would send each horse out for a series of breezes at intervals on a single morning, and, he noted, "I will never forget that when we walked them back, they were the most tired horses I ever saw."

Race riding of the day reflected the rough-hewn society. Many years later, as the 1961 Honor Guest at the Thoroughbred Club of America's tes-

timonial dinner, Hirsch reviewed the scene of just before and during his
early riding days:

> The first couple of years when I was around the track, there were
> great jockeys like Snapper Garrison and Fred Taral, and that was a
> little after Isaac Murphy was riding. You can see from the old pic-
> tures that in those days they rode horses with the long stirrups and
> wore sharp spurs and carried big whips and came down the stretch
> slashing their horses unmercifully. The blood ran out of their sides.
> Just about my time, they started not to punish their horses so much.
> Then along came Tod Sloan. He was not what you would call a good
> horseman — I mean by that he could hardly manage his horses in
> his morning gallops. But he was smart, very clever [riding with short
> stirrups] ... Sloan convinced Pittsburgh Phil, the smartest and big-
> gest bettor of his time, that he would show him how he could make
> horses run kindly. He usually would take out an old sulky horse that
> had been whipped and spurred and play around with him, and with
> Sloan's light hands they would fly. It wasn't long before he was a
> sensation both here and in Europe ... Of course, everyone copied his
> style. Now you would call them different horsemen, and horses run
> kinder for jockeys now than they did in olden times.

On another occasion Hirsch described Sloan as the "first jockey to baby
his horse, cluck softly in his ear — that's why he leaned forward the way
he did — and the horse responded to kindness. Horses gave their best for
Sloan when they wouldn't run a lick for a strong-arm rider."

As for his own style, Hirsch called himself a "whoop-dee-do rider" and
once boasted he could "beat the gate like hell." The object was to go "to the
front as fast as I could, stay there as long as I could."

He confessed to his own shortcomings, but his record, said to be 123
wins in 1,117 races, was not bad. He rode sixty winners in 1896 and fifty in
1897. It was weight that ended his career, for he was not by nature destined
to remain a tiny fellow. Hirsch went to work as a groom, trying to learn
enough to become a trainer. One of his associations along the way was with
Tommy Griffin, who was a sort of pinhooker of the day. Griffin would buy
drafts of inexpensive yearlings, break them, and race them enough to show
some potential — he hoped — and then sell them. Hirsch was an astute
observer of just what type of yearling a man could turn into an attractive
racing prospect.

In an interview with Turf historian Neil Newman, Hirsch once described
his situation thusly: "The only reason I became a trainer of horses was
when I hung up my tack as a jockey, there was nothing else I could do to
make a dollar. All of my life had been spent around horses."

Hirsch scraped together the nerve and connections to launch out as a trainer, and his first winner in that context came on March 21, 1902, at Fair Grounds in New Orleans. He saddled F.J. Bukdevitz' Gautama to win a $300 purse for horses of all ages. Hirsch noted the first horse he had ever won on as a rider and his first winner as a trainer were both sired by Galore, a son of the noted English stallion Galopin.

Hirsch had made a start, but it was followed by some stops. The connection with his first owner did not last long, and he dropped back to working for another trainer, Tim Gaynor. Gaynor was in poor health, so young Max Hirsch more or less ran the show, although not as trainer of record. The star of the stable was Whimsical, who Hirsch said was really owned by a bookmaker, Mattie Looran, but raced in Gaynor's name. She won the Belles Stakes at Sheepshead Bay and other nice races.

Hirsch described the next phase as more lean years, marked by big runs and big losses with the bookmakers, but in 1905 he was able to buy a colt from James Ben Ali Haggin's yearling sale at Sheepshead Bay. This was a son of the champion Salvator, but it cost only $1,000. Indicative that his judgment on all matters might not have matched his growing judgment of horses, Hirsch was already a married man, despite his tenuous finances. He had taken on responsibilities of a husband and provider when he wed Kathryn Claire in 1905, and he named his yearling Beauclere in her honor.

Hirsch gave Beauclere plenty of time, despite the tightness of his own circumstances, but when he brought the colt out he gave him an unusual assignment. Beauclere was 60-1 at Belmont Park on October 16, 1906. He was more or less a prompter for the renowned Roseben, seeking a world record, which indeed was set, with seven furlongs in 1:22. Beauclere was an adequate prompter, and four days later he won a race with a purse of $770. After several more wins, Hirsch sold a half-interest in Beauclere to Brooklyn cafe owner Joe Lemaire, and the horse raced in Lemaire's name thereafter.

Beauclere was a frequent winner, and when he later won the Washington Cup, worth $1,580, at the Bennings track in Washington, D.C., Hirsch took home the large silver trophy, a punch bowl that Mrs. Hirsch later used to bathe their first baby. Hirsch noted that he had enjoyed a grand meeting (at Bennings) "and returned to New York with more money than I had ever had up to that time."

Still, good horses were rarities, and Hirsch did not hit upon another one for several years. In the fall of 1914, he bought a colt from what he recalled as a "weeding-out sale" of the high-class August Belmont II stable. He recalled that for about $450, he got the two-year-old Norse King (Fair Play—Nineveh, by The Ill-Used).

The following year, Norse King, also racing in F.B. Lemaire's official ownership, became Hirsch's first Kentucky Derby starter, but finished fifteenth of sixteen behind the filly Regret. He was nearly 40-1, and thinking of him years later, Hirsch realized "it may seem silly to say so now, but he should have won the Derby in a walk." Norse King showed he was cut out to be a good horse when he later landed a purse of $2,275 in winning the Brooklyn Derby (known today as the Dwyer Stakes), beating the Kentucky Derby third-place finisher, Sharpshooter.

Hirsch ran Norse King against older horses in the Suburban Handicap, but, as he recalled, "it was a very rough-run race in which August Belmont's Stromboli was the principal offender. Stromboli knocked Norse King down, sloughed Addie M., and then went on to win from Sam Jackson and Sharpshooter." Hirsch assumed that the fact the chairman of The Jockey Club owned Stromboli, while a struggling fellow similar to himself owned the runner-up, meant the stewards would certainly not change the finish order.

Hirsch also recalled the incident reflected the phenomenon that "horses seem to have an extra sense that enables them to remember people who have been good to them." Specifically, he recalled Dan Daniels, a "colored man" who worked for him for forty-five years. When Norse King was fouled in the Suburban, "he tumbled over the rails, tangling his leg and breaking it badly ... Norse King was in anguish ... but in all that crowd he sought out and found Dan, the man who had cared for him. It was a touching scene, in a tragic episode." The memory concluded with reference to the harsh reality of the time: "The horse, of course, had to be shot."

As for the next few seasons, Hirsch in retrospect combined colorful phrases: "Tough sledding; chicken today, feathers the rest of the week." It was a candy man who sweetened this scenario and helped Hirsch achieve a pattern of sustained success that lasted fifty-plus years.

TROPHIES HELD ALOFT

In 1915 George W. Loft took a limousine to Sheepshead Bay racetrack to look at the 1914 Futurity winner Trojan. He found a foreman who suggested that if Loft were interested in owning racehorses, he might look up a fellow named Hirsch, at a nearby barn. Loft owned a candy manufacturing firm and was a banker and Tammany Hall politician whom the *Saturday Evening Post* identified as "the first fat cat Max had encountered during his many years of hope."

Loft's candy firm had a slogan, "Penny a Pound Profit," and he slipped a commercial name past The Jockey Club registration process in using the acronym, Papp, for a colt he and Hirsch bought for $3,700 in 1916. The colt was a son of Peter Quince—Phebe G., by Mazagan, and had been bred by J. Hamlet and Jack Keene. (By coincidence, Hirsch had ridden Keene's first winner, a fact Hirsch referred to years later when the Thoroughbred Club of America honored him at Keeneland, of which Keene had been progenitor.)

Reflecting on his connection to Loft, Hirsch clearly saw it as a milestone: "… I made a connection that really put me on the racing map and on the front pages of the racing papers — and, without bragging, I have never looked back since."

Papp proved a bargain when Hirsch sent him out to win more than $40,000 at two. The juvenile Papp won seven races, including the Futurity Stakes, Flash, United States Hotel, and Sanford Memorial. However, Sun Briar had enough wins over Papp to secure historic placement as the best two-year-old of the year. Papp was a major disappointment at three, when he won only once in nine starts. (Illustrative that his was a different era, Papp's failure led to his castration, after which he was sent to France to become a hurdler. He was euthanized after an accident in a jumping race.)

Among the other successful horses Hirsch trained for Loft was On Watch, who was to have a connection to the trainer's future that could hardly have been imagined at the time. On Watch was the best racing son of James R. Keene's Colin, the latter an unbeaten champion who would prove a shy breeder but a lasting influence. Years later Hirsch sold King Ranch an On Watch mare of his own who would produce the champion Stymie.

On Watch (Colin—Rubia Granda, by Greenan) was bred by James Corrigan, and when Corrigan's Wickliffe Stud was dispersed in January 1918, Hirsch was there to buy the colt for his own account for $1,400. He later turned the colt over to Loft, a pattern of now-he's-mine/now-he's-yours that would prove repetitive in Hirsch's career.

Racing from two through five, On Watch notched twenty-one victories including the National Stallion, Yonkers, Rainbow, and Paumonok among ten stakes wins. In 1920 On Watch gave Hirsch his first placing in the Kentucky Derby when he finished third behind Paul Jones and Upset. Another of Loft's horses, Donnacona (Prince Palatine—Kildonan, by Ladas), finished fifth in the stable's 4-1 entry. Later that spring Loft and Hirsch stepped up to take their beating and accept $1,500 in place money, by sending Donnacona out to lose the Belmont by twenty lengths to Man o' War. In the Miller Stakes at Saratoga that year, Donnacona got second, that time beaten "only" six lengths by Man o' War. Stablemate On Watch had encountered Man o' War before the latter reached superstar status, running second to the budding champion in his first two stakes at two, the Keene Memorial and Youthful.

Like many a horsemen of the time, Max Hirsch had a memory of flirting with purchasing Man o' War when the yearling was offered by August Belmont II at Saratoga in the summer of 1918. Ironically, his specific knowledge of the family, and his own professionalism, contrived to warn him off the legend. Hirsch said he remembered a full sister to Man o' War's (probably Masda) that had speed but was a problem filly. On one occasion, Hirsch told columnist Red Smith years later, the filly had to be scratched from a race because she refused to be saddled. On another occasion, however, she wheeled around when the barrier was sprung but recovered and came on to win.

Still, Hirsch had had good experience with other Belmont horses. He told Smith he had purchased seven or eight from the distinguished stable when he was training for Quincy Stable not long before then, and "they all won stakes, so I was interested in anything Belmont had. I was training for Loft, who was pretty big in the horse business and also the candy business, and I could just about buy what I wanted." Hirsch had liked Man o' War when he first saw him as a yearling, but "on the day of the sale I had lunch and started over [to the sale] but then thought I'd take one more look at the colt. I hopped the fence and went to his stall. Well, that horse had dug himself a hole clear up to his shoulders. He was snorting and pawing with his front feet like a crazy horse. I supposed what stirred him up like that was being put in strange quarters for the sale, but I looked at him and I thought about that headstrong sister of his, and I backed off. Sam Riddle bought him, and you know what he got."

Hirsch had developed a friendship with John E. Madden, the leading breeder and leading trainer who had climbed the ladder of success by breeding and selling large numbers of horses. Madden did not spend a lot of time around fellows who were not rich, Hirsch recalled, but he was impressed and flattered by the young trainer's close attention to Madden's horsemanship. Madden was keen on taking care of feet and was amused that Hirsch would come over to watch his horses being shod. Hirsch eventually began to visit Madden's Hamburg Place in Kentucky during the winters, and they would discuss breeding philosophies.

Hirsch credited Madden with beginning "to feed everybody," on the racetracks for he had horses at all price ranges and would sell some on the cuff, the payment to come from future earnings, if any. In Hirsch, Madden saw a young man with the potential to become a good customer, and such would prove to be the case. Hirsch had the sense to buy from Madden frequently, and in 1919 he became frustrated with protracted negotiations and made a deal with the master horseman:

"Give me the horses' breedings and price. Lead them out of the barn and walk them around in a circle and back to their stalls. If I say 'okay,' about a horse before he gets back to the stall, he's mine. If I let him pass, he's still yours."

Madden agreed, and within a few minutes Hirsch had purchased nine yearlings. The standout was a son of the developing champion sire, Star Shoot, out of Miss Minnie, by Meddler. This was an impressive yearling that was not a candidate to be purchased on the cuff. The price has often been reported at $10,000, although some accounts have it that another horse was thrown in for that price.

The Star Shoot colt, named Grey Lag, began racing for Hirsch's own account at two in 1920. He did not break his maiden until his fifth start, but Hirsch did not grow discouraged, and the colt then came to hand very quickly. In his next race Grey Lag finished third behind Step Lightly in the Futurity, and Hirsch thought him unlucky in the running.

Sam Hildreth was buying up horses for Harry Sinclair's new Rancocas Stable at the time, and he came calling. Hirsch put a price tag of $40,000 on Grey Lag. The dollar figure did not stop Hildreth, but discovery of an odd patch of white hairs normally covered by the saddlecloth did. For some reason, this blemish aroused Hildreth's superstitious streak and sent him scurrying from the shed row.

Three days after the Futurity, Hirsch had Grey Lag in the Champagne Stakes, the colt's fourth race in ten days. Hirsch already had a reputation that brought other horsemen to seek his advice on form, whether he trained for them or not, and Sinclair bemoaned a streak of bad luck with the books and implored Hirsch to put him onto something good. Hirsch admitted that he thought well of Grey Lag's chances in the Champagne. "I don't know how much he bet," Hirsch later recalled, "but his runners went every which way." The colt, indeed, came home by six lengths, to the pleasure of Sinclair as well as Hirsch himself.

When Sinclair later inquired of a price, Hirsch owned up that the man's trainer had already turned down the colt. Sinclair dismissed this as no obstacle. Hirsch quickly added $20,000 to the asking price, and so Grey Lag moved over to the Rancocas barn. He was to be the champion three-year-old and overall champion of 1921, co-champion older horse with Exterminator in 1922, and champion older horse again in 1923. Madden regarded Grey Lag as the best horse he ever bred, which put him in high company as the others included Triple Crown winner Sir Barton and four other Kentucky Derby winners. Grey Lag earned a total of $136,715, but Hirsch had made a good deal by getting $60,000 plus the purses he had already won.

The year after he sold Grey Lag, Hirsch found a quicker way to make a fortune than to race, or sell, a horse. He was involved in what has been called the greatest (honest) betting coup ever known on the Turf. Among his clientele at the time was Arnold Rothstein, a shadowy character said to have fixed the 1919 World Series. This sort of reputation was the drawback to dealing with Rothstein, for the association might negate the twenty years Hirsch had kept a clean reputation. Hirsch did the manly thing and began having his horses run with the name Willie Booth on the program as trainer once he personally had purchased them.

Any thought that this tactic would keep the association with Rothstein out of the public's or officials' minds ended on July 4, 1921. Rothstein had a colt named Sidereal who had bad feet and had not accomplished much but who outworked Morvich one morning. (In one of his rare miscues, Hirsch got rid of Morvich, who went on to win the 1922 Kentucky Derby while still unbeaten.) Hirsch knew that big money would be in town for the Dempsey–Carpentier fight, and instead of scratching Sidereal from the last race that day as he had planned, he sent word to his wife to have the horse brought over from Belmont to Aqueduct.

Rothstein had a team to run his bets, but because they were men who frequently made major bets with the bookmakers, a lot of money was down on Sidereal at 30-1 or so before word got around the betting ring, and the price started dropping. Eventually, Sidereal was 6-5 before he was taken off the bookmakers' board. Hirsch recalled years later that word raced through the grounds to the extent that police had to be asked to help keep the crowd at bay as he saddled Sidereal. This may not be a completely accurate memory, as he was engaged in subterfuge about the trainer's identity.

The horse stumbled leaving the gate, but recovered — as did Hirsch's heart — and strolled home. Rothstein's and Hirsch's take was $770,000, of which $200,000 belonged to the trainer. To compare what it would take for a trainer, at 10 percent of a winning purse, to accumulate such a total, Hirsch could have done so by winning the rich Futurity that year and every year thereafter through 1948.

Mrs. Hirsch was quoted as having told a friend, "Max came home that night and said, 'Mamma, here's the bet I win [sic] today,' and he laid more cash money on the table than I ever saw in all my life."

About six weeks later, Hirsch prepared Sporting Blood to win the historic Travers Stakes for Rothstein's Redstone Stable. The horse had only one rival, H.P. Whitney's champion filly Prudery. Sporting Blood had been bred by August Belmont II and was in the draft of 1919 yearlings purchased by Claiborne Farm for later resale. He was by Fair Play—Felicity, by Rock Sand, thus duplicating the sire/broodmare pattern that had produced Man o' War. That a colt of such heritage bred by the distinguished Belmont wound up racing for such a suspicious character might be regarded as odd. By the time Sporting Blood won his final race of the year, the Latonia Special, the sequence had been extended to an ownership pattern of aristocrat to gangster to cartoonist. The horse was sold to Bud Fisher, creator of the *Mutt and Jeff* comic strip. With Booth still down as trainer, Sporting Blood got in a victory for Hirsch over his own former star, Grey Lag.

Although the Sidereal caper was apparently on the up and up, Rothstein did not so much have the heart of a gambler as the larcenous soul of one who wanted a sure thing. This led him toward attempted race fixing, and he was later instructed to sell his horses and stay away from the racetrack. His adherence to this decree was assured when he was murdered in a hotel room as the climax to what the *Saturday Evening Post* described as "an unsuccessful peace conference between feuding gamblers."

Two years after the Sidereal score, and three years after he sold Grey Lag, Hirsch came upon his next great horse, Sarazen. Bred by Dr. Marcus Johnston, Sarazen was by the intensely inbred bleeder High Time (by a grandson of Domino and out of a daughter of Domino). Colonel Phil T. Chinn bought Sarazen (whose dam was Rush Box, by Box) and another High Time yearling for $2,400. Gene Sarazen had won both the U.S. Open and PGA golf tournaments, and he was saluted in the naming of the youngster, who won his first three races, at Hawthorne and Saratoga, at two in the summer of 1923.

That time, Hirsch was on the buying end and bought Sarazen for $35,000 on behalf of another major client, Mrs. Graham Fair Vanderbilt's Fair Stable. Chinn regarded himself as a sucker for accepting the price for a horse really "worth $100,000," although Sarazen was a gelding.

Mrs. Vanderbilt traveled to the races in a private train car, sometimes needing two for herself and her entourage. She was of the ilk that garnered for Hirsch the reputation for training millionaires as well as their horses. A newspaper account in 1926 identified him as the trainer for fifteen millionaires at the same time. Among the names were Bernard Baruch, Herbert Pulitzer, Mrs. Parker Corning, and A.H. Cosden, in addition to Loft and Mrs. Vanderbilt.

Geldings were ineligible for a considerable number of races, including the Futurity, at the time, and St. James and Wise Counsellor were reckoned the co-champions at two. Sarazen, however, continued winning and wound up the year ten for ten. The seven races he won after Hirsch took over included the Champagne, Laurel Special, and National. At that time, there were some all-age races staged late in the year, and Hirsch was not averse to racing a two-year-old against older horses. In Sarazen's final start at two, he got in with a hundred pounds and beat the three-year-old General Thatcher (120) and six-year-old Blazes (126) at a mile in the Fall Serial #2 at Laurel Park.

Sarazen never grew much beyond 15 hands and was said to weigh less than seven hundred pounds, but he was the winter-book favorite for the 1924 Kentucky Derby. He lost his debut at three, however, and Hirsch stopped on him for two months. He came back to win eight of his remaining eleven starts at three, including the Carter, Saranac, and Manhattan handicaps.

Sarazen's greatest victory came in an international race at Latonia.

JAMES ROWE SR.

James Rowe (left) trained numerous champions including Kentucky Derby winner Regret (below, Rowe on left with owner H.P. Whitney on right)

Rowe also trained the undefeated Colin (below with Joe Notter up at Saratoga)

Sam Hildreth

Sam Hildreth (above and left); Kentucky Derby winner Zev (below), a champion for Hildreth

H. Guy Bedwell

H. Guy Bedwell in his later years (above, on right) and at the height of his training career (left with Cmdr. J.K.L. Ross). Bedwell trained Triple Crown winner Sir Barton (below) for Ross

John E. Madden

Opposite: John Madden (left) with fellow horseman Max Hirsch; (above) Hamburg, the horse who paid for Madden's Kentucky farm; (below) Madden (middle) in a jovial moment with trainer Sam Hildreth (right)

MAX HIRSCH

Max Hirsch (left) with King Ranch owner Robert Kleberg

Max Hirsch with Assault in the Kentucky Derby winner's circle (above); Hirsch, the "Dean of Thoroughbred Racing," at age 84 (right)

James "Sunny Jim" Fitzsimmons

Sunny Jim Fitzsimmons with Bold
Ruler and jockey Eddie Arcaro
in the Preakness winner's circle
(above); Fitzsimmons with some
of his many trophies

H.J. "Derby Dick" Thompson

H.J. "Derby Dick" Thompson (right) with Sunny Jim Fitzsimmons

Thompson with Burgoo King, one of four Kentucky Derby winners Thompson trained for E.R. Bradley

PRESTON BURCH

(above) Preston Burch and son Elliott Burch; (right) a young Preston Burch (on left) with his father, W.P. Burch

(above) Bold, shown in the Preakness winner's circle with Eddie Arcaro up, was one of Preston Burch's greatest training achievements; (below) Burch (on right) with owner Isabel Dodge Sloane and Leslie Combs II at the 1951 Keeneland yearling sale

Ben And Jimmy Jones

Ben Jones (top, center) and his son, Jimmy Jones (top, left), helped Calumet Farm dominate horse racing in the 1940s and '50s, with horses such as the great Citation (above)

Ben (far left) and Jimmy (far right) with Calumet owner Warren Wright (left), Arlington Park general manager John D. Jackson, and jockey Doug Dodson; (below) Ben Jones poses between the Twin Spires at Churchill Downs

HIRSCH JACOBS

Hirsch Jacobs (left and above with one of his charges);
Stymie (below) helped launch Jacobs into the big time

Even after he had won three Kentucky Derbys, four Belmonts, and a Triple Crown, Hirsch said he often thought back to that race as "my biggest moment in racing." The event brought a crowd of 60,000 to watch the French champion Epinard contest the third of a series of International Specials staged that year. Epinard had been second in the first two but was considered to have excuses in each, and he was favored for the third one. Sarazen, trying one and a quarter miles for the first time, was 6-1 in a field that also included the redoubtable champion mare Princess Doreen.

Chilhowee set a fast pace for six furlongs, but Sarazen caught him and pulled away. Hirsch's gelding kept Epinard at bay, winning by one and a half lengths in a spectacular time of 2:00 4/5, beating the track record by nearly two seconds. Hirsch extolled it as "the most thrilling race I have ever seen or hope to see." He explained that no small part of his satisfaction was in seeing an American-bred defeat a European champion. Hirsch harbored strong feelings that Europeans failed to respect American blood sufficiently, although many of their best horses had some American influence in their pedigrees.

Sarazen was regarded as the three-year-old champion and Horse of the Year. He repeated the latter status as champion older horse of 1925, when he won only half of his ten starts but defeated the top competition of the day, including Sting, Aga Khan, Princess Doreen, and Mad Play. He won the Dixie, Fleetwing, and Arverne handicaps with weights up to 130 pounds.

Sarazen was champion older horse again at five, when he won four of fourteen, including another Dixie running and the coveted Metropolitan Handicap (129). Sarazen was said to have become cunning and preferred to avoid the exertions of a race. By the time Sarazen had suffered through winless campaigns at six and seven, Alex Gordon had taken over training for Mrs. Vanderbilt. The owner then gave Sarazen to Kentucky breeder Tom Piatt, who provided him a good home until his death in 1940. (Sarazen participated in a parade of distinguished geldings at Keeneland in 1937.)

Hirsch was well spoken, despite limited formal schooling, but employed some colorful phrases. He adhered to the backstretch custom of using the word "win" for all tenses of that verb — "he'll win today; he win yesterday; he win six in a row." He also used the phrase "grab off" in reference to victories, as in his praise of Sarazen: "In fifty-five starts, he grabbed off twenty-seven firsts." Sarazen earned a tidy career total of $225,000.

THE CLASSICS

Sir Barton won the Kentucky Derby, Preakness, and Belmont Stakes in 1919, but it was eleven years before these three races became widely spoken of as a series, the Triple Crown. Nevertheless, each had considerable prestige, and Hirsch broke through by winning one of the classics in 1928. This was with A.H. Cosden's Vito, who captured the Belmont Stakes.

The colt won the Grand Union Hotel Stakes at two, and Hirsch ran him in the Kentucky Derby the following spring. Vito finished twentieth and his stablemate, Sortie, was twenty-first.

In five races at three, Vito won an allowance race and the Belmont Stakes. In the classic, a pair of the better three-year-olds in a smart crop, Victorian and Sun Beau, dueled each other into defeat, and Vito came on to defeat Genie and Diavolo. Reigh Count led that exceptional crop, and Vito's Belmont score did not earn him high ranking among the three-year-olds. He broke down soon after the Belmont.

The year after Vito won the Belmont, Hirsch won another of the traditional New York races, the Alabama. His winner was Mrs. F. Ambrose Clark's Aquastella (Cudgel—Waterblossom, by Waterboy), who had been beaten a neck by Sweet Verbena for another great filly race, the Coaching Club American Oaks.

The latter twenties also saw major success for Hirsch with Happy Argo, from distinguished financier Bernard Baruch's Kershaw Stable. Happy Argo (Argosy—Happy Hours by St. Monans) was an Irish-bred whom Matt Brady imported and later sold to Hirsch, who was acting on behalf of Baruch. Happy Argo won the Carter, Speed, Fall Highweight, and Fleetwing handicaps in 1927–28. Baruch was a bothersome personality. It was said that the self-confident, loquacious Hirsch became diffident and quiet only around Baruch. Baruch was the sort to take as a given his horse would win whenever his trainer lent any encouragement the horse *might* succeed, and he would push for details as to how long the winning margin might be. Hirsch was even quoted to the effect it would be better if Baruch simply did not own racehorses, so ill designed was his personality for the pursuit. This did not square with other observations that Baruch and Hirsch were close friends.

By 1929 Hirsch had established a physical presence at Belmont Park as well as a reputation for success. He was photographed in the stylish straw boater hat of the day. The columnist W.K. Wheatley spoke of the Hirsch barn as far from "a sanatorium for aged and crippled horses. Hirsch is a busy man, and he has no time to devote to racers that fail to measure up to the best standards. His quarters are big and airy and he has several open-air paddocks where he likes to keep his charges out of doors as much as possible. (He had forty-eight horses in the complex at the time.) He is a strong believer in fresh air, and the record of his stable is ample evidence of his ability as a conditioner of the Thoroughbred. His bungalow is attractively furnished, and the owners of the Thoroughbreds in his care are almost daily visitors."

The 1930 season marked the fourth as a stakes winner for Sortie (On Watch—Kippy, by Broomstick), who stepped up at five to win his most important race, the Brooklyn Handicap. Sortie's five earlier stakes included the Pimlico Spring Handicap.

Sortie raced for A.C. Schwartz, whose brother, Morton L. Schwartz, also had his separate stable of runners with Hirsch. This was to be a key connection that led directly to Hirsch's first Kentucky Derby winner and indirectly to his two later ones.

A.C. Schwartz' earlier horses with Hirsch had included the English-bred Kentucky II (Royal Canopy—Naisha, by John o' Gaunt). In 1927 Kentucky II had upset the Belmont Stakes and Withers Stakes winner Chance Shot in the Dwyer, and he won three other stakes at three and four.

Morton Schwartz leased Elsmeade Stud in Kentucky, a farm then managed by Cy White. Elsmeade also was to be the first farm at which the mares of Ogden Phipps were boarded before White's health led him to convince young Phipps that he could no longer take proper care of them. Phipps transferred his mares to Claiborne Farm, where his mother's broodmare band was boarded. Elsmeade later became known as Plum Lane Farm and for many years was run by White's son, Henry White.

The early 1930s saw what appeared to be Hirsch's best shot to date at the Kentucky Derby. In 1932 he started the 9-5 favorite in Loma Stable's Tick On, a son of Hirsch's former stakes winner On Watch and out of Sox, whose sire, Donnacona, had been a contemporary of On Watch. Loma Stable was the stable name for Louis G. Kauffman, for whom Tick On had won the Hopeful Stakes at two.

Tick On's Derby experience still rankled Hirsch years later. The temperamental colt was particularly difficult around the starting barriers then employed, and Hirsch had carefully contrived a technique of schooling him with a noseband and light string twitch to get him to the post. Hirsch's daughter Mary was assisting her father at the time, and one morning at Churchill Downs the track's starter questioned her about the device used before a workout. "Oh, you Easterners, always with some darn contraption that isn't needed," was Hirsch's memory of the ensuing reaction. Without the subtle bit of equipment, Tick On was a terror to be forced into the line-up and at the break of the Derby he not only got away slowly, but also banged a shoulder into the "gate," as the term was then applied. The official race chart upheld at least part of Hirsch's memory, noting that Tick On was "much used at the gate." The colt finished sixth behind Colonel E.R. Bradley's victorious Burgoo King.

A week later, Hirsch noted that the shoulder injury had resulted in an abscess, which came to a head at an awkward moment — he was in the paddock prior to starting in the Preakness. Hirsch's instinct was to pull out a knife and lance the abscess on the spot, but with so many onlookers, he decided not to wield such a field expedient. He regretted that cautious attitude after Tick On — a gentleman at the gate with the string twitch employed — lost by a head to Burgoo King. Hirsch was convinced his horse was capable of having won the first two legs of the Triple Crown. He was ill starred afterward as well:

> Tick On, incidentally, is a good example of how fast the lights can go out on you in this business. Tick On and his (paternal) half brother, On Post, belonged to Mrs. Kauffman. I held On Post out of the Derby and Preakness that year, although he was as good a horse as Tick On. After the Pimlico classic, I decided to give Tick On a rest and bring in On Post [who had won the Walden Stakes at two.] He ran in an overnight and was beaten by a neck in one of the fastest races of the year. He was just hitting his stride. The next morning, Tick On, who had been working well, bowed a tendon. A week later, the same thing happened to On Post, and Mrs. Kauffman was out of business for the year.

Tick On did not win another stakes until he was disposed of to the West Coast and won a pair of added-money events at seven and eight. On Post was sent to England, where he won the Newbury Summer Cup at five.

In 1931, the year before Tick On's Derby attempt, Morton Schwartz' Clock Tower (Snob II—Daylight Saving, by Star Shoot) won the Washington, Southampton, and Maryland handicaps at three. (Daylight Saving was a star mare, whose other foals included stakes winner One Hour, later the dam of Kentucky Derby winner Hoop, Jr., bred by R.A. Fairbairn and raced by Fred W. Hooper.)

The following year, 1932, while Hirsch was struggling with Tick On and On Post, a half brother to Clock Tower came on strongly. This was Gusto, an American Flag—Daylight Saving colt who won only five of fifty-five starts in his life but at three showed a nice nose for the money. Gusto won the Arlington Classic's first-place purse of $76,600 and the American Derby's prize of $48,200 before returning to the East, where the prestige of his Jockey Club Gold Cup victory outstripped the comparative purse of $9,950. He was the leading earner among three-year-olds, although Burgoo King and Faireno were deemed co-champions of the division.

In 1934 Hirsch won another of the historic races, the Travers Stakes, with Morton Schwartz' Observant, also a son of On Watch. Observant (out of Sunny Sal, by Sun Briar) also won the Wilson Stakes. It was a big Saratoga meeting for Hirsch and Schwartz, for they also took the Alabama with Hindu Queen (Sickle—Maharanee, by Brown Prince II).

Twice during the early 1930s some rather bizarre medical concepts were accepted by Max Hirsch, one with lasting benefit and another with apparently a lethal possibility.

One of Hirsch's owners at the time was Buckley Byers, who twisted an ankle and went to an avante garde Park Avenue physician. He was prescribed the latest fad, radium pills, which were intended to cure the painful problem and rejuvenate the whole body at the same time. Byers gave some of the pills to Hirsch, who not only took them on blind faith, but fed them to a horse of Byers' named Knapsack, who suffered from splints. Knapsack seemed to improve, but then went out and broke both front legs during a race. Hirsch took one look at the forlorn scene and concluded on the spot that neither he, nor any of his horses, would partake of any more radium pills.

Flash forward a few decades, and with the development of the atomic bomb and then the hydrogen bomb, radiation had taken on a somber name. A Dr. Jay Lieben and his team at MIT came across records of Byers' doctor and his whim of the 1930s and had thirty patients exhumed, many years after their deaths. The remains were found to be highly radioactive. By 1964, Hirsch was the sole survivor found, and he was convinced to undergo a breath test. Indeed, the test was positive for radioactivity and left scientists pondering just how he had survived in such robust health. As compensation for his relenting to take the test, Hirsch was assured of health care at a New York hospital for the rest of his life. He seemed unconcerned, and he lived for another quarter-century.

Three years after the radium pills Hirsch came under the spiel and spell of ex-jockey Clarence Buxton, who was hawking the benefits of the naturally occurring iodine in South Carolina's soil and water. Hirsch knew the kindness of South Carolina winters, having hunted there with Bernard Baruch, and as good horses were coming out of winter quarters in South Carolina with sustained success, he could not ignore the possibilities. He eventually began wintering in Columbia, South Carolina. "It takes about ninety days to get a horse in shape properly," he said years later. "If you race them sooner, they usually wear out fast. I found that Columbia, South Carolina, had the kind of ninety days I wanted. Its winter weather is like New York's early spring climate. Therefore, the horses aren't affected by the change as we move north.

"I had wintered in Columbia only three years when I won my first Kentucky Derby, a comparatively early race in the season."

THE DERBY AND KING RANCH

In addition to iodine in the winter, another circumstance in his first Derby was his discernment that Morton L. Schwartz' prospect, Bold Venture, would require gentle handling if he were to stay sound. Bold Venture (St. Germans—Possible, by Ultimus) came along at a time when Schwartz had given up his lease on Elsmeade and was selling off most of his horses.

The colt was consigned to an auction at Belmont Park.

Hirsch's recollection was that he stepped in to buy the untried two-year-old on his own behalf for $7,500 when bidding lagged below expectations. Schwartz assumed Hirsch was saving the horse from the sale and thanked him. Hirsch demurred, stating that he would not be so presumptuous as to bid the other man's money without prior instruction and said he had intended to buy the horse for his own account. However, Schwartz wanted the horse, and so Hirsch wound up training him for the original owner. Another version held that Schwartz had placed a value of $20,000 on the colt and had his friend Isidor Bieber step in to buy him back on his behalf when bidding lagged, the hammer price being $7,100.

Although owned by Schwartz, Bold Venture was assigned to race at two in the name of Admiral Cary Grayson, another of Hirsch's clients. He won three races from eight starts and had several harrowing experiences. Prior to a prep for the Arlington Futurity, Bold Venture stumbled and fell during the pre-race rituals and was bruised and badly shaken. Then he dumped his rider and ran away in the mud on the day of the Arlington Futurity itself, and after being caught trailed in last. En route back East, Bold Venture narrowly escaped death when the train car he was riding in caught fire.

Still, Bold Venture had seemed competitive with top-rung juveniles, and Hirsch thought him a fine prospect if he could be held together. Schwartz, in whose colors the colt raced at three, looked toward a schedule including the Wood Memorial, Kentucky Derby, Preakness, and Belmont. Hirsch advised that the colt could not take that much racing so close together and that, "if you want him to run in the Wood, you'll have to skip the Derby."

Like any other owner, Schwartz put the Derby above the Wood, and Bold Venture went into the classic at 21-1 off a single allowance win at three. Hirsch had run seven horses in the Derby, and had only one placing, On Watch's third in 1920. For his eighth attempt he put teenage apprentice Ira "Babe" Hanford in the saddle, and the kid kept his cool pretty well when Bold Venture got away slowly. He let him roll around the first turn and took the lead on the backstretch, after which Bold Venture held on gamely to stave off favored Brevity and win by a head.

Hirsch was defensive about the win, taking umbrage at suggestions that others suffered more than his colt in the ragged start. Brevity was said to have gone to his knees, while Granville dumped jockey Jimmy Stout. Hirsch challenged some aspects of the official chart and said Hanford moved too soon, but the suggestion that Brevity was unlucky was not accurate, for the pair had raced nose and nose for the last part of it: "I'll say now that Bold Venture was in just as much trouble as the other horse — maybe more."

With Brevity bypassing the Preakness, Bold Venture was the favorite despite widely held opinion that he had been a lucky Derby winner. The odd happenings from his juvenile days continued when Hanford's leathers broke and he fell to the ground during a work, but Bold Venture did not go running wildly or dangerously around the track. Hanford was suspended at the time of the Preakness, and so the renowned George Woolf replaced him. By Hirsch's retelling, every ounce of savvy from the veteran was needed on Preakness Day:

"No horse could have had more difficulty than Bold Venture did in the Preakness ... He was pinched off at the start and had little running room. Woolf couldn't find an opening. When they hit the stretch, Granville, one of the horses some figured should have taken the Derby, was in front by three lengths. Woolf, in desperation, cut to the outside. Brother, did Bold Venture move! He sped from last to first ... It was one of the greatest stretch runs I have ever seen. "

Granville fought back gamely, and Bold Venture's margin was only a nose. The Preakness, though, brought out Hirsch's concerns about the colt, and it was to be the end of Bold Venture's career. He bowed a tendon during preparation for the Belmont, in which he would have tried to follow Sir Barton, Gallant Fox, and Omaha as the fourth Triple Crown winner. Bold Venture won six of eleven races and earned $68,300. Granville won the Belmont to launch a winning streak that secured Horse of the Year honors and the three-year-old championship.

Schwartz sold Bold Venture to King Ranch for $40,000 and thus destined Hirsch to train the best of his offspring. The horse initially stood in Kentucky but was disappointing for a number of years and was moved to Texas.

Hirsch had developed a connection to King Ranch the previous year, when the filly Split Second — the first stakes winner from the Schwartz mare One Hour, dam of Hoop, Jr. — was sold to the great Texas ranch. King Ranch was under direction of Robert J. Kleberg Jr., a cattleman, oilman, and horseman who had become smitten by Thoroughbreds and had begun a stable. Hirsch continued to train Split Second, and late in the year the juvenile filly by Hirsch's old runner Sortie won the Selima Stakes. The Maryland race was one of the most important for the division at the time, and it came late in the year after the New York season had closed down. The following season, Split Second was second in the Coaching Club American Oaks.

In 1937, the year after Bold Venture's pair of classic victories, Hirsch and King Ranch had their first champion together. Dawn Play was the only important horse sired by Hirsch's former stakes winner Clock Tower. She was out of a Man o' War mare, Gun Play, and was among the astute purchases Kleberg made from the stock of Morton L. Schwartz. Dawn Play cost $4,100.

At three in 1937, Dawn Play won the Acorn and CCA Oaks, two of the top filly races in New York, and shipped to Chicago to defeat colts in the American Derby. War Admiral, the Triple Crown winner of that year, did not contest the Chicago race, but the filly met a strong field including Case Ace.

Saratoga was a special place for Max Hirsch, but he had his tragedies there, too. In the summer of 1937, Hirsch was sitting in his office in his barn when a summer storm sent a streak of lightning through the stable. He recalled that it seemed to hit his foot, but it did not damage him personally, although it dashed through several stalls, knocking horses to the ground. Dawn Play was one of them. She survived and eventually produced foals, but not for five years, and she never had a stakes winner. (Twenty years later Hirsch and King Ranch won the Alabama at Saratoga with Here and There, only to see the filly die in a barn fire later that same evening!)

King Ranch was to be Hirsch's primary client until his death in 1969.

A young Kentuckian, Stanley D. Petter Jr., was taken under Hirsch's wing in the latter phases of the trainer's career and spent considerable time around him. Hirsch's friendliness and helpfulness to Petter illustrate the trainer's sense of loyalty. Petter was introduced to him by John Wesley Marr, at whose Clarkland Farm in Kentucky the young man had been working. Marr's father had been among those to help Hirsch when he wound up stranded in the East as an adolescent after his precipitant departure from Texas. Hirsch for many years encouraged owners to send their mares to the family's Clarkland, and now he was willing to let a Marr employee hang around and learn — while conveniently doing duties as chauffeur.

Petter said Hirsch had great admiration for Kleberg, tempered by the logistical bother that resulted from the rancher's belief that a racehorse had to have at least some of his preparation or freshening on Texas soil.

Hirsch also had "a monarchist's reverence" for The Jockey Club and its members, Petter recalled, and he was dismayed when a member failed to live up to the expected standard. "Mr. Hirsch would say, 'you and I might skin somebody, but no member of The Jockey Club has the right to skin anybody.'" With Kleberg he presumably had no complaints on that score.

Despite the close association with King Ranch for so many years, Hirsch always maintained a public stable. He had never wanted to have only a single boss, because being sacked by one of one meant a trainer was out of a job whereas being sacked by one of several meant a trainer could still be in business. Among the owners he trained for in addition to King Ranch were Arnold Hanger and John A. Bell Jr. and John A. Bell III of Jonabell Farm.

In 1937 one of Hirsch's other clients, Mrs. Parker Corning, won the Lawrence Realization with another horse bred and purchased from Schwartz. This was Unfailing (American Flag—Science, by Star Master).

Two years after Dawn Play won the American Derby, Hirsch and Kleberg showed their willingness to challenge colts with a filly again when another foal from Science, Ciencia, won the Santa Anita Derby. Ciencia that winter was assigned to one of Hirsch's sons, Buddy, who for years had a West Coast division for King Ranch. Ciencia was technically the first stakes winner bred by King Ranch, for the dam, Science, had been among those Kleberg bought from Schwartz. Science, by Star Master, was in foal to Cohort at the time and foaled Ciencia the next spring. Ciencia won the Autumn Day Stakes at two.

Over the next decade a series of family tragedies befell the Hirsches, starting in 1939. Mrs. Hirsch passed away that year, and thus Hirsch did not have the support of a wife on that terrible day a few years later when news reached him that one of their sons, Harold, had been killed in action during World War II. The other sons, Max Jr. and Buddy, also were in the war, but they returned and took up the craft of their father. Hirsch's daughter, Mary, had been his assistant, and in 1935 she famously was announced as the first female trainer licensed by The Jockey Club (which then held that authority for the state of New York). Two years later Mary sought another level of history when she ran No Sir in War Admiral's Kentucky Derby, but he finished thirteenth.

More tragedy was in the offing for the Hirsch family. Max Jr. had experimented with a career in color photography but eventually turned back to his roots. The youngster who had been bathed in a racing trophy as an infant took up training and in 1947 won the Coaching Club American Oaks, with John J. Watts' Harmonica. This involved both following in his father's footsteps and smacking the old man at the same time, for Max Sr. ran King Ranch's But Why Not, who was in the beaten field. The following winter, Max Jr. drowned when his car ran into a drainage canal near Hialeah racetrack.

Through these emotionally draining ten years the senior Hirsch continued his sustained success at the racetrack, and it was during that time that he reached a pinnacle by winning the Triple Crown.

One of Hirsch's loyal runners in the early 1940s was Mrs. Corning's homebred Attention (Equipoise—Fizzaz, by Bubbling Over), who won the National Stallion and United States Hotel Stakes at two in 1940 and added a single stakes a year for the next three seasons. Attention's wins included the Arlington Classic over the Triple Crown winner Whirlaway in 1941 and the Metropolitan Handicap in 1942.

In 1940 Hirsch won the Wood Memorial and finished third in the Derby with Dit (Transmute—Ingrid, by Crimper). Dit had been bred by Tom Piatt and was purchased by Hirsch for $4,000. He raced for W. Arnold Hanger and the following year won the Grey Lag, Sussex, and Continental handicaps. (He was killed in a stable fire.)

In 1941 a mix-up designated Max Hirsch as the breeder of Stymie, a colt he did not actually breed and who would come to haunt him. Kleberg was fascinated by genetics and developed the important beef breed of cattle he named Santa Gertrudis. He was an advocate of line breeding, a form of inbreeding that Hirsch described as "an incestuous process involving the mating of a stallion and mare between whom a close relationship exists." Kleberg was looking for the right pattern in which to breed a stallion named Equestrian, who was a product of the Domino male line and out of a Man o' War mare. Hirsch had some mares of his own and told Kleberg about one of them, Stop Watch, who also was by a Domino male line sire (On Watch) and out of a daughter of Man o' War.

Kleberg jumped on the idea, and he and Hirsch made an arrangement whereby Stop Watch would be taken into the King Ranch fold. Hirsch did not recall the exact details but was aware that the King Ranch office was late in making the transfer official through The Jockey Club. Thus Hirsch was the official breeder of record of the 1941 Equestrian—Stop Watch foal, who was named Stymie. Having been highly attracted to the breeding pattern, Kleberg and Hirsch got a horse they concluded was too mean to accomplish much. At least that is one version in a tale far too fascinating to have been handed down in a consistent version over the years. Others held that Kleberg was upset that Stymie was claimed and urged Hirsch to get him back.

Stymie showed little early on and was famously haltered by Hirsch Jacobs for $1,500, after which he emerged as a public idol and eventually financed Jacobs' and partner Isidor Bieber's segue from leading owners to high-fashion breeders.

Two unfortunate human characteristics were involved in the losing of Stymie and the stubborn refusal to get him back, at least by the telling of the story in the *Saturday Evening Post*. The sequence of events was launched when the colorful racetracker and owner Bieber, as was his wont, became so determined to back a winner that he ventured into the saddling stall with Hirsch in hopes of determining if the horse in question was a good thing. Hirsch dismissed him, upon which the riled Bieber instructed his partner, Hirsch Jacobs, to claim a horse off Hirsch whenever he could. The story goes that the count reached ten. Stymie was one of them, taken for $1,500 from his third start, on June 2, 1943, at Belmont Park. Stymie had been scratched two days earlier from a race in which the claiming price would have been $2,000. If pique were in fact the force driving the claim, however, it seems unlikely Bieber would have held his cards for a mere $500.

If this account is true, it downplays any qualities of a seer in Jacobs or Bieber, and Stymie did run for a price ten more times, but Jacobs showed he knew what to do with a good horse when the colt began to come to hand. Stymie wound up the leading money earner and a popular champion whose stretch runs carried him to thirty-five victories from 131 starts. Hirsch later admitted that he had held back from reclaiming the horse for $3,500 because he hated the thought of helping Bieber make a profit.

Adding to the irony was that Stymie and King Ranch champion Assault would become rivals.

While that claim was one Hirsch regretted, there were other times when he went to lengths to make sure a horse *was* claimed. Petter described the elaborate system Hirsch employed when he wanted to get a horse taken. Hirsch still used the old-fashion term "selling race" instead of "claiming race," but he knew how to work the system.

"I'm training him to sell" was Hirsch's way of describing the routine, which began by telling an exercise rider to "ride like hell" regardless of what the trainer did. During the work Hirsch would make a point of looking down at his watch and pretending to flinch back in stunned surprise by what he saw. He would then reach for an oversized handkerchief on his person for the occasion, and wave it with some urgency to suggest the horse was going too fast. Hirsch would then inquire of the official timer of his own clocking of the work, and whatever the answer, he would quip curtly, "You need to get a new watch." Clearly the word would get out that this was a bargain about to slip through Hirsch's hands.

"He would get this hint of a smile on his face and say, 'They all think they're going to get another Stymie, but they ain't going to get one.'"

ASSAULT ON THE TRIPLE CROWN

In addition to the prestige of winning the Triple Crown, Assault summoned one of the most superb jobs of horsemanship Hirsch ever displayed.

Assault came from a family that had been plagued with bad luck. His dam, Igual, was so sickly as a foal she nearly died and was thought unable to stand training. One full brother to Assault, Air Hero, broke down in a race and could not be saved, while another had wind problems. Assault found his own way of expressing the family jinx. Hirsch recalled that "the oil people at the ranch had some pipeline stakes and other gear around the property, and Assault stepped on one of the spikes, running it through his foot badly when he was a suckling. Before long he had a contracted hoof. Practically everyone concerned figured he was finished as a racer before he even started ... But Assault early showed a quality of all great champions — he refused to let adversity get him down. He was all heart."

Assault also represented high-quality breeding. He was by the Derby winner Bold Venture, whose softness Kleberg sought to compensate for in this case through inbreeding to Domino. Igual was sired by the great champion Equipoise, and her second dam was Masda, a full sister to Man o' War. If ever a horse deserved persevering with despite injury it was the little chestnut Assault.

Hirsch spoke glibly that when time came for the King Ranch crop to be sent to him, "they had room in the train car and they thought they'd see what I could do with him." The horse actually stumbled and fell on occasion in early training. The injury had meant the hoof wall was extremely thin, and as it contracted it raised the frog off the ground. Hirsch first blistered the foot to draw blood to the area and to promote growth. He then employed a device he had first seen used by master hoof specialist John E. Madden ("no foot, no horse"). This was a spring, a V-shaped device that fit onto the hoof with the open end forcing the contracted hoof wall to spread and let the frog down to the normal position. Back in 1921, prior to his big score with Sidereal, Hirsch quickly had had such a device removed the afternoon the horse ran and won.

Hirsch could tell right away that Assault had talent, but the colt had contrived ways of compensating for the deformed foot. When walking, trotting, or at a slow gallop, he continued to look like a horse that had something hurting him, but he seemed to ignore the injury at a gallop, although he cut his hocks severely. Hirsch experimented with various shoeing patterns until, "finally, I had a different shoe on every foot," and he often ran the horse in boots to help protect his hocks. The precise placement of nails in the right fore, with its thin wall, would remain a delicate matter.

The patient got to the races on June 4, 1945, and did not break his maiden until his fourth attempt. Two races later he won at 70-1 in the Flash Stakes for his only stakes win or placing at two. He won two of nine and was ranked eighteenth on the Experimental Free Handicap.

Hirsch would often employ a pattern of breezing a horse every other day, which helped get a horse ready for a big race without many preps. Assault came back the next April off a six-month layoff and won the six-furlong Experimental Free Handicap #1. Eleven days later he won the Wood Memorial by two and a quarter lengths from the highly regarded Hampden, and he was on his way to Kentucky. Hirsch chose to run him once more, in the one-mile Derby Trial on Tuesday of Derby week. The track was muddy, and Assault's boots became heavy and waterlogged, and he slipped back into longshot Derby status by running fourth behind Rippey and Spy Song. Even so, he was closing in the final furlongs.

On Derby Day, Assault and jockey Warren Mehrtens were 8-1 in a field of seventeen. Spy Song led for a long way, while Mehrtens had the King Ranch colt racing along in fifth. After a mile Assault was third, and he ran past the leaders in the stretch. While Spy Song held on for second over Hampden, Assault simply ran off from both of them. He won by eight lengths, matching the Derby margin of 1941 Triple Crown winner Whirlaway. The margin has been matched by others, but never exceeded. (The closest to it in recent years was the six and a half-length margin in 2006 of Barbaro — whose trainer, Michael Matz, is married to a granddaughter of Kleberg of King Ranch.)

Since his victory with Bold Venture, Hirsch had tried the Derby with Dit (third) and Dispose (sixth), so Assault's win left him with a record of two wins from eleven starters. Hirsch later admitted the falsehood inherent in his often-expressed attitude that "the Kentucky Derby is no more than the seventh race on a Saturday card at Churchill Downs. This statement, I must now admit, is not overly endowed with the truth. Every trainer likes to stand with a tired but proud Thoroughbred in the winner's circle after that great racing classic."

The 1946 Derby result was surprising to many, and we also have heard the story that it was particularly vexing to one J. Graham Brown. While we cannot vouch for the legitimacy of this tale, the story goes that Brown was renovating a bar at his Brown Hotel in Louisville and decided to wait to name it after the winner of the upcoming Derby. Names such as Hampden, Lord Boswell, maybe even Spy Song, would have been attractive. Brown probably hoped that neither Knockdown, Wee Admiral, nor With Pleasure would win. Even worse, though, was the victory of a horse named Assault. Figuring the wrong sort of business might transpire if a lady accepted a gentleman's invitation to meet in "the Assault room," Brown scotched the naming idea.

The Preakness was then run only a week after the Derby, and Assault was finally the favorite, at 7-5. Spy Song was not in the field, and Mehrtens moved Assault up from third to take the lead after about six furlongs. They turned for home with a one and a half-length lead and lengthened it to four by the eighth pole. Then Lord Boswell began cutting into the margin and Assault ducked from Mehrtens' whip. The jockey figured he better not hit the colt again, and he was desperately hand riding when they reached the wire with only a neck to spare.

As had happened to War Admiral in his Triple Crown of 1937, an easy Derby victory had been followed by a desperate Preakness win. Three weeks later, when post time came up for the Belmont Stakes, the comparison was not to War Admiral, but to Gallant Fox inasmuch as both he and Assault were Derby-Preakness winners who were not favored for the final classic. The Preakness stretch run had invited the thought that extra distance would help Lord Boswell more than Assault, and the other colt was a slight choice. Assault stumbled at the start, but that was his only difficulty. Neither Hampden nor Lord Boswell could make a race of it once Mehrtens gunned Assault to the lead in the stretch, but Natchez made a game fight before fading to trail by three lengths.

For all his admission of his reverence for the Derby, Hirsch was a New York trainer and like many others placed the Belmont on a pedestal. Now he had won two of them, nearly twenty years apart. The next two would come within eight years.

Assault did not get a break immediately after the Triple Crown and next added the Dwyer in an easy race two weeks later. He had then won four in a row and six of seven at three, but a stunning defeat and a prolonged drought lay ahead. Given a break of six weeks after the Dwyer, Assault next appeared in Chicago, where he was 7-10 for the one and one-quarter mile Arlington Classic. He finished dead last.

After the race, Assault lay down in his stall "with his eyes on fire — he liked to died," Hirsch recalled. Dr. Nelson Southard diagnosed "urinary thrombosis." Hirsch realized that the colt had been susceptible to kidney problems all along: "He takes care of himself. He'd lay down after a race, and I used to think he was taking a rest (because) he has so much sense. He'd just lay there like he was dead, then he'd get up and eat like hell. He never showed any pain, but this was bothering him all the time."

Assault was away from the races for only about five weeks, and when he returned the losses continued to mount. Twice he was overhauled in the stretch by none other than Stymie. While Hirsch conceded Stymie was a great horse, he was convinced Assault could withstand his charge and turn him back if ridden a certain way. After Stymie left Assault behind in the Gallant Fox Handicap, Hirsch and Kleberg decided to change riders. Aside from his first start at two, under Jimmy Stout, Assault had been ridden by Warren Mehrtens in every race of his career. Now, the masterful Eddie Arcaro would get a chance.

Prior to the Pimlico Special, Hirsch lectured Arcaro to wait, wait, wait for Stymie. Arcaro followed instructions, with the result that Assault had plenty left and turned back the older champion before drawing away to win by six lengths. He made one more start at three, winning the Westchester Handicap handily over the high-class Lucky Draw. Thus, Assault righted his record just in time and avoided the possible ignominy of being the only Triple Crown winner in history that was not named Horse of the Year.

It probably rankled Hirsch that, even in the year he won a Triple Crown — Assault's $424,195 was a single season record — it was Hirsch Jacobs who led the trainers' list in earnings for the first time, largely off the success of Stymie!

At four in 1947, Assault built upon the foundation of a Triple Crown. As a handicap horse, he proved truly great. He won his first five races, including the Suburban Handicap under 130 pounds and the Brooklyn under 133. (He did not contest the Metropolitan and thus was unable to attempt to become the only horse in history to win the Triple Crown and the New York Handicap Triple.)

When the weight went up to 135 pounds for the one and three-sixteenths mile Butler Handicap, Assault was poised for his greatest race. He was giving nine pounds to Stymie, fourteen to Rico Monte, and eighteen in actual weight to the Amazon Gallorette. Arcaro waited a bit too long and had to drive between the leader Stymie and Gallorette to salvage any chance at victory. He got up to beat Stymie by a head, while Gallorette fell back to be third, beaten two lengths.

Assault had now won seven races in succession, but that was the end of his greatness — and of his soundness. He swerved during the running of the International Gold Cup when beaten into third by Stymie and Natchez, and he was so sore that a match race with Calumet Farm's Armed had to be postponed. When it was finally time to stage the match race, Hirsch took the unusual step of taking the Calumet trainers Ben and Jimmy Jones to his stall to show them how lame Assault was: "Jimmy didn't say anything. Ben said, 'He might be all right tomorrow.'"

The $100,000 match had just become easy pickings. The Jones boys' mouths were watering, and Kleberg was too much the sportsman to duck the issue. Armed won by eight.

Assault was through for the year, and his earlier heroics could not stave off Armed's bid for division championship and Horse of the Year honors.

Hirsch and King Ranch did have a champion on hand in 1947, however. But Why Not (Blue Larkspur—Be Like Mom, by Sickle) had been acquired the year before at two, as part of the bounty King Ranch received when Kleberg, Ogden Phipps, and Greentree Stable purchased and divided a large draft of horses from the estate of E.R. Bradley. Hirsch's friend Petter recalled that Hirsch liked to take more than a little credit for this transaction. Kleberg was keen for the Bradley stock but could not afford them. Hirsch suggested splitting the venture, and when Kleberg countered that any proposed partners would want the same mares, the idea was struck to rate the horses into categories and then take turns drawing for them category at a time, somewhat like a pro sports draft.

At three in 1947, But Why Not underwent a stern campaign of major tests in which she gained a measure of revenge for Assault's failure in the Arlington Classic. Taking on males, she won the rich Chicago event from Calumet's Fervent.

The Classic came amidst a four-race winning streak for But Why Not, which included a win over older fillies and mares in the Arlington Matron and victory over other three-year-old fillies in the historic Alabama at Saratoga. The streak concluded with a nose victory over Miss Grillo in the Beldame Handicap. But Why Not had won the Pimlico Oaks and Acorn earlier in the year, and she was elected champion three-year-old filly. That same year another from the Bradley breakup, Bridal Flower (Challenger II—Big Hurry, by Black Toney), won the Westchester and Lady Baltimore handicaps for Hirsch. She had won four major races at three before Bradley's death.

At five Assault won his first start and then was unplaced in the Widener Handicap, coming out of it with a wrenched ankle and a second recent splint. He was sent to stud in Kentucky. The racetrack had seen the last of a great champion — or so it seemed.

In 1948, the year Assault was retired at five, Hirsch and Kleberg won the Coaching Club Oaks together for the third time. The victory of Scattered (Whirlaway—Imperatrice, by Caruso) followed the Oaks wins of Dawn Play (1937) and Too Timely (1943). They were to win it a fourth time, with a King Ranch homebred, Resaca, in 1959, but an additional CCA Oaks winner bred by Kleberg, Miss Cavandish (1964), had been sold as a yearling because she was so crooked.

GRAND OLD MAN STATUS

By 1949, when his next future classic winner came to the barn, it had been four decades since Beauclere had become Max Hirsch's first major winner as a trainer. Hirsch was among the New York horsemen still around whose racetrack careers had begun the previous century. He was nearing seventy, although, as it turned out, he still had two more decades of repeating success.

Hirsch's lone surviving son, Buddy, had established himself as a major horseman in his own right and still had a division of King Ranch horses on the West Coast. Daughter Mary had given up training, but her marriage kept a close connection to the sport. Her husband was racing secretary Charles McLennan, for whom the second-most important handicap race at Hialeah was named.

Hirsch rankled a few fellow trainers whose owners sought him for advice on selecting yearlings. Still, to others, he was a grand old man and a soft touch. Once, when it was discerned he had doled out maybe $5,000 to some needy racetrackers, he was challenged as to why he did not require signed IOUs. Hirsch snorted that if the acceptors were honest, they would pay him back; if they were not, what good would a piece of paper do?

What Hirsch might have been best known for — aside from winning big races — by that time was the pleasantries offered up every morning by his kitchens. Especially at Saratoga did it become one of the rites of the backstretch for many who knew Mr. Hirsch — and some who did not — to stop by for a glorious breakfast. Even so commonplace an offering as cold milk was extolled as taking on special pleasures when poured from Hirsch's large, metal pitchers.

Stanley Petter, who became a breeder, consignor, and adviser, said he heard the story from the man himself: The breakfast tradition had begun when some Saratoga high rollers noted their hunger as dawn announced the end of their evening at the tables of the local casinos then in vogue. Hirsch invited a group to his backstretch kitchen, and a tradition was born. Some of the "customers," including Bernard Baruch, treated breakfast at Hirsch's as a fitting prelude to sitting in the shade to study the *Racing Form*. Hirsch made many feel welcome, but one of his expectations was that if you came for breakfast you show enough interest to stay and watch the horses work. Mrs. Tad Legere took on an important role in organizing these breakfasts and other matters, and she was also Hirsch's long-time companion. With his family grown, Hirsch virtually lived on the racetrack. He had a cottage at Belmont Park but stayed at the Wade Hampton Hotel for his winters in Columbia, South Carolina.

On occasion, social gatherings could get out of hand. His bookkeeper, Irene Frost, was nonplussed on the day Assault won the Belmont, for Kleberg spent a great deal of time walking back and forth to the racetrack, where he seemed to find more and more friends to invite to the barn after the race. Meanwhile several planeloads of Texans arrived. What would have happened had Assault failed to win the Triple Crown apparently was not factored into the schedule.

In 1949 the fresh bunch of King Ranch juveniles included Middleground. Like Assault, he was a son of Bold Venture and in due time would give his sire the distinction of being the only Kentucky Derby winner who sired two Derby winners.

Middleground (Bold Venture—Verguenza, by Chicaro) had seven crosses of Domino within eight generations. Middleground won four of five at two and was third in the Arlington Futurity. His final win came in the Hopeful, before which Hirsch had announced that oncoming ankle trouble meant it would be the colt's final start at two.

Actually, Middleground almost missed the Hopeful. On the morning entries were to be taken, Hirsch and Kleberg wandered away from the barn and got into a long discussion about King Ranch matings for the next year. Meanwhile, Mrs. Legere fielded racing secretary Jimmy Kilroe's phone call reminding them that it was four minutes before the deadline. Mrs. Legere took it upon herself to say "put him in," as "Maxie" was nowhere to be found. Kilroe spotted an opportunity and also talked her into entering four other horses to help fill out the supporting card. When Hirsch returned to the barn, Mrs. Legere began telling the story in sequence but had to break in and say everything thing was fine when she sensed Hirsch might be headed toward heart failure.

By stopping Middleground in August, Hirsch ceded two-year-old championship status to whoever else might step up with later triumphs. Hill Prince and Oil Capitol shared honors in voting, but Middleground was the Experimental Free Handicap highweight. Meadow Stable's Hill Prince and Middleground were on a collision course for the following year's classics. Middleground failed to become Hirsch's second Triple Crown winner, but he did win two out of three.

The 1949 season also saw the return to racing by Assault, it having been determined that he was sterile. Despite his age and a series of problems, Hirsch had Assault ready to win as important a race as the Brooklyn Handicap in only his second start. That was his only win from six starts at six. The following year Assault was sent to Hirsch's son Buddy and won in his first start at seven. After finishing unplaced behind Noor, Hill Prince, and others in the Hollywood Gold Cup, Assault was permanently retired as a pensioner on the Texas spread where he had been foaled and raised. His final record was eighteen wins in forty-two starts and earnings of $675,470. During his four-year-old season, Assault had briefly edged ahead of Stymie as the all-time leading earner, but Stymie surpassed his total and eventually earned $918,485.

In the spring of 1950, Middleground was second to Hill Prince in the Wood Memorial, then second again, to Black George, in the Derby Trial. The gloss was definitely off his reputation, and his odds on Derby Day were nearly the same as Assault's had been. The King Ranch entry, also including On the Mark, went off a dime shy of 8-1. The speedy Californian Your Host had been impressive enough to go off as the 3-5 favorite, with Hill Prince at 5-2.

Hirsch again had entrusted his Derby fortunes to an apprentice, as Texas-born teenager Bill Boland rode Middleground. Boland placed Middleground fifth early as Your Host battled Mr. Trouble in front. The King Ranch contender passed Your Host on the stretch turn and held off Hill Prince's later bid, winning by one and one-quarter lengths. The time of 2:01 3/5 missed Whirlaway's Derby record by only one-fifth of a second. Hill Prince got his revenge in the Preakness Stakes, and then underscored that win by defeating Middleground again in the Withers. At one and a half miles in the Belmont Stakes, though, Middleground again won the glory.

He raced ten times at three and won only twice, but those wins had come in the Derby and Belmont. He later was third in the Leonard Richards Stakes before being retired with six wins in fifteen starts and earnings of $235,475. Hill Prince won four more major stakes, including the Jockey Club Gold Cup, and again took honors, both as champion three-year-old and as Horse of the Year.

The season of Middleground's classics also marked the fourth and final stakes-winning campaign for King Ranch's hardy Better Self. Another from Bradley's estate, Better Self (Bimelech—Bee Mac, by War Admiral) was versatile enough that his ten career stakes victories ranged from sprints such as the Paumonok Handicap and Saratoga Special to the one and one-quarter mile Saratoga Handicap.

The nation's top two-year-old of 1950 was Battlefield, and Hirsch had flirted with the possibility of owning that champion. Battlefield was bred by John A. Bell Jr., one of Hirsch's Kentucky owners, and Hirsch tried to help the breeder by mentioning to George D. Widener that the Jonabell consignment had a nice son of War Relic in the Saratoga yearling sale of 1949. The colt was out of Dark Display, whose half sister, Dark Discovery, had landed the Gallant Fox Handicap for Hirsch at long odds in 1942. Widener did not seem interested, but he came to the sale and sat beside Hirsch. The trainer had no intention of letting the colt slip away; he would buy him for one of his clients, or for himself. When Hirsch noticed Widener was his only rival in bidding, however, he realized how it would look if he were assumed to be bidding up the other man on behalf of a client. Although he was in no way bidding for Bell, Hirsch felt compelled to back off, and so Battlefield won a juvenile championship and many other races for Widener.

(In as long a career as Hirsch enjoyed, any horseman would certainly have some miscues. In addition to the aforementioned dismissal of Morvich and Stymie, other opportunities not grasped included turning back a colt that he thought had poor wind. Given the taunting name of Revoked by the consignor, that yearling became a major winner and useful sire. Another that got away was Market Wise, a high-class 1940s handicapper. Hirsch bought his dam but passed on the colt because he had "a little bad spot on him.")

Four years had elapsed between Assault's classic victories and Middleground's. Another four years later High Gun emerged to provide Hirsch his fourth and final Belmont Stakes.

One of the highlights in the intervening years was his victory in the Jockey Club Gold Cup with John S. Phipps' homebred Level Lea (Bull Lea—Level Best, by Equipoise). Level Lea was another case requiring sage horsemanship, along with a bit of luck. At one point during that year, he began to lose weight so alarmingly that a blood transfusion was administered. Still, he seemed destined for an early death, as his legs swelled, which was taken as indicating malnutrition. Hirsch tried what he knew or guessed he should, placing the colt on a diet of corn instead of oats and grazing him as much as possible. *American Race Horses of 1953* also mentioned that he dosed the horse "with a tonic he had known for half a century." Due to, despite of, or unrelated to any of these measures, Level Lea recovered in time to get back in action at Saratoga.

Hirsch had some health problems of his own and was hospitalized for surgery, so he had called on son Buddy to come in from California to run the stable. The old man was out and about in time to supervise Level Lea's late-season run of stakes, which included the Discovery and Edgemere. The horse just would not stay healthy, however, and contracted boils in his mouth and nostrils, which made handling the reins a very delicate matter. He was third in the Lawrence Realization but came back to win the two-mile Jockey Club Gold Cup under Bill Boland.

Ten days after the Jockey Club Gold Cup, Max Hirsch brought out an unraced two-year-old for which he had high and urgent ambition. The Garden State Stakes, one and one-sixteenth miles for two-year-olds, had been made the richest race in the world. Coming up in three weeks, the Garden State promised a winner's purse of more than $150,000, and Hirsch would leave no stone unturned with that kind of money on the line.

Central figure in this ambition was High Gun, who had been bred by brothers Paul and Kellar Little, and Cary Boshamer. Hirsch spotted the colt at Keeneland in the summer of 1952. He liked him, although the colt's dam, Rocket Gun (by Brazado), had once been in the King Ranch stable and was not considered worth keeping as a broodmare. Other than Rocket Gun's status as a lifelong maiden whose best effort was running second for a tag of $4,000, there was much to like about the colt's breeding. He was a son of the rising Hyperion stallion Heliopolis, and behind his dam was the family of Stymie. Rocket Gun was out of Sunset Gun, second dam of the claimer-turned-champion. For $10,200, Hirsch dipped into the Keeneland catalog to buy the son of his own cull and, thereby, got his fourth and final Belmont Stakes winner.

Although most of the stock handed him had been bred at King Ranch, Hirsch never lost his keen ability to judge a yearling. Petter told the story of attending sales with Hirsch in 1968 and how the old man studied one particular colt at length on several occasions and even paid attention to the responses of others there to look at the same yearling. Hirsch eventually said, " 'I'm not going to bid on that colt.' I asked him why, and he said the colt's nostrils were not wide enough. The horse was Silent Screen."

Silent Screen was the champion two-year-old of 1969, but when owner Sonny Werblin set him on the Kentucky Derby trail at three, "Hirsch muttered, 'That's a mistake.' Sure enough, Silent Screen couldn't get enough air for the longer races." He never won from a half-dozen starts at more than a mile, although he placed in the Wood Memorial and Preakness. He was fifth in the 1970 Kentucky Derby.

The yearling to be named High Gun represented one of Hirsch's most astute buys. The colt was given time to mature but then was rushed. He debuted at two on October 20, only eleven days before the Garden State. He won at first asking, going five and a half furlongs. Hirsch pushed him right back into the entries, and four days later he finished fifth, beaten eight lengths, going a mile and one sixteenth at Garden State. Hirsch took the hint and gave up his dreams for the big race. High Gun got a break of two weeks instead of one, and then won an allowance race at Jamaica, also at one and one sixteenth miles.

High Gun trained well over the winter at Columbia but was not pushed into the Kentucky Derby after finishing second in his comeback race and then third in the Wood Memorial. (After Middleground and On the Mark in 1950, Hirsch had one more Derby starter in Sonic, fourteenth in 1951. He thus had three wins from fourteen starters. He stands in a tie for third in number of wins and a tie for fifth in number of starters.) With two great targets having been passed, Hirsch set his sights on the Belmont. High Gun was second in another overnight race, third behind Jet Action in the Withers, fourth in a division of the Delaware Valley, and third in the Jersey Derby.

With zero wins from six starts at three, High Gun needed to earn his way into the Belmont. A week before the June 12 classic he did just that, coming from seventh to defeat Fisherman by three lengths in the Peter Pan Handicap at one and one-eighth miles.

Hirsch clung to an old-fashioned custom and worked High Gun the full one and one-half mile distance of the Belmont during the week between the Peter Pan and the classic. Eric Guerin had ridden High Gun in the Peter Pan, and convinced that he was on a good horse, he rode him very confidently in the Belmont. Fisherman had finished off Correlation not long after they straightened for home, but Guerin had dead aim on him. Although he had not been closer than twelve lengths to the pace after a mile, High Gun was gaining at a satisfactory rate, and Guerin hand rode him as he closed in on, and passed, the tough little Fisherman. High Gun won by a neck. Hirsch posed in the winner's circle with Kleberg and The Jockey Club chairman, George D. Widener. With his battered fedora held out of sight behind his back, the trainer in his three-piece suit looked as distinguished as anyone else in the photo. He had won his fourth and final Belmont, putting him in a tie for fifth in most winners of the classic through 2006. Hirsch was to have two more major contenders in Black Hills and Buffle, but the fates were against him in both cases.

High Gun had six more races at three and won four. First came his win in the Dwyer against other three-year-olds, followed by wins in the Sysonby, Manhattan, and Jockey Club Gold Cup over older horses. In the Gold Cup, he had a three-length edge on Fisherman, and Eddie Arcaro, who rode him that day, said his arms were numb from trying to rate the colt.

Kleberg and Hirsch, who had aimed for the Garden State the previous fall, were game to switch the horse to grass for another newish event, the Washington, D.C., International, but High Gun strained a muscle working out two days before the race and was put aside for the year. He was voted champion three-year-old of 1954.

King Ranch was the leading owner in earnings, with $837,615, but with some of its earnings attributed to Buddy Hirsch, Max did not lead the trainers' comparable statistics. (He never did lead that list, in fact.)

At four in 1955, High Gun did many of the things a great handicap horse is asked to do, but somehow the stamp of true greatness did not seem to come his way. Hirsch brought him out for the Metropolitan Handicap without a prep, and High Gun carried 130 pounds to victory. He gave fifteen pounds to Artismo but beat him by four and a half lengths. With the weight boosted to 133 for the Suburban, High Gun was asked to give five pounds to another very good Heliopolis colt in Helioscope and failed by only a head.

High Gun dropped back to sprinting and was unplaced in the seven-furlong Carter Handicap but toured in front throughout the Brooklyn Handicap to win by three and a half lengths under 132 pounds. He gave twenty-five pounds to runner-up Paper Tiger and sixteen to the accomplished Straight Face. With 135 up and still giving weight (four pounds) to Helioscope, High Gun again went down to defeat, by one and a half lengths.

Once again Kleberg and Hirsch answered a challenge, finally getting a chance to run High Gun on grass, a context rapidly gaining in prestige. (The grass course division had been added to the championships in *Daily Racing Form* balloting in 1953.) High Gun carried 130 pounds and finished only seventh in the Arlington Handicap.

For what proved High Gun's final start, Bill Boland replaced Arcaro, who chose to stick with his champion three-year-old of the year, Nashua. The race was the weight-for-age Sysonby, run at one and one-eighth miles and with a purse upped to $100,000 in the unrealized hope of attracting not only Nashua, but also his great rival, Swaps.

Kleberg once recalled telling friends watching the race that he did not know what had happened to his horse, he was so far back in the slop, but there was a good contest going on up front and they should watch that. Hirsch was not dismayed, however, for he had counseled Boland: "When you leave the gate, let the others go — the faster they run, the better it suits me. Just wait as long as you can, and then do the best you can."

It was not long before the picture began to change, and Boland brought High Gun up in a prolonged rally that nailed Jet Action by a head on the wire. Nashua was third, the first time in his life he finished worse than second. Better yet, Helioscope was farther back in the classy field.

Despite High Gun's failure in his one start on grass, Kleberg was said to be considering an adventurous trip to the Prix de l'Arc de Triomphe in France. One of High Gun's suspensory ligaments had been worrying

Hirsch for some time, however, and although the horse was not lame it was decided to retire him. He had won three of seven at four and was voted champion older horse, and he had a career mark of eleven wins and earnings of $486,025.

He was a two-time champion in his age divisions, but Hirsch was rankled that High Gun was not voted Horse of the Year at either three or four. He could understand that Native Dancer's laurel at four in 1954 was in recognition of his entire career of twenty-one wins in twenty-two starts, although he ran only three times that season. Hirsch did not accept graciously that the younger Nashua held sway in the voting over his older star, who beat him at weight-for-age in their only meeting. "Somebody was wrong," he said tersely of the voting process.

A DISTAFF PARADE

In the fourteen years of his remaining life, following the career of High Gun, Hirsch trained one more champion, the wonderful filly Gallant Bloom. Several among the best of his other remaining stakes winners were also distaffers, although he had very nice colts such as Black Hills and Buffle.

When High Gun was three, Hirsch and King Ranch had won the Acorn with Riverina (Princequillo—Bee Mac by War Admiral), a half sister to Better Self. The following year, High Gun's supporting cast included W. Arnold Hanger's Rico Reto, who won the historic Alabama. Rico Reto, by Rico Monte, was foaled from Harmonica, whom Max Jr. had trained so successfully.

The 1956 season was the first of four stakes-winning seasons for a rugged distaffer named Dotted Line. Although she was never voted a championship in any division, Dotted Line (Princequillo—Inscribe, by Brazado) was good enough to beat males going a mile and a half on grass in a division of the first Man o' War Stakes. That triumph, in 1959, was the fifth stakes win of her career, and the others included the Delaware Oaks on dirt. Dotted Line won eleven of sixty-seven races and earned $324,159.

Given his lengthy stint with a consistently successful breeding operation, Hirsch might have expected more frequent examples of training good horses produced by his good horses of the past. He did have some of these experiences — most notably Bold Venture and his two Derby winners — but an ongoing pattern worked against him. In addition to the loss of Stymie through claiming and the infertility of Assault, there was the similar fertility problem of High Gun, the injury to the filly Dawn Play, and the death of the highly promising classic contender Black Hills. Middleground, while not sterile, had reduced fertility. He did get seven stakes winners, and King Ranch bred all of them.

The pattern of horses having sub-normal fertility naturally created whispers of improper medication in a sport in which believing the worst often trumps the courtesy of doubt until proof is offered. Petter said Hirsch was aware of such rumors and on a couple of occasions witnessed someone ask Hirsch about it to his face. He recalled Hirsch's motions were slow in general by that time, but that he had a very expressive flinch that seemed to engage his entire body when something distasteful presented itself. This involuntary spasm and a grumbled harrumph were of a nature to make his opinion of the accusation clear.

It was also in 1956 that a gathering of the most distinguished leaders on the Turf organized a birthday celebration for Hirsch, complete with a three-quarters-inch-thick program tracing his career. Max had established a tradition of several birthday parties per year — one on the date he for years thought was his birthday, one on the real date, and one based on when the Travers was run. Thus, it was appropriate that a slightly offbeat big deal was made of his seventy-sixth birthday, whereas seventy-five is usually the preferred mark of distinction. Noted Turfman John W. Hanes authored the introduction in which he described Hirsch as a "superlative trainer of jockeys, horsemen, and horses (and perhaps I should add, owners) … his high moral standards and impeccable conduct have shone like a beacon … I am proud to call myself his friend."

Given the location of King Ranch, Kleberg employed a large number of Hispanics, and Hirsch's staff included a high percentage as well. Petter recalled the ritual whenever Kleberg arrived, or left, Saratoga. Each time an assistant would have the Hispanics lined up and the owner would go down the line, shake hands with each one and make some comment about a member of the fellow's family. The departure produced many requests to check on this or that back at the employee's family home, and Petter felt confident Kleberg followed up on his promises to do so.

Hirsch never seemed to judge anyone based on his or her ethnicity, although he would employ someone's origins in his identifying them in conversation. Nevertheless, ethnicity was not to be escaped in his life, for Hirsch had physical characteristics that invited thoughts that he had Jewish blood. Some took it as a given, but Petter recalled being visited after Hirsch's death by one of the grandsons, inquiring if the friend thought the old man had been Jewish.

Three of Middleground's best fillies won major stakes in the latter half of the 1950s. The aforementioned Here and There, victim of a fire only hours after she won the 1957 Alabama, was a daughter of Middleground, as was 1965 Acorn Stakes winner Ground Control. The best of the Middlegrounds was Resaca, who came to hand with championship credentials in the summer of 1959 but could not sustain her form long enough to earn a title.

Resaca (Middleground—Retama, by Brazado) won the Coaching Club

American Oaks over champion Quill and the Delaware Oaks over champion Silver Spoon, with Quill farther back. *American Race Horses of 1959* states without qualification that, "On two occasions ... Resaca was the best three-year-old filly in America." She had had her ankles fired at two and when asked to face the best three-year-old colt of the year, Sword Dancer, in the Travers, Resaca became lame again and finished last. She had but one more start and was unplaced, after which she was retired. Silver Spoon and Royal Native were co-champions of the division.

Another instance of winning a major race with the offspring of an earlier stakes winner occurred in 1961, when Resaca's half sister Tamarona won the Selima Stakes. Tamarona, by Better Self, added the Vineland Handicap at three. Contrasting with the pattern of King Ranch generations was another Selima victory, that of La Fuerza, in 1959. La Fuerza was an example of Kleberg's occasional importations, for she was a daughter of the English Derby winner Never Say Die and out of Solar System II, by Hyperion. La Fuerza was imported in utero.

The National Museum of Racing had established its Racing Hall of Fame in 1955. Most of first few years went about catching up on some obvious inductees from the past. In 1959 Max Hirsch was enshrined. Despite the honors and victories, however, the year 1959 had a dark shadow. During the spring, the colt Black Hills (Princequillo—Blackie II, by Congreve) emerged to win the Peter Pan and went into the Belmont Stakes as the 3-1 third choice behind the classic-tested Sword Dancer and Royal Orbit. The track was sloppy, and after Black Hills had rallied strongly from sixth to third under Arcaro, he fell at about the five-sixteenths pole. Lake Erie ran directly into the fallen horse. Black Hills was so severely injured that he was euthanized, a grim reminder to Hirsch of Norse King of so many seasons ago.

It was the very next week that King Ranch and Hirsch won the CCA Oaks with Resaca. In addition to the freshness of the sad memory, there was another reminder, for Arcaro was still in the hospital, so Manuel Ycaza rode the filly.

Among the stakes winners of the early to mid-1960s that must have been highly gratifying to Hirsch were the wins of Saidam, owned by Kleberg's daughter, Helen, and the sequence of victories by Indulto, owned by long-time client Ed Lasker. Indulto won the 1966 Withers among his five East Coast Stakes, prior to being sent west, where he won five more stakes through the age of nine. His dam, Moment of Truth II, was voted Brood-mare of the Year.

The 1966 season brought another tantalizing three-year-old onto the classic scene. Buffle represented Kleberg's beliefs both in his own King Ranch families and the importance of foreign infusions. During the 1950s,

Kleberg had traveled to England and convinced Lord Derby to let him send a few King Ranch mares to the great, but aging, stallion Hyperion. One of them was a half sister to Stymie, a mare named Timed. She produced the Hyperion colt Zenith, who showed such potential that Kleberg thought he could win the Kentucky Derby until he bowed a tendon. Zenith then contracted an infection, and he was nine years old when his son Buffle put him on the map as sire of a classic contender. Buffle was out of a Bold Venture mare, Refurbish.

In the spring of 1966, Buffle finished third behind Amberoid in the Wood Memorial. By breeding and running style he seemed to be a colt that would get better as the races grew longer, but Hirsch did not want to go for the Kentucky Derby. The King Ranch family was a large one, and although Kleberg was in charge, he was not free of pressure from relatives. The *Thoroughbred Record* took the reader through a scenario whereby one lady in the family was so adamant that Buffle be sent to the Derby that Hirsch atypically yielded to pressure and actually shipped the colt to Louisville. He quickly announced, however, that the colt was ailing, and he was returned to New York. Hirsch was coy in his explanations, claiming the attending veterinarian never diagnosed the "mysterious illness."

If, in fact, Hirsch had invented a phony problem, the racing gods prescribed a cruel irony, for that autumn Buffle did, indeed, come down with a mysterious illness. His condition was described as a partial paralysis, accompanied by an inability to swallow. Veterinarians and brain surgeons were consulted, but he died within a few days. An autopsy found brain lesions, whose origins and causes could not be explained.

Before that latest strike at the fates of good King Ranch horses, Buffle had come on to finish second to Amberoid in the Belmont Stakes. He next won the Suburban Handicap, becoming the first three-year-old to win that event since Crusader, exactly four decades earlier. Buffle was no match for the great Buckpasser in the Brooklyn Handicap or Travers, but he did score another rich triumph before his death by taking the $250,000 New Hampshire Sweepstakes. In addition to his own loss as a stallion prospect, Buffle proved an anomaly in the career of Zenith, who sired only one other stakes winner.

Two years later came the ninety-ninth and hundredth stakes winners credited to Max Hirsch in *The Blood-Horse* files — starting in the late 1920s and missing a couple of decades after his first major score. A total of six horses he trained were voted, or considered, champions: Sarazen, Dawn Play, Assault, But Why Not, High Gun, and Gallant Bloom.

In talking of Hirsch's training, Petter dismissed reports that Hirsch had a pattern of working horses every other day. He treated each horse individually.

Petter was struck by Hirsch's attention to, and retention of, detail: "After the horses were put away, he would walk slowly back into his cottage, slump down in his chair, shut his eyes, and slowly massage his temples. Then an assistant would read off the names of the morning's workers and Mr. Hirsch would recite the fractions, final time, and a comment, on each one." None of this had been jotted down as the morning unfolded.

His last two stakes winners were both fillies, and one of them was his last champion, Gallant Bloom, perhaps the best distaffer he ever trained. A daughter of Gallant Man—Multiflora, by Beau Max, she won a quarter-mile exhibition race (no betting, no purse) during the annual Palmetto Trials' at Hirsch's Columbia winter quarters in March 1968. Her first official start came at Belmont Park in June. She broke her maiden at first asking and then added her first stakes win, in the National Stallion Stakes. There followed three dismal efforts, in which she finished no closer than eleven lengths behind the leader, but she turned her form around to win four of her remaining five races, including the Matron and Gardenia. She defeated Shuvee in the Gardenia and managed to get a share of the juvenile filly championship, along with Process Shot. Remarkably, the last full year of his career was Hirsch's best from a monetary standpoint, and his earnings of $914,356 led all other trainers in earnings in New York. (Eddie Neloy was the national leader with $1,233,101.)

Max Hirsch was trainer of record for Gallant Bloom at two, and thereafter his son Buddy Hirsch was credited with her brilliant campaign. By the end of the 1969 season, she had extended her winning streak to ten. Although she spotted Shuvee the New York Filly Triple Crown and the Alabama, Gallant Bloom's late season brilliance secured her the three-year-old filly title. On April 2, 1969, Hirsch was trainer of record of a final starter, Heartland (Bold Ruler—Equal Venture, by Bold Venture), then died that night at Long Island Jewish Hospital. Heartland, whose dam was a full sister to Assault, had been among his final stakes winners, winning the 1968 Test Stakes and 1969 Distaff and Bed o' Roses handicaps. She was disqualified from the 1968 Alabama, that grand old race.

Petter said Hirsch was crestfallen after the disqualification, realizing that a career of six decades would not likely go on much longer. After all, he had first won the Alabama back in 1928 with Aquastella and ran his total to five, adding Hindu Queen, But Why Not, Rico Reto, and Here and There. "He walked with a sense of purpose, but slowly, by that time," Petter recalled of the day of the disqualified Alabama winner. "As we were walking past the dining room on the way out, one of the stewards, a big tall man, came over and said how sorry he was to have had to take Heartland down. Mr. Hirsch said something like, 'I understand. You were just doing what they pay you to do.' The steward then said how well Mr. Hirsch was taking it. Hirsch snapped, 'Of course I'm taking it well, you blind son of a bitch' and jumped on the man with both hands. Some nearby waiters had to break it up."

The winning streak of Gallant Bloom reached into her four-year-old season when she won two winter stakes at Santa Anita before concluding with a pair of losses. True to his upbringing, Buddy Hirsch ran her a final time against males, in the Suburban Handicap. She fell back to be unplaced and was retired.

Buddy Hirsch followed his father into the Hall of Fame, elected in 1982. His own son, Billy, for a time continued the tradition of training into another generation. In addition to Buddy and his famous racing sister, Mary, Max Hirsch's survivors included his other daughter, Katherine Reynolds.

Available records showed 1,933 wins for Hirsch and earnings of $12,203,270. These verifiable figures leave no reason to doubt Hirsch's own estimates that he won more than two thousand races and had earnings of more than $15,000,000.

"He showed us how to race," declared King Ranch's Kleberg. "He had the character, guts, and heart of the greatest sportsmen. The last horse he ran won. That's what he came from, and that's what he had. He ran his best all the way."

King Ranch's Kleberg died in 1974, but his legacy remains strong in the early twenty-first century as his daughter, Helen Groves, and her daughters remain prominent and successful in breeding and racing.

CHAPTER 6

JAMES "SUNNY JIM" FITZSIMMONS

One of American racing's most beloved characters, James E. Fitzsimmons embodied the persona of the grand old gentleman. He was nearly fifty years old before he landed the first of two jobs that lavished succor upon him for the rest of his professional career. For the next forty years a succession of good horses came his way as he built respect and veneration on the Turf.

We might see this as payback for years of struggle and uncertainty, years that had tested his mettle as a man and as a professional and found him worthy of every laurel wreath a fickle sport deigned to bestow. Fitzsimmons had scuffled around the lesser tracks as a jockey, flirted with the taint of Tammany Hall characters as owners, and almost conceded that the game was too tough — all this before he found a classic stage. By then, Mr. Fitz was already becoming harshly bent in posture, but his smile had a stayer's grace.

"Mr. Fitz" would win a record thirteen races of the series known as the Triple Crown, he would train ten champions, six Belmont Stakes winners, and three Kentucky Derby winners, and he would be central in victory in one of the crescendo events in all the history of his sport.

Sunny Jim they called him, a name picked up from a cartoon, but a nickname of respect and affection.

CHAMPIONS IN SIGHT, BUT NOT AT HAND

James E. Fitzsimmons was born in 1874 on Long Island, New York. He was not born in a racetrack stall, but he might just as well have been, for the world of Thoroughbred racing moved in on him. The house in which he was born was destined to be recalled as "on the site" where the Coney Island Jockey Club built the handsome Sheepshead Bay racetrack in a day when grand arenas of the Turf were elevating

New York to the status of the "Big Apple."

Fitzsimmons' destiny as a figure in the world of horse racing could not be said to be preordained, but it surely made sense that his first job would be on the Sheepshead Bay track. He was not quite eleven when he took on summer work doing stable and kitchen chores for the Brennan brothers' stable. He moved on from there.

No youngster susceptible to the magic wand of the racehorse could fail to envy James E. Fitzsimmons for the contacts he would make. As a teenager he worked for the renowned owners Mike and Phil Dwyer. That was during the era when the Dwyers' Hanover charged to twenty wins in twenty-seven starts at three in 1887 and Miss Woodford reigned as the first $100,000 earner. As articulated by Kent Hollingsworth in *The Great Ones*, Fitzsimmons would be counted many years later among veteran horsemen who still regarded the Dwyers' Miss Woodford as the best distaffer they had ever seen. Fitzsimmons would have been flirting with puberty about the time of Miss Woodford. This is not to say, however, that memories of the grand mare could not legitimately keep their pride of place over the years as he trained the likes of Vagrancy, High Voltage, and Misty Morn, and watched the wonders of Top Flight, Twilight Tear, Gallorette, and Real Delight in other stables. If Fitzsimmons placed Miss Woodford above the others, then that was an opinion to be taken seriously.

As a youth, Fitzsimmons contracted malaria. Afterward, he experienced at least one episode of heart palpitations, this during the heyday of Hanover and right after Miss Woodford's racing career. A physician in Long Branch, New Jersey — in the environs of Monmouth Park — advised that he should "give up racing. Stay away from the excitement or you won't last long with that heart." The young lad's responsible nature about his own health apparently prompted Fitzsimmons to ponder this advice seriously, and he did withdraw from active participation on the Turf — seventy-six years later.

Fitzsimmons moved from the kitchen and stable to the racetrack itself and presumably had been exercising horses before the day he suddenly had his first shot as a jockey. Hardy Campbell had a division of the Dwyer horses, and one day at the Brighton Beach, New York, racetrack he asked if Fitzsimmons could ride a race. The lad was about fifteen at the time. With little preparation but a share of trepidation, James E. Fitzsimmons rode Newburgh to finish fourth.

Working for the Dwyers sounds glamorous, but assignment to a lesser division of a stable that used top-level jockeys such as Jimmy McLaughlin meant that getting live mounts was an unworkable proposition. Fitzsimmons broke out on his own to make his fortune as a jockey.

In an article in *The Blood-Horse* in 1963, the writer George F.T. Ryall

— Audax Minor was his nom de plume for years for delightful *New Yorker* columns — portrayed the hustle-bustle of the young rider's place in racing for the next few years: "Outlaw tracks were thicker than blackberries, and Mr. Fitz had a go at all of them. 'No matter where there was racing, I was there,' he says."

The names that rolled out of Fitzsimmons' memory and Ryall's typewriter hardly bespoke the stretch-run thunder of Hanover and Miss Woodford. Instead, they were places called Gloucester and Guttenburg in New Jersey; Saint Asaph and Alexander Island in Virginia; Maspeth out on Long Island; Elkton, Marcus Hook, and Sunny Side in Maryland; Barksdale and Carnegie in Pennsylvania. While year-round racing in the Northeast and Mid-Atlantic states is popularly tagged as a modern diminution of sporting principles, parts of this circuit operated during the winter even then.

The term "outlaw tracks" needs some tempering, however. It does not connote only gyp outfits, beleaguered horses, and rampant chicanery. Actually, Aqueduct was regarded as an outlaw track when it opened in 1894 — the same year, coincidentally, of the formation of The Jockey Club, which did much to consolidate the regulation of Eastern racing.

Another great trainer, Sam Hildreth, made a point in his memoirs to defend some of those same tracks on the basis that the quality and degree of legitimacy of the racing there rose far above the presumptions implicit retrospectively in the term "outlaw." Also, a reference to the days when yet another great trainer, James Rowe Sr., was in an interim period as a starter, identified him as plying that trade at Saint Asaph.

Fitzsimmons told Ryall for that 1963 article that he could recall only two occasions when he was asked to manipulate the results of a race. However, one of his grandsons, Jack Fitzsimmons, recalled for the author in 2005 the memory of a tale his grandfather had told him years before: Going to the post one day on a heavy favorite, young Fitz noted that the term "heavy" had a double meaning. An audible sloshing emanated from the gut of his mount. It was clear that the horse had been given an abundance of water not long before the race, more or less guaranteeing he could not win, and it was just as obvious that the only reason for someone to have done that was to win a bet on another horse. As they approached the finish, with Fitzsimmons' mount well out of it, he steered over to the outside rail. There were two sound reasons. First, he knew that any sentiment toward acts of vengeance from the crowd would naturally be directed first at the rider, so leaping off the horse at the outside rail gave him a head start at running for cover. Moreover, it also gave him a jump at running down the horse's trainer — presumably in on the deal — to demand his fee. Fitzsimmons' very telling of the tale to his grandchildren was ample evidence that he had survived the incident, and he also told young Jack that he did, in fact, wrest his fee from the trainer.

Another tale that came down through the years and gave some hint of the atmosphere of racing as the young Fitzsimmons had known it took place at a track on the Maryland-Pennsylvania border. One state had blue laws that prohibited drinking on the grounds. So, management simply extended the length of the bar to cross the state line.

The young man who had dismissed a doctor's advice to leave racing for the good of his heart also found that his heart was susceptible to other aspects of youth. He was seventeen when he and Jennie Harvey were married. With the additional responsibility, he fought weight to continue his career as a jockey. Fitzsimmons devised a sweatbox in his own home, but he also used the method of sweating before a brick kiln. His family was to grow up with the thought that this practice commenced the gradual curving of his posture. He once lost eleven pounds in one day for a chance to earn $100 in a single race, and he won not only the battle with weight but also the race itself, although he recalled being "pretty shaky."

Fitzsimmons owned and trained some of the horses he rode and thus gained experience that might help him when the inevitable victory of weight over determination took place. By the time he was in his mid-twenties and with a wife to support, he had begun to despair of succeeding in such a tenuous career. As a new century began, he accepted a steady job with the Philadelphia street railway. Perhaps this seemed to him the end of dreams or perhaps it was the beginning of new ones.

It never quite came to that, for a few days before he was to begin his new job he heard that a prominent Philadelphia citizen was looking for a horse trainer. In landing that job working for Colonel Edward de Veaux Morrell, he resumed employment at the races and took a step up in prestige on the coattails of his prominent new boss. Being acceptable as an employee to those in high ranks was to be key to the future.

Fitzsimmons trained for Morrell for about four years. One measure of the young man's success was that he was the leading trainer at Pimlico in Maryland for a meeting in 1904. This was far from the glamour of the future, but it was a step or two up from Marcus Hook. Around this time, Fitzsimmons got the nickname "Sunny Jim" from George Dailey, the *New York World* sports editor to whom it occurred that the name of a popular cartoon character was appropriate for the man.

In 1906 Fitzsimmons launched his own public stable, headquartered at Aqueduct. This hint at the big time was diminished somewhat by the fact that some of his owners were said to have connections to the Tammany Hall scandal. Fitzsimmons was not alone among racing folk in having a Tammany Hall connection. One of his bosses from his teenage days, Mike Dwyer, became a partner with Tammany Hall's "Boss" Richard Croker years after he and brother Phil Dwyer had gone separate ways. (Boss Croker knew nothing of Teflon, but the underlying nothing-sticks concept appealed to him. Most of his Tammany Hall cronies were prosecuted, but he managed to slip away to Ireland, taking plenty of loot with him.)

Nothing about New York racing was settled for long in those days. In 1911 and 1912, anti-gambling legislation shuttered the tracks. Moneyed owners had the option of repairing to England or France. Fitzsimmons was not of that ilk. He hit the road to Canada and again down to Maryland. Racing came back in New York in 1913, under an imaginative concept of betting among friends being legal, but precluding anyone from establishing a set spot on the premises at which to do business. Any bookmaker who actually followed those rules must have become a sort of roving minstrel, offering odds instead of odes and "befriending" all who were willing to reach for their wallets.

The sport did not spring back to its former level of health and vigor immediately, and among steps to boost it was a plan developed by some of the Eastern hunt clubs. This involved taking advantage of the depressed horse market in Kentucky — that, too, in part a result of the New York ban. The clubs would purchase racehorses and parcel them out to their members. It is merely conjecture here, but it seems likely that Fitzsimmons' association with a prominent Philadelphian would have been an advantage, for he wound up training for some of these good folk. Among those who sent him horses were Herbert L. Pratt, president of Standard Oil of New York; Joseph E. Davis, president of Island Creek Coal Company; and Vernon Castle, a famous on-stage dancer of the ragtime era. As recalled in Ryall's retrospective, Fitzsimmons won fifty-one races in 1915.

In 1917 another positive step came when Fitzsimmons was hired by James F. Johnson to train his Quincy Stable. This outfit was one of the larger stables of the time and by 1920 included fifty horses, split into several divisions. After years of scuffling at outlaw tracks and leaving tracks when racing itself was outlawed, Fitzsimmons perhaps had license to feel a comfort level he had never known. Johnson was in the sugar business and a force on Wall Street, and he was a big bettor at the races. For Quincy Stable, Fitzsimmons in 1922 won the important Suburban Handicap, a race the likes of which, earlier in his career, he had only seen others win. The horse to do it was Captain Alcock, who defeated Kentucky Derby winners Paul Jones and Exterminator in the Pimlico Cup that same year. The success of Captain Alcock took some crafty backstretch remedies by Fitzsimmons. Captain Alcock had the problem of getting away slowly in his races, but Fitzsimmons solved this by frequent treatments of hot applications of olive oil, apparently working through a stiffness that merely warming up before a race could not solve.

A year before those victories, however, Johnson ran into a situation in which he felt he was treated unfairly by the legal system and that demoralized him to a degree about the game. Johnson had made what seemed a master stroke when he purchased Playfellow, a full brother to Man o' War. Playfellow (Fair Play—Mahubah, by Rock Sand) was a foal of 1918 and was a year younger than the other colt. Dorothy Ours' 2006 biography of Man o' War notes that Fitzsimmons later claimed to have bid $4,000 on Man o' War himself as a yearling in 1918 and regretted that his boss, Johnson, was not in attendance, implying that the man with the money perhaps would have gone further. (There was no dearth of other claims to have been an underbidder to the $5,000 that Sam Riddle paid for Man o' War.)

Reports of the purchase of the year-younger Playfellow as a yearling invite the thought the colt must not have been impressive physically. The *Thoroughbred Record* of 1921, looking back, placed the purchase price at $1,800. August Belmont II, Man o' War's breeder, had sweated and stewed over whether to include Man o' War in his yearling consignment of 1918, and the colt had fetched $5,000. Even if the sale of the next year's version had come prior to Man o' War's June debut — which seems unlikely given the market schedule for yearlings — a price of $1,800 would appear modest. A.B. Hancock Sr. of Claiborne Farm purchased a large draft of that crop of yearlings from Belmont, to resell them at Saratoga in August. Hancock's advertising of thirty-three yearlings in his consignment included five Fair Play fillies but no Fair Play colts. Had he turned down Man o' War's full brother himself?

At any rate, Johnson bought Playfellow. At two, in 1920, by which time Man o' War had made headlines, the younger colt started nine times and could not win a race, placing three times. At three in 1921, however, Playfellow came to hand suddenly for Fitzsimmons and won two races impressively. Oilman Harry F. Sinclair had launched a major stable with trainer Sam Hildreth and started negotiations for the suddenly hot full brother to a superstar. Many accounts place the purchase price at $100,000, but the *Record* identifies that figure as Sinclair's bid price, as against Johnson's original asking price of $125,000. The publication's issue of June 25, 1921, reports the deal was struck at $115,000.

Sinclair and Hildreth were on a major buying spree and also bought from Johnson the colt Knobbie for $25,000. A few days after the transaction, Knobbie and Playfellow ran first and second in Sinclair's colors in the $3,500 Carlton Stakes at a mile at Aqueduct. This would hardly indicate any physical problem, but after Playfellow then finished third and last in his next start, Sinclair called foul. The tale has been told that he had chosen that race to bet enough on Playfellow to recoup the rather handsome purchase price.

Sinclair sued, alleging that the horse cribbed. Fitzsimmons and Johnson countered that Playfellow, having won his previous two races and then placing in a fairly important stakes, was certainly equipped sufficiently to be a racehorse, and the first trial ended in a deadlock. The appellate court judge was said to have done everything but dictate a directed verdict on behalf of the defendant, but the jury decided in Sinclair's favor. Johnson duly paid $102,000 to refund most of the purchase price, plus costs, and Playfellow was returned to Fitzsimmons' barn.

Although supporters might contend that Fitzsimmons and Johnson were victimized, it must be noted that Playfellow ran four times at four and four times at five, without winning. (At stud he sired more than one hundred foals but got only one stakes winner. Playfellow was simply a younger brother without a lucky star of his own.)

AN EXACTA IN LIFE

With Johnson's disillusionment and discontent, the future again looked murky to Fitzsimmons, and, indeed, Quincy Stable would soon fade out of the picture of major racing. One day in 1923, however, William Woodward Sr. saw Fitzsimmons at the races and offered him the job of training his developing Belair Stable. In an article in the *Maryland Horse* many years later, historian Joe Hickey described the deal as simple as this:

Woodward: "Fitz, would you be interested in training my horses?"

Fitzsimmons: "I'd love to."

Woodward: "Do you want a contract?"

Fitzsimmons: "Don't believe in them."

[Handshake. Then exit stage left. Reassemble in morning to work out details.]

Within a few years, Woodward allowed Fitzsimmons to add another client, Mrs. Henry Carnegie Phipps' new Wheatley Stable, without interrupting their own association.

Fitzsimmons was to train for forty more years, and he never again would have a season without a brigade of highly bred, expertly raised young Thoroughbreds being sent to his stable. With such instruments set before him, he would conduct lovely and thrilling symphonies.

Even if a trainer were to lapse into daydreaming about perfect owners, he would probably think himself foolish to imagine having both a Woodward and a Phipps as owners.

Woodward was a handsome, Victorian sort of fellow who had been bemused by the thought of racing horses since he was ten or eleven and his father was talking at the breakfast table about Pierre Lorillard being the only American at that time to have won the Epsom Derby in England. Young Woodward also coveted memories of coaching with his father out to Belmont Park for the Belmont Stakes during the 1880s.

Woodward further solidified his love of racing, tradition, and England when he served abroad as secretary to Ambassador Joseph Choate. Returning to a business career centered in New York, he ascended to the top spot at Hanover Bank, and he inherited from an uncle a historic property, Belair, in Maryland. Woodward's first fledgling efforts in racing involved raising and training horses at Belair, but he soon began boarding mares at Arthur Hancock Sr.'s Claiborne Farm in Kentucky. He bred in the name of Belair Stud and raced as Belair Stable.

His young horses were sent to the Maryland farm after weaning, and on weekend visits he delighted in watching them. Woodward's dream of winning the Epsom Derby was never realized, but neither was it ever abandoned. Woodward annually sent several two-year-olds abroad, and part of the selection process was based on discerning which colts romping in his undulating paddocks looked likely to be nimble enough sweeping down the hill at Tattenham Corner and into the straight at Epsom.

Woodward already had scored some major victories before hiring Fitzsimmons. His Lion d'Or had won the Toboggan Handicap in 1920, and the next year Woodward's Flambette had won the Coaching Club American Oaks. The Oaks had been established in 1917 with Woodward one of the founders of the club for which it was named. In 1924, the year after Woodward hired him, Fitzsimmons won the Alabama Stakes for his new boss, with Priscilla Ruley. He had known a grand champion mare of the past, Miss Woodford; now he was defeating another champion, Princess Doreen, runner-up in the Alabama. Given that Woodward specialized in the longer races, it also was appropriate that another victory of 1924 came in the mile and five-eighths Lawrence Realization.

In 1926 The Jockey Club member J.E. Davis suggested to Gladys Mills Phipps that she consider Fitzsimmons for the trainer of the stable she had begun with three yearling purchases at Saratoga the year before. Mrs. Phipps was the daughter of Ogden Mills, whose father, Darius Ogden Mills, had prospered in the West during the California gold rush and had then migrated to Wall Street. On her mother's side, Gladys Mills had ancestors whose stamp on America included signing the Declaration of Independence and handling the Louisiana Purchase. Gladys was married to Henry Carnegie Phipps, whose father had been associated with industrialist Andrew Carnegie.

Gladys' father and twin sister each raced horses in partnership with Lord Derby's French division, and she herself was an accomplished rider. She was encouraged by Harry Payne Whitney to enter Thoroughbred racing, and after that initial purchase of yearlings she acquired eight from Whitney's own crop of homebreds.

This was a gold strike to rival those made by customers of Darius Ogden

Mills. They included the champion two-year-old Dice, Jockey Club Gold Cup winner Diavolo, Wood Memorial winner Distraction, and Alabama winner Nixie. Mrs. Phipps chose to race in the name of Wheatley Stable, initially with her brother, Ogden Livingston Mills, and after his death she continued on her own.

Over the years with Belair and Wheatley, Fitzsimmons would have in his stable quick and brilliant juveniles and maturing stayers at the same time. He proved adroit at the entire range.

Sadly, his and Mrs. Phipps' experience with Dice demonstrated the fragility of success. Dice (Dominant—Frumpery, by Chicle) raced to five wins in five starts in the spring and summer of 1927. Victories included the Juvenile, Keene Memorial, and Great American. Then Dice suffered an internal hemorrhage and could not be saved. He was rated co-champion with Reigh Count among two-year-olds that year.

As would happen at other times, Fitzsimmons' stable had stars for both his distinguished owners in 1929. That was the year the four-year-old Diavolo, one of the Wheatley purchases from Whitney, won the two-mile Jockey Club Gold Cup. The son of Whisk Broom II—Vexatious, by Peter Pan, won four other stakes that year, the Dixie and Saratoga handicaps and the Saratoga and Pimlico cups.

On the Belair side of the aisle, a big, rakish colt with the handsome name of Gallant Fox was creating an impression that he might develop into just the sort of classic horse Woodward was seeking. He was in the first crop of Sir Gallahad III, a French colt Hancock had imported to stand at Claiborne Farm. Woodward participated in the partnership that bought the stallion prospect.

At two in 1929, Gallant Fox, who was out of the Celt mare Marguerite, won two of seven races, including a win over Caruso in the Flash Stakes. As Saratoga races go, the Flash was hardly the most important, but it must have been a sweet moment for Fitzsimmons. His jockey's memory reached back to 1893, when he rode William T. in the Flash: "He finished second, and it might have been my fault."

Gallant Fox added the Junior Champion at a mile in his last race, the distance adding credence to the thought that this was the sort of classic colt Woodward was trying to breed.

(The image of Fitzsimmons as a quick-action opportunist in business is not what has drifted down through the years. It was also in 1929, however, that he leapt at the chance to form a company to produce a backstretch liniment that survived the years under the brand name Bigeloil. Perhaps longing for an improvement on hot olive oil as a treatment, Fitzsimmons purchased a sample of the liniment outside the equine realm. Bill Macbeth, who had been a hockey player in Canada and was then a sports writer in

New York, told him that the managers of major league baseball's New York Giants and Brooklyn Dodgers used the stuff for their players, so, surely, it was good enough for horses. Fitzsimmons tarried but finally began using it on a horse named Best Man, whose lameness in the hind legs had befuddled his visiting veterinarian. The liniment acted as a light blister, creating a scurf, which was followed by improved form. Ryall's profile of Fitzsimmons recalled that the same liniment worked well on a Wheatley Stable filly named Erin, and it soon became a staple in the Fitzsimmons barn. Erin won the 1929 Rosedale and 1930 Gazelle and in time was to become the third dam of Ruffian. Not long after being converted by the benefits of the old baseball rub, Fitzsimmons bought the formula from its inventor, a Dr. Barker, and with him and another partner formed a company to produce and sell Bigeloil. Fitzsimmons Leg Paint was later added as an additional backstretch product, and the Fitzsimmons family was involved in the ownership of these products until about the next turn of a century.)

Seven months after Gallant Fox's last race at two, Fitzsimmons had him ready to test the notion that he possessed classic potential. Woodward was high enough on Gallant Fox that he coaxed the great jockey Earl Sande back from training to return to the saddle for the colt's campaign.

Gallant Fox came out in the Wood Memorial, which he won by four lengths over Crack Brigade. Both colts went to the Preakness, which that year was run before the Kentucky Derby. The result again was Gallant Fox first, Crack Brigade second, but the margin was only three-quarters of a length.

At Churchill Downs, the Derby played host to Lord Derby, one of whose ancestors had been the reason so many races around the world are named Derby. It was an earlier Lord Derby for whom the Epsom classic was named when inaugurated in 1780. The old star Sande and Gallant Fox came down in front by two lengths. Woodward hosted Lord Derby for a dinner at his New York home during the first phase of the dignitary's American visit and then happily received the Derby trophy from Lord Derby some days later.

Harry Payne Whitney's 1929 juvenile champion Whichone awaited when Gallant Fox returned to New York for the Belmont Stakes. Despite having won the Preakness and Derby, Gallant Fox was not even favored, so impressive had the Whitney colt been in winning the Withers Stakes in his first start at three. Also, Whichone had beaten Gallant Fox the previous year in the Futurity.

Despite Gallant Fox's image as a stayer and not a speed horse, Sande put him on the lead. The colt turned back the efforts of Whichone and Questionnaire and won by three lengths. Thus, he had duplicated Sir Barton's 1919 sweep of the Derby, Preakness, and Belmont Stakes. *New York Times* writer Bryan Field called the event the "Triple Crown" in the next day's edition.

Gallant Fox added the Dwyer and then shipped to Chicago for the Arlington Classic before he and Whichone got into their famous duel in the Travers and both went down to the longshot Jim Dandy. Gallant Fox rebounded to win the mile and three-quarters Saratoga Cup, mile and five-eighths Lawrence Realization, and two-mile Jockey Club Gold Cup. (Fitzsimmons thus had won back-to-back runnings of the Jockey Club Gold Cup, one for each of his patrons.) Gallant Fox had won eleven of seventeen races — including ten of his last eleven — and earned $328,165. This was a record for the time, and the bulk of it had come at three, when he became the first horse to earn $300,000 in a single year. Gallant Fox boosted Fitzsimmons to the top of the trainers' list in earnings, for the first of five times in his career. The trainer's total for 1930 was $397,355, topping by some $5,000 Sam Hildreth's previous record total.

Woodward, who was elected chairman of The Jockey Club in 1930, kept separate, private journals of his American and English stables. He also wrote and published a book on Gallant Fox. Therein he suggested that the colt might be compared to Man o' War, but Woodward stopped short of saying Gallant Fox was better.

Once she had entered the racing game, Mrs. Henry Carnegie Phipps was quick to get into breeding as well. (With Woodward's influence, she, too, chose Claiborne Farm as the place to board her mares and, eventually, stood stallions there as well.) She was the breeder of record of the 1928 foal by English stallion Blandford and out of the imported English mare Flying Squadron, by Light Brigade. She named the colt Blenheim, a name that had been given by the Aga Khan to another Blandford colt overseas. The second Blenheim won the 1930 Epsom Derby and became Blenheim II when imported for a distinguished stallion career at Claiborne.

In the meantime, Mrs. Phipps' Blenheim came to hand at four in 1932, when he won a distinguished list of a half-dozen stakes — the Brooklyn, Empire City, Brookdale, Aqueduct, and Edgemere handicaps and the Whitney Gold Cup. Blenheim was second in the Jockey Club Gold Cup for the second year. (The handicap division of 1932 was so strong, however, that Blenheim was not listed among the leaders, who included Equipoise, Mate, Jamestown, and the Australian champion Phar Lap.)

Once again, Fitzsimmons was providing plenty of trips to the winner's circle for both Wheatley and Belair. In 1932 he won for Woodward his second Belmont. The classic that year went to Faireno (Chatterton—Minerva, by Ambassador IV), who also won the Lawrence Realization, Saratoga Handicap, Dwyer, and other stakes and gained recognition as co-champion three-year-old with Burgoo King.

Woodward never stressed breeding for early juvenile success, but Hancock understood that speed is part of the equation of any successful horse in major racing. That year Belair's Happy Gal was regarded (retrospectively) as the best juvenile filly. The daughter of Sir Gallahad III—My Reverie, by Ultimus, won the Juvenile and Flash stakes and the Saratoga Special. This willingness to run a filly against colts netted a win over the top juvenile male, Ladysman, in the Special. Fitzsimmons repeated as the leading trainer, with $266,650.

The following year, 1933, saw several major scores for Mrs. Phipps. Wheatley's Dark Secret (Flying Ebony—Silencia, by King James) had a highly active campaign and won eight stakes. These included the Jockey Cup Gold Cup, in which he defeated Equipoise, but none of this was enough to dethrone C.V. Whitney's horse, beloved as "the Chocolate Soldier." Dark Secret's other wins included the Washington, Brooklyn, and Manhattan handicaps, and the Whitney Gold Trophy. Dark Secret had been purchased for $5,700 from the Gifford Cochran dispersal in 1931.

Also in 1933, Wheatley took one of the most coveted races in New York, when Edelweiss captured the Coaching Club American Oaks. In her previous start, in the Acorn, Edelweiss (Chicle—Helvetia, by Hourless) had gotten caught in the webbing of the starting contraption then in use but came on to finish second. Wheatley won the race, anyway, with Iseult. Edelweiss defeated Colonel E.R. Bradley's Kentucky Oaks winner Barn Swallow in the CCA Oaks but later lost to her in the Alabama, and the Bradley filly was rated the division champion.

On the Belair side, the former classic winner Faireno won four major handicaps at four in 1933.

In 1934 Dark Secret added the Saratoga Cup and another Manhattan Handicap before attempting a second Jockey Club Gold Cup. In that race the Wheatley runner defeated Belair's Faireno. Any tendency toward jocular comment about the result and their shared trainer, which either owner might otherwise have summoned, was put aside by the grim fact that the winner injured himself and could not be saved. (Starting with Diavolo in 1929, Fitzsimmons had thus won four of the last six Gold Cups.)

A SECOND CROWN

The 1934 season also saw a big, lengthy colt from the first crop of Gallant Fox come to Fitzsimmons. This was the Belair homebred Omaha, who was out of Flambino, by Wrack. Omaha epitomized much of what Woodward sought. He was a golden horse who grew to 16.3 hands and weighed 1,300 pounds. He was large but not gross, and the fact he needed time to develop fit Woodward's goal of aiming for the classics.

As his sire had done, Omaha gave Fitzsimmons and Woodward encouragement at two, while not being able to defeat the best of his young contemporaries. He won only once in nine starts, but he was often around, running second in the Sanford, Champagne, and Junior Champion and fourth in the Futurity, Hopeful, Saratoga Special, and United States Hotel. Somewhat at odds with the concept of giving a horse time, Fitzsimmons must have thought Omaha needed action, for he ran the big colt four times at Saratoga between August 4 and September 1.

Omaha came out at three in late April and won an allowance race before finishing third to Today in the Wood Memorial. That completed his preparation for the classics. Omaha rolled through them all; the Kentucky Derby by one and a half lengths over Roman Soldier, the Preakness by six over Firethorn, and the Belmont by one and a half lengths, again over Firethorn. In the midst of this ascent, Omaha dropped back to a mile and was second to Rosemont in the Withers, but Rosemont could not handle him in the Belmont Stakes.

Smokey Saunders rode Omaha through the Triple Crown, and W.D. Wright was the jockey for his remaining American races. Omaha tried older horses in the Brooklyn Handicap (114 pounds), but he was third behind Discovery (123), who was then rounding into the form that would prove him to be one of the great handicap horses of all time.

Omaha's three-year-old season concluded early, on July 20. After the Brooklyn, he won the Dwyer and then shipped to Chicago to win the Arlington Classic. His chances for more glory at Saratoga and in the fall were eliminated by a baffling, recurring soreness that Fitzsimmons was unable to diagnose, but Omaha was clearly the champion of his age. Fitzsimmons and Woodward had achieved something no one else had in winning their second Triple Crown. (Ben Jones and Calumet Farm would later duplicate the feat, with Whirlaway and Citation.) Also, Gallant Fox became the first (and remains the only) Triple Crown winner to sire a Triple Crown winner.

Woodward had retired Gallant Fox at three but decided to bring Omaha back at four, despite his problems. This did not mean he would return to Fitzsimmons, however, for Woodward chose to send Omaha abroad. His aim would be the Ascot Gold Cup, in those days the central target of the top English classic colts, which were kept in training at four. It was not a classic colt that Omaha had to deal with, however, but the filly Quashed. They waged an epic duel for the Gold Cup, the American barely losing. Omaha won two races and placed in another from his four English starts.

A minor stakes winner at two in 1935 was the Wheatley homebred Seabiscuit (Hard Tack—Swing On, by Whisk Broom II). Sent to a lesser division, Seabiscuit ran thirty-five times that year, which had much to do with the reputation Fitzsimmons developed for preferring rigorous campaigns. As Ryall noted years later:

"Training methods have always been divided into two distinct schools, the severe and the lenient, towards which individual trainers veer one way or another. Because it was the one he was brought up in, Mr. Fitz quite naturally inclined to the hard — now called the old-fashioned way. His horses were freely and often extended in their morning workouts, and if they stood up to their preparation they seldom failed on the racecourse in the afternoon. Of course, many fell by the wayside before they got that far, but that was to be expected. Provided they are not out of the ordinary in temperament or constitution, racehorses adapt themselves to the ways of their trainers. 'But each one is different,' Mr. Fitz says, 'and you've got to watch them for any peculiarities. A horse with bad habits, usually finishes second.' "

Various examples besides Seabiscuit's thirty-five races at two can be pointed to as evidence of Fitzsimmons' employing a pattern of frequent racing. From the beginning of his association with Woodward, Fitzsimmons must have received the owner's blessing on that technique, for he raced the filly Priscilla Ruley twenty-seven times at three — harking back to the misty past and Hanover for the Dwyer Brothers. Conversely, none of the six horses Fitzsimmons trained to win the Belmont Stakes ever raced more than a dozen times at three, and, late in his career, one of his masterpieces of horsemanship was bringing Nashua up to win the Widener Handicap without a prep in his debut at four. As the man said, "Each one is different."

Seabiscuit, famously, was sold to Charles S. Howard and became an American idol, his fame regenerated by a book and a movie some sixty years later.

THE GLORIOUS DECADE CONTINUES

The first two crops of Gallant Fox gave cause to think the young stallion was on his way to lasting greatness, as was his own sire. The second crop of Gallant Fox colts for Belair included Granville (out of Gravita, by Sarmatian), who more or less fit a familiar pattern. At two, he had only an allowance win from seven races but was tried against the best and placed in the Babylon and Champagne, although he was unable to make any mark in the Futurity.

At three in 1936, he came out to win an allowance race by daylight and then hooked up with Wheatley's Teufel and lost by a nose in the Wood Memorial. Both colts proceeded to Churchill Downs, for the Kentucky Derby, along with another Belair colt, Merry Pete. It proved a dismal trip. Having the same trainer, the Belair/Wheatley horses were coupled, and the entry went off at about 11-1 in a field of fourteen. Teufel finished eighth, never in contention, and Merry Pete had a similar trip to be tenth. Those were the highlights of the day for Fitzsimmons and the respective owners, however, because Granville was bumped and unseated jockey Jimmy Stout very early in the proceedings.

Unscathed and reunited with Stout, Granville went on to Pimlico, where he got to within a nose of the Derby winner, Bold Venture. Stepping out of the division, he tried older horses in the Suburban Handicap and was beaten a nose by Firethorn. Thus, from his last four races, Granville's record read one off-the-board loss and three nose losses.

A streak of a rosier kind was in the offing, and by the end of the year Granville was voted Horse of the Year as well as champion three-year-old in the first year such designations were certified by ballot. The winning streak began when Granville got on the plus side of those nose-to-nose photos, edging Mr. Bones in the Belmont Stakes. This was the fourth win in that signature New York event for Fitzsimmons and Belair. In the Arlington Classic, Mr. Bones was again runner-up, but finally Granville got some daylight between himself and another horse, winning by two and a half lengths. The Classic was run at a mile and a quarter at that time.

Back east Granville added the Kenner, Travers, and the mile and three-quarters Saratoga Cup, all at Saratoga. In the Cup he did what Omaha had not been able to do the previous year when he defeated the older Discovery. Getting ten pounds, Granville won by eight lengths in a two-horse field. He concluded his campaign, and career, with his sixth consecutive win, taking the Realization. Granville had won eight of eighteen races in two years and earned $111,820. Fitzsimmons returned to the top of the trainers' list, with $193,415.

The year 1937 was a good one for Wheatley, highlighted by victory in one of the top New York handicaps, the Metropolitan. The winner was Mrs. Phipps' Snark (Boojum—Helvetia, by Hourless), a half brother to the CCA Oaks winner Edelweiss. In addition to the Metropolitan, Snark won two other stakes that year. Wheatley came close to the juvenile filly championship that season when homebred Merry Lassie (Stimulus—Iseult, by Sir Gallahad III) won the Polly Drummond at the new Delaware Park and then took two of the best of the established New York races, the Spinaway and the Matron. Jacola, however, was voted the division title.

Also in 1937, Mrs. Phipps for the second consecutive year won the Wood Memorial, with Melodist and made another run at the Kentucky Derby, getting a better result as the colt finished fourth behind Triple Crown winner War Admiral. It would be twenty years before Bold Ruler became Wheatley's next Derby runner.

The following season, Snark added another of the best New York handicaps when he won for Wheatley the historic Suburban. He also won the Paumonok in a campaign in which he had to deal with War Admiral several times.

The year 1938 was Belair's turn to win the Wood Memorial. The vehicle was a colt named Fighting Fox. Since Gallant Fox, Woodward had been duplicating the match of Sir Gallahad III and Marguerite, and Fighting Fox was the resulting foal of 1935. He had won the Grand Union Hotel Stakes at two. The Wood Memorial win earned him a Derby trip, but he could finish only sixth. He won no further stakes at three but would prove an admirable handicapper.

The Belair two-year-olds of 1938 included one that would develop into the stable's fifth Belmont Stakes winner of the decade. Unlike Gallant Fox, Faireno, Omaha, and Granville, this colt, Johnstown, was not a homebred. The son of Jamestown—La France, by Sir Gallahad III, was acquired from Hancock of Claiborne Farm. Johnstown started in April and had twelve races at two. He won four of his first eight and then ran fourth in the Futurity. He ended the year on a serious roll to implant himself into consideration for the next year's classics. In his final three starts at two, Johnstown won the Richard Johnson Stakes in Maryland, the Remsen in New York, and the Breeders' Futurity in Kentucky.

He apparently was the sort of horse that Fitzsimmons thought needed a bit more action than his others. He started him back at three in a less orthodox way than before. Johnstown came out sprinting against older horses and won by six lengths. Before the Wood Memorial, Fitzsimmons squeezed in another race, an allowance race at a mile and seventy yards, which Johnstown also won by six. Four days later he won the Wood by eight.

Johnstown was 3-5 in the Kentucky Derby, and everything went smoothly this time — or almost. Johnstown did swerve at the start but avoided any mishap and soon had a clear lead. He dominated throughout and won by eight lengths — a winning margin that has been matched but never exceeded in the Derby.

After six straight victories by Johnstown, a third Triple Crown seemed perfectly within the realm of practicality. In the Preakness, however, Johnstown caught a muddy track, and while he led early he soon weakened and fell back to fifth. Maryland-bred hero Challedon won it for his home state. Wheatley's Gilded Knight, winner of the Chesapeake Stakes, finished second.

Johnstown thus had three major races on three consecutive Saturdays, but the thought that his Preakness loss hinted at fatigue was apparently not Fitzsimmons' reaction. He proved correct. The Belmont Stakes was three weeks away, but before then Fitzsimmons squeezed in the one-mile Withers Stakes, which Johnstown won by six. The Belmont brought another dominating performance, the Belair colt winning by five.

Two weeks later Johnstown added the Dwyer, in which Challedon was third. In Chicago, however, Challedon won the Arlington Classic while Johnstown again faded, coming in third. A wind affliction was noted, and

Johnstown would race no more. He had won fourteen of twenty-one races to earn $169,315. However, Challedon kept going and accomplished enough in the latter part of the season that he prevailed in voting for three-year-old championship honors and for Horse of the Year.

Fitzsimmons led the trainers' list in 1939 with $266,205, his fourth title of the 1930s. Along with Johnstown, the Belair contributors to that total included Fighting Fox, whose five stakes victories included the $50,000 Massachusetts Handicap. Fitzsimmons' total was not all from Belair horses, of course. A highlight for Wheatley in 1939 was the Acorn Stakes victory by Hostility. This filly was one of the few fillies or colts by Man o' War (Playfellow's brother) that Fitzsimmons trained. Hostility's dam, Marguerite de Valois, by Teddy, was out of the great French producer Plucky Liege, dam of leading sires Sir Gallahad III and Bull Dog, Epsom Derby winner Bois Roussel, and Grand Prix de Paris winner Admiral Drake. This was surely illustrative of the commitment to top quality Fitzsimmons' patrons harbored.

A LULL, BY COMPARISON

The 1940s did not continue the level of success that the 1930s had seen. Nevertheless, the relationships between Fitzsimmons and Mrs. Phipps and between Fitzsimmons and Woodward were supported by strong enough bonds that they endured. Over the years Mrs. Phipps developed the frequent habit of motoring to the barn and visiting with "Fitz," as she called him. A hint at the personal connection between Fitzsimmons and Woodward came from the owner's recollection of a moment on the day of Gallant Fox's stunning defeat in the 1930 Travers: "I went to the stable after the race and was glad to find the horse in very satisfactory shape. I had not been well for a week or ten days and Fitzsimmons asked me how I felt. I told him I was better, and in his usual smiling, friendly way, he told me we could well afford to lose the Travers as long as 'W.W.' felt better."

The excellence of Gallant Fox's early foals was not followed by a continuing pattern of major winners. After Omaha and Granville, there was little of note on the American side. Abroad, Gallant Fox was represented by Flares, who avenged his full brother, Omaha, by winning the Ascot Gold Cup in 1938. For the most part, Woodward's pattern of developing classic winners and then sending them to stud came afoul of a pattern that Hancock must have recognized: late-maturing types that need a distance of ground to excel tend not to be the kind that succeed at a highest level as stallions. Woodward as a young Turfman had been advised by the distinguished figure August Belmont II, "Billy, breed to stoutness! When you get one that has some speed, you have a very good horse." Hancock and his son and grandson found more success in a different version: Never neglect speed, and when you find one that has speed and can also stay a bit, you have a very good stallion prospect. A.B. "Bull" Hancock Jr.'s preference for the latter led to his importation of Nasrullah, and that stallion got the only Futurity winner Woodward bred as well as the only truly outstanding sire (Nashua). But as the 1940s dawned, that was well in the future.

The decade was not dismal but definitely below the high standards enjoyed in the 1930s.

The decline was not immediately noticeable. In 1940 Belair's homebred Fenelon (Sir Gallahad III—Filante, by Sardanapale) won a nice series of prestige stakes: the Travers, Jockey Club Gold Cup, Lawrence Realization, and Empire City Handicap. The next year, he added five more including the Brooklyn, Manhattan, and Whitney.

Also in 1941, Fitzsimmons confronted an unusual situation when figuring what to do with a horse named Foxbrough. Another full brother to Gallant Fox, Foxbrough had been the top-ranked two-year-old in England but had not trained on to be a major winner thereafter. Today, breeders would know what to do given this set of circumstances: full brother to Triple Crown winner, top juvenile in England, comes out with a disappointing race at three. Well, you retire him immediately, and the trainer is quoted as being dismayed that (fill in the injury) has ended the budding career of as brilliant a prospect as he has ever seen. In the days of Foxbrough, that was not so frequent an attitude. Woodward had kept him in training, and there he was in Fitzsimmons' barn at age five, converted to American dirt racing. Fitzsimmons got a rich score out of Foxbrough in the $25,000 Butler Handicap and another stakes, the Yonkers.

A key figure for Belair was Vagrancy (Sir Gallahad III—Valkyr, by Man o' War). This filly's career came down on the side of Fitzsimmons liking vigorous campaigns. From April through October of 1942, Vagrancy went into battle twenty-one times at three and won eleven races. Her wins ranged from seven furlongs to a mile and a half and brought home a distinguished collection of major trophies — the CCA Oaks, Alabama, Beldame, Ladies, Test, Delaware Oaks, and Pimlico Oaks among nine stakes. She was voted champion three-year-old filly and also champion handicap filly under the format used for *Daily Racing Form* balloting at the time.

Vagrancy won fifteen races from forty-two starts in her career and earned $102,480. She made a major mark as a producer, but her most distinguished foal raced abroad. Woodward sent her 1945 foal, Black Tarquin, to England, where he won a classic, the St. Leger. (In 1946 Vagrancy's half sister, Hypnotic [by Hypnotist II], won the CCA Oaks and Alabama, but Bridal Flower was voted the division championship.)

In 1944 Belair and Fitzsimmons were figures in a unique moment. When Belair's Bossuet came to the line even with Wait a Bit and Brownie in the

Carter Handicap, it marked the first — and still the only — instance of a triple dead heat in a major stakes.

In 1946 Wheatley Stable laid the groundwork for future championship success. Mrs. Phipps had established her own broodmare band over some two decades and did not often revisit sale rings anymore, but she paid $35,000 for a Mahmoud—Planetoid, by Ariel, filly. It was the highest price paid for a yearling filly that year, but the cost was well worth it. Named Grey Flight, the daughter of the 1936 Epsom Derby winner won the Autumn Day Stakes and, more importantly, produced no fewer than nine stakes winners. Fitzsimmons' career lasted long enough that he trained six of them.

Both Wheatley and Belair were producing stakes winners as the latter 1940s proceeded, and one was Bonnie Beryl, who won the Frizette Stakes for Belair.

There was another branch of the stable beginning to make waves by then, however. Mrs. Phipps' son, Ogden Phipps, had begun racing his own horses, separate from his mother's, as early as the 1930s. A budding business career, and then World War II, intervened, and there was a gap of more than a dozen years between the breeding of his first stakes winner, White Cockade (foal of 1933), and his second, The Admiral (1946).

Ogden Phipps' interest in the breeding operation of Colonel E.R. Bradley led him to some early purchases and eventually a major share of the Bradley estate. Fitzsimmons also trained for the younger Phipps, whose 1947 filly Striking (War Admiral—Baby League, by Bubbling Over) won the 1949 Schuylerville Stakes at Saratoga before launching a distinguished breeding career.

It was not until the next decade, however, that additional championship banners would again festoon the lengthening legacy of Sunny Jim Fitzsimmons.

RULERS GALORE

At the dawn of the 1950s, Ogden Phipps' Busanda (War Admiral—Businesslike, by Blue Larkspur) was three, and she won the historic Alabama Stakes for Fitzsimmons and the breeder.

For Woodward the decade began on a thrilling, but frustrating, note. His dream since childhood of winning the Epsom Derby came as close to reality as it ever would when his homebred Prince Simon finished only a head behind Galcador in the seminal classic. Prince Simon also had lost by only a head in the Two Thousand Guineas. That he won enough to be ranked the top three-year-old in England that year was perhaps some consolation. Of course, none of it had a direct bearing on Sunny Jim Fitzsimmons.

In 1951 Ogden Phipps' Busanda moved far up in the hierarchy of distaffers handled by Fitzsimmons. She won the historic Suburban Handicap, as well as the Saratoga Cup, New Castle Handicap, and Top Flight Handicap. The following year she beat males in the Saratoga Cup a second time and also won the Diana. Busanda won ten of sixty-five races and earned $182,460. (Her great son Buckpasser came to the races only two years after Fitzsimmons' retirement.)

Arguably the best horse William Woodward Sr. ever bred was foaled in 1952. He was a colt by the recently imported Nasrullah and out of Segula, a Johnstown filly who had won six of twenty-nine races as a three-year-old. (Segula was to foal Alabama Stakes winner Sabette, but the latter was only a yearling at the time Segula was sent to Nasrullah.)

Woodward had in mind sending the Nasrullah—Segula colt to England, but the old gentleman died in 1953 when the colt was a yearling. Woodward had many daughters, but only one son, and it was William Woodward Jr. who was named to take over Belair Stud and Belair Stable. The younger man concluded that having one stable was enough to deal with, so he did not send any youngsters to England. Thus, the Nasrullah—Segula colt would race in this country, carrying the name of Nashua.

With the death of Woodward and the loss of Fitzsimmons' own wife two years earlier, the trainer, as he headed into his eighties, might have dwelled on thoughts that his road, too, was nearing its last curves. The passage of time was inexorable.

Fitzsimmons had six children and seventeen grandchildren, however, and through much of his career had various relatives in his employ. As for the instinct to pity him because of his posture, two of his grandsons have told us that they believe he was spared much pain from the curvature of his spine. It did become so severe, however, that their "Grandpop" preferred to have conversations seated so he could better look a person in the eye.

With much to remember but much to live for, Fitzsimmons soldiered on, and Nashua was the sort to speak to a horseman's soul. A large, powerful colt, he had quirks that led to the nickname of "Mickey" around the barn and to some snide comments from his regular rider, Eddie Arcaro, but did he ever have speed — and class! He won six of eight starts at two in 1954, when he was the champion two-year-old.

Fitzsimmons had never won the Futurity, and as Nashua's victories in such as the Juvenile, Grand Union Hotel, and Hopeful led him toward that storied old race, leaders of New York racetrack management dared superstition by creating a special trophy in advance. Nashua did not let them down, winning the Futurity in a frothy battle with his season-long rival, Summer Tan.

During the winter and spring he was three, Nashua showed ability, but such tricks as propping in the final furlong or waiting until it seem too late to get down to business tempered his riders' regard for him. Nashua won the Flamingo and Florida Derby for Arcaro, who was serving a suspension on the day Ted Atkinson barely got him to rush past Summer Tan in time to win the Wood Memorial.

In his early eighties, Fitzsimmons felt the trip to Kentucky for the Derby was a grueling exercise he could miss without diminishing Nashua's case. His son John, a key assistant, went with Nashua and his groom, Alfred Robertson. Nashua was the favorite, but a threat from the West Coast had developed in the brilliant Swaps. Bill Shoemaker put this California phenom on the lead, and Arcaro and Nashua could not wear them down. Summer Tan was a distant third.

With the chance of a third Triple Crown out the window, Nashua went on to Pimlico. There he was tested by a nice colt with the historic name of Saratoga, and Nashua was forced to a track record (1:54 3/5) to wear him down and win by a length. Swaps had gone back to California to continue building an extraordinary status.

Fitzsimmons had last won the Belmont Stakes in 1939. Now, sixteen years later, he saddled Nashua to win in a nine-length gallop, giving the young Woodward his first as an owner and the trainer his sixth. Only James Rowe (eight) and Sam Hildreth (seven) have more.

Nashua went on his merry way, winning the Dwyer and then the Arlington Classic, as Fitzsimmons resumed the quarter-century old practice of sending his classic three-year-olds to Chicago during the summer. There turned out to be need for a return trip to Chicago, too, for public demand for a match race with Swaps had been building to a national fervor, and fever.

As Seabiscuit had taken the track early against the supposed front-runner War Admiral in their acclaimed match in the 1938 Pimlico Special, the prevailing wisdom about match races was he who strikes the first blow has the edge. Prior to the $100,000 winner-take-all affair set for Chicago's Washington Park, it was easy to assume that Rex Ellsworth's Swaps was the natural speed and that Nashua would be chasing him. Fitzsimmons, however, put plenty of speed drills in Nashua, and the big colt was ready to gun from the start. Moreover, Arcaro had discerned a preferred path in the heavy, drying out track.

When the break came, Arcaro went to the whip, got Nashua away first, and steered him to the best footing. Nashua held sway, turned back Swaps' sequence of challenges, and drew off to win by six and a half lengths. Fitzsimmons was not one to make a big deal out of winning one more horse race after all those years, but he was quoted once as allowing himself to call this "the moment of a lifetime."

The Nashua–Swaps match race was hardly off national television screens before reports that Swaps had not been at his best began to chip away at its status as a definitive event. Nashua lost his next race, challenging older horses and trailing High Gun and Jet Action in the Sysonby. Then, in his final race of the year, he added another chapter to the old Fitzsimmons legacy by winning the gentleman another Jockey Club Gold Cup.

From those middle 1950s days Fitzsimmons' family harbored revered memories of summer visits to Saratoga. Fitzsimmons had a summer place up there and established a trust to preserve what Joe Hickey described in the *Maryland Horse* "as a rustic compound of four cottages and a bunk-house." Racing writers, jockeys, and fellow trainers were guests, and there were tales of Fitzsimmons once offering Grey Flight's blanket to an over-night stayer to combat the upstate evening chill.

In the Woodward family, however, tragedy lurked. Late in Nashua's Horse of the Year season at three in 1955, William Woodward Jr. was shot and killed by his wife. The family's place in high society assured massive coverage and later prompted Dominick Dunne's fictional account, *The Two Mrs. Grenvilles*. Mrs. Woodward's explanation that she had mistaken her husband for a burglar was accepted by the legal system.

The senior Woodward's estate was still not completely settled, and now a new generation of executors' decisions would be needed. The breeding and racing stock, save Nashua, was consigned to public auctions. Nashua was placed in a special category and sealed bids for him and him alone were invited. Kentucky breeder Leslie Combs II put together a syndicate, which made the winning bid of $1,251,200. Combs announced that Nashua would remain in training at four and that Mr. Fitz would still train him.

Fitz had his horse back, but no longer in the old Belair colors of white, with red polka dots, red cap. With the death of William Woodward Jr., these colors would be taken over by one of his sisters, Mrs. Edith Bancroft, and their mother, Mrs. Woodward Sr. They would once again be carried to glory by their Damascus and later by horses raced by Mrs. Bancroft's sons, Thomas and William, but by then Mr. Fitz had passed away.

The career of Nashua made the most headlines in the years 1954 and 1955, but the Wheatley Stable fortunes also had taken a sharp rise. In 1954, when Nashua was the two-year-old colt champion, Wheatley had the corresponding juvenile filly champion in High Voltage. In 1955, when Nashua was three-year-old colt champion and Horse of the Year, Wheatley had the corresponding three-year-old filly champion in Misty Morn.

The gray High Voltage (Ambiorix—Dynamo, by Menow) had an even dozen starts at two, between April 2 and November 2. She broke her maiden in her second race, stepped up to win the Rosedale Stakes, and was off and running on a busy stakes regimen. She also won the National Stallion (filly division), Colleen, Matron, and Selima. Her season ended with a fourth behind Myrtle's Jet in the Frizette, but in winning six of twelve she had done enough to secure the juvenile filly championship.

The following year High Voltage proved her ability to maintain a presence at the top of the crop at three. In rapid succession she won the Acorn, Black-Eyed Susan, and beloved Coaching Club American Oaks (a mile and three-eighths). She ran dismally in the Top Flight but rebounded to win the Delaware Oaks. Four for five in major stakes at that time, she then won only two more out of ten remaining starts, and only one of those was in a stakes, the Vineland Handicap.

This opened the way for her stablemate, Misty Morn, to wrest the three-year-old filly title, which she did. Misty Morn was by the emerging champion stallion Princequillo (sire of Belair's Prince Simon) and was the second stakes winner and first real star foaled from Grey Flight. Misty Morn was not precocious. She made fifteen starts at two and three before her first stakes attempt and did not get her first added-money victory until her twenty-fifth race, the Providence Stakes at Narragansett in New England. Then she won the Molly Pitcher over Clear Dawn, was second to the high-class colt Saratoga in the Saranac, and won the Monmouth Oaks and Diana. Misty Morn still had eight more races, and she won only two, but she saved her best for last and defeated not only males, but older ones, going a mile and five-eighths in the Gallant Fox Handicap. It was her twenty-second race of the year, and that win put her on top in voting for three-year-old filly championship.

Fitzsimmons was the leading trainer for the fifth and final time — and first time since 1939 — with earnings of $1,270,055.

So, when Nashua headed to Florida by train with the glamour and clamor of being the first million-dollar Thoroughbred purchase, the Thoroughbred version of a Pullman car also had champions Misty Morn and High Voltage aboard.

In a training feat starkly contrasting his reputation for heavy campaigns, Fitzsimmons had Nashua ready to win the Widener at a mile and a quarter off works alone. The champ carried 127, and it took a supreme effort by him and Arcaro to win by a head in a four-horse blanket finish witnessed by a record crowd of 42,000 at Hialeah, the epicenter of Eastern winter racing. The superb field included, in order of finish, Social Outcast, Sailor, and Find.

Nashua had never finished worse than third until his next race, the Gulfstream Park Handicap, and that race signaled a lessening of his consistency. He threw in several more dismal races, and Fitzsimmons put blinkers on him for the first time since early in his three-year-old year. Nashua awakened to win the Suburban Handicap in one of his best performances. He also won the Monmouth Park Handicap but lost the Woodward before finishing with a flourish, setting a track record for two miles in Fitzsimmon's revered Jockey Club Gold Cup. A spring victory in the Camden Handicap had put Nashua ahead of Citation as the all-time leading earner. Nashua won six of ten at four, which was not enough to forestall the sensational campaign of Swaps, whom he never met again, to be Horse of the Year. Nashua was retired with twenty-two wins in thirty starts and earnings of $1,288,565.

(That autumn, Swaps suffered a life-threatening fracture in a hind leg during a work at Garden State Park in New Jersey. None other than his rival's trainer, Sunny Jim, volunteered the sling, which was rapidly dispatched to help those attending him. Swaps proved amenable to the sling and survived for a significant stallion career. At the end of that career, he and Nashua were both standing at Combs' Spendthrift Farm.)

Both Wheatley distaff champions High Voltage and Misty Morn failed to add to their distinction at four in 1956. Misty Morn did not place from five starts and was finished by June. High Voltage had a season difficult to reconcile with commonplace management of top horses. She had seventeen races from February into August, and her only win came in an overnight handicap after four defeats. Early in her campaign, however, High Voltage placed in the Columbiana and Black Helen handicaps, perhaps encouraging the thought she could come around, but she failed to place in any additional stakes.

Nevertheless, the year 1956 was a bellwether one for Wheatley. As Belair-bred Nashua left the stage, Wheatley's Bold Ruler was coming to the fore. Bold Ruler was a dark bay or brown, by Nashua's sire Nasrullah, but a racy, leggier sort. His dam, Miss Disco, was a stakes winner by Discovery and had been purchased by Mrs. Phipps from Bull Hancock. The Claiborne owner had offered Mrs. Phipps the opportunity when he had been unable to buy a mare he was looking for on her behalf.

As a young horse, Bold Ruler injured his tongue, presumably on a stall chain, and this made his mouth sensitive and at times caused him to refuse to rate kindly. Nevertheless, he was a highly efficient machine for two-year-old racing, and he launched his campaign with five straight dashing victories. Two came in stakes, the Youthful and Juvenile. Bold Ruler then had back trouble, which forced Mr. Fitz to leave him idle at Saratoga, but after dropping an allowance race, Bold Ruler won his final Futurity prep. On the day Nashua bowed out with his second Jockey Club Gold Cup, Arcaro guided Bold Ruler to victory in the Futurity. After so many years of the Futurity eluding Fitzsimmons, the octogenarian had won it twice in three years.

Bold Ruler seemed to have the juvenile colt title wrapped up, but Fitzsimmons and the Phippses chose to run him in the mile and a sixteenth Garden State Stakes. Originated in 1953, this New Jersey race had been the richest race in the world, and the top stables responded enthusiastically to it. Bold Ruler ran up on the heels of a fading pacemaker and was pushed back in the ruck, finishing seventeenth as Calumet Farm's Barbizon came on to win. A later failure by Bold Ruler in the Remsen cleared the way for Barbizon to win the colt championship.

The 1957 season saw Fitzsimmons at perhaps his best. He had a problem colt with distance limitations, and he seems to have gotten the most out of him. Bold Ruler swapped winter triumphs with Calumet's Gen. Duke, nosed out Gallant Man in the Wood Memorial, and proceeded to Churchill Downs. Fitzsimmons, who had not won a Derby since Johnstown eighteen years before, that time made the trip. Mrs. Phipps had never won it and had had no runner in two decades.

Jockey Arcaro always afterward blamed himself for fighting Bold Ruler to keep him off the lead. Had the colt been allowed to go on early, he likely would have used his speed too early. Fighting him discouraged the colt, though, and he finished fourth as favorite behind Iron Liege, Gallant Man, and Round Table.

At Pimlico, Arcaro let Bold Ruler run more freely and he had control throughout. It was the first win in a classic for Wheatley Stable, but the thirteenth for Fitzsimmons, his fourth Preakness to go with six Belmonts and three Kentucky Derbys. Other trainers had won more of each of the classics, but none had matched the aggregate. Fitzsimmons' thirteen Triple Crown races stood alone as the record for forty-three years, until Commendable won the 2000 Belmont Stakes to become the thirteenth classic winner for D. Wayne Lukas. Through the Triple Crown of 2006, Fitz and Lukas remain tied for first.

Bold Ruler's free-running style made it easy to devise a strategy against him in the Belmont's mile and a half. John Nerud employed Bold Nero as the pacemaker, and then stablemate Gallant Man came along and won impressively after Bold Ruler was softened.

For all his brilliance, Bold Ruler had his problems. He was stiff and sore and some even conjectured there was a flaw in how the muscles over his back aligned. That was probably a stretch, but Fitzsimmons used the newly developed medication Butazolidin on the horse, to good effect. Use of Butazolidin for racing was condoned at the time, as it is today, and Fitzsimmons on occasion also took the unusual step of having Bold Ruler jogged under a rider from the barn to the paddock, further to ensure he warmed out of stiffness.

Bold Ruler had a spectacular late summer and fall, winning six of seven. His only loss, though, came in the Woodward, behind Dedicate and Gallant Man, again calling into question his effectiveness at a mile and a quarter.

Bold Ruler's other performances included plenty of evidence that Mr. Fitz and Mrs. Phipps respected the history of American handicap racing. Bold Ruler won the Jerome and Vosburgh under 130 pounds, the Queens County under 133, and, finally, the Benjamin Franklin under 136.

The season culminated in a three-way battle with Round Table and Gallant Man, compatriots in what is recognized as one of the most superb collections of three-year-olds ever seen. Bold Ruler stole away to a big lead early and swept through the stretch to win the Trenton Handicap by two and a quarter lengths from Gallant Man, with Round Table struggling in the off going. Finally, Bold Ruler had won at one and a quarter miles, and he clinched the three-year-old championship. By that time there were two major polls, and he split with Dedicate as Horse of the Year.

The colt's nagging problems continued, and Mr. Fitz missed the winter Hialeah targets. He got Bold Ruler back to win the Toboggan to launch his four-year-old career in 1958. A report by William Conklin in the *New York Times* gave a charming look at Mr. Fitz combining family and professional agendas:

"Mr. Fitz watched the race from a spot on the lawn ... 'Can't see much from here,' he said [and one can imagine how difficult it would be to watch a race from any vantage point given his bent posture], 'maybe the last quarter-mile ...'

"While the field was going to the post, the dean of American trainers was concerned about his two and a half-year-old granddaughter, Dotty May, who had found something to cry about. He produced a few pennies to dry her tears, turned his head up the Widener stretch, and said, 'Well, I guess they're about ready to go.' "

A few minutes later, having seen what he thought was a victory, he asked for verification: "Have they put up the numbers? Somebody might have got to him just there at the end."

Nobody had caught Bold Ruler, and he was launched onto one of the gamest of handicappers' seasons. He lost his one meeting with Gallant Man, carrying 135 to the other's 130 in the Metropolitan Mile, and he finally was stopped by his leg problems, and 136 pounds, in the Brooklyn in his finale. All his other races produced notable victories that year, though, the Carter under 135, the Stymie under 133, the time-honored Suburban Handicap under 134, and the Monmouth Handicap under 134. The Suburban and Monmouth were run at one and one-quarter miles.

Round Table's great campaign won year-end honors, but Bold Ruler went to stud at Claiborne with a reputation enhanced by his four-year-old form. He had a career record of twenty-three wins in thirty-three starts and earnings of $764,204.

Fitzsimmons was frequently pushed to evaluate his best horses, of course.

He tended to say that Bold Ruler would be best at a mile; Nashua slightly best, over Gallant Fox, at a mile and a quarter; and, at least on occasion, he gave Gallant Fox the nod at a mile and a half. He never failed to appreciate that it was the horses and their owners that had made his career:

"Nobody can make a bad horse good. The main object is to avoid making a good horse bad, and a lot of it is just a matter of luck … I came into this game with nothing to give it … Racing gave me the happiest life you could want. Racing doesn't owe me a thing, but I owe the game a hell of a lot."

THE FINAL YEARS OF WINNERS

Bold Ruler was to be a sensation at stud, leading the sire list seven times consecutively and a total of eight times. Both Wheatley Stable and Ogden Phipps in separate colors turned out a succession of champions in the 1960s, many of them by Bold Ruler.

Fitzsimmons stayed at the game long enough to enjoy the first of the Bold Rulers and win a few races with them, but he announced his retirement in 1963, when the oldest of that line were three-year-olds. Nevertheless, Bold Ruler's retirement had not meant the last of Fitz's major victories.

In 1959, with Bold Ruler at stud in Kentucky, Wheatley won the revered Alabama with High Bid (To Market—Stepping Stone, by Princequillo). High Bid also won three other stakes that year, and her younger half brother, Progressing, by Bimelech, won the Pimlico Futurity. The two-year-old filly Irish Jay (Double Jay—Irish Witch, by Bold Irishman) won the Spinaway, Demoiselle, Fashion, and a division of the Schuylerville.

The next year, 1960, Irish Jay won the Acorn, and in 1961 Ogden Phipps' Funloving (Tom Fool—Flitabout, by Challedon) won the Mother Goose and Black-Eyed Susan.

New York and New Jersey had deep holds on the life of Sunny Jim Fitzsimmons, and they were the scenes of his final stakes triumphs. On June 15, 1963, the Bold Ruler filly King's Story won the Miss Woodford Stakes at Monmouth Park, New Jersey. It had been at the old Monmouth that the wide-eyed young Fitz had seen the namesake of that race, Miss Woodford herself. What memories must have been his for private savoring if he allowed himself to think back on seventy-eight years of working around horses.

Records are incomplete for one whose career spanned the years his did, but from available resources a total of 149 individual stakes-winning horses can be identified. One calculation has him winning 2,267 races and having trained earners of $13 million.

At the time of Fitzsimmons' retirement, Ogden Phipps spoke of his family's having had "such a wonderful association with Mr. Fitz for thirty-eight years. The record speaks for his skill as a trainer, but what has been more important to us has been Mr. Fitz the man, a man of great character whose outlook on life and concern for his fellow man endeared him to all fortunate enough to know him."

Bill Winfrey succeeded Mr. Fitz as the Phipps family trainer. The old gentleman continued to follow the races until his death at ninety-one in 1966. (Mrs. Phipps passed away in 1970.)

One of Fitzsimmons' grandsons, Jack Fitzsimmons, gave us a succinct summation of his memory and respect for one upon whom the nickname Sunny Jim fit so well and yet was so devoted to the profession of the shed row: "I never saw him upset with anybody — unless they had put a bandage on incorrectly."

CHAPTER 7

H.J. "DERBY DICK"
THOMPSON

The Kentucky Derby originated in 1875, imitating an event born in England (the Epsom Derby) nearly a century earlier. The English race had taken on such prestige that, as racing spread from country to country, each nation tended to come up with its own imitation in attempting to create a structure for its own program. The United States was no different although the country was large enough, and regionalized enough, that more than one pattern was set into play in the hopes of duplicating not only the English Derby but also the system of other classic races.

None of these set plans took hold. Willy-nilly, the Kentucky Derby came to the fore as one part of the pattern, and Maryland's Preakness and New York's Belmont took on the roles as acts II and III to complete the venerated Triple Crown (although into the 1930s the Preakness on occasion came before the Derby).

Thoughts of a Triple Crown mean getting ahead of ourselves, however, when we address H.J. Thompson, trainer for Colonel Edward Riley Bradley. Bradley was a Derby man. He was a wandering sort who had sought, made, and managed fortunes for some years before the world of horse racing became one of his prime playthings. Bradley bought a farm in Kentucky and came to love and covet the Derby. Well, why not? To a man such as Bradley, the Derby grew to have everything — prestige (which expanded from regional to national), tradition, excitement, and charm. Then, too, it hit a personal jackpot with that Circean beckoning to Bradley's earthly spirit — a winter book!!

It was not that Bradley needed someone else handling the wagering action, but the winter book assured that people might begin thinking of the Derby months in advance. Ah, the bets that could be made! Some of them germinated at Bradley's Palm Beach, Florida, gambling club, where

Bradley could play the roles of host, proprietor, entrepreneur, Christian protector of the great unwashed, and hell-bent gambler. Derby bets might range from "who will win" to "who will beat whom regardless of where they finish," and on down to "can you name a horse today that will even show up at the start in May?"

We are aware that winning a purse is not the only motivation of the race-horse owner of yesterday, today, or tomorrow. However, we can presume that training for a fellow like Bradley — and there have been many of them — adds to the sense of moment for a trainer when a horse sallies out for a specific event. H.J. Thompson said as much in a succinct quote:

"Colonel Bradley is a hard-betting man, so I have to train his horses hard. I have to have them ready to run when he's ready to bet."

Bradley, in turn, expressed his confidence in his trainer: "If Dick can't get them ready, nobody can."

FROM BALDWIN TO BRADLEY

Herbert John Thompson was born in Detroit, Michigan, on September 21, 1881. He was fond of horses as a youngster, and his first jobs around them were with Standardbreds. He went to work at fourteen for Edward F. "Pop" Geers, one of the top trotting-horse trainers, and also had a stint with Dave McClary. Thompson had connections with the highest level of Standardbreds, those on the Grand Circuit.

By 1902, he had shifted to Thoroughbreds and went to work for E.J. "Lucky" Baldwin. Given that his later association was with Bradley, Thompson staked claim to having worked for a pair of the most famous and flamboyant individuals on the Turf.

Baldwin, like Thompson, began life as a Midwesterner. Born in Ohio in 1828, Baldwin at eighteen won $200 at a local fair with his trotting horse Lovely. There was something else lovely in Baldwin's life, for he eloped with a farmer's daughter — no joke. He changed careers, and wives, with some frequency, trying real estate, horse trading, supplying provisions to miners, and investing in stocks. He got the nickname Lucky after a trip to India to hunt tiger. Baldwin had taken with him the key to his strong box, precluding his agent from following instructions about selling some stock. By the time Baldwin returned to San Francisco, the stock had risen so dramatically that he found himself a multi-millionaire.

Baldwin bought the eight-thousand-acre Rancho Santa Anita and got into horse racing in a big way. By his association with Baldwin's outfit, Thompson got another look at the better type of horse; he was still with Baldwin in 1907, when the entrepreneur opened the original Santa Anita racetrack.

From one self-made American legend, Thompson threw in with another.

In 1909 (the year Baldwin died), he went to work for Bradley, whose trainer was Cliff Hammond. If Bradley's tale were to be pitted against Baldwin's in a contest of rambunctious color and charm, the Colonel's side would rest upon such as:

Origins in Pittsburgh, Pennsylvania, 1859; a foray west, where he befriended Wyatt Earp and Billy the Kid; duty as an Indian scout and cowboy; a career path finally meandering to establishment of a series of gambling clubs from Texas to Chicago to Florida. Famously, Bradley testified in Congress that his profession was gambling.

Acting on a physician's advice that he establish some fresh-air activities, he launched into breeding Thoroughbreds in Kentucky and racing them on the best circuits of America. As a farmer, breeder, and racehorse owner, a man could breathe healthy air by day and still be a gambling impresario by night! No wonder Bradley loved God.

The strident contrasts in this Colonel's march were once addressed as follows in a commentary in *The Blood-Horse*:

> He was a combination of cold mathematics and groundless superstition, of gambling and godliness, inscrutable as night and plain as sunshine. He was always coldly calculating, and yet he earned the affections of people more completely than any [other] man on the Turf of his time ... He operated a gaming house from which he earned millions, in a state and country where gaming is definitely against the law. Yet the priest who delivered the eulogy at his funeral called him 'this saintly man' ... A good loser himself, he quickly marked poor losers off his list ... As far as he was concerned, the judges were always right. There was no duplicity in him. He was a gambler. He stood his ground.

Colonel Bradley — the title was a Kentucky courtesy, not military — bought his Kentucky farm in 1906 and built it to more than a thousand acres under the name Idle Hour Farm. His silks were green and white.

Thompson was promoted to head trainer after nine years with the stable when Hammond died at Saratoga in July 1918. Bradley raced no horses at Saratoga that year, so Thompson's first win was put off until September, by which time the outfit had shipped down to the Kentucky Association track in Lexington. On September 20, 1918, he sent out Blue Paradise at odds of 7-10 to win the first race of the day, a $800 purse. In his late thirties at the time, Thompson was destined to stay with Bradley for the rest of the trainer's relatively short career. Various photos of the times suggest that Thompson dressed well and was a distinguished-looking man. He seems comfortable in the background of Bradley, whose straw boater connotes a flair the trainer did not share.

A BREAKTHROUGH IN THE DERBY

Bradley and Thompson made their first Derby foray two years later, in 1920. That was a year that the star of America's three-year-old crop was not in the race, but the Bradley entry, By Golly, could not cash in on the absence of mighty Man o' War. By Golly finished seventh as part of the 13-1 mutuel field while the 16-1 Paul Jones edged Man o' War's one-time conqueror, Upset.

The 1920 season saw the emergence of the tiny filly Bit of White, who won the Debutante at two that year at Churchill Downs. Years later Thompson still would at times declare she was the best filly he trained, pointing especially to her five-length victory at three in the two-mile Louisville Cup.

In 1919 Commander J.K.L. Ross had made Derby history by owning the first two under the wire, Sir Barton and Billy Kelly. In 1921 Bradley was to match that feat as he made his triumphal first trip to Derby glory. Perhaps it was symptomatic of being a gambler first and a horseman second, but Bradley came out of a one-two Derby triumph with a grievance.

As the foal crop of 1918 developed, a colt with the unhandy name Believe Idle Hour had won the Clipsetta Stakes, and stablemate Behave Yourself won the Queen City Handicap. Over the winter, however, it was another of Bradley's homebreds, Black Servant, who became the *beau ideal* of his owner's ambitions for the Kentucky Derby. However awkward the naming pattern is when seen from today's perspective, Black Servant was an obvious choice, for he was by Black Toney, a Bradley horse who had been a nice sort of runner but only marginal as a sire prospect. A major winner in Black Toney's column would be a boon. (Bradley early on established a penchant for giving his horses names beginning with the introductory letter of his own surname.)

Peter Chew's book *The Kentucky Derby: The First 100 Years* (Houghton Mifflin, Boston, 1974) addressed the combination of sportsman and gambler that Bradley embodied: "Although the Derby's prominence has been traced to the 1915 victory of Harry Payne Whitney's great filly Regret, Bradley always credited Emil Herz, who opened the first Derby winter book two years later. Other winter books opened in succeeding years, and in 1921, bookmakers in St. Louis, Chicago, Louisville, and New York quoted Derby odds."

Chew further pointed out that because a horse was in a winter book, regardless of who owned it, there were no odds-slashing entries. Thus, he records, it was possible to get 40-1 on Black Servant and 100-1 on Behave Yourself at times during the winter of 1920–21, even though they had the same owner. Confusingly, Chew avers that while much of Lexington was on to Black Servant early, Bradley did not bet heavily, waiting to take the 9-1 on his two-horse entry at post time.

At any rate, Black Servant defeated Behave Yourself in the Blue Grass Stakes a week before the Derby. Then, in a Derby field of twelve, Black Servant, with jockey Lawrence Lyke, put the Bradley colors on the lead while Charles Thompson lagged back in eighth with Behave Yourself. Both numbers in Harry Payne Whitney's favored entry, Prudery and Tryster, were in mid-pack early. (Harry Sinclair's Grey Lag had been scratched or else he might have been the favorite.)

Black Servant turned back the early runners-up, Muskallonge and then Leonardo II, and turned for home in front. Meanwhile, Behave Yourself had been advancing position by position. Chew's research revealed a telling incident "… as the two Bradley colorbearers ran for the wire. Suddenly, a hat skimmed past Black Servant's head. He pricked his ears, momentarily losing stride, and (jockey) Thompson seized the moment to spur Behave Yourself ahead, even though he was well aware that Colonel Bradley wanted Black Servant to win. When Lyke realized Thompson was trying to steal the race, he shouted 'Take back, you son of a bitch.' But Thompson wasn't about to take back, and Behave Yourself held on to beat Black Servant by a nose."

To split hairs, the official margin was a head. The favored entry finished third and fourth.

Bradley was furious, in part because he thought, incorrectly, that one of his particular friends had lost a bundle on the race. (In fact, this fellow, one J. Leonard Replogle, had covered himself handsomely with pari-mutuel backup on the entry.)

Thus, the scenario on Derby Day 1921 was this: (1) The winning breeder and owner had fulfilled an ambition he had set upon about fifteen years earlier, and he was furious. (2) A jockey had ridden a clever, waiting race and had come on to win what many were already considering the most important event on the Turf, and he was sacked.

Bradley did the honorable thing, of course, for he delivered the winning jockey's share of the purse along with the jockey's walking papers. Given these reactions, the report that Bradley had done the bulk of his own betting through the pari-mutuel system, getting 9-1 regardless of which of his horses won, invites skepticism.

(The subject here is the trainer, but one more extraneous detail of Behave Yourself's win is too gossipy to exclude. Behave Yourself was by Marathon—Miss Ringlets, by Handball. The dam had been owned by a gambling crony of Bradley's, a fellow known as Caesar Young. In due course, the breeding stock of this Mr. Young came onto the market because the show girl with whom he had been involved shot and killed him one night. Eventually, Bradley acquired Miss Ringlets, and from her he bred Behave

Yourself. Purchasing mares formerly owned by dead friends might be difficult to fit in with any popular breeding theory, but in this case it produced a Derby winner.)

Meanwhile, trainer Thompson presumably was held blameless for finishing two-one in the Kentucky Derby instead of one-two.

Behave Yourself never won another race in eight starts and was given to Bradley's brother with the idea that the Derby winner might sire some useful polo ponies. Black Servant won only one later stakes at three and, after missing his four-year-old season, won a single race at five. The decision to retain him for the stud at Idle Hour, however, was pivotal to Bradley's success, for Black Servant sired the best horse Thompson ever trained, Blue Larkspur, and a half-dozen other stakes winners bred by Bradley.

After the 1921 Kentucky Derby, Bradley's wife, Agnes Curry Bradley, apparently did not share her husband's discomfiture with how he had happened to dominate the race. She was said to remark airily that running one-two could only be bettered in terms of fun if they ran three horses in the race. It is almost certainly a coincidence, but the next year Bradley did just that. His Bet Mosie finished second behind unbeaten Morvich, while the others in the 3-1 entry, By Gosh and Busy American, ran ninth and last, respectively. Busy American had broken down in the early running.

Once he zeroed in on the Derby, Bradley apparently had no scruples about running just to be running. In 1923 he was tenth in a field of twenty-one with 28-1 Bright Tomorrow. The next year, he ran another three-ply entry, at 10-1, and finished third with Beau Butler, seventeenth with Baffling, and nineteenth and last with Bob Tail. In 1925 the stable was eleventh of twenty with 51-1 Broadway Jones.

There was more to Thompson's assignment than the Derby, of course. For a man whose identity would be linked to a specific race that was largely the province of males, he was showing a deft hand at lightly training fillies as well. He had won the 1920 Latonia Oaks with Busy Signal, and he was to repeat in that important stakes in 1924 with Befuddle, who defeated Princess Doreen.

In 1922 Thompson sent out the Bradley juvenile filly Blossom Time, by farm stallion North Star III, to beat colts in a division of the Pimlico Futurity, and she was rated second to Sally's Alley among juvenile fillies. In 1923 Beau Butler, who was third in the next year's Derby, got in some good moments as a two-year-old, including his own victory in the Pimlico Futurity.

In 1924 Thompson had Blue Warbler, another by North Star III, contending for honors among two-year-old fillies. She won the Spinaway and Matron but then was upstaged for championship honors by Harry Payne Whitney's pair of Mother Goose and Maud Muller.

The next year Thompson was bringing along what would prove to be his second Kentucky Derby winner. Bubbling Over was by North Star III—Beaming Beauty, by Sweep. At two in 1925, he was rated close to the year's top juvenile colt, Pompey. Bubbling Over set out with five consecutive victories to start his campaign, but none of them were in stakes. He then was beaten in his first stakes attempt but won the Nursery Handicap and Champagne Stakes before finishing second to Flight of Time in the Breeders' Futurity in Kentucky.

In 1926 Bradley was back in full force for the beloved Kentucky Derby, and, once again, he not only won it but also ran first and second. Stories handed down on this race emphasize Thompson's point that he was training for a fellow to whom winning bets might supercede other benefits of winning races. Happily, however, the pressure appears to have been all about winning rather than manipulating a loss today to get a price tomorrow.

Bradley brought to Thompson's task some distractions as well, for the Colonel was ever keen to try out innovations. From time to time, Thompson was instructed to experiment with goggles and windshield-wiping devices on his horses, and with a saddle with springs meant to alleviate pressure on a horse's breathing apparatus except when extra tightness was needed on turns. None of these caught on. Bradley also experimented with ultraviolet ray machines back at the farm to promote equine conditioning.

Not everything he tried was a demonstrable failure, however. Whether it was cause and effect is doubtable, but he did win a Derby with Burgoo King after instructing that the horse be given cod liver oil and dried fish and subjected to ultraviolet light in a special stall. Moreover, when he became involved in racetrack ownership, Bradley put money into some of the early starting gates leading toward the modern contraptions, and he brought over from Australia a type of protective cap for jockeys that was an early version of the skull caps later adopted.

As the 1926 Derby approached, Bradley was said to have been so egged on about the fine reputation of Pompey that he got down $100,000 on Bubbling Over. Further, he promised Bubbling Over's jockey, Albert Johnson, that the rider would get $10,000 if he won and $5,000 even if he lost provided he finished ahead of Pompey. By that time, the Derby's winning purse constituted good money, too, at $50,075.

Bubbling Over had been brought out by Thompson to win the Blue Grass Stakes, and with stablemate Bagenbaggage also on board, the Idle Hour entry was the 1.90-1 choice over 2-1 Pompey. Bubbling Over went to the front early and turned back Pompey's bid. As the previous year's two-year-old champion faded to finish fifth, Bagenbaggage came on from mid-pack to finish second, as Bubbling Over soared home by five lengths.

Author Chew estimated that Bradley left Churchill Downs up by $311,000, comprising the $50,000 winner's purse, $6,000 for second place, a trophy worth $5,000, and $250,000 in winning wagers. Thompson had done a nice spring's work.

Though neither Bradley nor Thompson ever led any of the breeder, owner, or trainer standings statistically at the end of a year, there was an admirable multiplicity of success during many seasons. The 1926 three-year-old division was a case in point. Bubbling Over was overshadowed eventually in championship terms by Samuel D. Riddle's Crusader, but there was strength in numbers in the Idle Hour fold. Derby runner-up Bagenbaggage won the Latonia Derby ($25,000, a major purse at the time), Louisiana Derby, and St. Valentine Handicap. (Bagenbaggage was by Under Fire and out of Blushing Beauty, a half sister to Derby winner Behave Yourself.) Moreover, Idle Hour had another three-year-old whose earnings for the year outstripped the Derby darlings. This was Boot to Boot (North Star III—Padula, by Laveno), a half brother to Black Servant. Boot to Boot won the American Derby and Ohio Derby and exceeded $100,000 in earnings that year, en route to a career total of $120,954. This was considerably more than the $78,552 career earnings of Derby winner Bubbling Over, whose lack of soundness restricted his record to thirteen starts, of which he won ten.

From today's perspective, the concept of a trainer keeping his two-year-old prospects in Kentucky through the winter and preparing them on the farm for the Derby the following spring is difficult to fathom. Thompson's technique of the 1920s and into the early 1930s eventually became obsolete, for the fashion changed to Derby winners coming out of prolonged training in warmer winter racing climes, such as Florida, California, or — for a time — South Carolina.

In 1934 (as it turned out only three years before his death), Thompson laid out his schedules for breaking and training horses in general and specifically for preparing a Derby candidate. The lengthy presentation for *The Blood-Horse* is a reminder that, for the racehorse trainer, the basics must go before the glamor:

> The yearlings at Idle Hour are generally picked up about July 1. Mr. Thompson believes the most important feature in the early training of a yearling is "to get a mouth on him. A horse's mouth is the tenderest thing in the world and must be handled with delicate care. Few are aware that when whiskey stimulant is necessarily administered, unusual care must be taken in its dilution, or it will seriously scald the interior of the mouth."
>
> To Mr. Thompson, the first and most important thing to stop is biting. A bit is put in the yearling's mouth, and he is led around on a shank [daily] for about 10 days. After this, a pad and surcingle

are put on. The surcingle takes the place of a girth, and for four or five days the youngster is walking about in this manner. At the end of this time, a boy is put on him (or her), but no stirrups are allowed until the yearling is thoroughly accustomed to the saddle. The yearlings are kept [for their lessons] under the enclosed shed for about three weeks. At Idle Hour Farm, plenty of time is taken in the breaking of yearlings for, as Mr. Thompson said, "any bad habit contracted at this time sticks for life.

The yearlings are next started in to gallop, and are gradually worked, beginning slowly, until, by easy stages, the distance and speed is increased to a quarter-mile and until they are ready for their trials, about the middle of September. After the preliminary trials, two or three weeks are taken to let them down, and during that time they are schooled in starting and receive their first training in good post manners. The yearlings are never shod, unless the ground is baked, in which case plates are put on to keep their hoofs from cracking.

About the middle of January, the older horses are taken up, followed by the two-year-olds the first of February. By this time, Mr. Thompson knows the characteristics, and peculiarities, of each individual. He says, "a horse has as much character as a man." By March 1, the horses are breezing a quarter-mile. All early work at Idle Hour is done in an open field. A track is improvised on the turf. There, the horses are galloped and breezed until weather conditions permit them to work on the training track. Mr. Thompson says he has not, he believes, been on the training track more than three times during March in the past three or four years.

Gradually, the horses are increased from a quarter to a half. If a horse is being "prepped" for the Derby, he is naturally taken along faster, but it takes until the middle of April to get him up to a mile. A stiff work is given seven or eight days before the race, at Derby distances, and a race or two is given, if possible at shorter distances before the classic.

"Horses," says 'Derby Dick,' "change greatly between their second and third years … You must always allow yourself to be guided by your horse's conformation, and the way he does in the saddle."

Mr. Thompson believes in feeding little at a time, but feeding often. He advocates giving a horse anything he will eat: [in addition to oats], plenty of hay, green stuff, carrots, etc. He also feeds corn during the winter. He says a horse has the smallest stomach, his size considered, in the animal kingdom and therefore he feeds little and often. In March, the horses are fed four times a day — 3:30 a.m., 11 a.m., 4:30 p.m., and 9 p.m. The feed box is only left in the stall for an hour, and is then removed whether the feed is consumed or not. When he walks through the barn at 10 p.m., if all is well, the horses have finished their feed and are stretched out in repose ...

Mr. Thompson insists that all his horses' legs be rubbed thoroughly after they are walked [following a work]. This is to reestablish normal circulation. No horse is bandaged when he is put away, unless he is suffering from leg trouble ...

The article goes on to say that Thompson regarded seven quarts of grain a day as typical for a three-year-old filly while noting that colts would eat more. The champion Blue Larkspur, for example, ate ten quarts daily during the summer.

Thompson's schedule for getting a Derby horse ready was in stark contrast to that developed by a contemporary, Ben A. Jones. Once Jones hit on the idea of winter racing, in Florida mainly, he took the technique of heavy racing to the point that he and son Jimmy ran Tim Tam ten times at three before the colt won the Derby in 1958. Even taking into account the truism that all horses are different, this is certainly far from Thompson's idea of keeping them through the Kentucky winter and getting one or two prep races. (The decree that the Derby be run the first Saturday in May did not come along until 1932, but it was not run much more than a week later during Thompson's experience.)

Today, Thompson's technique seems impossible, but Jones' campaigning of Tim Tam is equally far from trainers' minds. In the early twenty-first century, we have a trend of three or four prep races for many Derby hopefuls. The cliché about there being many ways to prepare for the race is certainly supported by history.

THE IRONY OF BLUE LARKSPUR

Bradley and Thompson ran another entry in the Derby the year after Bubbling Over beat Bagenbaggage. Buddy Bauer was sixth, and Bewithus, fourteenth. Buddy Bauer was a decent sort and won the Fairmount Derby that year and six more stakes through the age of six.

In 1928 Idle Hour had no Derby entrant for the first time since By Golly made that first attempt in 1920. The following year, though, 1929, brought out the best horse Bradley had bred and raced to that time, the mighty Blue Larkspur. Several years after Thompson's death Bimelech would come along to challenge Blue Larkspur for pride of place among all the Bradley-bred colts.

Blue Larkspur was by Black Servant and was out of Thompson's and Bradley's good filly Blossom Time, by North Star III. Thompson brought him out at two in New York in mid-May, and Blue Larkspur needed two races before winning the Juvenile Stakes in his third start. He added the National Stallion Stakes and Saratoga Special, by which time he had three wins over rival Jack High.

The Hopeful found Blue Larkspur carrying 130 pounds and giving three to Jack High, and that time the tables were turned. Then, Blue Larkspur was kicked prior to the start of the Futurity and finished eighth of twenty-four. He was lame at the finish and was through for the year. High Strung won the Futurity and prevailed as champion.

So, in addition to his usual routine of winter and early spring, H.J. Thompson had some treatment of Blue Larkspur to achieve if he were to produce the colt as a Derby horse. Perhaps owing to a lack of communication throughout the racing world, Blue Larkspur prevailed, nonetheless, as the Kentucky Derby favorite. Once again, betting competed with horsemanship in Thompson's day-to-day menu of things to worry about. Nevertheless, Thompson, true to the schedule as set out above, had Blue Larkspur sharp enough to win his spring debut, defeating Clyde Van Dusen in his prep in Lexington.

The Derby of 1929 had side drama, as Derbys are wont to do. Thompson was matter-of-fact about what happened: "At the time I was sick and so failed to have Blue Larkspur shod properly, so the best horse I ever sent forth had to take a beating."

Other versions, including Chew's, were more dramatic. Thompson underwent an emergency appendectomy two days before the Derby. Torrential rains on the afternoon of the race itself brought out blacksmiths to put mud caulks on a number of the Derby starters. With Thompson not on the scene, his assistant, Guy "Chappie" Hastings, was beside himself. The regular blacksmith had declared a change in shoes unnecessary and had driven back to Lexington, a factor in later rumors that this craftsman was at odds with Thompson over something.

Hastings implored Idle Hour farm manager Olin Gentry to authorize him to find another blacksmith to change Blue Larkspur's plates. Gentry was never a shrinking violet, but he understood that the farm manager had no standing to authorize such an action in the racing stable. Gentry told Hastings to confer with the boss himself, Bradley. "I've seen Bradley," Hastings retorted, seeing his last resort go awry. "He says the horse shoer ought to know what he's doing."

This showed considerable coolness for an owner who allegedly had bet $125,000 on Blue Larkspur and was seeing the moment of truth approach amid a veritable tempest of rain, lightning, and thunder.

In a field of twenty-one, Blue Larkspur and Bradley's Bay Beauty formed the favored entry at about 9-5. Blue Larkspur struggled with the footing, and although he was in a contending spot from the beginning, he could not mount a true challenge. He finished fourth as Clyde Van Dusen skipped home at 3-1 (destined to seventy-four years of distinction as the most recent gelding to win the Derby).

Thompson brought Blue Larkspur back to run in the one-mile Withers Stakes, and the result suggested a possibility that the Derby had seen a short horse that benefited from the demanding race. Blue Larkspur charged back after being challenged and won by a neck from Chestnut Oak, with Jack High third. The time of 1:36 was only three-fifths of a second off Man o' War's record for the stakes.

Blue Larkspur's Derby defeat might have invited worries about him in off going, but he was favored for the mile and a half Belmont Stakes although a sloppy track surface prevailed. He also was fighting the perception that horses of the Domino male line were unsuited for the distance. (Domino was generations removed on the top of the pedigree.) Blue Larkspur again was kicked in the milling around before the start, but he prevailed by two lengths over African, with old rival Jack High third.

Despite his mishap, Blue Larkspur came back in three weeks for the Dwyer. His defeat was not laid to any lack of soundness in the minds of many observers but instead to the inattentiveness of jockey Mack Garner, who allowed Grey Coat to slip up on the rail and win by a head.

Chicago racing took on major-league status that year with the opening of Arlington Park. A race named the Arlington Classic offered a purse of $59,900 for its first running, which compared favorably with the $53,950 for the Kentucky Derby, $52,325 for the Preakness, and $59,650 for the Belmont. Illustrative that sportsmen and sportswomen who like tradition also like money, in its first eleven runnings the Arlington Classic was won by seven horses that had won Triple Crown events during their spring campaigns.

Blue Larkspur found a heavy track for the mile and a quarter inaugural Classic. The lingering memories of his Derby failure and his defeat in the Dwyer contributed to the champion filly Rose of Sharon being the betting favorite. Blue Larkspur brought to happy fruition any betting action Bradley might have had on board, winning by five lengths. The demanding nature of the going was illustrated by the final time of 2:14 2/5.

Blue Larkspur was sent to Saratoga, where he bowed a tendon while being prepared for the Miller Stakes. He was through for the year, but with four wins in six starts and earnings of $153,450, he was adjudged the top three-year-old and Horse of the Year for 1929.

Bringing a horse back from a bowed tendon was not then, nor is it now, a high percentage proposition, especially in a case where it is the intent that a high-class horse return to more or less his best form. Thompson proved himself able to achieve this in the case of Blue Larkspur.

The following summer the colt was back at Arlington Park. After being beaten in a prep race at his return, Blue Larkspur won the Stars and Stripes Handicap over Misstep and Sun Beau. Although Arlington Park was only a year old, his track record of 1:49 2/5 for nine furlongs was impressive.

Following Blue Larkspur's lead, the top three-year-old of 1930, Gallant Fox, shipped out to win the Arlington Classic once the top Eastern three-year-old races of the spring were completed. The Arlington Cup, a weight-for-age opportunity, came up a week after Gallant Fox won the Classic, but trainer Sunny Jim Fitzsimmons did not hang around to challenge the older Blue Larkspur. The Bradley colt won by three and a half lengths, beating Petee-Wrack, Toro, and Sun Beau at level weights over a mile and a quarter.

A few days later, however, Thompson noted that the vehicle of his admirable training feat again was amiss. Blue Larkspur had a filling in an ankle, so he was retired to Idle Hour. Blue Larkspur shared handicap male championship status with Sun Beau. He had won ten of sixteen races and earned $272,070.

"I would consider myself mighty fortunate if I was ever able to train another horse like Blue Larkspur," Thompson said about that time. A few months before his death, an article in *The Blood-Horse* stated without qualification that, still, "of the host of winners trained for Col. Bradley, he is certain … Blue Larkspur … was the best." (As a true horseman, Thompson was able to separate admiration for horses in his care from recognition of another man's champion. He regarded Man o' War as the best colt he ever saw race, and Artful as the best filly.)

Bradley and Thompson had another champion in 1930, the year Blue Larkspur was four. The juvenile filly Baba Kenny provided the trainer another opportunity to show his ability with the more delicate gender at the same time he was prevailing with the powerful, high-appetite older male.

Baba Kenny (Black Servant—Betty Beall, by North Star III), like Blue Larkspur, represented the breeding pattern of Black Servant on a North Star III mare. Her key victory at two was in the Matron Stakes. At three the following year, Baba Kenny won the first running of the Acorn Stakes.

While Blue Larkspur and Baba Kenny were winning major prizes for Idle Hour in 1930, Bradley and Thompson had tried another two-ply challenge on the Kentucky Derby, running twelfth and thirteenth with the 9-1 entry of Breezing Thru and Buckeye Poet behind Triple Crown winner Gallant Fox.

The next season Idle Hour had no Derby runner. It was not a totally blank year, however, for in addition to Baba Kenny's Acorn Stakes, Thompson won the Wilson and Yonkers with Blind Bowboy and a lesser stakes with Bathorse.

"DERBY DICK"

The following two years brought Bradley's and Thompson's third and fourth Kentucky Derby winners.

The colts from the foal crop of 1929, which Thompson was wintering as 1931 gave way to 1932 included a son of Bubbling Over. The colt in question was Burgoo King. Thus, Thompson had his hands on a potential Derby winner sired by a horse with whom he had already won a Derby.

Burgoo King (out of Minawand, by Lonawand) was bred in partnership between Bradley and the owner of a neighboring farm, Horace N. Davis of Bluegrass Heights. The mare had been so unsuccessful that Davis, when offered Minawand, said he would only take her if Bradley provided a season to Bubbling Over and the pair shared the resulting foal. Bradley later inspected the colt and liked him enough to buy out Davis' interest.

He gave him a name that fits well into the history of all things Kentucky. The colt was named for James T. Looney, who used to travel through Kentucky and prepare the unique stew known as burgoo for private parties.

Burgoo King won four races from twelve starts at two. Although he was campaigned as if he were a real contender, his only stakes placing was a third in the Pimlico Futurity. He was unplaced in a half-dozen stakes, including the Futurity, Champagne, and Hopeful.

Valley Lake Stable's Burning Blaze, the juvenile male champion of 1931, was injured in a prep race the week before the Derby and never raced again. Meanwhile, Thompson had produced Burgoo King out of his winter design, the colt needing only a single race before being ready to win. In the Derby, Burgoo King was part of the ubiquitous Bradley pairing pattern, going off at about 11-2 along with stablemate Brother Joe (who finished nineteenth of twenty). Burgoo King was always among the leaders, and he passed early front-runner Economic and pulled off the win by five lengths. Economic held on for second by a head over Stepenfetchit.

Some history had been made, although it would be surpassed in twelve months' time. Bradley was the first owner of three Derby winners, and Thompson was the first trainer of three.

The Derby was run on the first Saturday of May that year, and the Preakness, often run before the Derby, was held a week later. The Derby favorite, Tick On, had become upset before the start and then was in traffic during the running, finishing sixth. He was still widely regarded as the best colt coming out of the race. Accordingly, Tick On was the Preakness favorite, but Burgoo King outbattled him to win by a head.

The hubbub created by a Derby–Preakness double in 1932 was nothing approaching what it is today. Still, the fledgling Triple Crown conclusion, the Belmont Stakes, loomed ahead. Burgoo King, however, made his next start in the Withers, in which he caught a sloppy track and was unplaced. He was not sound enough to contest the Belmont Stakes and did not race at four.

The Derby–Preakness winner was regarded as co-champion three-year-old, sharing the honor with Belair Stud's Belmont winner Faireno. In the two-year-old filly division, Belair prevailed with Happy Gal as champion, although Idle Hour and Thompson got in a major win with Barn Swallow in the Matron.

Burgoo King came back at five to win two minor races from four starts, and he had a career record for Thompson of eight wins in twenty-one starts and earnings of $110,940. The attention of the stable, of course, turned to the three-year-olds, and Burgoo King's successor as a Derby winner was under Thompson's shed row.

Brokers Tip (Black Toney—Forteresse, by Sardanapale) was a horse destined for a double dose of Derby history. For one thing, he was a maiden when he won, just as Sir Barton had been in 1919. Whereas Sir Barton went on to be a Triple Crown winner, Brokers Tip retired with his Derby victory as the only win of his life, from fourteen starts in three years. Then there were the amazing circumstances around the running of the 1933 Derby, which has gone down in history with such tags as "The Fighting Finish" and "Rodeo Derby."

Olin Gentry was for many years the farm manager at Idle Hour for Bradley and later manager on the same property when it was known as John W. Galbreath's Darby Dan Farm. He recalled for Chew that Brokers Tip was such a weakling as a foal that veterinarians devised a leather-cast support for his legs, accompanied by a prescription of calcium supplement.

Brokers Tip got to the races at two but was unable to win from four starts. Thompson, however, produced him in time to contest Latonia's Cincinnati Trophy on July 16, 1932. He was left at the post but rallied dramatically to be third, within a length and a half of winner Head Play. Brokers Tip was 9-1 for the Derby, in which the W.R. Coe entry of Ladysman and Pomponius was favored at 3-2.

Don Meade, who for many seasons was the contract rider for Bradley, brought Brokers Tip up from eleventh to contest the issue with Herb Fisher and Head Play, who had raced forwardly and had taken the lead before turning for home.

What ensued displayed the Thoroughbred's fighting courage, which is widely admired, laced with mankind's flagrant rule breaking, which sports laws are intended to contain. Meade and Fisher grabbed at each other's saddlecloths and hands, and Fisher took a swipe with his whip at the rival rider. They charged under the wire together. Brokers Tip was declared the winner. Stewards reviewed the situation but made no disqualification. Both riders were suspended thirty days for what had transpired on the track, and Fisher got an extra five days for leaping upon the victorious Meade back in the jocks' room.

H.J. Thompson thus had won four Kentucky Derbys and embedded the nickname "Derby Dick" more deeply into racing lore. (The nickname was said to have become colloquially popular after the trainer won his second Derby.) Two had been won amid a swirl of animosity, what with his owner furious with the winning jockey after one win and the winning jockey involved in a melee in another.

In addition to their added distinction as first owner and first trainer to win four Kentucky Derbys, Bradley and Thompson gleaned additional distinction that spring. Not only did they win the Derby, but they also were the first to win the Derby and Kentucky Oaks the same year, for Barn Swallow won the fillies' counterpart. (Calumet Farm and trainer Ben Jones matched the feat in 1949 and went one up on Bradley and Thompson with another double in 1952.)

Thompson was to win no more Kentucky Derbys in the four remaining years of his life, but it was not for lack of trying. He had an entrant in each of the remaining runnings of his career. He was ninth with Bazaar in 1934, sixteenth with Boxthorn in 1935, fifth with Bien Joli in 1936, and twentieth with Billionaire in 1937. These ran his total to twenty-four runners, of which four were winners.

FINAL CHAMPIONS

Thompson's 1933 Oaks winner, Barn Swallow, had won the Matron at two. At three, the daughter of Black Servant—Blue Warbler, by North Star III, later added another historic triumph when she took the Alabama Stakes. She was regarded the champion three-year-old filly of 1933.

That same year, Idle Hour's Bazaar shared juvenile filly honors with Mata Hari. Bazaar defeated future Preakness winner High Quest and future handicap champion Discovery in the Hopeful and beat future Derby winner Cavalcade in the Spalding Lowe Jenkins.

At various times Thompson was quoted that Bit of White was the best filly he trained, but in some quotations he favored Bazaar.

Thompson generalized that fillies "are more delicate [than colts] and, therefore, unable to stand as much prepping. A filly can be trained on just one-half the work that it takes to get a colt ready." Bazaar (Tetratema—Silver Hue, by Lemberg) was an exception among fillies. She was big and rangy, built like a colt, and Thompson ran her in the Kentucky Derby off a work over the full distance in 2:04 4/5. Thompson harbored the thought that had he not had to delay that work until three days before the race, because jockey Meade was unavailable until then, she might have run better than her ninth-place finish.

After the Kentucky Derby, Bazaar added victories in the Test Stakes and Mount Washington Handicap, and she shared a second championship with Mata Hari.

The year Bazaar was three, Thompson also trained the champion juvenile colt for Bradley. The two-year-old Balladier had a stamp of pedigree that by then was identified as Idle Hour excellence. He was by Black Toney—Blue Warbler, by North Star III. He was a highly unlucky colt, but history accords him honors among juvenile males of 1934.

He was the sixth champion Thompson had trained, following Blue Larkspur, Baba Kenny, Barn Swallow, Burgoo King, and Bazaar. To the citizens of Kentucky, however, Thompson's list of champions was probably less significant than his winning their Derby with Behave Yourself, Bubbling Over, Burgoo King, and Brokers Tip.

In 1934 two-year-old Balladier won the United States Hotel Stakes at Saratoga but stumbled at the start of the Hopeful and was unplaced. In the Futurity he again had a difficult start, and he was beaten by four lengths by Chance Sun. Balladier, however, defeated the promising Omaha by a nose in the Champagne. His record read: five starts, three wins, two excuses. He was to be an exceptional stallion, but Thompson did not live to take any of his runners to the races.

The year Balladier and Bazaar were champions, Thompson had other major victories. Bird Flower won the Albany and Adirondack stakes and Boxthorn won the Saratoga Special.

The following year Beanie M. won the Adirondack and Matron; Bien Joli won the East View Stakes; and Boxthorn added the Commonwealth Stakes.

In 1936 Bow and Arrow won the Sheridan Stakes at three. Thompson's three other stakes winners that year were two-year-olds, which was an interesting development inasmuch as that was a crop Bradley had decided to sell.

For the first time, Idle Hour yearlings were offered at Saratoga in 1935 and such was the status of the stock that Bradley's consignment topped all others. A total of thirty-one yearlings was recorded as sold for $152,050, to average $4,905. The highest-priced yearling in the auction was the colt later to be named Brooklyn, at $20,000, and the second-highest price was the colt to be named Biologist, at $13,000. They were listed as sold to George Read, agent, and Frank E. Brown, respectively.

Perhaps Bradley had not fined-tuned the art of running up bids without something going wrong. Or, perhaps, at certain moments of truth at the sale, Bradley just could not stand the thought of a colt he had bred striding home in the Derby under other silks. It was reported that prominent owner Mrs. Ethel V. Mars, who owned Milky Way Stable, made a live bid of $19,500 on the sale topper but did not hear the subsequent bid of $20,000 and so did not realize her bid had been topped.

At any rate, the Saratoga sale "toppers" came home to receive their "B" names and became stakes winners for Bradley and Thompson at two. Brooklyn (Blue Larkspur—Knockaney Bridge, by Bridge of Earn) won the Walden, and Biologist (Bubbling Over—La Troienne, by Teddy) won the Albany. A third yearling brought home by the breeder also won stakes at two for Thompson and Bradley. This was the grandly named Billionaire (Black Toney—Forteresse, by Sardanapale), who was knocked down to "F.E. Brown" for $8,500. Thompson won the Wakefield Handicap with him.

For the most part, these years were somewhat anticlimactic for Thompson in that no champions emerged after Balladier and no Derby winner after Brokers Tip. Brooklyn, however, had raised great hopes. In addition to winning the Walden, he inherited second in the Pimlico Futurity through a disqualification. Oddly, track handicapper John B. Campbell assigned Brooklyn top weight of 126 pounds on the Experimental Free Handicap, a pound above the voted champion Pompoon, who won the Belmont Futurity and other stakes. Bradley bet Pompoon's owner, J.H. Louchheim, that Brooklyn would finish ahead of Pompoon in the 1937 Derby. Bradley got slightly the better of the odds, putting up $10,000 to the other man's $11,000.

Brooklyn was finished first, all right, but not in the right sense from Bradley's point of view. The colt failed to train on well enough to run in the Derby whereas Pompoon was second in the classic. Billionaire was the lone Bradley runner to make it to the 1937 Derby but finished last behind War Admiral.

The fact that George Woolf rather than Don Meade rode Billionaire in the Derby reflected trouble that had struck the Bradley stable the year before. Meade, still Idle Hour's contract rider, was caught at Hialeah phoning bets to Newark on horses he was riding against. As recorded in the diligently researched manuscript produced on Bradley by racing and farm journalist Charles Koch, Meade was grounded and the case referred to the Florida Racing Commission:

"I went up to Palm Beach to see Mr. Bradley," Meade said later. "He asked me if I did what the stewards said I did. I said, 'Yes, I did.' Tears ran from his eyes. He said, 'Don, I don't see how you could do that. How could you do that?'

"After that he told me to go up to the farm and help break yearlings and he'd work to have me reinstated. And he did."

Koch wondered how that could have been accomplished: "Meade doesn't pretend to know. Still, he says, 'As long as the Colonel lived in Palm Beach, there was never a governor elected without Bradley behind him. I think the Governor had to show his gratitude in some way. Perhaps that was it.' "

Meade was reinstated, but he was to be in and out of trouble several times before effectively being banned for life in 1945. That year, he was ruled off in Mexico, and the decree was recognized by United States jurisdictions.

Amid all he accomplished, Bradley's greatest lasting contribution to the Turf was probably the importation of the French mare La Troienne. Thompson, however, saw only the beginnings of the vast influence La Troienne was to exert on the bloodstock fortunes of Bradley and other breeders. The mare's tail-female descendants have produced more than eight hundred stakes winners (and still counting in 2006).

Thompson missed the glory with the first of La Troienne's brood, the champion filly Black Helen. Bill Hurley, who had been training the second string, was assigned Black Helen, who went south for a Florida winter campaign. The little filly turned out to be top drawer. Black Helen won the Florida Derby, American Derby, and Coaching Club American Oaks and was the champion three-year-old filly of 1935.

Thompson won the one stakes with La Troienne's Biologist, but the trainer passed away suddenly on November 12, 1937. He was in Baltimore with a division of the stable while Bill Hurley had another draft in Florida, preparing for the winter season by then in vogue. Eight days before his death, Thompson had won for the final time. The winner, at Pimlico, was Baby League, destined to be one of the greatest of La Troienne's producing daughters (dam of champion Busher, etc.)

Thompson's activity had been reduced due to heart trouble, and he suffered a fatal heart attack. Thompson was survived by his widow, Dorothy. Bradley expressed shock at the news. The body was sent to Idle Hour, where the funeral was held, and Thompson was buried in Calvary Cemetery in Lexington.

Thompson's career predated various aspects of record keeping, but it can be documented that starting in 1928, he won stakes with eighteen horses and from 1919 won 373 races, earning $1,296,761.

H.J. Thompson trained six champions. "Derby Dick" Thompson won the Kentucky Derby four times, and that stuck as his signature identity. He held the record for trainers in number of Derby wins by himself from 1932 until Ben A. Jones matched Derby Dick with his fourth in 1948. The following year, Jones won his fifth, and he added a sixth in 1952. Only D. Wayne

Lukas has won as many as four in the interim.

Thus, seventy-three years after Brokers Tip, Derby Dick Thompson is still tied for second in victories in the greatest of American racing goals.

CHAPTER 8

PRESTON
BURCH

P reston Burch literally wrote the book on training Thoroughbred horses. Or, more accurately, he wrote *a* book on training that became a definitive treatise on the subject.

Training Thoroughbred Horses was published in 1953, three years after Burch led the nation's trainers in earnings. The book was as succinct and unpretentious as its title. It was published by *The Blood-Horse* and has been reissued several times over the years.

At the time the book was first published, Preston Morris Burch had more than a half-century of experience as a horseman. His key mentor had been his father, William Preston Burch. In turn, Preston Morris Burch's younger son, Elliott Burch, followed sire and grandsire into the Hall of Fame. Jimmy Kilroe, renowned and revered for his years as a racing secretary and racetrack executive, once stated, "No other family can show a century of greater contribution to racing than the Burch family."

It had all begun with a one-eyed Rebel.

GENERAL WADE HAMPTON'S COURIER

William Preston Burch was born in 1846 in Cheraw, South Carolina. According to a snippet in a *Thoroughbred Record* of 1900, the preteen W.P. Burch had lost vision in one eye in 1857 when some sort of powder he was holding in a bottle exploded in his face. (Forty-three years later Burch began to notice a swelling in one side of his face. A physician discovered a piece of glass that had been lodged there without causing mischief for all those years. Upon its delayed removal, the shard took on status as a unique personal souvenir.)

General Wade Hampton was either unaware of, or unconcerned about, the limited vision of the young man who served as a courier during the Civil War. What Hampton liked about W.P. Burch was that the soldier owned a swift Thoroughbred mare. What troubled the general was Burch's attendant interest in racing said mare.

Racing horses was against regulations in the Confederate Army but was not unknown in that organization. Burch family tradition held that Gen. Hampton's threats to have young Burch shot were overstated and never consummated. (Well, one could hardly have a family tale handed down from one generation to the next alleging that a direct ancestor had been killed before the opportunity to become an ancestor.)

Preston Burch would tell of Gen. Hampton recounting to him years later how "I nearly had your father shot many times." Gen. Hampton's "threat" usually went thusly:

Hampton to soldier Burch: "They tell me you've been horse racing."

W.P. Burch: "Yes, sir."

Hampton: "You know that's against regulations."

Burch: "Yes, sir."

Hampton: "Burch, I've a good mind to have you shot."

Burch: "Yes, sir."

Hampton: "Did you win?"

Burch: "Yes, sir."

Hampton: "Well, that's right, Burch. Don't ever let them beat you."

The younger Burch, of course, had to append that "My father won every race he ran during the war."

W.P. Burch's home was in the path of Union General William Tecumseh Sherman's marches through Georgia and South Carolina. With no workable homestead surviving, Burch set out after the war to make some money with the one asset he had left, his trusty mare. This led to a career as a racehorse jockey and then trainer.

At the end of a long career, the *Thoroughbred Record* obituary recalled that W.P. Burch "began with quarter horses shortly after the [Civil] War and raced them through the 'fair' circuits of the Far West and Middle West. About 25 or 30 years ago, Burch became associated with the late Francis Hitchcock, a steward of The Jockey Club, and trained his Thoroughbreds. When Hitchcock practically retired, Burch took over the horses owned by Samuel D. Ross of Washington, D.C. … For the last three years, Burch had been in poor health."

Burch was elected into the National Museum of Racing's Hall of Fame in its inaugural balloting, in 1955. His major winners had included Biggonet, winner of the 1885 Spinaway Stakes and 1886 Withers Stakes (over champion Inspector B.), and Grey Friar, winner of a division of the 1902 Matron Stakes. He also had a gelding with his own name, Burch, with whom he won stakes for five years.

Burch lived the wandering life of the horseman, a lifestyle his younger son would embrace but would later try to dissuade his own issue from adopting.

"Mother followed father as long as she could stand it," Preston Burch once told columnist Red Smith, "then she settled down in Washington (D.C.) … I was one of three children, and mother often told us how she would put all three of us to sleep in the bureau drawers of a hotel room. I saw that new Spencer Tracy movie the other night, and there was a baby lying in a bureau drawer. I had to laugh. 'That's me,' I thought, 'going to the races.' "

W.P. Burch lived to the age of eighty. He passed away in 1926, in a sanitarium at Saratoga Springs, New York, the city where he had shipped his stable in anticipation of that year's meeting. His widow, Emily Burch, lived until 1943.

At the time of the elder Burch's death, his stable included the high-class My Own, owned by Admiral Cary Grayson, a partner in Blue Ridge Farm. The Jockey Club cited Grayson, who had been President Woodrow Wilson's personal physician, for his sportsmanship in making My Own available in 1923 to race against Epsom Derby winner Papyrus in a special $100,000 match race at Belmont Park. As it turned out, Zev was selected as America's representative in that event and duly won it. However, My Own was past his best days by the time he came into W.P. Burch's care, and the trainer died soon afterward.

In addition to his career with horses, W.P. Burch was venerated for schooling a number of important horsemen. Among them were the trainers Andrew Jackson Joyner, Gwyn Tompkins, and George Odom. The last-named had the distinction of riding and also training Belmont Stakes winners. Burch also helped launch his sons, Preston and Selby, into training careers.

The *American Racing Manual* of 1927, looking back on W.P. Burch's death in 1926, wrote of a "quiet, soft-spoken gentleman, whose years in racing had been many and whose knowledge of the Thoroughbred was ultimate and comprehending."

Preston Burch looked back on his father as one who "didn't care any more for money than some of the old boys that used to ride the rails. If the man he was training for had good horses, well, he was pleased to train them. If the man couldn't afford good horses, he'd train them just the same."

A SON AND APPRENTICE

Preston Morris Burch was born in Augusta, Georgia, on August 25, 1884. He left high school at the age of eighteen and was put to work by his father. Despite his youth, Preston Burch had an inkling that actually owning a horse would intensify the learning process. He purchased a horse named

Stuyve and with him won his first race as an owner and first as a trainer, at the Gravesend track in New York. His silks were blue, with orange cuffs and orange cap, and Stuyve carried them to four more wins before the end of the year.

Young Burch was still not on his own, for he went to California as stable agent for his Uncle Green B. Morris, while training a couple of horses himself. "Uncle Green" is not the most comfortable reference or salutation within a family, and, Burch pointed out years later, Morris was known mercifully to his kin as "G.B." A self-made success from Mississippi, G.B. Morris had gone west as a driver of the sort of conveyance known as a prairie schooner as part of a wagon train. He later retraced his steps to the East, where he developed a racing stable so good that he was America's leading owner by earnings in 1902.

The 1898 volume *The American Turf* describes Morris as "conspicuously a representative of a class of hard working, practical racing men, who have done as much as any of their associates to develop and improve the sport." Nephew Preston Burch eventually worked for the elite among racing sportsmen, but he, himself, also would make his way as a "hard working, practical racing man."

Back east, Preston Burch had another stint with his father and then took some of the lesser horses in the stables of several major owners to race them in Canada. His patrons were John E. Madden, Francis Hitchcock, and Newton Bennington. Burch recalled ruefully of this adventure that he "won twenty-seven races, but left owing everybody."

In 1906 Burch, at the age of twenty-one, took the job as trainer for the Chelsea Stable of Russell Tucker and Ernest La Montagne. He started strongly, winning the Amateur Cup at Belmont Park with The Cricket, and had solid success. In 1908 he had a day that attracted particular attention when he won four races at Pimlico.

New York was the top racing circuit in North America, but a series of political steps fostered by anti-gambling sentiment threatened the sport. In 1911–12, there was no racing in New York. La Montagne had died and the Chelsea Stable was dissolved. Preston Burch was among Americans who looked overseas, and he landed in France, where he had horses for John Sanford, William Astor Chandler, C.P. Eustis, and La Montagne's kinsman, Harry La Montagne. Burch, by then, was approaching his thirties, and photos of the era show a tall, large-framed young man with a spare, unfurnished look that promised handsomeness later.

In those days in France, it was the norm for a trainer to have both a steeplechase stable and a flat stable. Burch's major success came in the Grand Steeplechase International in Milan, with Sultan VII, and he also saddled winners in Germany, Switzerland, and Belgium, as well as in France. Sultan VII's Italian Grand Steeplechase involved some post-race drama when an inquiry resulted from the actions of "the little boy who had been getting up on horses for me," as Burch recalled. The kid had been shut off and herded persistently by a champion rider, who subsequently claimed foul after Sultan VII somehow got home first.

"Mr. La Montagne came rushing up to us — he was real mad — and asked my boy if he had fouled that other rider," Burch recalled for a dinner gathering more than sixty years later. " 'No, sir. He fouled me. Ran me all over the course.' Mr. La Montagne seemed satisfied ... A few minutes later, they put our number back up there, and we were declared the winner; and then my boy turned to me and said, 'You know, when I was trying to keep that rider off me, I *did* get in one good lick — caught him with my whip right across his nose.' "

Rumblings of war were developing, but Burch remained naïve. Perhaps his father had been one of those Southerners who had looked upon the Civil War as a grand adventure that would be won in a hurry. At any rate, Preston Burch admitted, "We in France thought the Germans were going to fold up quickly, but Sanford was in London and was getting the right information. I had the horses at Maisons-Laffitte, near Paris. After I had balked at moving them to the (Sanford) Normandy farm, I got a cable from Sanford I'll never forget. It said: 'Dear Burch: In spite of your private opinion of the war, ship my horses to Normandy at once.' When we did go to Normandy, we took a road that paralleled a German cavalry outfit only 20 miles away most of the trip."

Burch served as a volunteer ambulance driver in France, then in 1914 returned to America. His ship, the *Lusitania*, had only a few more passages before it went down the following May.

"I loved it (in Europe)," Burch would say later, "and I never would have left but for the war."

John Sanford was an American with a farm and stable based in New York. By 1913, racing had returned to the state. Sanford had an American trainer, Hollie Hughes, but found a spot for Burch as stable agent.

One morning at Saratoga in 1915, Sanford was observing his horses in training. Burch, leaning on the rail, diverted attention from Hughes' string and pointed to a colt in another: "That colt is going to beat every three-year-old in the country next year." Sanford jumped for the bait. "Who is he?" he asked, and immediately authorized a purchase, without establishing a price limit. Burch said the colt, George Smith, could not be bought at the time, but he commented that the owner did not tend to be solvent on a consistent basis and that an opportunity might arise in the future.

Burch generally seemed to possess total recall through much of his life, and it was atypical and bothersome to him years later that he could not remember the name of the owner from whom he purchased George Smith for Sanford. It was also atypical of the gentlemanly Burch that he would repeat to Turf writer Bob Horwood, as he did in 1957, the salacious story that the former owner of George Smith at one point had been denied a license in Maryland because of an unpaid bill to a Baltimore madam. Burch had forgotten the name, but not the spice.

That owner whose identity slipped Burch's memory was Edward McBride of Baltimore, who bought the colt in 1914 as part of a package of yearlings. George Smith had been bred by Fred Forsythe of Harrodsburg, Kentucky, and by his brother-in-law, Christopher Chinn, brother to the storied horseman, gambler, and raconteur Colonel Phil Chinn.

Burch and Sanford bided their time and, sure enough, before the year (1915) was out, they were able to buy George Smith for $20,000. "It was too much money for a poor man to refuse," McBride said, "but Mr. Sanford [of a noted textile business] can afford to pay it after he sells a few more rolls of carpet."

George Smith won nine of twelve starts at two and the following year fulfilled Burch's prediction when Hughes sent him out to win the Kentucky Derby. It was an indication that this Burch fellow had developed an eye for a horse and a feel for his craft.

George Smith was still in action as a five-year-old, when responsibility for the stable passed into Burch's hands following expansion of the outfit and Hughes' departure for wartime military service. The horse had never been totally sound after his Derby, so Burch went to a blacksmith whom the noted trainer Sam Hildreth — himself a former farrier and a stickler on feet — was reported to pay $5,000 annually for his expertise. Burch had a bar plate made for George Smith, and the horse soon landed a milestone prize for himself and an ever-lasting memory for his young trainer. Under 130 pounds, George Smith won the mile and a half Bowie Handicap, defeating two other Kentucky Derby winners, Omar Khayyam and Exterminator. He gave fifteen pounds to Omar Khayyam and ten (in actual weight) to the three-year-old Exterminator. The exceptional fifteen-horse field also included Stromboli, The Porter, and War Cloud.

Aside from the hoof trouble, Burch revered George Smith as "a perfect race horse, in disposition, in health, in everything. He never coughed in his life, though we had two epidemics in the stable when he was there."

The son of Out of Reach—Consuelo II, by Bradwardine, won three other stakes at five that year. George Smith lingered as a special hero in Burch's memory. In 1978 *Daily Racing Form*'s obituary of Preston Burch mused, "To his death, Preston Burch was not sure that George Smith, on his best days, was not the best American Thoroughbred of all time." Man o' War, Citation, and Secretariat had been amid the innumerable caravan of champions in the interim, but the imprint of a special racehorse in one's own hands can be a lasting, beloved image.

Burch later described Sanford as a gambler who was drawn especially to getting a price on maidens. He recalled being stunned by instructions resulting from an uncommon string of success with young horses: The non-starters and other non-winners were to be sent home so Sanford would have some maidens to bet on the next spring!

In 1920, two years after George Smith's victories at age five, Burch took a new job. Aside from George Smith, there had been few major successes for Sanford. Burch's new boss was the Nevada Stock Farm of George Wingfield. Burch once remarked on the range of his owners: "John Sanford was a bettor. George Wingfield was a Nevada political boss. Mrs. Sloane was a grand sportslady." (Mrs. Isabel Dodge Sloane was his last boss as a trainer and one of several distinguished patrons of the Turf for whom Burch trained.)

The relationship with Wingfield lasted eight years. The best horse Burch trained for Wingfield was General Thatcher, who won six stakes from Maryland to Canada in 1924 and 1925. General Thatcher gained more prestige from a loss, however, as he ran second to Vigil in the 1923 Preakness Stakes. Two years later Burch won the Hotel Sinton Stakes and Christmas Handicap with General Thatcher's two-year-old half sister, Miss Thatcher. A 1951 article by historian Joe Palmer identified Miss Thatcher as the first filly to record a time as good as 1:11 for six furlongs in a race around a turn.

By 1929 Burch had moved on to train the Dixiana Farm stable of auto-body manufacturing tycoon Charles T. Fisher. During the 1920s *The Blood-Horse* stakes-winner tracking system kicked in, and in 1928 Burch was credited with the first of sixty-eight stakes-winning horses under that system. That year he won stakes with Chicleight and Voltear. Chicleight won the Pimlico Nursery and Voltear won the American National Juvenile (at $10,000 a considerable prize at the time) and Dearborn Stakes. The following year Voltear won the $10,000 Chesapeake Stakes. In 1929 Strolling Player won the Pimlico Fall Serial for Burch.

BREEDER, OWNER, TRAINER

In 1930 Preston Burch was training a public stable, and his owners included himself. That year he brought to the races his homebred Tambour, a daughter of General Thatcher. Tambour's dam, Castanet, had been a purchase that came with a bonus. She was entered in a Saratoga sale with the presumption that she had failed to get in foal to the cover of the great stallion Fair Play, sire of Man o' War and a good deal more. Castanet was by Frizzle, a son of the great mare Frizette. Burch evaluated Castanet as a breeding prospect he might get for between $600 and $800, but he kept going when she exceeded that range, and he bought her for $1,300. It turned out that she was in foal to Fair Play, after all, and Burch sold her resulting foal for $7,000.

To the cover of his old star General Thatcher, Castanet produced a 1928 filly whom Burch named Tambour. He was breeder, owner, and trainer of Tambour, and when she won the Selima Stakes in the fall of 1930, he had a very nice filly and an owner who could cause him no trouble. The Selima was only five years old at the time, but with champions Fair Star and Bateau already among its winners, it had considerable prestige. The winner's share of $26,070 (more than three times George Smith's Bowie Handicap purse) might well have made the Selima Preston Burch's favorite race at the time. The owner's 100 percent minus the trainer's 10 percent still came out to 100 percent. (Of course, jockey Laverne Fator had to be paid, too.) Burch had lost his father only four years before and must have wished W.P. could have seen that moment.

The following year, 1931, Tambour became Preston Burch's first champion, as trainer, breeder, owner, and — in the language of proxies — any and all of them. (She would be the only champion he ever trained.) The key victories in Tambour's three-year-old season came in the Coaching Club American Oaks and the Potomac Handicap. The CCA Oaks had been inaugurated in 1917 and because its founders included a number of distinguished Eastern horsemen and coachmen, it was a highly prestigious race from the inception. Its added money in 1931 was only $3,500 as compared to the Potomac Handicap's handsome $20,000, but the first prize for the Oaks was $15,000.

The Potomac found Tambour facing older males, including the Preakness winner Mate. Also in the field was the popular Maryland distaffer Tred Avon. Going a mile and one-sixteenth, Tambour was 13-1 in such company, but she beat Tred Avon by a length to win it. Mate was third.

Despite the glamour Tambour brought to his career, the workaday horseman years later, as author, used her to make a point about so mundane a topic as capped hocks: "Now and then a horse will kick the walls of his stall or otherwise injure the back of his hocks, and develop what are called capped hocks. He generally will carry this blemish for the rest of his life, but it won't interfere with his racing. Both hocks on my good mare Tambour were slightly capped. A great many horses in Europe have capped hocks, caused by bumping their hocks against brick stable walls, as nearly all the stables in Europe are built of brick."

In 1933 Tambour, at five, added the Delaware Handicap, a race name that under a modern revival would represent one of Preston Burch's last great moments before retirement. Tambour won thirteen of thirty-one races in her career and earned $80,415.

Other stakes winners trained by Burch in the late 1920s and early 1930s included Sweep All, with whom he won the 1930 Endurance Handicap for Fisher. The owner decided to concentrate on Midwest racing, and Burch gave up the horses. The following year Sweep All, trained by Clyde Van Dusen, finished second to Twenty Grand in the 1931 Kentucky Derby.

The year 1932 saw Burch win stakes with a half-dozen individual horses. His owners included one of the most distinguished Turfmen of the day, Walter M. Jeffords Sr.

Jeffords was undoubtedly impressed by Tambour, for he was a great fan of the CCA Oaks, which he had won three times within four years a few seasons earlier. In the late 1930s Burch would win a running of the CCA Oaks for Jeffords with Creole Maid. Other owners to send horses to Burch included Cary Grayson and Samuel Ross, who had also had horses with Burch's father, plus William du Pont Jr. and du Pont's sister, Mrs. Randolph Scott (better known as Marion du Pont Scott).

Burch's highlights in 1932 included landing one of New York's top prizes, the Suburban Handicap, with White Clover II for du Pont's Foxcatcher Farm. White Clover II also won the Riggs Handicap. For Jeffords, Burch won the Withers that year with Boatswain, a Man o' War colt. Burch also had kept his hand in the steeplechasing game and that year won the Billy Barton Steeplechase with Tereus.

The next year, 1933, saw an episode Burch still found amusing enough to recall when he was honored by the Thoroughbred Club of America in 1973. His stable in 1933 included a pair of steeplechasers for Mrs. Scott, Annapolis and Battleship. Both were sons of Man o' War, who was a linchpin in Mrs. Scott's breeding patterns through many years. There was a two-day hunt meeting in Brookline, Massachusetts, and both horses were sent up. On day one, Battleship won the National Hunt Cup under future Hall of Fame jump jockey Carroll Bassett. (Mrs. Scott later sent Battleship to England, where he won the Grand National Steeplechase for trainer Reginald Hobbs.) The next day's card included two races that Burch thought fit Annapolis, both on the flat. Burch asked Mrs. Scott which one she would prefer to win, and she gave the savvy answer that the easier one would be fine but asked what Burch thought. He said he thought Annapolis could win both.

"Oh, you wouldn't run Annapolis in two races [in one day]," Burch recalled as her response. "That wouldn't be sporting." To which Burch replied that he thought it would be very sporting, indeed.

Burch continued: "About that time, S.J. Holloway, one of the old trainers, walked by, and Mrs. Scott asked him if he thought Annapolis could win two races on the same day. Holloway thought a moment and then asked, 'What does Burch think?' Mrs. Scott told him that I thought Annapolis could do it all right: 'Then I think so, too,' Holloway said."

So, on June 17, 1933, Bassett brought Annapolis home by five lengths in a mile and one-sixteenth flat race, the first event on the card. The seven-year-old horse was returned to the barn, walked under a cooler, and given a carefully monitored amount of water. He was resaddled for the third race, at a mile and a half. Bassett remounted and brought him home by four lengths.

In 1934 Burch gave up his public stable and signed on to train for the Jeffords stable as private trainer. He recalled that Tommy Hitchcock asked him around that time if he still had horses for Mrs. Scott. Burch said he did not, that his brother Selby was training for her, and that he, Preston, was only connected in an advisory capacity.

"Oh, just interfering, eh?" was Hitchcock's reply, which Burch remembered later and quipped, "I often think of that comment now, when someone asks for my advice on training or breeding."

In 1934 Burch launched the highly successful career of the Jeffords homebred Firethorn (Sun Briar—Baton Rouge, by Man o' War). At two that year, Firethorn won the Walden Handicap, and the following season he climaxed an excellent season when jockey Eddie Arcaro brought him home in the two-mile Jockey Club Gold Cup. Firethorn had been second to Omaha in both the Preakness and Belmont. With the Triple Crown winner on the sidelines, Firethorn also won another of the autumn distance tests, the Lawrence Realization, as well as the Washington Handicap. He was rated second to Omaha among three-year-olds.

The following year at four, Firethorn won only one stakes, but it was a big one, Burch's second Suburban Handicap. Again at five in 1937, Firethorn won only one stakes, but it was a second Jockey Club Gold Cup. He followed Mad Hatter and Dark Secret as the third horse to win two runnings of that event, which had been inaugurated in 1920. Firethorn won only eight of thirty-five races, but several of the eight were highly significant. He earned $74,750.

The year Firethorn was five and won his second Gold Cup, his juvenile half sister Creole Maid, by Pharamond II, won the Schuylerville and Adirondack, both Saratoga fixtures. The next year, 1938, Creole Maid won the revered Coaching Club American Oaks. Creole Maid was beaten later as Brookmeade Stable's Handcuff added the Delaware Oaks and Alabama to a pair of other major wins. Burch one day would train for Brookmeade, but in 1938 the stable was a competitor at the highest echelon, and Handcuff excelled above Burch's candidate and was the three-year-old filly champion.

In 1936 Burch won the Pimlico Futurity with Matey and the Matron with Wand, both Man o' War juveniles and Jeffords homebreds. The following year he saddled yet another Man o' War filly, Regal Lily, to win the historic Alabama Stakes. Regal Lily also won the Gazelle that year.

A drought of two years without a stakes winner ensued after Creole Maid. Burch went back to a public stable. In 1941 he broke through again with the first of four stakes-winning campaigns with Deering Howe's Cassis, who won the Christiana Stakes at two that year. Cassis would win a total of eight stakes over the years. Speed was his hole card, and he won two runnings of the Fall Highweight Handicap and one of the Vosburgh (in a dead heat with Paperboy). The career of Cassis overlapped that of Howe's True North, whom Burch saddled for stakes victories in three seasons spread from 1942 through 1946.

In 1945 True North defeated the emerging Calumet Farm champion Armed in the Fall Highweight while carrying 140 pounds. The following year True North carried 130 and was second to his barnmate Cassis (116) in the same race. True North won a half-dozen stakes, of which one had sentimental value, for it was the W.P. Burch Memorial in Maryland. Preston Burch also had won that race in 1936, with Indomitable.

The 1943 season had been a strong one for Burch, for he won stakes with four horses. Three of them were juveniles, and two won major events. Mrs. Ames darted to early victories in the National Stallion, Fashion, and Astoria stakes for Henry Lustig's Longchamps Stable, and Rodney Stone won the Sanford Stakes for Harry La Montagne.

The following year Mrs. Isabel Dodge Sloane invited Burch to succeed Hugh Fontaine as her trainer. Burch accepted, and he thus set out on what would prove the last thirteen years of his career as an active racetracker. He was by then a handsome gentleman of sixty. He had a countenance somewhat reminiscent of John Wayne, but with less of the bravado inherent in the iconic actor's persona. In photographs, sans hat and with spectacles, Burch could bring to mind a kindly professor.

THE BARD OF BROOKMEADE

Mrs. Sloane was the owner of Brookmeade Stable and a decade earlier, in 1934, had become the first female to lead American owners. Her horses that year included Kentucky Derby winner Cavalcade, and Brookmeade horses earned a total of $251,138. Mrs. Sloane was a daughter of a co-founder of Dodge Motor Company, and in 1920 she received an inheritance valued at $7 million. A few years later the value of her holdings increased markedly when a bank syndicate bought the Dodge firm for $146 million. Mrs. Sloane had a lovely farm, Brookmeade, in Virginia, and also boarded mares in Kentucky.

Press announcements at the time Burch was named to succeed Hugh Fontaine as Brookmeade's trainer indicated that he would be giving up all his other horses. However, Burch continued to win major stakes for others as well as Brookmeade for several more years.

The year 1944 found Burch saddling seven stakes winners. For Brookmeade, he sent out Dare Me against one of the most potent fillies of all time, Calumet's Twilight Tear. Dare Me was second to the champion in the CCA Oaks and late in the season got in a victory over Twilight Tear in the Maryland Handicap.

Despite Twilight Tear's dominance, her early autumn break provided a window of opportunity for other three-year-old fillies. Burch took advantage with Donita's First, owned by Longchamps Stable. Donita's First won the Beldame Stakes and Ladies Handicap, two of the most important distaff races in New York.

Also in 1944, Burch won the late-season juvenile race, the Remsen, with Brookmeade's homebred Great Power.

The following year saw the first of four stakes-winning campaigns of a champion Preston Burch bred but did not own or train. Gallorette, like Tambour, was among nine stakes winners Burch bred as part of his sideline, and she was a champion extraordinaire. The trail that produced Gallorette illustrated the reality that good Thoroughbred female families are revered but that individuals from those families might elude high visibility and fall toward obscurity. It also demonstrates that Preston Burch was a pedigree maven, something his son, Elliott Burch, later said appealed to him about his father.

In 1930 William du Pont Jr. had paid $11,000 for Gallette at the Saratoga yearling sale. The filly, bred and offered by William Woodward Sr.'s Belair Stud, developed ankle trouble, so Burch recommended that du Pont give her time. When Burch next saw her, Gallette had been relegated to a jumping race, and then du Pont put her in a sale, where she brought only $250. Burch was unaware of the opportunity to purchase the filly who had a superb pedigree, being by the rising champion sire Sir Gallahad III. The fact that Gallette was a half sister to the dam of Triple Crown winner Omaha was not yet known.

A couple of years later Burch saw the mare advertised in *Morning Telegraph* as part of a two-mare package, and he bought the two for $2,500. He returned Gallette to training and ran her in claiming races, but a friend notified him that there was talk about her attractive pedigree and Burch had better not risk her again. Burch began to use the mare in foal-sharing arrangements. Several such deals produced disappointing results, but then W.L. Brann came onto the scene. Brann had bred the 1939 Preakness winner and two-time Horse of the Year Challedon by crossing his stallion Challenger II with a Sir Gallahad III mare. It was an easy cross to bear.

"I know where there is one [a Sir Gallahad III mare]," Burch said. "I've got her."

Fending off Brann's entreaties to sell him Gallette outright, Burch worked out a sharing plan, owners of mare and sire to alternate ownership of the foals. Thus, in 1942, Gallette foaled a Challenger II filly whose breeder of record was Preston Burch but whose owner would be W.L. Brann. She was named Gallorette, and she was such an enduring champion that she was voted the best American distaffer of the first half of the twentieth century in a poll of the American Trainers Association. Burch was a mainstay in that organization — its president for seven years — and therefore felt constrained from voting for a horse he had bred.

Gallette's later foals included Gallita, a full sister to Gallorette. Gallita foaled Claiborne Farm's Garden States Stakes and American Derby winner Nadir. Burch's foals out of the alternating sequence from Gallette were a modest winner and a foal that never raced, prompting a friend to scold, "I thought you had more sense than to go partners with a millionaire."

In 1946 Burch was still training some horses for other owners, and his two-year-olds included Howe's exciting prospect Donor (Challedon—Orissa, by Purchase). Donor was entered in a $7,000 claiming race in his debut, a bit of risk management employed because the Jamaica (New York) meeting was only four days old; few would have heard about Donor and few owners would be eligible to claim him (legally, anyway) because only owners who had started a horse at the meeting could enter claims.

Donor won his debut, escaped the halterman, and by year's end had won seven of twelve, including the Champagne, Sapling, World's Playground, Sanford, and Albany. In the Champagne, the runner-up and third-place colts were destined to be classic winners the next year, i.e., Belmont Stakes winner Phalanx and Kentucky Derby winner Jet Pilot. Despite that record, Donor was rated behind ten other colts on the Experimental Free Handicap, which was topped by Double Jay, Cosmic Bomb, and the filly First Flight.

Donor was to win nine more stakes through the age of five and earn $367,560 to rank among the leaders for some years. Burch, however, only trained him at two. By the time Donor won stakes at three, he had been turned over to George Odom — former student of Burch's father — as Preston Burch concentrated on Brookmeade horses.

Ironically, until that time, in the years since signing on with Brookmeade, Burch had been identified as the breeder of another owner's contemporary champion and as trainer of a number of winners at least as important as anything Brookmeade had.

Among the gems in the Brookmeade broodmare band when Burch came aboard was the Sir Gallahad III mare Omayya. She was the dam of the major winner Pomayya, who predated Burch's appointment, and also of Dare Me, with whom Burch defeated Twilight Tear in the 1944 Maryland Handicap.

Omayya's 1945 foal was the Whirlaway gelding Dart By, with whom Burch won the Mayflower Stakes. Although the New England circuit today is decidedly below the top racing in this country, that was not the case then, and Dart By's 1947 Mayflower offered $25,000 in added money. Dart By ran a total of 126 times and won sixteen races. He won no further stakes until he was five and burst out with another $25,000-added triumph, in the All American Handicap, as well as two other scores to do his bit for the team's emergence as the leading stable.

In 1947, the year Dart By won the Mayflower, Burch's total of five stakes winners in the stable also included another major two-year-old winner. Inheritance, a daughter of Triple Crown winner War Admiral, won the Matron Stakes on the disqualification of champion filly Bewitch. Inheritance, who ran a fine race to be beaten by only a neck, earned $36,060 in that victory. She had been purchased from breeder Hal Price Headley for $25,000 as a yearling. Burch was involved in yearling selection as well as advising on matings for Brookmeade.

Also in 1947, Burch won another important juvenile filly race, Slumber Song's Frizette, and the juvenile gelding Inseparable won the Tremont and Sanford. (Inseparable had been bred by Elmendorf Farm and was a high-priced Keeneland summer sale yearling at $32,000. He won stakes again at three, then later was sold to Hasty House Stable as an older horse and continued winning, for trainer Harry Trotsek.)

In 1949 Burch again won stakes with five horses. One of them was More Sun (Sun Again—The Damsel, by Flag Pole), who won the $25,000 Graduation Stakes and the Saratoga Special and Grand Union Hotel stakes at two. Another was Chains (by Firethorn and out of champion Handcuff), who won the $25,000 Dixie Handicap, $20,000 Merchants' and Citizens' Handicap, and Olympic Handicap.

That same year Burch's communications skills were tapped by *Daily Racing Form*, which asked that he fill in for columnist Charlie Hatton who was on vacation. A number of individuals in racing were recruited to fill in for Hatton's column, entitled "Judge's Stand."

Preston Burch's piece was articulate, intuitive, and informative:

"Most people around the race track will tell you that no two men train alike and that it is almost impossible to get two trainers to agree on anything. This, of course, is only partly true. Because horses are as different as people, no two can be trained in the same way. One must never lose sight of the fact that he is dealing with a live animal, who feels, sees, hears, and thinks. A horse can read voices like people read books. He understands at once from your tone of voice whether you intend to be friend, ugly, timid, or firm. Seldom is a horse found who will not respond to kind treatment. On the other hand, a horse with any spirit at all will fight back if badly treated."

The column went on, setting out easily grasped, logic-supported detail similar to the flow of chapters in the book that would follow only a few years later.

TOPPING THE LEADER BOARD

Mrs. Sloane had first won the title as America's leading owner in 1934. Now, in 1950, she returned to the top. Brookmeade horses earned $651,399, and trainer Burch led his profession's standings, too. The numbers were almost identical, for few earnings were accrued to Brookmeade-owned horses sent to other divisions. Burch's total as trainer that year was $637,754. He was credited with ninety-six wins.

Despite his success, 1950 also was a year in which Burch had health problems that consigned him for a time to a hospital. Much was made of his studying condition books while bedridden. Elliott Burch, the son who eventually would succeed him, recalled that, "Dad was sick, but had horses all over the country. He had a foreman [Clarence Parrish] and three assistants, including myself, and I helped serve as his eyes and ears. He knew what all the horses were doing at all times, and he placed them meticulously, like an expert chess player." Parrish, the key assistant, was in daily phone contact with the boss.

Highlights of the year included the triumphs of Greek Ship. A son of Heliopolis—Boat, by Man o' War, Greek Ship was bred in Kentucky by Harrie B. Scott, at whose Shandon Farm Brookmeade boarded mares, and the colt was purchased for Mrs. Sloane and Burch by Kentuckian Cy White for $23,000 at the Keeneland summer sale.

At two, Greek Ship won four of nine races, with his three stakes scores coming in the Mayflower, Wakefield, and Flash. He was assigned 120 pounds on the Experimental Free Handicap, tied for ninth, six pounds below topper Middleground.

The typical Brookmeade routine at the time prescribed spending the winter in Aiken, South Carolina, but during the winter of 1949–50, Greek Ship was one of three horses Brookmeade sent to Hialeah. Such a move indicated they were being looked upon as potential Kentucky Derby horses. The others were Sunglow and More Sun. Mrs. Sloane had won the Derby in 1934 with Cavalcade, but Burch had had no luck in the race. His record was sixteenth with General Thatcher in 1923, sixth with Voltear in 1929, tenth with Commonwealth in 1935, and tenth with Liberty Road in 1947.

Greek Ship and Sunglow found the competition at Hialeah tough enough that Burch repaired to Louisiana, where Greek Ship won the Louisiana Derby with Sunglow second. Yes, indeed, this was a better place, but one cannot be a Derby horse and avoid the best forever.

Mrs. Sloane had fond recollections of the Chesapeake Stakes as a prep for the Derby, as Cavalcade had won it over the same two that were second and third to him in the Derby. Also, the Chesapeake had been won in 1937 by emerging Triple Crown winner War Admiral and in 1948 by another Triple Crown winner, Citation.

To Maryland went Greek Ship and Sunglow, and they ran one-two again, but in reverse order, Sunglow winning the Chesapeake with a seven-pound pull in the weights. The historical importance of the race notwithstanding, Joe Palmer observed in *American Race Horses of 1950* that the field "was not really a strong one and Greek Ship was shipped to Kentucky with no more than a faint hope."

The hope was extinguished when he ran fourth in the Derby Trial, and he was taken out of the big race. Sunglow was third in the Trial and was left in the Derby, in which he ran well enough to be fourth, beaten about four and a half lengths at 27-1 as Middleground won in the second-fastest clocking to that time, 2:01 3/5.

Any thought that Sunglow thus had taken over as Brookmeade's top three-year-old proved mistaken. Sunglow (Sun Again—Rosern, by Mad Hatter), an $8,000 yearling bought from Mereworth Farm, was destined to greater distinction, but it was not as a racehorse in 1950. He added two more stakes wins to his Chesapeake, winning the Discovery and Saranac, whereas Greek Ship made a pattern of beating older horses more often than beating other three-year-olds.

Within a month of having been sent, as it were, slinking out of the Kentucky Derby picture, Greek Ship audaciously whipped his elders in one of the most important of New York handicaps, the Metropolitan. The field was a good one, including My Request, Piet, and Cochise, and although Greek Ship carried only 106 pounds, nothing in the field was giving him weight when the weight-for-age scale was considered.

Thereafter, Greek Ship won two more important races against his elders and only the Choice Stakes against his own age group. The victories against older horses came in the Monmouth Handicap and the Empire City Gold Cup. In the Gold Cup, he and Sunglow formed the favored entry, and Greek Ship came rushing up to win by a half-length over Palestinian, with Better Self third. The $39,700 purse was his largest and raised his total to $140,175, which led the stable in that year of pre-eminence.

In the two-year-old filly division Mrs. Sloane and Burch had a star in 1950 in Atalanta. She was another from Omayya and was sired by the 1943 Triple Crown winner Count Fleet. Atalanta won early at two and later picked up two important stakes wins, in the Schuylerville and Matron — the latter regarded at that time as the filly counterpart to the Futurity. She was beaten in the Demoiselle and Marguerite, however, paving the way for Aunt Jinny to prevail as champion two-year-old filly. (Atalanta was sold to

John W. Galbreath, owner of Darby Dan Farm, for whom she won her later stakes victories.)

The remaining stakes winners for Brookmeade and Burch in 1950 were Ouija, a three-year-old filly who won the Diana Handicap, and Going Away, who added the $25,000 Atlantic City Turf Handicap and $15,000 Pageant Handicap to the stable's coffers.

THE PROBLEM-CHILD CLASSIC WINNER

Burch might have been able to direct the workings of the stable from his sickbed for a time in 1950, but his triumphant remolding of Bold into a Preakness winner the following year required Burch to be there in person.

Bold made for interesting reading in *Training Thoroughbred Horses*. If Burch had been tempted to invent an example of horses' individualities and repertoire of problems to make his points, he hardly could have come up with a plausible case to match Bold. The deal was, of course, that Bold was a real horse.

As Brookmeade homebreds went, Bold was not particularly well bred, being by By Jimminy—Little Rebel, by John P. Grier, but by coincidence the pedigree had meaning to one Preston Burch. The fifth dam of Bold was Red Cross IV, whom Burch had purchased for $25,000, a record price in France at the time, back when he was working overseas for John Sanford. The outbreak of World War I precluded Red Cross IV from racing, but she became an important progenitor, and her descendant Little Rebel was a Brookmeade mare.

Prior to trainer-author-professor Burch addressing the subject of Bold in print, Joe Palmer noted in *American Race Horses of 1951*, that, at two, "Bold was always regarded as a colt with a good deal of ability, and he showed up excellently at the Aiken Trials in March. But after this he was a trial himself. Through most of 1950, he alternated with bucked shins and colds, and at one time popped a splint, for variety."

Nevertheless, when Bold finally got to the races late in his juvenile year, he won one of three and finished first in the Endurance Handicap, although disqualified for interference after the stakes. He was noticed on the Experimental Free Handicap, on which his 115 assignment was eleven pounds from Uncle Miltie's top rank and behind a total of ten colts.

In his book on training, Burch took up the subject of Bold, who "was troubled with splints, bucked shins, and sore feet, and moreover was a difficult colt to restrain in his works. However, he had exceptional speed, as some of the workouts indicate. He usually was walked the day after a work, then was galloped until the next workout."

Burch provides a daily log, of which highlights include such head-shaking, tight-lipped excerpts as:

Inclined to bear out ... hard to control ... a bit too fast for the stage of preparation he was in ...

A one-cup blinker was tried, but he still was hard to hold and showed an inclination to bear out slightly ...

(March 19) four furlongs, barefoot, reverse way of the five-furlong training track, :56 2/5 ...

(April 5) tired badly ... boy couldn't hold him during the first part of the work ...

(April 14) Belmont Park training track, reverse way ... galloped out five furlongs in 1:03 4/5, pulled up. Bold's preparation was in view of the Toboggan Handicap ...

Then came an extraordinarily bright moment:

"(May 1) one mile, right way of the track ... one mile, 1:40 2/5, eased up nine furlongs in 1:55 4/5 ... This work led to decision to start Bold in the Preakness."

Burch, perhaps wondering if he would be sicker in 1951 than in 1950, shipped Bold to Pimlico, where the horse won an overnight race by twelve lengths on May 9. In the Preakness Prep on May 14, Bold was beaten a neck by Alerted at a mile and one-sixteenth, and the trainer noted what a bad ride he got.

Then, more finesse was needed:

(May 15) Shoes pulled because of sore feet. Walked. Feet treated.

(May 16) Walked. Feet treated.

(May 17) Galloped barefoot. Shod that afternoon.

(May 18) Five furlongs, eased up, in 1:02.

(May 19) Won 1 3/16-mile Preakness by seven lengths, leading all the way. Counterpoint second, Alerted third. Wore one-cup blinker which he always wore when racing or working the right way of the track ... [Jockey Eddie Arcaro was called in to ride Bold in the Preakness.]

Bold got clear of the field on the run to the first turn of the Preakness, and he was comfortably turning back bids most of the way. In the stretch he simply continued as Arcaro felt plenty of horse under him and was in complete control, winning by seven lengths. The victory was worth $83,110.

Bold bucked his shins again in his prep for the Belmont and bore out badly. He got back about a month later and won the Saranac Handicap.

Bold's body, or mind, could not stay right for long, however. After the Saranac, he bore out in his prep for the Travers and missed the big Saratoga race. He went through the rail in a workout, injuring a rider, and then fell back to twelfth of thirteen in the Empire City. Bold finished the year with three wins in seven starts and his career record was four wins in ten starts and earnings of $107,460.

The year after Bold's Preakness victory, when Burch thought he had him nearing a return to the races, the colt was turned out in a paddock at Brookmeade in Virginia. He was struck dead by a bolt of lightning.

Bold was one of nine stakes winners for Brookmeade in 1951. Aside from the Preakness, the most important event won by the stable that year was the $50,000-added Widener Handicap, in which Sunglow finally moved up a major prestige notch in defeating Three Rings and County Delight.

Also in 1951, More Sun, mentioned earlier as a tentative classic consideration at three the previous year, came back from a blank stakes year to add the Fleetwing Handicap. Greek Ship, the star of 1950, was back at four to win the $25,000 All American Handicap; at five in 1952, he would win that race again as well as the Atlantic City Turf, Ocean City, and Royal Palm handicaps as he raised his earnings to $312,050.

Also in 1951, Picador won the Atlantic City Turf and Ocean City handicaps en route to a career of four stakes wins as he would add the Bougainvillea and Hialeah Turf Cup on Hialeah's classy grass course.

Other stakes winners for Burch in 1951 included Steadfast, who took the $30,000 Jersey Handicap, and War King who won the Vosburgh Handicap.

THE FINAL YEARS

Preston Burch was nearing his seventieth birthday when *Training Thoroughbred Horses* was published. He was four years from retirement as active trainer for Brookmeade, but such was his status that he would be called upon as an adviser by various parties for many years. He lived another quarter-century after the book was published and was accurately perceived as one of the sport's treasures.

In the final half-dozen years between his classic win with Bold and his retirement as trainer, Burch continued to have a strong stable of stakes winners every year. There were never fewer than four stakes-winning horses attributed to him annually in those years until 1957, the year he handed the baton to son Elliott.

During those seasons:

Sky Ship won Gulfstream Park's first running of the Florida Derby, quickly established as a major classics prep; Tritium won Burch another running of the revered Selima; the durable Sunglow added two more stakes at the age of six.

Turf specialist County Clare won five stakes; First Aid won the Hibiscus and Bahamas at three, then worked on through three more stakes-winning seasons that included wins in the Merchants' and Citizens' and Whitney.

Capeador won the Tropical Handicap and three other stakes at four in

1954; Gandharva won the 1954 Spinaway at two and three more stakes at three and four; Encore won three Florida stakes at two and four.

Floral Park won the last stakes credited to Preston Burch, the 1957 Bellerose Handicap.

The obvious bellwether performances of those years, however, came with Preston Burch's handling of Flower Bowl and Sailor. In 1956 this pair contrived to win three of the greatest races the man had ever won in his half-century-plus training. What an exclamatory farewell it was to have Sailor defeat Nashua in the Gulfstream Park Handicap and add the John B. Campbell Memorial Handicap and then to plot so long in advance toward Flower Bowl's victory in the richest distaff race in existence at the time.

Around the time Preston Burch was to be honored as Testimonial Dinner honor guest of the Thoroughbred Club of America, his son Elliott, by then a famed trainer in his own right, was asked to write a column for *Daily Racing Form*. Elliott keyed in on Sailor and Flower Bowl:

> Sailor had an innate ability, but also a strong predisposition to unsoundness. Basically, the horse was a sprinter, but through careful handling, Preston Burch got him to run several top races at 1 1/4 miles ...
>
> Flower Bowl was a lovely mare with a good disposition, who did not break her maiden until she was three. I remember my father training her for a stakes race in 1956. He told the exercise boy to go a good mile on the Tuesday before the race, and the boy went too slow. She was returned to the barn, and walked for twenty to thirty minutes. Dad then put another boy on her, and he took her to the main track where she stepped a sharp five-furlongs. I remember saying to Dad that people would say that he was crazy and had ruined the mare; but his genius prevailed. The following Saturday she ran the race of her life to win the Delaware Handicap.

Sailor (Eight Thirty—Flota, by Jack High) was a foal of 1952, in the same wonderful American foal crop as Nashua, Swaps, Summer Tan, Saratoga, Traffic Judge, and Bardstown. He was a problem from the beginning, but Preston Burch was a problem solver with many years experience. Sailor had osselets at two but came on as a stakes-class horse early at three to win the Toboggan Handicap. He grabbed a quarter in that race, however, and was put aside again. At the end of the season, at three in 1955, he put together an impressive series of wins in the Fall Highweight, Roamer, and Pimlico Special.

The following winter at Hialeah saw a record crowd of some 42,000 turn out for the four-year-old debut of 1955 Horse of the Year Nashua in the Widener Handicap at Hialeah. Sailor (119 pounds) was in the fray to the very end and was third in a four-horse blanket finish as Nashua (127) prevailed by a head over Social Outcast.

In his next race, the Gulfstream Park Handicap, Sailor got ten pounds from Nashua and won by nearly two lengths. He dueled with Find early and drew out, as Nashua finished fifth.

The John B. Campbell Memorial Handicap in Maryland was then one of the winter's top handicaps in the East, and Sailor was sent back to the state where Preston Burch had won so many races during his long career. Sailor led all the way to win over a strong field that included Joe Jones, Fisherman, and Jet Action, but he bobbled near the sixteenth pole. The Brookmeade star was finished, with a broken bone in the left fore. He was sent to stud at John W. Galbreath's Darby Dan Farm in Kentucky with twelve wins in twenty-one starts and earnings of $321,075.

Flower Bowl (Alibhai—Flower Bed, by Beau Pere) was challenged by Preston Burch to contest races against the best of her division, but at the end of her three-year-old season in 1955 she had won only three of thirteen races. The next year, Burch continued to test Flower Bowl against the best, and she won two of nine races prior to the one and a quarter-mile Delaware Handicap. The richest distaff race in the world at that time, the Delaware offered a purse of $115,000.

Carrying 112 pounds, the four-year-old Flower Bowl received weight from most of a strong field that included Miz Clementine, Searching, Dotted Line, High Voltage, Blue Sparkler, and Amoret. Flower Bowl put in the powerful closing performance Burch had long felt she was capable of doing, and she came from eleven lengths back to win by two. Twenty-three years after Tambour had won the Delaware Handicap in a totally different context, Burch had won the race again in its exalted status.

Flower Bowl later won the historic Ladies Handicap to prove her crossing the Delaware winner's circle was well deserved, and she was retired with seven wins from thirty-two starts and earnings of $174,625.

EPILOGUE

The year following those smashing victories by Sailor and Flower Bowl, Preston Burch retired. His son Elliott took over. Preston continued as an adviser to Brookmeade and others and, one hopes, enjoyed his status as a revered icon of the Turf. He lived to the age of ninety-three and passed away in 1978. He had been preceded in death by his brother Selby, also a trainer, and by his first wife. His widow, Mary, survived, as did sons William and Elliott.

As set out in the introduction of this volume, the focus is on trainers whose careers can be placed logically in the first half of the twentieth century. Were the focus toward a later era, Preston Burch's son Elliott would command a chapter of his own. Elliott took over the Brookmeade horses in 1957 and within a few years had had his hands on more truly outstanding horses than his father and grandfather together had enjoyed in almost a century in racing.

Elliott's career on the racetrack came after his father relented to helping him, for Preston Burch had thought the travel demands of a racehorse trainer were antithetical to the pursuit of a supportive family life. "He just followed me and watched what I did, and he was a natural horseman," Preston said of Elliott. "Horsemanship; that's natural with you. If you have it you have it, and if you haven't got it you can't get it. I think we all love our horses. I think we were, all three of us [father, son, grandson], more for saving our horses and having them in good condition, rather than running them as much as we could to win as much money as we could."

The Brookmeade two-year-olds of 1958 included Sunglow's son Sword Dancer, who the following year came within a photo of winning the Kentucky Derby for young Elliott Burch. Sword Dancer then won the Belmont Stakes among a series of major triumphs that included a showdown win in the Woodward over older stars Round Table and Hillsdale. Sword Dancer was Horse of the Year, and the following year Bowl of Flowers harked back to Preston Burch's final glories when she emerged as champion two-year-old filly. She was by Sailor and out of Flower Bowl. Bowl of Flowers repeated as champion at three for Elliott and eventually joined Sword Dancer in the Hall of Fame.

Mrs. Sloane died in 1962, and Elliott Burch then was hired to train Paul Mellon's Rokeby Stable. The trainer took Rokeby to new heights, with the Belmont victory of Quadrangle and Horse of the Year campaigns of Arts and Letters (his third Belmont winner) and Fort Marcy, as well as other championships by Run the Gantlet and Key to the Mint. Arts and Letters and Fort Marcy also became Hall of Fame members.

Elliott Burch had to relinquish the Rokeby horses due to illness in the 1970s, but he came back to train for C.V. Whitney and won major races with horses such as Silver Buck and State Dinner before Whitney's retirement from the sport. A son, William Burch, made a promising start as the fourth generation of Burches to train, but he died as a young man.

Elliott Burch had an abiding love and respect for his father and the ability to express those sentiments:

"Although Preston Burch never had the 'great' horse in his care, he managed to stay at the top of his profession for all his active years ... Were I to characterize the man, I would mention his infinite patience, with people and horses; his complete kindness, and, to use a current word, his unflappability. As his son, I am terribly proud of him, and have never been otherwise. I count myself blessed for having such a father."

>⊱┄◈┄○┄◈┄⊰
CHAPTER 9
>⊱┄◈┄○┄◈┄⊰

BEN AND JIMMY
JONES

R
acing's most famous father-and-son training duo achieved renown at the helm of America's grandest stable. But they served their apprenticeship on the hardscrabble plains of the Midwest, getting the most out of cheap stock and learning the kind of common-sense horsemanship that would prove invaluable with the highly pedigreed horseflesh that would ultimately come their way.

"If you didn't learn, you didn't eat," Ben A. Jones once said, in recollecting his early days. "What I learned about training, I learned pretty much by myself."

Jones' father primarily concentrated on raising cattle, not racehorses. The son gradually altered emphasis on horses from a sideline to a scuffling existence and, finally, to the vehicle for a sustained level of success that by some measures was without equal.

Benjamin Allyn Jones was born on December 31, 1882, on his parents' cattle ranch outside Parnell, Missouri. In their delightful volume on Ben Jones and his son, Jimmy, co-authors Joe Hirsch and Gene Plowden identified Black Beauty as part of the beginning of the saga. *In the Winner's Circle — The Jones Boys of Calumet Farm* (Mason & Lipscomb, 1974) hastens to explain that the horse Black Beauty in the life of young Jones was not from the tale by Anna Sewell.

This specific Black Beauty was brought to town by a horse trader known as Gypsy George. Ben Jones, then in his early twenties, recognized the horse was unsound but thought he could get her right and paid $100 for her. The catch was that Gypsy George added the condition that whenever he returned he would have the option of buying her back for $150. This was all on the side of the Gypsy, for if the mare were still worthless, Gypsy George would not owe a dime whereas if Jones made something of her, there would be little profit to reward his trouble, care, and feed.

When word came that Gypsy George was about to return, the mare was in such good shape that Ben wanted to keep her, but he knew Gypsy George would want her back. He decided to drive a nail slightly into a hoof so she would walk lame. Gypsy George passed on her. It was not the last time Jones would find a way to convince a marauder to leave a certain horse alone.

Jones' father, Horace, had been something of a success story but was not so successful that his son was spared having to work his way up his own ladder. The elder Jones moved from Indiana while on his way to live in Texas and fell for the countryside of Missouri. He became a buyer for a meat packer and then developed his own cattle operation enough to open a bank and a school house. Ben attended that school, at least until a tornado demolished it, and he got through high school and played football at Colorado Agricultural College. He came out of that experience with a slight limp that lasted a lifetime.

Ben felt strapped in by the routines of a cattle ranch, and although he attended his chores, he found that racing horses — pacers or runners — had more appeal. Gambling and the occasional brawl were not distasteful in his mind, either.

The Jones Stock Farm was a cattle operation first, but it also had a half-mile track. Locals and visitors would race runners and trotters around this circuit, and such events might be tied to festive occasions also involving tents where lemonade, dances, and, eventually, contraband Prohibition drink were purveyed.

Then, the idea about a horse-racing career became more exotic. When a track opened down in Juarez, Mexico, Ben A. Jones' wandering eye regarded it as a far-off target.

Ben Jones eventually made Juarez a regular winter stop, and it was there that one of the enduring tales of his life occurred. In 1916 Pancho Villa was ravaging Mexico with his rebel magnetism, and word reached the racetrack that he and his revolutionaries were gathering up black horses wherever the animals might be found. Jones had a worthwhile black horse named Lemon Joe. Once Ben made sure his own son, Jimmy, had been hustled across the Rio Grande safely, Jones went to work on saving his meal ticket, too. He wrapped one of Lemon Joe's legs in a potato sack, which was partially filled with mud, and bandaged the ensemble to the leg. Every step Joe tried to take made him look hopelessly lame, and Pancho's lads passed him by.

One of the ironies in the Jones tale is that he would one day become identified as the master of getting a three-year-old ready to traverse a mile and a quarter in May. Some regard this as pushing a young horse. Well, for Jones the Missouri traveler, by the time a horse was in May of his three-year-old year, he should be a veteran competitor.

"I used to think a half-mile was a long race," Jones said many years later, reflecting upon the days of two hundred- and four hundred-yard county fair matches for the horses he trained. Later, when he had fallen into the racetrack life as his meal ticket, he still had to expedite the careers of his horses.

The stallion Seth was standing in Texas when he was recommended to Jones. Seth (Adam—Purity, by Deceiver) was leased for two years to stand at the Jones Stock Farm. Later, Jones saw a good thing developing and returned to Texas to buy the horse outright.

"I needed to win in a hurry," Jones said about that era. "Needed money, living day to day." Seth was his guy. The stallion turned out horses that could win at two, and winning early was such a big deal that Jones toward the end of his life would recall only one instance when he purposely kept a horse from racing at that age.

Seth turned out enough winners that he ranked among America's twenty leading sires — in earnings — from 1925 through 1928. As an example of Seth's style of statistical leadership, in 1927 he was twentieth in earnings with $128,638, while the 170 wins by his progeny totaled almost one hundred more wins than were recorded by the offspring of the earnings leader, Fair Play. Seth had fifty-four starters that year, and a dozen of them ran in thirty or more races each in the single season. Two of them topped forty starts each. That same season, however, 1927, Seth slipped and fell on a slick spot in his paddock and broke his neck. He was nineteen.

Two years later the deceased Seth tied Stefan the Great as the national leader in juvenile winners, each with thirteen.

Ben Jones was breeding and racing his own, and with the impetus given by Seth, he ranked among the top ten breeders nationally from 1923 through 1931.

With Seth dead, however, and the Depression coming on, the Jones enterprise fell on hard times. By that time, Jones' son, Jimmy, had become his assistant, at least during part of the year.

Horace Allyn Jones (known as Jimmy) had been born on November 24, 1906. Ben A. Jones was not quite twenty-four at the time and was in a winning dice game when urgent word reached him that his wife was in labor.

Jimmy meandered through youth for some time. He attended Northwest Missouri State Teachers College, but his heart, like his father's, steered him elsewhere. He was a groom, blacksmith, even a jockey at times. His college was within twenty miles of Parnell, so he could attend to mares and the breeding operation while his father was at the racetrack, and then the son would join up with his dad wherever he happened to be during the summer. It might be Louisville, or it might be Omaha.

Descriptions of Ben's and Jimmy's careers often seem to meld, as if they represented brothers rather than two generations. This was due to Jimmy joining Ben at an early age rather than father handing son the mantle. For a big, stout-looking fellow whose signature fashion was a wide-brimmed Stetson and whose lifestyle engendered tales of manly fist fights, Ben Jones was actually subject to more than his share of health problems. As early as 1926, Jimmy received a call to go down to Fair Grounds and help his father, who had become ill. Ben later was diagnosed as diabetic, but whatever his illness in 1926, it apparently was short-lived.

When word of his father's illness reached him, Jimmy and some friends had left college and were learning that working a threshing machine job in Battle Creek, Michigan, was not an answer to life's dreams. Once he got to New Orleans, Jimmy Jones took out a trainer's license in his own name. In 1926 he received credit for his first official victory, courtesy of a horse named Nose Dive (fittingly, another word for plunge). "It was quite a thrill — as much to me then as the big ones we were to win later on," Jimmy said.

Jimmy told some wild border tales from this era. Shipping horses to Mexico involved hiding all but one authorized attendant per railroad car, so that horsemen of the day might be smuggling people into Mexico — as odd as that might sound in 2006. After crossing another border, into Canada, Ben once got into fight over what he regarded as an illegal attempt to claim his horse. He was charged with biting his opponent, and the situation required considerable tact on Jimmy's part to get his father released. Once back on American soil, Jimmy recalled, Ben never ventured into Canada again.

Ben Jones had always run his own horses for the most part, and low purses meant it was as important to win bets as it was to win races.

Jimmy recalled his father winning $15,000 from betting on a single race, but the thought that this "was all the money in the world" soon proved unfounded. Racing had a great many downs, as well as such a rare up, and the Wall Street crash of 1929 sent many Americans into a negative spiral.

In 1932 when Ben told his son he had a chance to work for Herbert Woolf, a successful Kansas City department store owner who had owned horses for a time and wanted to develop a major outfit, the younger man's counsel was direct: "Hell yes, take it. We're going to go broke the way things are going."

The idea was for Jimmy to stay on and sell off the Jones horses while his father jumped right into working for another man.

Because of the Depression, giving a horse away was not much easier than selling one. Not only did Jimmy have the racing stable to dispose of, but mares back in Parnell to get rid of, too. When he got back to his home town, the economy was so bad that the locals hit on the idea of making Jimmy the mayor. He served a term and managed to provide jobs with federal subsidies, putting Parnell citizens to work, he recalled, "paving streets, building sidewalks ... cleaning up parks and working along the Platte River."

THE KENTUCKY DERBY

Meanwhile Ben Jones jumped into his new job, succeeding Dan Stewart as trainer for Woolf's Woolford Farm. He took over when the stable was in Florida that winter but spotted some good opportunities at Oriental Park in Cuba. He shipped the two-year-old filly Lucille K. to win the Cuban Juvenile and Lady Broadcast to win the closing-day Cuban Grand National. These were Ben A. Jones' first stakes victories recorded in *The Blood-Horse* archives, and they were of good class. Oriental Park in Cuba was a highly fashionable place at the time.

After his short stint in politics, Jimmy rejoined his father, and aside from the younger man's World War II service, they were training partners for the rest of Ben's life. Jimmy had married Peggy Keenan in 1929.

In his first four years working for Woolf, Ben Jones (the trainer of record) won stakes with eight individual horses. Some raced in the name of T.C. Worden or Leonard Wilson, but most of his stable ran in the name of Woolford, the farm Woolf had developed on the Kansas-Missouri border.

Back at the scene of Jimmy's first win, father Ben won the 1934 New Orleans Handicap with Wilson's well-bred Slapped (Pompey—Smack, by Sweep On), a tough customer who was four at the time. Slapped ran 131 times and won thirty-four races, earning $28,615. Although Ben Jones did not have him all the way, he was a rugged Jones sort of horse. Jimmy recalled that the Jones team and Woolford made some headlines, too, by winning sixteen races in sixteen days at the Arlington Downs track in Texas.

Three times in his life did a particular stallion undergird the career of Ben A. Jones. Seth had been the first, and the ultimate was to be Calumet Farm's five-time leading sire Bull Lea. In between came Insco.

Griffin Watkins named the horse for his International Shoe Company. Insco's career was as abbreviated as his name. He was a flashy stakes winner at two but disappointed at three. He then broke down and after Watkins' insurance firm precluded his euthanizing the horse — and collecting a $25,000 payoff — he bred a few mares to him before ordering Insco sold. Jimmy Jones went to the sale with Rush McCoy, an agent for Woolf. He vividly recalled that a thunderstorm was brewing on the night in 1932 when Insco was led to the outdoor ring where Fasig-Tipton Company held its Lexington sales at the time. McCoy entered a bid of $500. A bolt of lightning caught the crowd's attention, thunder resounded almost immediately, and torrential rain chased most of the customers away. Insco drew no further bids.

The first stallion Woolf acquired for Woolford Farm would sire a Kentucky Derby winner. From Insco's third crop, Woolf delivered to the Joneses a Kansas-bred colt named Lawrin, out of Margaret Lawrence, by Vulcain. Jones gave the colt a long two-year-old campaign, fifteen races from April in Texas to December in Florida. Lawrin won three races, was second six times, and earned $3,060.

The Woolford horses were wintered in Florida, where Hialeah attracted major stables to a glamorous setting. Lawrin won some races but was struck on a leg by a competitor during another. He was written off for the big feature for three-year-olds, the $25,000 Flamingo Stakes, but Jones did not concur with that conventional wisdom.

Although this was Jones' first foray into such territory, he apparently did not flinch in the face of top-class racing, vis-a-vis the grist mill variety of horses he had known all his life. Jones sent out Lawrin in a mile race against older horses, and his victory caused a shuffling of public opinion. Lawrin was favored for the Flamingo Stakes, which he duly won.

Jones had his first Kentucky Derby horse, but Lawrin had been in heavy action for a year. He needed a rest, but the trainer could not rest him too long. Two months after the Flamingo, Lawrin came out for a purse race on opening day at Churchill Downs and finished third. Again the public was down on him, but three days later he ran The Chief to a head in the Derby Trial in a swift 1:35 4/5.

Behind the scenes, Ben and Jimmy Jones struggled with a hoof problem. As Jimmy Jones related it in the Gene Plowden–Joe Hirsch book, *In the Winner's Circle—The Jones Boys of Calumet Farm*, the case of Lawrin gives insight into the trainers' acute knowledge:

> That spring, after the stable shipped to Kentucky, Lawrin had some trouble with one foot. A separation developed between the hoof wall and the main portion. Dirt probably had worked its way up in this separation, like a splinter driven under a fingernail, and an infection developed. We had to find the pocket of infection, open it, and let it drain. We kept working up between the wall and the hoof with a knife until we reached the pocket. Once it started to drain, the pressure was relieved.
>
> Such antibiotics as penicillin and streptomycin were not available in those days, so we began to tub the foot in hot water to get the infection out. Now, when a horse's hoof is tubbed in hot water it softens the foot to the danger point. So we had to harden Lawrin's foot again. We used iodine and turpentine, which are hardening agents. They have a tendency to make the nerves recede and to harden up the foot. Those old-time methods might be scoffed at today, but they were effective, and we didn't have a big vet's bill, either.

There was another bit of horseman's savvy in Ben Jones's repertoire that spring. He fitted Lawrin with a bar shoe on the problem hoof. That device helps hold a hoof together but works slightly against getting the maximum traction. Despite Lawrin's exceptional effort in the Derby Trial, Jones determined the bar shoe should come off and, incidentally, a fellow named Eddie Arcaro should go on.

In today's world, the fact that a hot young rider like Arcaro would be available for a Derby mount during the middle of Derby Week is difficult to comprehend. In a time when many riders had contracts with specific stables, however, they were not free to negotiate a Saturday stakes mount well in advance; what if their contract stable had a horse in the same race or another important event the same day?

Arcaro was a young star who had ridden Calumet Farm's first champion, Nellie Flag, when she was beaten as favorite in the 1935 Kentucky Derby. He had not been in the race since, but Jones called on him because Arcaro's contract holder, Greentree Stable, did not have a horse in the 1938 Derby. Lawrin was 8-1.

Many years later, Jimmy Jones described the Derby as follows: "Eddie rated Lawrin nicely off the pace during the early stages, saving ground along the inside. But when Lawrin gave him a big move on the turn to pass horses, Eddie made too much use of him. Lawrin opened a three-length lead at the eighth pole, which was too much too soon for the long stretch at Churchill Downs, and he was a very tired horse in the drive. Lawrin drifted out from sheer fatigue as Dauber came on with a tremendous rush. However, Lawrin and Arcaro managed to hold Dauber safe and won by a diminishing length. The Jones boys had their first Derby!"

Well, a fellow has to be pretty grim by nature, or have won a bunch of these things, to be so critical of a Derby victory, even in retrospect. Jimmy had more than sixty years left to be asked about such matters. As for Ben, one of his most colorful summations of his first Derby win was: "He had a heel separation and I had had a bar shoe on him. [Reshod] with regular shoes, he scampered home in the Derby like a barefoot boy in the spring."

Another quote attributed to Ben years later might possibly have alluded to the evening of Derby Day 1938, to wit, "I used to stay up all night after a Derby win, but I don't do that anymore. I take a drink or two and go to bed early."

Over the years the senior Jones was known as Ben, B.A., or Plain Ben. Clearly, there was nothing "plain" about the big, two-fisted fellow in the broad-brimmed Stetson.

Son Jimmy agreed and pointed out that the writer Tony Betts contrived the idea of using the nickname in recollection of an actual prize fighter, Plain Ben, from many years earlier.

There would never be a day when money did not mean a lot to the Jones boys, and Jimmy years later savored the fiscal aspect of Lawrin's Kentucky Derby. Owner Woolf had been betting on his horse in the winter books from time to time and somehow still got 20-1 after Lawrin had won the Flamingo. Given the purse of $47,050, the $5,000 trophy, and a sequence of personal bets, Jimmy figured Woolf had a $200,000 afternoon. Woolf handed Ben Jones a check for $10,000 — more than double the trainer's routine 10 percent of a winning purse.

War Admiral had become the fourth Triple Crown winner the year before Lawrin's Derby, so the sequence of Derby–Preakness–Belmont was becoming solidified on the Turf as a major deal. The Triple Crown was not yet universally seen as a natural target of all horse owners, however, and Lawrin had not been nominated for either of the two other races.

Thus, Jones took him west to a new track called Hollywood Park — a name and location redolent of the glamour of the California movie scene. There he eked out a tough win in the Hollywood Trial. This led to a race for which management had grand ambitions and a grandiose name — the American Invitational Three-Year-Old Championship Stakes. It had a $50,000-added purse. Dauber, who had won the Preakness, shipped west for a rematch, but he bowed a tendon before the race. Lawrin thus caught a weak field for the big event and won handily, but he, too, soon bowed a tendon just as prospects for a meeting with the older Seabiscuit had become intriguing. Lawrin never raced again. He had won nine of twenty-six races and earned $126,275.

Training siblings, half siblings, and sons and daughters of good horses would become commonplace for Ben A. and Jimmy Jones. An early example was Lawrin's juvenile full sister, Unerring, who was sent out to win the Starlet Sweepstakes and five other races that same year.

The first champion trained by Ben A. Jones also was in the Woolf barn in 1938, but it was neither Lawrin nor his full sister. Stagehand upstaged Lawrin when voting for three-year-old champion was compiled, but in the juvenile filly division Woolf and Jones had one better than Unerring. This was Inscoelda (Insco—Griselda, by Wrack). Ben A. Jones was still in the mode of early racing of two-year-olds, and the warm-climate tracks accommodated him. Inscoelda debuted in a three-furlong dash at Hialeah on January 12, several months before she was two by the calendar. By February 11 she had broken her maiden — in her fourth start.

Inscoelda eventually ran sixteen times at two, and she won six races. With key victories in the Arlington Lassie and the Walden, she was voted champion juvenile filly. While the name Inscoelda hardly nudges in among the Whirlaways and Citations of the Joneses' later distinction, she is the only one who can claim to have been Ben Jones' first official champion.

(Unerring, who had begun her career under Ben Jones, was to be named the champion three-year-old filly of 1939, but by the time of her key triumphs that year the Jones boys had moved to greener employment pastures. R.O. Higdon is given credit as trainer of Unerring as a champion.)

Early in 1939, a year after Lawrin's distinction, Ben Jones won the Flamingo again, with Technician, and, accordingly, another Kentucky Derby beckoned. Jones had given this candidate a busy winter, as he had with Lawrin, and thereafter prescribed a rest before the Derby. The Flamingo was run on February 25, and Technician did not face the starter again until April 29, when he won an allowance race. On May 2, he was second in the Derby Trial. In the Derby itself Technician ran near the middle of a small, eight-horse field and could never challenge. He finished fifth as the 6-1 second choice to 3-5 winner Johnstown.

The Woolford assignment was clearly a good one. The owner was having success, and with Insco having sired Lawrin, Unerring, and Inscoelda right off the mark, he looked like the sort of stallion that would support long-range prosperity. In the winter of 1939, however, Insco was injured in his paddock, and blood poisoning developed. He died at the age of eleven.

Meanwhile, Jones had attracted the attention of Warren Wright Sr., whose high ambitions for his Calumet Farm had not been fulfilled by results to date. On July 14, 1939, Jones announced the end of his association with Woolford Farm. There was apparently some subterfuge in his announcement: "I leave the employ of Mr. Woolf on most friendly terms. I informed him of my decision to resign several days ago, and my plans for the future are indefinite."

It was only a few days later, of course, that Wright announced that Jones was to replace Frank Kearns as trainer for Calumet at the end of the Saratoga meeting. Trainer Ross Higdon was in position to take on the Woolford horses right away, so Jimmy and Ben drove to Saratoga, figuring on some pleasant vacation time at the old Spa. However, Kearns had already found a new position by the time they reached Saratoga. So, the Joneses went right to work, familiarizing themselves with their horses but not running yet.

Their new boss was a tycoon from Chicago. Wright was the son of William Monroe Wright, who had established the Calumet Baking Powder Company. Late in his life the elder Wright bought property in Kentucky and launched Calumet Farm as a Standardbred operation. Warren Wright had been handed the reins of the family business in 1913, and by 1928 he had transformed it into something the forerunner of General Mills considered was worth about $40 million. The sale was made.

Upon inheriting Calumet Farm after his father's death in 1931, Warren Wright Sr. turned it into a Thoroughbred operation. He already had some connections to the game. Warren Wright was a friend of taxicab mogul and rental car pioneer John D. Hertz and had accompanied him to Churchill Downs in 1928 to see the Hertz stable's Reigh Count win the Kentucky Derby. Warren Wright Sr.'s wife, Kentuckian Lucille Parker Wright, recalled the first time she met Ben Jones: "I remember our first words. Mr. Jones wore a big hat, and when I introduced myself to him and shook his hand, the big hat came off in an instant, and he put it under his arm. 'I know all about you,' I said, 'and the one thing I want more than anything else is to win the Kentucky Derby.' He leaned down and kissed me, and said, 'That's what I want, and we will get it.' " Many years later, in an interview for *Sports Illustrated* in 1978, she recalled that it was she who first called Jones to see if he would consider taking over the Calumet string.

Jones hit the ground running when he took over the Calumet string. Jones saddled his first starter for Calumet on September 20 at Aqueduct and was second. By October 5, however, he had saddled a total of ten starters, and seven of them had won. It was not until October 11 that Jones had the experience of starting a Calumet horse that failed to place, and after that he bounced back to have two winners of his next five starts. *The Blood-Horse* stated the summary as: sixteen starts, nine wins, four seconds, one third, two unplaced. On October 5 Jones saddled three winners for Calumet at Belmont Park, one of which was Easy Mon, winner that day of the historic Jerome Handicap.

Although Calumet Farm was not then perceived as occupying the pedestal to which it would ascend, it was already a luxurious exemplar of the romance of the Bluegrass. In fact, Jimmy and Ben had visited it the Sunday after Lawrin won the Derby. Jimmy recalled that, "I thought to myself, 'how lucky a fellow would be if he could be connected with an outfit like this!' Later, in the car, B.A. admitted he'd had the same thought, but neither of us ever dreamed anything so wonderful would happen."

Ben Jones curtailed his own breeding operation after accepting Wright's job. With the success of his Woolford days, he had replenished the broodmare band back at Jones Stock Farm, but that year he announced he was selling his twenty-one mares and the stallions Higher and Flint Shot. The farm, then covering 2,400 acres, was to be converted to growing crops. Runners bred by Jones continued to race for several more years, of course. By 1945, records showed him to have bred the winners of more than three thousand races and earners of more than $2 million.

WHIRLAWAY'S TRIPLE CROWN

In 1940 the Joneses took on the new Calumet two-year-olds. One of them was a chestnut colt named Whirlaway, a son of Blenheim II. The stallion was a high-fashion horse, an Epsom Derby winner who had been bought from the Aga Khan by a group put together by A.B. Hancock Sr. of Claiborne Farm. Wright was among the investors. Whirlaway was a future Triple Crown winner, and so the influence of Blenheim II would seem to be the best thing the breeding division of Calumet had going for it.

The greatest stallion in Calumet's future, however, was at the moment a question mark in the racing stable. When Ben Jones took over Calumet's runners, the four-year-old Bull Lea was still around but was not totally sound. He had won the Blue Grass Stakes in 1938 and had been eighth as second choice to Fighting Fox when Jones won the Derby with Lawrin.

During the winter of 1939, Bull Lea had covered a mile and a quarter successfully in winning Hialeah's rich Widener Handicap. Though a coveted race with a glamorous name, this running proved disappointing. After all, track management had tried to position it as the vehicle for a rematch between Seabiscuit and War Admiral after their famous 1938 match. Neither started, and truth be told, if either had it seems unlikely that Bull Lea would have had such an important victory on his escutcheon.

During the winter of 1939–40, Wright hoped that Bull Lea could come back at five.

"We had our doubts," Jimmy Jones recalled, "and one morning after we had breezed him ... at a very easy lick, the old tendon began to fill. We had to make a decision ... most of the stallions had their books full by that time. We had to decide whether to keep Bull Lea with the stable the rest of the year or ship him home and hope for some mares for him. Fortunately, we decided to send him to the farm."

Although he had disappointed in the Kentucky Derby and won an anticlimactic Widener, Bull Lea had an aura of appeal. He was by Bull Dog, an $80,000 import who was a full brother to the established great sire Sir Gallahad III. Bull Lea was out of Rose Leaves, a Ballot mare who had foaled three previous stakes winners. In one of the fateful moves of his life, Wright had outbid Mrs. Ethel V. Mars of Milky Way Stable, $14,000 to $13,600, at the Saratoga yearling sale of 1936. The prim fellow who used to own a baking powder company had won a hand that would make him more glamorous than the lady with the candy-bar connection!

Wright assigned ten mares to Bull Lea for 1940. Most of them were either stakes winners or sisters or daughters of stakes winners and presumably were diverted from booking plans to other stallions. Later, Brownell Combs announced that his champion Myrtlewood also would be in Bull Lea's first book.

Bull Lea was such a great stallion that he no doubt would have made his mark even had he been subjected to a disappointing five-year-old season at the racetrack. Still, the crop that resulted from the decision to retire him for the 1940 breeding season was an effective promotional unit, for it produced champions Armed, Twilight Tear, and Durazna.

For Ben and Jimmy Jones, of course, matters at the racetrack in 1940 dealt with horses that were there, as opposed to future offspring of one that was not. Whirlaway (Blenheim II—Dustwhirl, by Sweep) had his quirks, but he was the one among twenty youngsters who the Joneses recognized had substantial ability.

"A rugged little fellow with a long tail," Jimmy recalled, "and he had a lot of desire and fight in him." Ben Jones made a project out of the two-year-old. He got into Whirly's head to the extent that he recognized the horse appreciated routine. So, he would ask over and over in the morning what he expected of the horse in the afternoon.

Whirlaway tended to run so wide in his races that it was frequently said he went to the outside rail. This, of course, lost him some races, but he did win the Saratoga Special and the Hopeful at Saratoga. Jimmy recalled that the colt was struck in an eye by a stone kicked back during the Hopeful and that human ocular specialists were called in when it was feared the colt would lose an eye.

For all that drama Whirlaway was away from the races for only three weeks. When he came back to be fifth in an allowance race, the official chart caller had justification for dramatic language: "Swerved, impeded, hung late." Whirlaway then was third behind Our Boots in the Futurity, which was run on a straight course at that time and thus presented no opportunity for blowing a turn.

Jockey Arcaro recalled some years later than Ben Jones concluded that Whirlaway "was simply a dumb horse — that once out in the middle of the track where he couldn't see the rail, his mental processes became foggy and he got lost. That's why, Jones theorized, he bore out and did all sorts of crazy things."

At Keeneland, Whirlaway won an allowance race and defeated Our Boots in the Breeders' Futurity. Our Boots, however, was voted the championship among two-year-olds of 1940. Whirlaway pranced along his erratic way, eliciting chart comments "bore out both turns" for his third in the Pimlico Futurity, but then rated an "easily" for his win in the Walden.

Whirlaway had won seven of sixteen races at two, from June into November. He was given almost three months off before launching his three-year-old season with an allowance sprint. Although he won, the chart carried the admonition, "bore out stretch." He then lost two allowance races.

The trainers Jones also were devoting considerable intellect to the subject of training their owner. As Jimmy told it, they recognized something was not quite right with Whirlaway, but with the owner coveting that Flamingo Stakes trophy they needed something less vague by way of explanation. So, they fell back on the trainer's prerogative of announcing a lie.

Whirlaway, the world was told, had a splint. Obviously, he could not be trained for the Flamingo. A bit later in the winter, though, he was coming around and Ben Jones popped the supposed Derby colt into a race of five and a half furlongs. Owner Wright had been convinced to forget the Flamingo, but when fishing in nearby waters he read that his Derby colt was being returned to sprinting, he ordered a launch to shore and arrived at Tropical Park in time to contest the issue.

Plowden and Hirsch quoted Jimmy to the effect that tension filled the Calumet box. Wright reminded the trainer he was the owner and demanded he scratch the colt whereas Jones countered the trainer was there to make the decisions. Jimmy figured a job hung in the balance, for both were "mad as hornets." Whirlaway received the chart call "forced wide, just up" and won by a neck. Jimmy Jones' unofficial personal chart notes were that "the good Lord certainly had his arms around the Joneses that afternoon."

The win soothed Wright who welcomed the resulting sequence of congratulations from passersby at his box. Later that day he decreed — and we have only Jimmy Jones' testimony for this — "I'm never going to train another horse. From now on, you fellows are doing the training. Use your own judgment and do what you think is best."

Yet, Whirlaway remained a puzzle. Two weeks after the five and a half-furlong win he won a six-furlong sprint at Keeneland in Kentucky, but then he was beaten six lengths by Our Boots in the mile and one eighth Blue Grass Stakes. "Bore out turn, tired," quoted the chart.

On Tuesday of Derby Week, Whirlaway ran in the one-mile Derby Trial. He was in front midway through the race but was passed by Blue Pair. Jimmy Jones lamented that Whirlaway "ran out on the turn when he should have beaten Blue Pair easily."

As had been the case with Lawrin, Ben Jones when in trouble called upon Eddie Arcaro. Wendell Eads had ridden Whirlaway in four of his seven races at three.

The lore of Derby Week 1941 had Jones pronouncing that he would sit astride a pony at the stretch turn, near the rail, for a morning work and that Arcaro would bring Whirlaway breezing by between Jones and the rail. An oft-repeated detail of such tales has Arcaro declaring that, as the scenario unfolded, he said to himself "if that old man is game enough to sit there on that pony, I'm game enough to run him down!" Whirlaway, of course, skimmed the rail, whether Jones was situated where they turned for home or, as in another version, near the eighth pole.

Neither Jimmy's version in the Plowden–Hirsch book nor Arcaro's rendition in his own book supports much in the way of dramatics. The Joneses, though, mused on how a one-eyed blinker had recently helped with a problem horse named Quien Es. A horse is reluctant to veer in a direction he cannot see, so a blinker with a closed, or nearly closed, cup on one side will tend to discourage his going in that direction.

As Jimmy Jones recalled, the one-eyed blinker was tried on Whirlaway for the first time for his initial breeze under Arcaro.

The jockey's memory differed. In *I Ride to Win*, by Arcaro (as told to Jack O'Hara, Greenberg Publisher, 1951), Arcaro notes that Jones positioned himself on a pony at the furlong pole. "When I set Whirlaway down, he behaved like any other horse I had ridden ... he stayed right in on the rail. I should add that Whirlaway was equipped with regulation blinkers."

Arcaro adds that the breeze relieved him of "all fear that he would run out with me." He elaborated that his brief introduction had indicated that Whirlaway was a horse that responded well if the rider would "take a long hold on him and freeze with it. You just couldn't reach up and take a fresh hold when he wanted to turn in a run. Although I might look like a coachman, I found out pretty quickly that it was the only way to handle him." Arcaro praised Jones in that he "always plans his races well." Before the 1941 Derby, the rider noted, Jones was "exceptionally verbose" in his instructions. The morning of the race, Jones told Eddie he definitely did not want Whirlaway up with the early pace. He felt so strongly about this detail that Arcaro recalled him saying, "If you can get away badly, that will help." Jones was confident Whirlaway would get to the lead, and if it were at the sixteenth pole that would be fine. Getting to the front earlier might create a problem.

By Arcaro's telling, Jones had not mentioned the one-eyed blinker, but at the last moment he equipped Whirlaway with one that "shades only the right eye. The left cup has been torn off." Jones, he said, "didn't try to explain to me, but I knew what he had in mind ... That Jones, always thinking up new ideas."

All things considered, the Derby public still believed in the mercurial chestnut with the appealingly long tail flowing behind. It was a tentative sort of belief, but fans sent the Calumet devil's red and blue colors off at 2.90-1 in a field of eleven. Jones must have been happy to see Whirlaway blocked in the first furlong, for it meant he was in eighth place after a half-mile. After six furlongs, Whirlaway was still sixth, and Arcaro then moved him between horses. Running kindly, fast, and, oh so sweetly, Whirlaway gained the lead with alacrity. With radio announcer Clem McCarthy rasping out the pulse of his rally, Whirlaway did what Jones feared in that he got his lead well before the eighth pole. By the time he reached that point, though, he had put three lengths on the runner-up, and he continued his emphatic dismissal of his field.

Whirlaway won by eight lengths in a record 2:01 2/5. The time held as the Kentucky Derby record for twenty years; the margin has been matched but never bettered.

The Joneses had their second Derby; Calumet, its first; and Kentucky now had a horse to love without qualification.

When asked how he had, seemingly, cured Whirlaway of bad habits instantly, Arcaro remarked that, "I just shoved him between the two leaders ... he could neither run in nor out ... We just sailed along on the beam and anchored at the home port in record time."

Whirlaway had no serious challenges awaiting in the Preakness or Belmont. He won both, with a tune-up win in between. The worry about the Belmont was stamina, and although Jimmy Jones noted he was "a tired, staggering horse" at the finish, he had a two and a half-length margin as he completed the Triple Crown.

The Joneses were ambivalent about Whirlaway. In later years, after Citation came along, they stressed that Whirlaway should not even be spoken of in the same breath as that great horse. Still, Ben Jones years later remarked that "of all the Derby horses I had, I guess old Whirlaway was my favorite," although he was unstinting in the conviction that Citation was the greatest. The memory of Whirlaway perhaps reflects a tendency to fondly recall a problem child dealt with successfully.

Whirlaway won six consecutive races beginning with the Derby, but for the most part he was the sort of campaigner that raced hard and often and had frequent defeats as well as major victories. He wound up winning thirteen of twenty at three and was Horse of the Year as well as champion three-year-old. Ben A. Jones was the leading trainer in the nation with $475,318, featuring seventy wins, and Calumet Farm was both the leading owner and leading breeder in earnings for the first time each.

Whirlaway earned $272,386 at three, meaning that others in the stable accounted for more than $200,000. A goodly portion of this, $57,900, came from the victory of Some Chance in another of the top prizes in America, the Futurity Stakes. With Eads aboard, Some Chance (Chance Play—Some Pomp, by Pompey) defeated Devil Diver in the Futurity. Another juvenile, Sun Again (Sun Teddy—Hug Again, by Stimulus) contributed a nice purse of $34,655 when Eads brought him home in the Arlington Futurity. He also won the Juvenile Stakes.

Although neither of the Calumet youngsters could deny Alsab the two-year-old championship, they illustrated the growing strength of the stable. Calumet also won the Acorn Stakes that year with Some Chance's older half sister, Proud One, and the juvenile filly Mar-Kell won the Spinaway, while Beau James also won a stakes for the stable.

The next year, 1942, Whirlaway was a champion again. One of the most publicized phases of his campaign involved his meetings with the champion three-year-old, Alsab. In a match race at Narragansett, Alsab set the pace and held off Whirlaway and jockey George Woolf to win by a nose.

Jimmy Jones wrote that he could not remember another time his father was so disappointed. Most match races are climactic events in themselves, but such were the campaigning philosophies of the two camps that the pair met again two weeks later, when Whirlaway beat the younger colt in the two-mile Jockey Club Gold Cup. Only a week more passed before they met once more, Alsab that time winning the New York Handicap at two and a quarter miles. Nevertheless, Whirlaway, perhaps buttressed by the prestige of the Jockey Club Gold Cup, prevailed as Horse of the Year a second time.

He won twelve of twenty-two that year. Overall, he won thirty-two of sixty races and earned $561,161. Whirlaway passed Seabiscuit as leading money earner of all time and became the first Thoroughbred to win as much as a half-million. By the end of the decade, another homebred had owner Wright eyeing a milestone doubling that mark.

Greentree Stable had its own banner year in 1942, with Derby, Belmont, and Travers winner Shut Out, and took leading owner and breeder honors. Greentree's trainer, John Gaver, led trainers. Ben Jones would top that list the next two years.

In 1943 Whirlaway made two starts at five before his retirement early in the year. After three years of dealing with that fascinating star, the Joneses turned their attention to the first crop of two-year-olds by Bull Lea. That is, Ben did so. With the United States at war, not only were some race meetings interrupted but also men of Jimmy's age had duties to attend. H.A. Jones was sworn into the Coast Guard as a lieutenant on April 7, 1943. (He was associated with a fellow horseman, Humphrey Finney, in operations along the coast of northern Florida. This was the area where German saboteurs had come ashore some months earlier.)

Of Bull Lea's three champions in his first crop, only one came to hand for Ben Jones that year. Twilight Tear (Bull Lea—Lady Lark, by Blue Larkspur) gave a hint of things to come when she won the Arlington Lassie and was second in the Selima. She was beaten in the Selima by a Calumet stablemate, the Blenheim II filly Miss Keeneland. Championship honors for her division, though, fell to Brownell Combs, who got Durazna as his reward for sending Myrtlewood to Bull Lea his first year.

Calumet's status as having a champion each year was extended to a third season by Mar-Kell. Another by Blenheim II, Mar-Kell was out of Nellie Flag, Calumet's only champion in the pre-Jones days. Mar-Kell was a beautiful mare, large but refined, and she had been a stakes winner at two but ran in only one stakes at three.

Now, at four, Mar-Kell was ready to blossom into the sort her win in the Spinaway at two had promised. In an active campaign of eighteen races, she won half, and those nine wins included four stakes. The first was the

Washington's Birthday Handicap in New Orleans, where Mar-Kell's campaign began due to the wartime cessation of the south Florida racing season. She won the Top Flight in New York and Cinderella in Chicago. Late in the season, again in New York, Mar-Kell defeated champions Stefanita and Vagrancy in the Beldame to clinch honors as champion older filly or mare.

Jones made it to Churchill Downs with good prospects for the Derby and the Oaks. Ocean Wave won the Blue Grass Stakes and Derby Trial, and he was seen as the likely second choice for the big race, inasmuch as he was one major winner that favorite Count Fleet had not already beaten. Although the Derby Trial was on Tuesday of Derby week, Ocean Wave was back on the track again in serious enough work later in the week to come up slightly lame. Jones worked Ocean Wave a half-mile on Derby morning, and it was not until after the third race on the card that the decision to scratch was reluctantly made. Ocean Wave did little afterward.

Derby Weekend was not without its rewards for Calumet, however, for on Derby Eve, Nellie L., another from Nellie Flag, won the Kentucky Oaks. The Blenheim II filly, Mar-Kell's full sister, also added the Acorn that spring. Sun Again, like Mar-Kell, returned to win stakes at four after having done so at two, but not at three. In 1943 he won the Riggs and Drexel handicaps, and he was to be even more productive the next year. Ben Jones, who won seventy-three races, led the trainer's money list with a restricted wartime total of $267,915 while Calumet returned to the top of the owner's list. Claiborne Farm led the breeders.

TWILIGHT TEAR AND ARMED

The 1944 season saw Ben Jones and Calumet haul in another Kentucky Derby with Pensive, but such were the gathering riches on his team that Pensive was not Calumet's best three-year-old. That honor belonged to Twilight Tear, and she became the first three-year-old filly to be voted Horse of the Year. (Busher followed in that distinction the very next year, but there have been no others since.)

Pensive was by Lord Derby's distinguished stallion Hyperion out of Lord Astor's mare Penicuik II, by Buchan. Hyperion was an Epsom Derby winner, and Pensive's second dam, Pennycomequick, was an Epsom Oaks winner. A.B. Hancock Sr. purchased and imported Penicuik II; Wright bought her before she foaled and thus was the breeder of record of Pensive.

At two Pensive won two of five races. The second win was impressive enough to make him the favorite for the Futurity, but he was fourth behind Occupy. The next winter he won one of three starts in Florida and then moved to Maryland. Pensive had shelly feet, but Jones knew he could not pamper him and get him ready for a mile and a quarter in May. Less than a month before the Derby, Jones ran him against tough older horses in the Rowe Memorial at six furlongs, and Pensive was up to win by a head over six-year-old Porter's Cap. That was his first stakes win and remained his only one going into the Kentucky Derby, for of the three remaining races jammed in before the classic he won only an allowance race. During that active span, Pensive finished second against older horses in the Bowie Handicap and second again in the Chesapeake Stakes.

Greentree Stable's Stir Up was the Derby favorite at about 3-2, with contract rider Arcaro this time a foe of Calumet. Pensive was the second choice, at 7.10-1. Eight horses were grouped in the mutuel field, and with half the entire Derby cast available for a single ticket, enough of the public went for this deal to make the entity fourth choice at 7.70-1.

Jockey Conn McCreary was known for his late-closing style, and in Pensive he had a natural ally. The Calumet hope was thirteenth early, and when he began to close, there was room along the rail. At one point, McCreary thought about splitting Arcaro on Stir Up and Woolf on Broadcloth but took a more discriminating path and was able to slip through, sticking to the rail. Once in front Pensive established daylight and bore out only slightly while winning by four and a half lengths. As Ben Jones put it, "McCreary kind of squeezed in, just snatched Pensive over horses' heels, and came through on the rail." Broadcloth was second; Stir Up, third.

A week later Pensive swept from behind again to defeat Platter in the Preakness. Stir Up tried front-running tactics that time but was overtaken in the stretch and finished third.

Pensive now, of course, stood a mile and a half from concluding Ben A. Jones' second Triple Crown. However, he had run down on his back heels in the Preakness. He made a noble effort in the Belmont, but he was unable to hold off Bounding Home in the stretch and lost by a half-length.

Pensive's later campaign creates a sense that the racing fates were wise to deny him Triple Crown status. Had he won the Belmont and then undergone his remaining campaign just as it was, he would have been destined to be known as the most disappointing of Triple Crown winners. He did not win another race and at year's end had a season's record of seventeen starts and five wins. There were indications of oncoming tendon problems, and he was retired, having won seven of twenty-two races and earned $167,715. By Jimminy was the champion three-year-old male.

Meanwhile, Twilight Tear was fulfilling Jones' fondest hopes. She came out on February 29 at Hialeah and was third in the Leap Year Handicap. She would not know defeat again until August, by which time she had won eleven races in a row. The heart of this streak included the Pimlico Oaks, Acorn, and Coaching Club American Oaks, all by open daylight. In the CCA Oaks, then run at a mile and three-eighths, Twilight Tear dominated early, and McCreary brought her home four lengths in front of Dare Me.

During the usual Chicago summer for Calumet, Twilight Tear added the Princess Doreen Stakes and then Jones let her challenge colts. She was 3-10 when she won the seven-furlong Skokie Handicap, giving weight to Sirde and Challenge Me.

The main target in Chicago was the rich Arlington Classic. The Skokie had been run on July 6 and the Classic was set for July 22, but Jones thought she needed another race in between. In a one-mile allowance race, she teamed with her classics-winning stablemate and toured in front to beat Pensive by more than a length. In the Classic, Twilight Tear won by two lengths from Old Kentuck, with Pensive third.

Wartime disruptions assigned the Saratoga meeting to Belmont Park, where Twilight Tear next appeared, for the historic Alabama. But for that change of scenery, the 1944 Alabama presumably would be one of the blocks upon which is built Saratoga's reputation as "graveyard of favorites."

Despite McCreary's adeptness with closers, he did not fight the style of Twilight Tear, who had been showing speed from the start in her races. Sunny Jim Fitzsimmons spotted the Alabama as a good time to try a one-two punch. With Twilight Tear the top weight at 126 pounds, Fitzsimmons assigned Belair Stud's Thread o' Gold (117) the task of challenging early while stablemate Vienna (114) was to lie back. Thread o' Gold did not actually make the lead, but she pressured Twilight Tear through a quick pace, which tired her enough that Vienna came along and won the mile and a quarter race by three-quarters of a length. Twilight Tear had been 1-20, but her eleven-race winning streak had ended.

Ben gave her two months before she ran again. Four autumn starts produced three victories. After daylight margins in an overnight sprint and in the mile and one eighth Queen Isabella Handicap, Twilight Tear took up 130 pounds for the Maryland Handicap. Catching a muddy track on the deep Laurel footing and going a mile and a quarter, she led for six furlongs but tired and wound up unplaced for the only time in her life. She finished fourth to Dare Me, to whom she gave twenty-one pounds.

Jones was undeterred and accepted an assignment that put Twilight Tear over the top as Horse of the Year. This came in the mile and three-sixteenths Pimlico Special. She was facing not only a male, but an older one, and a champion at that. Greentree Stable's Devil Diver had been co-champion handicap male in 1943 and would repeat in 1944.

In one of the more stunning performances by a filly against a top colt in racing history, Twilight Tear opened a clear lead early and powered along in control, defeating Devil Diver by six lengths.

Twilight Tear's fans had remained loyal and, even in the face of her recent defeat, had made her the 65-100 choice. Doug Dodson rode her, as he had in her previous two races.

Twilight Tear had won fourteen of seventeen races and earned $167,555 at three. Jimmy Jones was discharged from the Coast Guard in the autumn of 1944 and quickly returned to the stable. He was not to participate in further glory with Twilight Tear, however. The filly bled during a morning work the next spring and was rested further. Then she bled again while losing an allowance race and was retired immediately.

A Horse of the Year and a Derby-Preakness winner formed a powerful pair, but they were far from the only good winners on hand for Ben Jones in 1944. A half-dozen others — Miss Keeneland, Good Blood, Hail Victory, Pot o' Luck, Teddy Haste, and Twosy — also won stakes for the stable. Jones set a record for earnings by a trainer, with $601,660, having won sixty races, and Calumet was the leading owner and leading breeder again.

Highlights for runners other than Twilight Tear and Pensive included the Champagne Stakes and Pimlico Futurity victories of two-year-old colt Pot o' Luck (Chance Play—Potheen, by Wildair). The older Sun Again, then five, had his best year, winning the Dixie, Equipoise Mile, and McClennan handicaps among five stakes wins.

In 1945 one of the Jones boys' most remarkable training achievements began to unfold. The year marked the first stakes victory for Armed, who by then was four. A member of that first crop of Bull Lea, Armed had ankle problems at two, and after an abbreviated period at the racetrack, he returned to the farm to be pinfired and gelded.

From the days of Seth, and even before, Ben Jones was programmed to race two-year-olds. Not only was there economic pressure in those days, but many trainers regard a Thoroughbred's learning curve to mandate racing at that age. We once heard a prominent trainer put it as, "there's nothing dumber than an unraced three-year-old."

Ben Jones would recall that Armed was the only horse he deliberately left unraced as a two-year-old. While back at Calumet, Armed had purpose, however, for he was kept in some form of exercise by the farm's yearling man, Rufus Schilling, who rode him back and forth to the gate while accompanying the new yearlings.

Armed (Bull Lea—Armful, by Chance Shot) got to the races in late February of his three-year-old season. He made an immediate splash. In his debut he ran off with Eddie Arcaro and won by eight lengths, and after he won for McCreary the next time out, the enthusiastic rider urged Ben to "go in the Derby with this one." Armed was still a work in progress, however, and won only one of his remaining five starts at three.

At four Armed was an important handicap horse but not quite the champion he would become. That year, 1945, he won ten of fifteen races. His first stakes score came in a division of the Sheridan, and he was second in four consecutive stakes before winning another one. Late in the year he won the Washington Handicap and two overnight races and then declared his arrival as a player in the handicap division by defeating First Fiddle and Stymie at level weights in the Pimlico Special.

The winter–spring of 1945 had seen disruption of racing. The cessation of Florida racing was a bother, with such targets as the Flamingo wiped off the slate, and the Kentucky Derby was delayed until June 9. Jones' Derby hope was Pot o' Luck, who trained impressively through a series of six- and seven-furlong works to compensate for the lack of racing. By April he was shipped to Kentucky, where Jones raced him into even better shape. Pot o' Luck was ready to win in his third race, the Ben Ali against older horses, but then was fourth while trying to come from last in the Blue Grass Stakes.

The Derby, however, found Pot o' Luck the slight favorite at 3.30-1, as Calumet's Derby aura was beginning to take hold. Hoop, Jr. was 3.70-1 and proved too much to handle, as Arcaro sent him to the lead early in the mud and won off by six lengths. Pot o' Luck rallied from fifteenth under regular rider Dodson and finished second.

Thereafter, Pot o' Luck had a highly useful campaign, winning several important races although losing frequently. He won the rich Arlington Classic, the two-mile Jockey Club Gold Cup, the Lawrence Realization, and Governor Bowie Handicap. He picked spots well, for he had only five wins from twenty-one starts.

Otherwise in 1945, Miss Keeneland was still around for her one annual stakes victory, and it came in a nice one, the Top Flight Handicap; Good Blood won the Queen Isabella; and the Bull Lea two-year-old High Shine won the Hyde Park Stakes.

Neither Jones nor Calumet topped the respective statistical lists.

In 1946 Armed continued improving and replaced Stymie as the champion older horse. He won eleven of eighteen races and was worse than third only once. With the war over and racing getting back into full force in Florida, Armed's first big target was the Widener Handicap at Hialeah. Under 128 pounds, he won by four and a half lengths and then followed up with both halves of a coupling called the Double Event at Tropical Park.

He beat champion Stymie in the Dixie Handicap and again in the Suburban Handicap. Under 130 pounds, Armed gave seven to Stymie in the latter race, but Dodson brought him along to win by two and a half lengths. Reply Paid beat Stymie for second. Three defeats followed, but Armed got in three more stakes scores, each under 130 pounds, to be voted champion older male. (Triple Crown winner Assault was Horse of the Year.)

By 1946 some horses won stakes with Jimmy as trainer of record; some, with Ben. This was due in part to the health of the elder man, who was diabetic and needed surgery. *Daily Racing Form*'s career past performances of Armed include a half-dozen notations of trainer change between father and son. In looking back from a distance, Jimmy placed his father's change of status from head trainer to general manager around this time. The following year, *American Race Horses of 1947* described their relationship as follows: "Since the two work together with no standing division of duties, it is entirely an arbitrary matter to say that any given horse is trained by one or the other." Nevertheless, it was not until 1956 that a Derby starter had Jimmy down as trainer of record!

Armed's earnings of $288,725 went a good way toward returning Calumet to the top of the owner's list, but the total of $564,095 indicates the help he got from other troops. All told, five Calumet horses earned $20,000 or more apiece, six others brought in at least $10,000 each, and eight more hit the $5,000 mark. Nevertheless, since the Joneses' earnings were not combined, Hirsch Jacobs (Stymie's trainer) was able to lead the trainers' list with less than the Calumet total, $560,077. (Mereworth Farm led breeders.)

Armed's development from ornery, ouchy youngster to full-fledged champion was completed in 1947. He won eleven of seventeen races, earned $376,325, and was voted Horse of the Year as well as a second handicap championship.

Armed's Horse of the Year drive began in high style as he took four in a row at Hialeah. These included the McLennan under 130 pounds and a second Widener, under 129. The Joneses then made a daring trip west, where a week after Armed had won Florida's biggest handicap race he tried for California's. Under 129 pounds in the Santa Anita Handicap, Armed finished fifth behind Olhaverry (116).

Three weeks later Armed was back in action in Florida to win the Gulfstream Park Handicap under 129 pounds. Thereafter, wins were interspersed with losses although he thrice put together victories back to back.

With the weights never exceeding 132 pounds regardless of his record, Armed added the Stars and Stripes, Arlington, Whirlaway, and Washington handicaps in Chicago. Back east he defeated Assault by eight lengths in a match race that had been postponed by the latter's tentative soundness. The $100,000 purse was a nice sum to accept even though Assault's questionable condition diminished the victory's significance.

Armed then added the Sysonby, and the sour note implications of a defeat in his final race, the Pimlico Special, were ameliorated by the fact the race was won by Calumet's Fervent.

As difficult as it is to imagine, Armed's entire championship campaign of 1947 could have been obliterated, say by injury, and Calumet still would have been the leading owner. Moreover, it still would have set a record in earnings!

No stable had ever accounted for $1 million in a single year, but Calumet Farm in 1947 found this barrier easily passed and raced on toward a second million. The total was $1,402,436. On the breeders' list the record total was $1,807,432, double all but two previous yearly totals for a breeder. A preponderance of the one hundred wins for the team, eighty-five, were attributed that year to Jimmy, and he led trainers with $1,334,805, which was more than double his father's previous record. He and his father had a sense of tidiness in records, for when they had approached the end of the year with ninety-nine wins, Jimmy cranked up Great Spirit a bit earlier than intended so he would win race number one hundred for Calumet that year, on December 29.

Aside from Armed, where had all this treasure of 1947 come from? Well, there were the champion two-year-old, Citation, and the champion two-year-old filly, Bewitch. Also on hand was a classic winner, Preakness victor Faultless, who also won four other stakes. Then, too, there was another three-year-old, Fervent, good enough to win the American Derby, Pimlico Special, and two other stakes, all ranging from $25,000 to $60,000 in added value. The Whirlaway filly Whirl Some won the Selima and Marguerite during the autumn in Maryland, prompting some suggestion that she was better than her champion stablemate, Bewitch. Pot o' Luck was back to win the Ben Ali, and Twosy added the Colonial. The two-year-old Free America won the $20,000 George Woolf Memorial, and Pep Well won three nice handicaps, including the Philadelphia.

One thing the year did not produce was a Kentucky Derby winner. Oh, well. The Calumet Derby effort that year was not bad, for Faultless was beaten only two heads, by Jet Pilot and Phalanx, while finishing third. Faultless had a special connection to the professional life of Ben Jones. He was by Calumet's rising super-sire Bull Lea and was out of Unerring, the champion-to-be in the Woolford Farm stable when Jones had left it. With Jones' encouragement, Wright had purchased Unerring as a broodmare.

In the Preakness, Faultless defeated both colts who had beaten him in the Derby. He then added the Withers but faded in the Belmont Stakes. Jimmy Jones thought he looked like a horse with back trouble and conjectured he had gotten cast in his stall, although the barn staff denied that explanation.

At any rate, Faultless won eight of twelve races at three. Fervent (Blenheim II—Hug Again, by Stimulus) won six of ten. This splitting of honors between friends left Phalanx to take the three-year-old championship.

In the two-year-old division of 1947, an arch example of Calumet's potency came in the Washington Park Futurity. Two Calumet colts, Citation and Free America, and their distaff companion, Bewitch, formed an entry that was sent off at 1-5. Jimmy Jones found himself in the unusual position of not only assuming he would win but also thinking how to run one-two-three. He counseled the riders against overuse of any horse so long as a stablemate was in command. The jockey fees would be split among them. Bewitch, the filly, had enough speed to lead all the way and won by a length from Citation, with Free America third.

Bewitch (Bull Lea—Potheen, by Wildair) had made her debut at Keeneland, winning by six lengths. She was still unbeaten at the time of the Washington Futurity, having won the Debutante by eight lengths, the Hyde Park by eight, the Pollyanna by five, and the Arlington Lassie by two and three-quarters lengths. Doug Dodson had ridden her in every race, and she was switched from the division credited to Jimmy to Ben's after three races.

Bewitch's unbeaten status was seemingly extended to nine races as she arrived home first in the Matron, but she bore in during the race and was disqualified to last. In her final race she faced Citation again in the Futurity but was unable to handle him by then and finished third.

Citation was a large, lengthy son of Bull Lea and out of Hydroplane II, a Hyperion mare whom Wright had purchased in England. He was one of two Bull Lea colts in the foal crop of 1945 that appeared the best among the forty or so youngsters in the crop when they were yearlings. The Jones boys, farm manger Paul Ebelhart, and contemporary yearling man Bob Moore all placed at the top the colts to be known to history as Citation and Coaltown.

Citation came to hand first, and by the time of the Belmont Futurity he had won six of seven, his only defeat coming at the hands of Bewitch. He had won the Elementary Stakes and Futurity Trial, and then in his eighth start, he was part of what seemed to be a five-horse battle late in the Futurity before he emphatically left the others behind and won by three lengths.

Citation then was stretched from sprint distances to the mile and a sixteenth of the Pimlico Futurity and won in the mud by daylight over Better Self and Ace Admiral. He had won eight of nine and earned $155,680 but was a better horse than the record showed!

THE GREATEST

At three, Citation won nineteen of twenty, and his one loss came under circumstances the rider might have overcome had it been a more important event. He elicited a lasting loyalty among many who saw him run. From Ben Jones came such declarations as "Citation can catch any horse he can see," and "he was the greatest horse anyone ever had the opportunity to fool with — the only Derby horse I was ever sure of." Jockey Eddie Arcaro declared Citation the greatest of the many champions he rode.

At two and three Citation won twenty-seven of twenty-nine and arguably could have won the two others had circumstances demanded. Thereafter, injury cost him a year and a bit of his greatness. Forty-nine years after his retirement, Citation was voted third behind Man o' War and Secretariat in polls of the best of the twenty-first century. Had he retired at three, as the two others did, he might have shouldered his way up at least one more spot.

In comparing the two of the three with whom he was familiar, Turf writer Joe Palmer famously called Man o' War "a living flame," Citation "a well-oiled machine." While the 16.2-hand Man o' War was a high-headed, shiny chestnut — a bronzed warrior — the 16-hand Citation was a flawless bay — a racehorse.

The sustained and sublime brilliance of Citation's three-year-old season was achieved despite the turmoil of a jockey change, a hastily escalated schedule, and even tragedy.

Doug Dodson had been riding well for Calumet and was the long-standing partner of Armed. From 1945 into 1948, he rode Armed in forty-nine of fifty-six races, and he won several races on Citation at two, including the Pimlico Futurity. Jimmy Jones noted, however, that Dodson seemed to have to urge on Citation more than did Albert Snider, who won five races on the colt, among them the Futurity. Jones had not figured out why this was the case when he decided to keep Snider aboard for Citation's early three-year-old races.

It was not until later, Jones recalled, he figured out Citation's hole card, as he put it: "He wanted his jockeys to have their hands very close together in his mane. If they spread their hands apart, as jockeys can do when taking a long hold, he wouldn't run as willingly."

In Florida, early in 1948, Jones had not wanted *any* jockey to ride Citation in a race very soon, but the competitive nature of owner Wright came into play. One of Wright's best friends and fishing companions was Edward S. Moore, who owned a colt named Relic. When Relic began to reel off some victories in dashing style, Wright went to Jones and said, by the trainer's memory, "Jimmy, I want to beat that horse of Eddie Moore's the very first time they run him against Citation."

As recorded by Kent Hollingsworth, in *The Kentucky Thoroughbred* (University Press of Kentucky, 1976), Wright also noted he did not want Citation to get beat in the process of preparing for this meeting. "I was a young man then ... and I kind of took that as an order," Jones recalled.

Jones found a spot, a tough one, for Citation on February 2, when the colt won an overnight race at six furlongs, and two days later Relic dashed home in the Bahamas Stakes. They appeared to be on a collision course in either the nine-furlong Everglades Stakes or Flamingo, the first only two weeks away. The Joneses thus took the unusual step of running Citation against older horses, and in so doing found out just what kind of colt they had. On February 11 Citation went out for the seven-furlong Seminole Handicap. Champion stablemate Armed was in with 128 pounds to the youngster's 112, and Faultless was in the race, too. Two other very good older sprinters, Delegate and Buzfuz, also took aim against the younger colt. This would almost universally be looked upon as a stern task for a three-year-old in February. Only Citation looked upon it differently, and his opinion was proven correct as he got home by a length over Delegate, with Armed third.

Jockey Snider had been warned not to abuse the colt in such a demanding situation, but afterward he quipped, "after a quarter of a mile, I was just playing with those horses."

Jones told Plowden and Hirsch, "At that moment, I realized I had a really great horse." Citation was ready for Relic, but the meeting was anticlimactic. In the Everglades Stakes, Citation won handily and Relic was unplaced. Thereafter, the Wright–Moore rivalry would have to be relegated to the fishing boat, for Relic went wrong.

Citation was in splendid fettle and picked up the Flamingo by six.

Then tragedy intervened. Jockey Snider went out on a fishing trip in the Florida Keys with two friends. A storm blew in, and the men were reported missing. Jimmy Jones had a pilot's license and took part in the search, but while the boat was eventually found, its passengers were not.

Dodson, upset over losing the mount on Citation, had left the stable, and Jones had immediately named Snider as first-string rider. With Snider suddenly gone, the Joneses turned again to Arcaro, even though he had made a Derby commitment on Ben Whitaker's My Request. Arcaro was urged into riding Citation in his next race, the Chesapeake Trial, at Maryland's Havre de Grace track.

Citation caught mud in the Trial. The colt had won seven in a row, but Jimmy stressed bringing him back safely above bringing him back first, if a choice had to be made. A colt named Hefty carried Citation wide repeatedly, and Saggy took advantage by opening a long lead. Citation closed to menace but was a length short. Arcaro might have gotten him home with a punishing ride, but the Chesapeake Trial was not the end game, after all.

Illustrative of how seriously Jimmy Jones took such matters, authors Plowden and Hirsch explained that the trainer went back through records and found that Hefty had never run wide before and that, afterward, he tracked the animal to the extent he was aware he never did so again.

Next was the Chesapeake Stakes itself, an event that for many years was a viable Derby prep. Arcaro was up again, but again there would be drama. Citation's special bit broke when a gate man grabbed his bridle. Starter Eddie Blind had him fitted with a regular D-bit, kept on hand for such emergencies. Citation was difficult to manage in the running and was all over the track, but he won by four and a half lengths. Arcaro, then, had two experiences with Citation: a loss and a disturbingly wanton journey to victory. Still, he had an inkling about what he was on and found a way to slip out of his plan to ride My Request at Churchill Downs.

The bit that broke was a device the Joneses had fashioned back in Parnell. "I had developed what was to become widely known as the Citation bit," Jimmy Jones said. "Actually, it was based on the old Norton driving bit used on many horses when I was a boy on the farm in Missouri. It was a double snaffle bit [with lines] up through the brow band and between the horse's ears. Two rings, one on either side of the bit, slid up and down, giving the rider better control of a robust horse." Jones had a worker at a boat yard replicate the device after the first one broke.

Of all the sentimental tales about Calumet Farm stored in the bosom of racing fans of the time, two probably stood out. One was the story of Whirlaway and the one-eyed blinker. The other was the springtime of Coaltown and Citation.

Although there apparently was no pecking order in terms of who had the better division of the Calumet stable, Citation was in the group that Jimmy Jones had when Ben shipped out to Kentucky with some others. The father's stable included Coaltown, yet another Bull Lea colt with a fascinating past.

As mentioned, Citation and Coaltown had been divined as the best of their crop early. Citation had lived up to such promise, but Coaltown fell flat — literally. When he was two and in training in Chicago, Coaltown caught a cold, which produced an abscess in his throat. The abscess broke during a morning work, and Coaltown collapsed on the racetrack.

"I rode over and looked at him," Ben Jones would recall. "He was lying there with blood and pus running out of his nostrils, and you wouldn't have given a hundred dollars for him. I wouldn't have bet we'd get him back to the barn."

Coaltown (Bull Lea—Easy Lass, by Blenheim II) recovered and got to the races in February at Hialeah. While the Joneses were busy producing their champion to Wright's satisfaction, Coaltown won a pair of races in spectacular style and was said to work a half-mile in :43 4/5.

Once Ben got Coaltown to Kentucky, things got serious. Like his stablemate, Coaltown made child's play of beating older horses sprinting, in the Phoenix Handicap, then won easily in his distance test, the mile and one eighth Bluegrass Stakes. Kentuckians had a hard time looking past him. They had heard about Citation, but they had seen Coaltown.

Six years earlier Eddie Arcaro had been given his choice between two Greentree horses in the Kentucky Derby. He had chosen Devil Diver over Shut Out and had watched from sixth as the other horse finished first. He was sensitive to such possibilities, and the Kentucky talk about Coaltown was nettlesome. He went to Ben Jones for assurance. As the jockey later recalled, Ben told him "the horse that Citation could not run down had not yet been born."

Citation tuned up by winning the Derby Trial. The Calumet entry for the 1948 Kentucky Derby was 2-5 and such was its dominance in a field of only six that Churchill Downs management, on the day of its great moment in the sport, took the businessman's route and eliminated place and show betting.

The track for the Derby was sloppy, a condition that creates a visceral uncertainty as horses go to the post, regardless of perceived form. Coaltown scooted to a rather large lead, which Arcaro noticed. In his autobiography he admitted, "Let me tell you that I was plenty scared back there while Coaltown was virtually skimming over the ground a way out in front. I was following my orders implicitly, but … Coaltown was running so easily."

Jimmy Jones visited the Churchill Downs backstretch during Derby Week for many years and never seemed to tire of telling stories of his Derbys. Unfailingly friendly, he would relive 1948 and many other Derby moments. One of his best memories, which the present author savored in hearing, was that, even he — the damned trainer, no less — had a moment when he watched Coaltown approach the far turn and "the thought flickered through my mind that that old man [his father] had been tricking me."

No worry.

True, Ben Jones was down as the trainer of record for both Calumet colts that day, which would allow him to win his fourth Kentucky Derby — and thereby tie Derby Dick Thompson for the record — regardless of who had handled Citation more frequently day to day. But Ben had not lied to son and jockey.

Citation went at Coaltown as he went at his competitive life, picking him up rather easily and dismissing the suggestion that here was some sort of threat. "After Citation … had stowed him away," wrote Arcaro, "I knew … Old Ben had called it right, again." Citation won by three and a half lengths, Coaltown was second, and Eddie's erstwhile partner, My Request, was third.

"This was a memorable day for me," Arcaro wrote. "I had broken the old jinx that Futurity winners never win Derbys. And I was the first jockey in history to win four Runs for the Roses."

(Arcaro had established a fund that dedicated a portion of Citation's earnings for Albert Snider's family. Calumet owner Wright, upon learning of this plan, pledged to match whatever Arcaro provided. Both were upset when word of the charitable plan was made public.)

The Triple Crown is conceived as a highly competitive, testing series. However, when a horse approaches the Derby already perceived as potentially great and then ratifies this thought by winning, the competition in the next two classics is not always particularly demanding. This was true in Citation's case.

With Jimmy restored as trainer of record for the rest of the Triple Crown, Citation was 1-10 for the Preakness. He rolled home by five and a half over Vulcan's Forge. In the Belmont he was 1-5 and defeated Better Self — and any lingering hope that distance would be an issue — by eight lengths. His time of 2:28 1/5 in the Belmont matched Count Fleet's stakes record, and we suppose there was a moment when Warren Wright Sr. enveloped his second Triple Crown and thought, "take that, John D. Hertz!"

At the behest of Gene Mori, who had established Garden State Park in New Jersey, as well as owning Hialeah, Jones ran Citation in the Jersey Stakes between the Preakness and Belmont. Citation won by eleven lengths.

As of the Belmont, Citation had won six consecutive races, and within a month he had won the Stars and Stripes Handicap in Chicago to increase the streak to seven. This skein would grow to sixteen and take several years to play out.

Not even for a Citation, however, would racing always be a snap. As Jimmy Jones relived it for Plowden and Hirsch:

> When Citation was in training for [the Arlington Classic] a little thing happened that might have ended his brilliant career just when he was in his prime. The horse was walking around the barn one morning when the manure truck came by, hit a tin feed tub, and caused a raucous clatter. It sounded like the sky was falling — in great junks of concrete and landing on tin roofs. Citation, alarmed by the noise, leaped high in the air and came down with a dull thud. The result was he pulled the big muscle that reaches from the hip-bone down to the upper leg or stifle. At the moment, nobody knew exactly what was wrong, but they realized he had been badly hurt. I had to take him out of training.

Happily, an incident that could have been an end was merely an interruption. Jones and a veterinarian he trusted, Dr. R.D. Coneley, treated the injury with what Jones called "inductothermy — a machine built up a heat field by means of electrical energy, and it penetrated to the deep-seated muscle injury that we figured was bothering the horse." It was a long way from the Norton driving bit, for Jones clearly was not a man tied only to tradition to the detriment of innovation. Citation was out of action for only six weeks, before winning a prep and then the American Derby. His goal back east was the Jockey Club Gold Cup, but there was a three-week gap.

Unlike today's trainers, Jimmy Jones said "I always preferred racing up to a major stake rather than training up. That way, you get a better look at your horse, and he benefits more mentally from the competition than he would in a workout."

Citation, naturally, by then would be a name that scuttled a race if it popped up on overnight entries, and Jones found himself with few choices. He wound up prepping Citation for the two miles on Saturday by running him one mile on Wednesday. Citation was unperturbed. He won the mile Sysonby over such horses as Spy Song and First Flight as his prep for the two-mile Jockey Club Gold Cup, in which he defeated the previous year's champion three-year-old, Phalanx, by seven lengths. Phalanx tried again in the mile and five-eighths Empire City Gold Cup and did better; he lost to Citation by only two lengths.

Citation had a walkover in the Pimlico Special. Though the Calumet stable routinely spent the winters in Florida, Citation headed to California, with his first target the Santa Anita Maturity, leading logically to the Santa Anita Handicap. This plan involved a rest of several months, but Citation was in such roaring good form that Jimmy acceded to the request of his friend Mori. The owner of Hialeah and Garden State had also purchased the Tanforan track in northern California. He called Jimmy Jones and said he would count it as quite a favor were Citation to run in his $50,000 Tanforan Handicap. Jones thought that looked like an easy spot and agreed. Citation had had slightly more than a month since the Pimlico Special, and a month and a half since a real race, so Jimmy gave him a prep at Tanforan, a sprint he duly won in the mud. Arcaro wrote three years later that "he didn't run with his usual fire and zest. I knew something was wrong. I expressed my opinion to Jimmy Jones, and he said not to let it worry me, that he would be sharper for his handicap engagement."

"We went to the well once too often," Jimmy lamented of the Tanforan Handicap. Citation won the mile and a quarter race by five lengths in track-record time, but, Arcaro noted in his book, "he was unable to extend himself and didn't seem to have the will to go on. I believe I hit him more in that race than in any other."

A few days later, an osselet, an enlargement in the fetlock caused by increased fluid of the joint, was observed. The horse returned to Florida, where a young veterinarian from Kentucky, Dr. Art Davidson, was brought in to fire the area. The procedure involves implanting hot iron or electric needles to the affected area to encourage healing blood flow. Jones later second-guessed Wright's decision that the horse stay with the stable. Jones thought horses that had been fired benefited from cold weather. Moreover, the colt in his idleness gained weight, despite Jones trying "to guard against it. A cripple should be kept on a starvation diet."

Although the year ended on a worrisome note, it had been another banner season. Calumet swept the honors, statistical and otherwise, in 1948. Citation, Calumet's second Triple Crown winner and the three-year-old champion and Horse of the Year, earned a record for a single season, $709,470.

Jimmy Jones did not break his own record but was the leading trainer with $1,118,670. Calumet led as owner ($1,269,710) and breeder ($1,559,850).

Oddly, the only other stakes winner attributed to Jimmy Jones in 1948 was In the Pink, a Bull Lea filly who won the $25,000 Misty Isle Stakes. Ben Jones, in addition to the times he was down as Citation's trainer of record, was credited with stakes wins by Bewitch, Coaltown, Faultless, and Fervent.

THE SUBSTITUTE CHAMPION

Citation was away from the races for his entire four-year-old season. Delete a Horse of the Year from the entries and most stables would accept the reality of seriously diminished prospects. In Calumet's case, it was a matter similar to the English royal succession: The Horse of the Year is hurt, all praise the new Horse of the Year.

Coaltown was still no Citation, and his Horse of the Year title had to be shared, but he did provide Calumet the sixth such title in nine years. Further, to perk up the troops who were missing Citation, the three-year-old Ponder came along to win the diamond anniversary running of the Kentucky Derby; he thus enabled Warren Wright to tie the owner's record for number of wins and Ben A. Jones to break the trainer's mark.

Ponder was a Derby winner sired by a Derby winner, being a son of Pensive—Miss Rushin, by Blenheim II. He had been obscure as a two-year-old in 1948, that division being the one weak squad among the Calumet troops. Ponder was showing some promise during the next winter, but it was indicative of his status at the time that Ben and Jimmy ducked the main winter target, the Flamingo Stakes.

At Keeneland, where he had been assigned to Ben Jones' spring division, Ponder was unplaced going six and a half furlongs and did not run in the Blue Grass Stakes. However, he was entered for the Derby Trial, apparently his last chance to earn his way into the Derby itself. The one-mile Trial was the longest race Ponder had run in, and while he posed no threat to the speedy favorite, Olympia, the extra furlong saw him come from behind to finish second, well clear of third-place Capot.

By 1949, Kentucky Derby watchers had a sense some magic might be in the devil's red and blue silks, but even with that in mind, it was sufficiently difficult to make a case for Ponder that he went off at 16-1. The wily Jones boys took an extra precaution against this particular colt becoming unsettled or distracted by the Derby crowd. Ponder was ridden, not led, from the barn area to the front side of Churchill Downs and then was ridden up and down the stretch a furlong or so to become accustomed to the hubbub, prior to proceeding to the indoor saddling paddock behind the stands.

Jockey Steve Brooks allowed Ponder to trail in last place as favored

Olympia set out on a trip beyond his best distance. The Calumet colt was still only twelfth after six furlongs but had advanced to sixth by the turn for home. Brooks chose to concede ground by staying outside rather than risk being blocked while trying to work through closer to the rail. Ponder's overland rally continued, and he gained the lead over Greentree Stable's similarly emerging Capot. The Calumet colt got home by three lengths for his first stakes win.

Ben A. Jones had his fifth Derby, to supplant Derby Dick Thompson as the leader, and Warren Wright had his unique Diamond Jubilee Kentucky Derby trophy, with its appropriate precious-jewel inlays.

Ben Jones, in his best W.C. Fields diction, commented some years later: "I was bothered in not being able to figure if Ponder's peak and the Derby would arrive simultaneously. They did."

In the Preakness, Capot did not have to chase a speed burner like Olympia, so the Greentree runner had plenty left, while Brooks — by his own admission — misjudged the pace and had Ponder too far back early to have any reasonable chance of getting into contention. Ponder finished fifth. In the Peter Pan at a mile and an eighth, Capot was drawn into a speed duel with some of the lightweights, which set things up for Ponder, who came along to overpower them all and win by three-parts of a length.

The spring classics concluded with Capot getting away with a controlled pace and just holding off Ponder to win the Belmont Stakes by a half-length. Brooks came in for some criticism for trying to get through on the inside turning for home and being blocked momentarily.

Ponder thereafter added some of the top prizes of Chicago and New York. He won both the Arlington Classic and American Derby in the Midwest and prevailed in the autumn distance tests of the Lawrence Realization and Jockey Club Gold Cup. He struck himself in the Gold Cup, and after some thought of trying to run him in the Pimlico Special, Ponder was retired for the year. He had won nine of twenty-one starts, but that was some nine!

While Ponder was winning his share of headlines in the glamorous three-year-old division, Coaltown had been racing through an impressive twelve-for-fifteen record as a four-year-old. The season started with Coaltown showing so much speed that it was decided he needed a stronger jockey. In his first start he broke poorly but swallowed the field to win. Then, poor Eldon Nelson ran into criticism for being aboard when Coaltown won by ten lengths and equaled the world record of 1:47 3/5 for a mile and an eighth. The fractional times included such anomalies for those days as 1:08 4/5 for six furlongs and 1:34 1/5 for a mile.

With Ted Atkinson, perceived as a stronger rider, aboard, Coaltown was more tractable in winning the McLennan Handicap by four lengths. He then proved himself at the Derby distance of a mile and a quarter when he toured in front to win the Widener Handicap by two lengths as part of a 1-20 entry with third-place Faultless.

Walkovers of the era tended to come late in the season. By then, when dominant champions emerged, various pretenders had taken their shots, and while lacking the historic perspective to use the phrase "*no mas*," they employed the equally compelling tactic of simply not showing up. In Coaltown's case, though, a race as early as April 23 produced no challengers, and he won the Edward Burke Handicap in a walkover at Havre de Grace despite being assigned 130 pounds.

Coaltown won two more stakes to run his winning streak to eight. Along the way, the Joneses declined handicapper John Blanks Campbell's compliment of 138 pounds for the Suburban, the name Blanks perhaps being turned against the perpetrator, as in "blankety-blank."

When Coaltown finally lost, it was while giving sixteen pounds to Star Reward in the Equipoise Mile. In his next two races, however, he beat the same horse giving the same or comparable amounts of weight, while also defeating his old-timer stablemate, Armed. In the Whirlaway, Coaltown lowered Equipoise's world mile record to 1:34 (Ponder was second), and he then added the Washington Park Handicap.

"At this point, he had won twelve of thirteen races, had broken four track records, and had set or equaled three world records," summarized Kent Hollingsworth in *The Great Ones* (The Blood-Horse, 1970). His speed was well documented, but he had never won a close race, never shown the courage needed in a battle. In the barn, Coaltown's nickname was "Wheezy," because of the rattle in his throat, so perhaps he had a physical inability to withstand the pressure of a heated race. His performance against the younger Capot did nothing to change his status of not having won a close one, for the youngster tracked him, tracked him, tracked him, and then went on by to win the Sysonby Mile by a length and a half.

The decisive race came in the Pimlico Special. Again, Capot would not let Coaltown's early speed dominate, and when Brooks tried to take his horse back off the pace, the younger colt romped away. Capot won by a dozen lengths. Coaltown was the obvious choice as champion older horse and won out as Horse of the Year as well on the Thoroughbred Racing Associations ballot, whereas Capot won the division title as well as the ultimate honor in the *Daily Racing Form* poll. The half-length between victory and defeat for Ponder in the Belmont might have been decisive in the latter poll.

Coaltown was but one of four champions for Calumet in 1949. The stable's Wistful and Two Lea shared honors in the three-year-old filly ranks, and Bewitch returned to win championship honors as the top older filly.

Wistful (Sun Again—Easy Lass, by Blenheim II) did her part in 1949 in giving Calumet one of its most sublime weekends when she won the Kentucky Oaks the afternoon before Ponder's Derby. Ben Jones and Calumet followed Derby Dick Thompson and Colonel Bradley as the second trainer and second owner to achieve this double. It would not be the last for Jones and Calumet.

Wistful, Coaltown's half sister, then proceeded to become the first to complete what was then regarded as the filly counterpart to the Triple Crown. Following the route of the colts, this entailed victory at Pimlico in the Pimlico Oaks and at Belmont in the Coaching Club American Oaks. It was not done intentionally, but Wistful handed off the baton to stablemate Two Lea in her next race, the Cleopatra Handicap. Wistful came out of the race with an osselet and did not start again at three, having a record of six wins in eleven starts.

Two Lea (Bull Lea—Two Bob, by The Porter) had won one previous stakes, the Princess Doreen, and thereafter she won the Cleopatra Handicap, had a rest, and tuned up for the next year with an allowance win in late December. She won six of seven at three, but it is difficult to reconcile her being voted equal distinction with the Filly Triple Crown winner.

Bewitch, who had been champion at two, earned her title at four by winning only four of thirteen races in 1949. The foursome consisted of the Churchill Downs Inaugural, Misty Isle, Beverly, and Vineland handicaps. Additional stakes winners for Calumet in 1949 were Pep Well, Faultless, Free America, Theory, and Duchess Peg. The richest races from this group were Duchess Peg's $25,000 Arlington Lassie and Theory's $25,000 Champagne, as Calumet broke through with juvenile stakes wins for the only time in two seasons.

Jimmy Jones was the leading trainer with $978,587 in 1949, and Calumet again led the owners' and breeders' list.

In 1950 Citation returned, but while he was a powerful runner he was not his old self. He won his comeback start, a six-furlong sprint at Santa Anita on January 11. This was his sixteenth consecutive victory, the start of the streak beginning with the Chesapeake Stakes almost two years earlier. That number took on more meaning forty-six years later when Cigar stretched his own winning streak to sixteen, matching Citation's as the longest in major American racing of modern times.

Citation was beaten in his next race and was consigned to a pedestrian-looking record of only two wins in nine starts that season. However, his defeats included some sterling efforts in his frustrating four losses to the emerging champion Noor. Citation's sole stakes win that year found him beating the speedy Bolero in world-record time of 1:33 3/5 in the Golden Gate Mile.

Such a promising effort, along with an earnings total flirting near the unprecedented milestone of $1 million, encouraged the decision to keep

Citation in training for a six-year-old season. This idea changed to a sentimental crusade when Warren Wright Sr. died on the last day of 1950. Mrs. Wright then thought of the $1-million goal in terms of a tribute to her husband.

Aside from Citation, 1950 brought additional major victories from some of the stars of 1949. Two Lea repeated as a champion, taking the older distaff honors. Two Lea won her first major target that year at Santa Anita, the Santa Margarita against her own gender and then joined stablemate Ponder in the Santa Anita Maturity (later renamed the Charles H. Strub Stakes). It is typical of the glut of success he had enjoyed that Jimmy Jones found the one-two finish in a $100,000 race irritating. Ponder won, with Two Lea second. Jones thought it should have been the other way around, but the race strategy acquiesced to the owner's preference that the stallion prospect get the victory if a choice were available.

Two Lea was third in the Santa Anita Handicap and second in her only remaining start before soundness problems stopped her for the year. Hers was an unusual record for a champion, two wins in five starts, of which only one came after February.

Wistful, co-champion at three with Two Lea, had an active campaign at four in 1950 but won only one stakes, the Clang Handicap. Two-time champion Bewitch won the Black Helen Handicap at five, and Derby winner Ponder won the San Antonio, Marchbank, Tanforan, and Arlington handicaps in addition to the Santa Anita Maturity. Theory won the Bahamas early but did not go on as a classic colt.

Calumet retained the leadership on the breeders' list in 1950, but Brookmeade Stable led the owners while its Preston Burch led the trainers.

MRS. MARKEY'S ERA

The key historic moment for Calumet Farm in 1951 came on July 14, when Citation as a six-year-old won the Hollywood Gold Cup. The purse raised his total earnings to $1,085,760 as he attained his late owner's goal of being the first Thoroughbred to earn a million dollars. It was not about the money so much as about the honor and status. Underscoring just what Calumet Farm was in those days, the runner-up purse of $20,000 that day made Bewitch the all-time leading money-winning filly.

Citation went out in a manner befitting his past glories. He lost his first four races of 1951 but then put together a curtain-call string of three major scores, taking the Argonaut and American handicaps before his four-length Gold Cup victory. Jimmy Jones said later that he had been training Citation mentally more than physically, "for his legs were gone." This must have been exaggeration, for Calumet hardly would have purposely exposed the horse to grave injury even for the millionaire goal; further, Jones also was quoted that Citation "was just getting good and there was a $50,000 race [the Sunset], just there for the taking."

Mrs. Wright, however, decided that climbing Mount Everest did not require an encore: "Jimmy," she said over the phone, "I wish you would call the press tomorrow and tell everyone that Citation has run his last race and will be retired. A million dollars was the goal of Mr. Wright for the horse, and now he has achieved it." Citation shared honors with Hill Prince as champion older horse.

Calumet clung to the leading breeder status in 1951, but Greentree Stable and trainer John Gaver again took the other honors. Aside from Citation's big days, two of his mates from the 1947 foal crops also added final stakes victories. Bewitch won the important Vanity Handicap and bowed out with twenty wins from fifty-five starts and earnings of $462,605. Coaltown, who had won only a purse race from four starts at five in 1950, was back at six to win the Art Sparks Handicap and Children's Hospital Handicap. He ran his record to twenty-three wins in thirty-nine starts and earnings of $415,675 and joined Citation on the same railroad car home to retirement in Kentucky.

Also winning stakes for Calumet in 1951 were Wistful, All Blue, A Gleam (Twilight Tear's daughter), and Hill Gail. The juvenile colt Hill Gail showed promise in winning the Arlington Futurity and running second in the Washington Park Futurity. (These two races were not merged, as the Arlington-Washington Futurity, until 1962.)

The year's Kentucky Derby effort had centered on Fanfare, who won the Derby Trial. A Pensive colt who was a half brother to Coaltown and Wistful, Fanfare raced with the front ranks of a twenty-horse Derby field but was then crowded and could not challenge. His fifth-place finish matched Technician's as the worst for any Derby entrant credited to Ben A. Jones.

As matters stood at the dawn of 1952, it could have been inferred that Calumet Farm was beginning to slip. Its major wins of the year just ended had in large part depended on six-year-olds, and while they now became fresh additions to the breeding stock, that is always an uncertain element. The stable had fallen from its place as leading owner, and its master, Warren Wright Sr., had passed away.

What happened in 1952 was quite the opposite. Calumet won another Kentucky Derby, unveiled another great filly champion, set a record in earnings as a breeder, and returned to the top of the owner and trainer categories. Along the way old Ben A. Jones went on an outrageous tear of winning fifteen consecutive stakes! On a personal front, Mrs. Wright wed Admiral Gene Markey, a charming novelist and raconteur with whom she launched into a glamorous life of travel and fulfillment that lasted nearly three decades.

The transfiguration of Hill Gail from problem horse to Derby winner saw the Jones boys again relying on the practical wisdom acquired during their Missouri days. As Jimmy told Plowden and Hirsch:

"Hill Gail was challenging me. I tried all kinds of equipment on him — Citation bit, overcheck, prongs, figure-eight, you name it. But he was stubborn, ill-tempered, and as mean-spirited as they come. He was strong as a bull, but with the disposition of a hornet. Nothing could hold him."

Jones thought Hill Gail's pedigree predetermined his disposition. Hill Gail was by the great Bull Lea, but his dam, Jane Gail, by Blenheim II, had been too erratic and high strung to be effective as a racehorse although capable enough to have worked five furlongs in fifty-seven seconds one morning.

With the Santa Anita Derby approaching and Hill Gail's manner unchanged, Jones harked back to Jones Stock Farm days:

"I recalled a trick we used in breaking a young mean workhorse. We would hitch the young tough guy between two old, large, well-broken workhorses and set the doubletrees so that he did most of the work. In a short time, he'd wear down and become a good boy." Something similar was tried on Hill Gail.

Hill Gail had won the San Vicente but lost the San Gabriel. After his Jones Stock Farm crash course in etiquette, he won the Santa Anita Derby, the big target for three-year-olds in the West and the California counterpart of the coveted Flamingo Stakes in Florida. Keeping Hill Gail busy, Ben and Jimmy won the Phoenix Handicap against older horses but skipped the Blue Grass in favor of an overnight race in which an apprentice got the mount and botched it. Hill Gail then won the Derby Trial, and he went into the Kentucky Derby as the 6-5 favorite. As Eddie Arcaro recalled it, one more bit of professor-of-horsedom played out in the paddock: "Hill Gail was an idiot horse. He got to acting up in the paddock before the Derby, and B.A. says to old 'Slow and Easy' (another revered Calumet employee), 'Slow, sorta point that horse toward me,' and then B.A. smacked Hill Gail right on the nose and staggered that horse not 10 minutes before the race. That settled him, though."

Arcaro recalled, too, that Jones gave him so many instructions, not all consistent, that he did not really know what B.A. wanted him to do. It made little difference, for Hill Gail was still Hill Gail, lessons or not.

"Hill Gail got away from me and ran off — he bolted. I thought sure he was going out the gap at the half-mile pole, so I stood up, trying to straighten him out, and when things settled down I found I was about 10 lengths on top. Well, we did just stagger home, barely holding off Sub Fleet. I came back to the winner's circle, and B.A. says, 'That's my boy! Rode him just like I toldja!' "

Derby memories deserve drama in the telling. The chart, however, makes no mention of a lead of more than five lengths, and the final margin was two lengths. Still, Arcaro had set the record for a jockey by winning his fifth Derby, and Jones had broken his own record with his sixth as a trainer.

Calumet Farm was credited with a record fifth Derby. One can assume that, had Bradley been able to communicate from the great beyond, he would have pointed out in gentlemanly fashion that he and Warren Wright each had won four Derbys and now the widow Wright had won one on her own, so that four remained the record. History generally has been kind to Bradley, but it has tended to combine all things Calumet into one column insofar as the Kentucky Derby is concerned.

Hill Gail came out of the Derby with a bruised left fore but was sent on to Pimlico. Before the Preakness, however, he developed an osselet, and he did not get back to the races that year. (He was stakes-placed at four and five but never won another stakes.) One Count came along to be three-year-old champion and Horse of the Year for 1952.

The day before Hill Gail's Derby, Jones and Calumet for the second time launched an Oaks–Derby double. The Oaks winner was Real Delight.

At three in 1952, Real Delight (Bull Lea—Blue Delight, by Blue Larkspur) won eleven of twelve races. Her lone defeat came in an allowance in which she was ridden by Donald Devine, the same ill-starred apprentice who had ridden Hill Gail to defeat.

Development of a splint near the knee in the spring of her two-year-old season had kept Real Delight from action that year. When she appeared at three, she was a well-grown, 16.2-hand filly, and she came out winning at Santa Anita. After two victories she shipped east with the Ben Jones division and, at Keeneland, won the Ashland Stakes by five before her Devine blip in the allowance race. Real Delight proceeded to sweep the Filly Triple Crown, taking the Kentucky Oaks, Black-Eyed Susan (as the Pimlico Oaks had been renamed), and CCA Oaks, all by daylight margins.

The eight-race winning streak that dominated her campaign continued through the Cleopatra, Arlington Matron, Modesty, Beverly, and Beldame.

Unlike many other great fillies, Real Delight never faced males. Also, a showdown with champion Next Move was scuttled when they drew into different divisions of the Beldame. However, Real Delight did defeat older females, and her 1:34 4/5 for a mile in the Beverly was the swiftest then on record for a three-year-old filly. She carried 129 pounds, giving twenty-four to runner-up Aesthete; the champion mare Sickle's Image was third.

Under the voting policies of the day, Real Delight was named champion in both the three-year-old filly and handicap distaff divisions on the *Daily Racing Form* poll, whereas Next Move was the older distaff champion on the TRA poll.

Real Delight's spring and summer were part of the amazing phase bracketed by the dates April 24 and September 16, during which Ben Jones sent out horses in fifteen stakes races and won them all. Meanwhile, Jimmy Jones had the other division in California and won fifteen stakes on his own, although his record for that phase was "only" 48 percent wins, for his runners merely placed in sixteen stakes. (Of course, in some instances, he was working against his own win percentage by running entries.)

Ben's other major winners included Mark-Ye-Well (Bull Lea—Mar-Kell, by Blenheim II), who developed into a sterling replacement for Hill Gail in the three-year-old colt division. Mark-Ye-Well's emergence might have precluded Real Delight's opportunity to run against males, as Twilight Tear had done, for Mark-Ye-Well won the Arlington Classic and American Derby, the two top targets for three-year-old colts in the Chicago summer. He also had won the Clang and later, in New York, added the Lawrence Realization.

Also attributed to Ben Jones' division, the juvenile filly Bubbley, a full sister to Real Delight, won the Debutante and Pollyanna Stakes.

In Jimmy Jones' West Coast division, the summer star was Two Lea, back at six and unbothered by an unsightly knot on an ankle. A mare of rugged inner constitution regardless of physical frailties, Two Lea defeated males in the Hollywood Gold Cup and Children's Hospital and San Mateo handicaps. Against other distaffers the old girl won the Vanity and Ramona handicaps. The Vanity marked a Calumet three-step, for Two Lea was followed by veteran champion Wistful and stablemate Jennie Lee. Two Lea had won championships with lesser seasons, but she could not crowd into the title honors in 1952. Her final record was fifteen wins in twenty-six starts and earnings of $309,250.

A Gleam proved herself to be up to the Calumet gender challenge, defeating colts in the Westerner, Cinema, and Debonair. She also beat older stablemate Two Lea in the Milady, and against her own sex and age, she won the Hollywood Oaks. Armed's little sister Lap Full won the Del Mar Debutante and Santa Ynez at two, and Dixie Lad won the Governor's Handicap at Sacramento.

Ben Jones had only twenty-nine wins in 1952, but his $662,137 made him leading trainer in earnings. As a breeder, Calumet became the first to reach $2 million in a given year. As an owner, Calumet set no records but passed $1 million for the fourth time; at the time, no other owner had reached that mark. (Jimmy Jones explained that the bookkeeping system lumped the farm and stable expenses and that it took about $600,000 in earnings in a given year to make the overall enterprise break even.)

Four years would pass before the next time a Calumet trainer topped the list. Likewise, Calumet would not be leading owner in three of those years, although continuing to hold sway as breeder. (In that statistic Calumet led annually from 1947 to 1957.) No Calumet runner made the Derby field between Hill Gail in 1952 and Fabius in 1956, although Chanlea won the Santa Anita Derby in 1953.

Times were not dismal, however. The last stakes winners credited to Ben A. Jones were Real Delight, who won the Arlington Matron in a short four-year-old campaign, and Miz Clementine, a two-year-old filly of 1953. Miz Clementine (Bull Lea—Two Bob, by The Porter), a full sister to Two Lea, won the Pollyanna Stakes that year.

The years 1953–55 saw Mark-Ye-Well add the Santa Anita Handicap, Santa Anita Maturity, and five other stakes to the earlier victories of his distinguished three-year-old season. He thus had a career record of eleven stakes victories, among fourteen wins from forty starts and exceptional earnings of $581,910. He was the only Calumet horse to win the Santa Anita Handicap, although such stalwarts as Citation, Ponder, and Two Lea had been sent out in the "Big 'Cap." The Jones boys had figured out that Mark-Ye-Well's tendency to throw out a stifle could be overcome to some extent by exercise. They took him out twice a day rather than once, and whenever he was shipped by rail they assigned him the entire end of a car so he could move around.

Miz Clementine proved of similar durability as her full sister Two Lea, although she never managed a season's championship. She won a career total of eleven stakes. Miz Clementine defeated males in the California Derby and won the Hollywood Oaks, New Castle, and Vagrancy. The highlight of her career would have been a victory over Kentucky Derby winner Determine in the 1955 Santa Anita Maturity but for a misstep that bothered Jimmy Jones for years afterward.

Jones had noted that the mare Two Bob and her foals had the peculiarity of sulking if hit hard on the right side. In the paddock prior to the 1955 Maturity, he had meant to remind Arcaro of that characteristic, but so many celebrities and other well-wishers had clustered around that his effort to be polite to one and all meant he did not get around to it. It must have slipped Arcaro's mind as well. When the whip came down hard on her right flank during the stretch run, Miz Clementine ducked severely toward the rail, bothering Determine, and although she recovered to be first at the wire, her number had to come down.

JIMMY'S DERBYS

The year 1956 saw Calumet return to the status of leading owner in earnings. Jimmy Jones did not lead the trainers, but he had a special year. It was the first time a Kentucky Derby entrant carried his name as trainer of record, and the highlights included a Preakness victory and the thrilling score by Barbizon in the richest race of the time, the Garden State Stakes.

For Barbizon, that victory clinched juvenile championship honors.

Calumet's key Derby colts in the winter of 1956 appeared to be Pintor Lea and Fabius, although Liberty Sun briefly injected himself into the picture when he caught an off track and won the Everglades Stakes. Pintor Lea and Fabius both made it to the big race, but Pintor Lea apparently was compromised by soundness problems, and he finished fifth. Fabius stepped up nobly and effectively enough to finish second.

Fabius was in the first crop of Citation and created the mistaken impression that the great horse was destined for success at stud. His dam was Shameen, by Royal Minstrel.

The Joneses had thought Fabius had promise at two, but he won only twice in eleven starts. He was not a robust colt, and they concluded he should avoid mud. Not only could he not perform at his best, but the rigors of battling an off track left him weakened for several weeks.

During the winter of 1956, Fabius was third behind Needles in the Flamingo Stakes and Pintor Lea was third behind the same horse in the Florida Derby. Fabius won two sprint races at Keeneland and then won the Derby Trial, and the Calumet entry was 4-1 second choice to Needles in the seventeen-horse Derby field.

Bill Hartack had come on board as Calumet's rider, and the 1956 Derby was his first. Fabius was in contention from the start and took the lead in the stretch, but Needles was able to negotiate through the entire field, coming from sixteenth to win by three-quarters of a length.

In the Preakness, Fabius ran back to his Derby performance, and that time Needles was unable to get to him. The Calumet colt won by nearly two lengths. There were four weeks between the Preakness and the Belmont at that time, and Fabius ran not once but twice between the classics. He won the Jersey Stakes and ran second in the Leonard Richards Stakes.

With jockey P.J. Bailey substituting for Hartack in the Belmont, Fabius ran a very good race but perhaps was used too much too soon. His seven-length lead at the quarter-pole did not hold up, and he finished third behind Needles and Career Boy.

Jimmy Jones regretted his later decision to run Fabius in the slop in the Ohio Derby, for the delicate classic winner not only failed in that race but did not thrive thereafter.

The day before the Kentucky Derby, Calumet had passed T.C. McDowell as the leading owner of Kentucky Oaks winners. McDowell had won the race four times between 1899 and 1915. Calumet's Princess Turia defeated champion Doubledogdare to bring home the stable's fifth Oaks.

Princess Turia (Heliopolis—Blue Delight, by Blue Larkspur) was a half sister to Real Delight. She added the Black-Eyed Susan but lost the Filly Triple Crown when Levee beat her a neck in the CCA Oaks. Princess Turia also won the Acorn Stakes and Cleopatra Handicap that year. The Acorn harked back to Calumet's most audacious days, for Princess Turia dead-heated for the victory with her own stablemate, Beyond!

In the older distaff division, Miz Clementine added the New Castle Stakes and Vagrancy Handicap. She was never a champion like her sister Two Lea was on two occasions, but Miz Clementine wound up with more career stakes victories, eleven to nine. In the older male division, Twilight Tear's son Bardstown won his first stakes at four, taking five handicaps, including the $75,000 Trenton and $50,000 Equipoise Mile.

The champion in Calumet's barn in 1956 was one who leapt to headlines quickly and quickly faded. Barbizon (Polynesian—Good Blood, by Bull Lea) did not get to the races until September. By October 27 he had been given a Jones-school-of-action campaign and was making his sixth start when sent out for the Garden State Stakes. He had won all but his most recent race, when second to the very speedy Federal Hill in the mile and a sixteenth Garden State Trial. Jimmy Jones thought Hartack had not ridden a particularly smart race, and he authorized the $10,000 necessary to make Barbizon a supplemental entry for the Garden State Stakes itself a week later.

Hartack brought Barbizon up from twelfth to nail Federal Hill by a nose at the end of a mile and a sixteenth in the Garden State Stakes. The purse of $168,430 was then the largest in racing history.

Horace A. "Jimmy" Jones was credited with his first Kentucky Derby winner the next year. Even though he was winning it for Calumet Farm, which already had the record in number of victories, Jimmy's first official Derby could hardly have been more of a surprise.

As 1957 began, Calumet seemed to have an exceptional hand in the three-year-old division. In addition to a champion two-year-old who seemed to love longer distances, Ben and Jimmy had been bringing along a highly exciting prospect named Gen. Duke and another nice colt named Iron Liege. Gen. Duke and Iron Liege were both by farm stallion Bull Lea, who already had two Derby winners in Citation and Hill Gail and who had been America's leading' sire five times (1947–49 and 1952–53.)

In 1954 the editors of a yet-to-be born magazine, *Sports Illustrated*, had approached Calumet with the idea of selecting a similarly yet-to-be-born foal for a photographic essay from birth until ... whatever. The ultimate fantasy, of course, was that the be-knighted youngster might make it to the Kentucky Derby. Since *Time* publisher Henry Luce was the godfather of this enterprise, it was taken seriously, and the War Admiral mare Iron Maiden was selected. She was, of course, in foal to the farm star Bull Lea. Thus, the birth of Iron Liege was duly attended by the photographer known as Ylla.

As the winter of 1957 played out, however, it was obvious that the Bull

Lea colt out of champion Wistful, by Sun Again, would have been the better photographic subject. Gen. Duke had won one of two races at two and had been put aside because of bucked shins. At three he won only four of ten races, but that had to do with the Jones pattern of racing a horse to his peak. The four races included two victories over Bold Ruler at a mile and an eighth, one in the Everglades Stakes and the next in a world record-equaling 1:46 4/5 in the Florida Derby. Iron Liege was a respectful distance back in both races, as he was when Bold Ruler beat Gen. Duke in the Flamingo and when second to Gen. Duke in the Fountain of Youth Stakes. (Barbizon was fifth in the Fountain of Youth and never won a stakes race after the Garden State, although campaigned aggressively.)

Jimmy Jones was quoted in *In the Winner's Circle*: "I was convinced that Gen. Duke was the best three-year-old we had had since Citation." However, things began to go amiss in the spring in Kentucky — just when they are supposed to go right for Derby horses.

Iron Liege defeated Gen. Duke in a seven-furlong race at Keeneland, and jockey Hartack told Jones he had felt a little bobble in the stretch. Jones ordered X-rays, but they did the devil's work that X-rays can do: They gave no answer. Jones was thus encouraged to hope that the problem was nothing more than a stone bruise, such as the colt had suffered before.

Jimmy discovered heat in a hoof and tubbed the colt repeatedly. He was able to run Gen. Duke in the Derby Trial, but the Derby hopeful finished second to Federal Hill. Iron Liege went in the Trial, too, but ran dismally, trying to get out on Dave Erb all through the stretch.

"I still had hopes of running Gen. Duke in the Derby," Jones recalled, "and continued to work feverishly with the able, young Louisville veterinarian Dr. Alex Harthill. We tried every sort of treatment, but the foot kept getting worse instead of better. At nine o'clock on Derby morning, with the windows opened for betting on the race, I reluctantly announced to the track management and the press that Gen. Duke would not run. I never felt more miserable in my life."

Enter, again, Iron Liege. Two years earlier, his dam, Iron Maiden, had taken on matriarchal status through a daughter, Iron Reward, whose son Swaps won the Derby of 1955. Now Iron Liege was the lone combatant from the once-powerful Calumet triumvirate of Barbizon–Gen. Duke–Iron Liege. Hartack took pride of place as stable jockey, so Erb — who had won on Needles — had no chance at a second consecutive Derby.

"I don't believe any of us had the faintest hope of winning with Iron Liege in a field that included Bold Ruler, Gallant Man, and Round Table," Jones said, and yet a horseman's devotion to his craft had created a seam in how the form was read. Jones had tended to place most of his attention on Gen. Duke, but he had paid enough attention to Iron Liege and his surprisingly bad Derby Trial effort that he had surmised that, unlike most horses, Iron Liege was braver when on the inside of horses — between them and the rail — rather than outside. He discussed this with Hartack prior to putting the rider aboard.

In a moment of frivolity reflecting the cold, dark day, Jimmy threw out the line, "I wished I'd taken a slug of brandy against the chill."

Well, Iron Liege was the slug of brandy against any chill. Hartack kept him tracking the pace, vamped briefly when blocked from taking the lead from Federal Hill, then drove to the front. Bold Ruler was fighting Arcaro that day and did not stay under the circumstances, and Round Table, while a very good colt, was not yet a great one. The threat was Gallant Man, charging toward Iron Liege. Willie Shoemaker, famously, mistook the sixteenth pole for the finish line and rose in his irons for a millisecond. Sitting back down without his colt raising his head, Shoemaker drove for the victory, but Hartack was driving, too, and Iron Liege won by a nose.

"I grabbed B.A. and whirled him around in pure excitement and joy," Jimmy Jones recalled. "It was an exhilaration impossible to put into words."

Arcaro had figured out Bold Ruler's hole card in time for the Preakness, and they put Iron Liege in his place emphatically. The one-time photo foal would always have the roses to his credit, but Iron Liege was not a championship contender. He did, however, add the Jersey Stakes, Sheridan Handicap, and Laurance Armour Memorial Stakes as a three-year-old.

Retelling how a three-year-old classic season plays out inadvertently suggests a concentration on one aspect of a trainer's job. At the same time Jimmy Jones was dealing with the so-called "next Citation" and his three-year-old teammates in Florida in the winter of 1957, he and his father also were reveling in the achievements of the older Bardstown.

An example of Calumet's understanding that a breeding farm could not depend solely on its own stallions, Bardstown was a son of the outside sire Alibhai and was out of the great homebred Twilight Tear, by Bull Lea. With his distinguished Calumet heritage, Bardstown was given the name of the Kentucky town that is the site of the "Old Kentucky Home" that comes to mind each Derby Day. For the first few years of his life, this seemed a wasted tribute. But Bardstown was a poster child for the Jones boys' patience and ability to overcome trouble. The horse had to overcome puffy ankles, splints, and back trouble, but by the time Bardstown was five, Jimmy Jones had him ready to challenge the best.

Bardstown won the $50,000 Tropical Park Handicap, dropped the McLennan Handicap to the accomplished Summer Tan, and then asserted his status by defeating the same horse in the Widener Handicap at Hialeah. Bardstown next added the Appleton Handicap, and then he (under 130 pounds) and stablemate Fabius cruised to a one-two finish over the latter's nemesis, Needles, in the Gulfstream Park Handicap. (Fabius added one stakes victory at four, taking the Armed Handicap.)

Having finally come out from under a blanket of misfortune, Bardstown suffered more trouble and was put aside with ankle trouble.

The 1957 season saw Jimmy Jones return to the top of the trainer standings for the first time since 1949. Calumet led the lists of both owners and breeders.

In 1958 Jimmy Jones won the Kentucky Derby a second time, with Tim Tam. To win Derbys back to back matched his father's duo of record, i.e., Citation and Ponder in 1948 and 1949. Tim Tam brought to an end the Jones boys' participation in the race they loved so much. Officially, Ben had run eleven horses in the Derby, winning with six; Jimmy had run four starters, winning with two. Collectively, then, the record was eight winners from fifteen starters, or, amazingly, more winners than losers. When it is considered that in 1948 and again in 1956 there were two horses entered, this record looks even better when expressed as thirteen Derbys, eight victories!

Tim Tam was from the multi-champion Two Lea, by Bull Lea. Calumet had sent Two Lea across Lexington to be part of the first book of mares covered by the 1953 Horse of the Year, Greentree Stable's Tom Fool. Tim Tam was the result.

Tim Tam was not rushed, and, in fact, had only one start at two, finishing fourth in a maiden race at Garden State on October 18, 1957. The next winter the Joneses set a stern campaign for him. He ran ten times at three before the Kentucky Derby! Of these, he won eight.

Uncomplicated were his wearing down of valiant pacemaker Lincoln Road in the Florida Derby and his victories in the Everglades, Fountain of Youth, and a variety of strategically placed overnights. Controversial was his ultimate victory over Jewel's Reward in the Flamingo, after the rival had fouled Tim Tam, delaying the trophy presentation.

Tim Tam was a machine who won the Derby in machine-like fashion, but, even so, there had to be drama. Regular rider Hartack was injured in a starting gate mishap on Saturday before Derby Day. Jimmy Jones selected Ismael "Milo" Valenzuela as Hartack's substitute.

In the Kentucky Derby, Lincoln Road returned to his role as pacemaker, and Tim Tam wore him down to win by a half-length. The script was followed again in the Preakness, and Tim Tam won more emphatically, beating Lincoln Road by a length and a half.

Give a Jones a Derby–Preakness winner on an eight-race winning streak, and he will want to be happy. In 1958 Jimmy Jones was in just that position, and yet he had a problem. Jockey Hartack thought he had recovered enough to ride Tim Tam in the Belmont Stakes. Jones, supported by a cable from Mrs. Markey on holiday in France, went with the guy who had just won the Derby and Preakness.

He offered Hartack 10 percent of the purse if Tim Tam won, but Hartack wanted the ride, not just the money. The relationship was severed.

No horse had won the Derby and Preakness since Citation's Triple Crown of ten years earlier, so the Belmont was an event of huge dimension, to Jones, Valenzuela, and the sporting world. Tim Tam was heavily favored, but he faltered in the stretch and was beaten by six lengths by the Irish colt Cavan.

"Tim Tam pulled up lame, and when I rushed down to the track to look him over, I am told there were tears in my eyes," Jimmy Jones recalled. "They carted him off in a horse ambulance, and I was absolutely devastated — crushed."

Tim Tam was never to race again, obviously, but he would be all right for stud duty. After his recovery, he was sent home to Calumet with a record of ten wins in fourteen starts and earnings of $467,475.

As glum as the situation with Tim Tam on Belmont Day had seemed, it was not as bad as the news that spring about Gen. Duke. That brilliant colt had come back to the racing stable and was apparently getting close to a start when Jones noticed a lack of coordination. Jones resisted, at first, the thought that a robust four-year-old could be a wobbler, but indeed Gen. Duke suffered from the syndrome and could not be saved.

Willie Molter, trainer of the prolific Round Table, was the leading trainer in 1958, and Claiborne Farm, breeder of Round Table, was leading breeder, but Calumet and Mrs. Markey prevailed as leading owner.

THE FINAL YEARS

Calumet Farm fell from the top of the owners' list in both 1959 and 1960. Oddly, when the stable returned to lead the list in 1961, the total earnings of $759,856 were so modest when compared to, say, nearly twice that amount as early as 1947, that even championship status bespoke a menacing decline. The 1961 season was the fourteenth, and last, as leading breeder for Calumet and the twelfth, and last, as leading owner. Jimmy Jones was the leading trainer in 1961, for the fifth and last time, beating his father's mark by one year in the cozy, organizational distinctions within Calumet.

The year after Tim Tam, 1959, saw Bardstown come back in full bloom, but, as always, his soundness was brief. During the Florida winter, the seven-year-old added a second Widener Handicap and a second Tropical Park Handicap, as well as a win in the Orange Bowl Handicap. Those races increased his stakes-wins total to thirteen, as he finished a troubled career with eighteen wins in thirty-one starts and earnings of $628,752.

Also in 1959 On-and-On, A Glitter, Rosewood, and Kentucky Pride won stakes for Calumet.

In 1960 the only stakes winner in the devil's red and blue was On-and-On, a son of the great Claiborne Farm stallion Nasrullah and out of Tim Tam's champion dam, Two Lea.

The year 1961 brought the death of Ben A. Jones, on June 13, at the age of seventy-eight. He was buried in the family plot back in Missouri, his origin. In addition to Jimmy, survivors were Ben's wife, Betty, a daughter, and a sister.

Ben Jones — B.A., Plain Ben — had been a storied figure in American sports. His record of six Kentucky Derbys probably stands highest among his distinctions, and it has not yet been breached. Records compiled by *The Blood-Horse* attribute stakes wins with fifty-two horses to him, although the method of attributions of Calumet victories obscures this as any sort of measure of his abilities.

Two years before Ben A. Jones' death the family friend Ben Lindheimer had assembled a gathering at his Arlington Park to pay tribute to both Ben and Jimmy Jones on the twentieth anniversary of their association with Calumet Farm. The son spoke: "My father absolutely would never try to talk before a group. Although I don't do it well, I will try on occasion ... I want to thank my dad for all he has done for me. He is the greatest horse trainer of them all."

Jimmy Jones' reign by himself as Calumet's trainer would last only three years before his own retirement from active training. During those last three years he had a sprightly group of stakes winners and, as stated earlier, Calumet led the owners' list in 1961, the year of Ben Jones' death.

Bull Lea died in 1964, but the decline of the stable had been underway despite the stallion's lingering days. "I tried very hard to make ends meet," Jimmy told authors Plowden and Hirsch, "but it was an impossibility. The horses simply weren't there. I felt very keenly about this, particularly in view of our record of 23 years in the black."

That autumn Jimmy Jones accepted the offer to become director of racing at Monmouth Park. On October 1, 1964, or twenty-five years and a month after old Ben had taken the Calumet job, the most famous stable in America would have a trainer not named Jones.

Ben A. Jones and Jimmy Jones had, collectively, led the trainer standings nine times and had trained a combined total of thirteen champions: Inscoelda, Whirlaway, Mar-Kell, Twilight Tear, Armed, Bewitch, Citation, Coaltown, Two Lea, Wistful, Real Delight, Barbizon, and Tim Tam.

After his retirement from Monmouth Park, Jimmy Jones remained a garrulous, gracious ambassador of racing for many years. He died at the age of ninety-four in 2001.

EPILOGUE

Calumet struggled through a number of trainers, but Mrs. Markey stood steadfastly through tough times. In 1968 Forward Pass provided Calumet an eighth Derby in a brief rally, and then in the late 1970s and early 1980s, under John Veitch, Calumet blossomed anew with the likes of Alydar, Davona Dale, Our Mims, and Before Dawn. (Again, we can only presume that in Bradley's calculation, three owners would today still be tied for first with four Derby winners each: himself, Warren Wright Sr., and Mrs. Gene Markey.)

Admiral Markey died in 1980; Mrs. Markey, in 1982. A granddaughter's husband, J.T. Lundy, then was placed in charge, but bankruptcy put the grand old farm on the auction block in 1992. Henryk de Kwiatkowski purchased Calumet, and as of 2006, his widow and children are maintaining the handsome property as a commercial farm.

CHAPTER 10

HIRSCH JACOBS

As a personality, Hirsch Jacobs had little in common with John E. Madden, but their careers followed similar climbs. Madden, big, brusque, outspoken, and proud, bought and sold his way up the ladder of the horse business until he was in position to establish and operate one of the most fashionable of breeding farms. Jacobs was a smaller, quieter gentleman, but his inner grit and ability to learn about horses equaled Madden's and allowed him to duplicate that same climb in his own manner.

Hirsch Jacobs was born in Brooklyn on April 8, 1904. His father liked to bet on the races occasionally, and that was the only connection the lad had to the sport of horse racing. Hirsch raised racing pigeons, a quaint fact that was repeated so often his family had to explain to members of the press years later that the pigeons were a youthful sideline and not how he got his start in a career. In the 1962 volume *American Race Horses*, the Turf writer and humorist Raleigh Burroughs noted wryly that "In his youth, Jacobs was a trainer of racing pigeons, and he must have been the world's greatest, because people are still talking about it." That's the point! It's not worth talking about! the family might well have responded.

A fascination for horse racing developed, and Hirsch Jacobs launched into the tenuous ambition of making a career of the racetrack. Two brothers, Eugene and Sidney Jacobs, also became trainers.

Hirsch Jacobs' first official winner came when he was twenty-two, on December 29, 1926, when Reveillon scored at Pompano Park. Those familiar with the community of Pompano today might assume there was a bit of chicness involved in racing there, but this was many years before Pompano became engulfed in the megalopolis that spans so much of south Florida. Pompano was a truck farming community whose school schedule was geared toward allowing students to work on parents' farms and whose high school football team for many years had the nickname of Bean Pickers. Although Reveillon was a son of Man o' War's sire, Fair Play, his initial victory for Jacobs was not a classy occasion, and the purse was $700.

Reveillon had been claimed by Jacobs for $1,500 and run back twice within four days of the claim. Jacobs then gave him something of a rest and ran him twelve times in thirty-four days. Reveillon's first win for Jacobs came in his thirteenth start for the young horseman.

That was his first victory of record, but *The Blood-Horse* in 1943 published an account that had Jacobs training as early as 1924 for a C. Ferrara, but with Ferrara's name down as trainer of record.

Unlike John E. Madden, Jacobs was to have a partner for much of his career, and in the persona of Isidor Bieber the Bieber-Jacobs outfit had a character all its own. It was Hirsch Jacobs and his wife, Ethel, who were close friends with Damon Runyon, but it was Bieber who elicited the adjective "Runyonesque."

Bieber was described by author A.J. Lawrence as "a character who, in his time, has played many parts: A bet-a-million, an improver of the breed, a Broadway barkeeper, a ticket scalper, a soldier, a crusader, and rough-and-tumble battler. In his heavier moments, he is as fair a Shakespearean scholar as ever put foot against a brass rail. Posterity is a sure shot to recognize Bieber because he is, above all, the discoverer of Hirsch Jacobs, leading trainer in the country."

Bieber said he recalled the grand opening of Belmont Park in 1905 and was smitten by horses for the rest of his life. He raced for a time as B.B. Stable, but then cringed angrily when it fostered the nickname "Kid Beebee." (Jacobs' daughter, Patrice, still refers to him conversationally as "Beebee" at times.) Bieber said in a 1952 interview that back in the days when bookmakers legally manned the New York tracks, he would bet as much as $50,000 on a single race but that he had become a moderate bettor. One of the tales of Bieber's action was of the day he parlayed $20 up to $120,000 at the Empire City track but lost it all on Bill Brennan in his fight against Jack Dempsey that night at Madison Square Garden. Bieber summed up his day, as, "Well, I lost twenty dollars." Another story around him was that he won $60,000 backing Woodrow Wilson against Charles Evans Hughes in another type of contest, the presidential election.

Jacobs first crossed paths with Bieber in 1927, when he overheard the older man bemoaning the bad racing luck that had cost him a big bet on a horse named Scat at the Jamaica racetrack in New York. In response to Bieber's tirade, Jacobs quipped, in the language of the racetrack: "What are you crying about? We had Corinth in the race, and if he don't get left at the post, he walks in."

The following year, however, when Bieber chanced upon Hirsch Jacobs at Oriental Park, his initial approach to the young man was based on fleet-ingly mistaking Jacobs for someone else whom Bieber knew. The conver-sation that followed the misunderstanding turned out to be meaningful. Bieber later recalled thinking, "This boy has such honest eyes I would trust him with my uncounted bankroll."

Bieber was forty-one and Jacobs twenty-four when they subsequently be-came partners on a handshake. It was a good match: financial wherewithal in one partner, steely determination and ambition in the other. Jacobs had already established himself and was training at the time for Johnny Mas-cia and Louis Sylvestri. He did not initially give up all other owners when he hooked up with Bieber.

By 1933 Jacobs reached the top in national statistics by leading all train-ers in number of wins, with 116, despite being based on the demanding New York circuit. He still was not yet training exclusively for the combine with Bieber. He also had horses for his friend Runyon and leased a couple of his own horses to race in his stable in the name of one of his brothers, Dr. Irving Jacobs, an eye surgeon. That years later the Bieber-Jacobs Stable would migrate to the top of the list of breeders in earnings is one of the most remarkable sequences in the history of Thoroughbred racing.

Companion and co-owner along that trail was Mrs. Jacobs. In 1933, the same year he led trainers for the first time, Jacobs married Ethel Dushock, whom he had met three years earlier. In a 1984 interview for *The Blood-Horse*, Mrs. Jacobs recalled that Jacobs was renting an upper level room in her family's home when they met. Miss Dushock was working in a bank.

"He took me to the races a few times," she said, "but I really couldn't go very often. After all, I was working."

Over the years, many of the Bieber-Jacobs horses ran in the name of Mrs. Ethel D. Jacobs.

Jacobs took up long-term residence atop the list of trainers in wins. After leading the list in 1933, he also led for the next six years, with totals rang-ing from a low of 106 wins in 1939 to a high of 177 in 1936. The 177 stood as a record until Willie Molter won 184 races in 1948. Jacobs' streak was ended — actually, merely interrupted — in 1940, and then he resumed as the leader in 1941. The answer to the trivia question implied by these facts is Daniel Womeldorff, who had 108 winners to second-place Jacobs' ninety-eight in 1940.

(On the list of leading owners by wins, the young wife of Hirsch Jacobs led in 1936 and 1937, as a number of the horses were raced in her name, whereas B.B. Stable had been the leader in 1934.)

In January 1943, under the heading "Death and Taxes and Jacobs," *The Blood-Horse* remarked that "about the easiest prediction for any given year in recent American racing was that Hirsch Jacobs would be the leading trainer, judged by the number of winners he saddled. In 1942 Jacobs won with 133 winners, which was just sixty more than the runner-up, Ben Jones, could supply ... When Jacobs came on the scene, the sustained flight record was held by H. Guy Bedwell, who had led in 1909 and for six consecutive years beginning in 1912. Jacobs ran the consecutive years record to seven (1933–39) and now has raised the total years to nine."

That report was issued after Jacobs led again in 1942, and he continued to lead through 1944, giving him eleven titles in twelve years.

PRELUDES TO STYMIE

The wholesale-wins aspect of Hirsch Jacobs' career during those years is often simplified by the phrase "claiming trainer." This is deceptive. While it is true that Isidor Bieber did not often pay handsome prices and that claiming was a key part of the operation, the stable in those days was not without high-class horses. *The Blood-Horse* statistics show Jacobs winning a stakes race as early as 1929, although it was also a claiming race. A horse named Jack Biener won the Garden City Claiming Stakes that year. Through the 1930s, Jacobs had one stakes-winning horse, and one only, each year except for 1935 when he had none and 1938 when he had two.

Most of his stakes success continued to come in the claiming stakes then frequent, but in 1933 Jacobs had a brush with higher-class races when he saddled Character to win two three-year-old stakes at fashionable Hialeah. These were the Hialeah Stakes and Bahamas Stakes.

Bieber and Jacobs had claimed Character from Mrs. W.T. Anderson for $2,500 the previous October and he raced in the name of B.B. Stable. After the Hialeah Stakes, *The Blood-Horse* noted that the "painfully inelegant little gelding has paraded into the winner's circle after nine of his last ten essays." The Bahamas made that ten of eleven, but when stretched out to a mile and one-eighth in Hialeah's chief classic prep, the Florida Derby, Character was unplaced. (The Florida Derby was then the name of the top three-year-old race at Hialeah. That race was later renamed the Flamingo Stakes, making way for Gulfstream Park to launch its own Florida Derby in 1952. The Gulfstream version is the Florida Derby that is still run.)

The next year the fellow with the reputation for quantity over quality came out early in the New York season with a stakes-winning juvenile when Angelic won the Youthful Stakes. Angelic raced in the colors of the Jacobs' friend, Patrice (Mrs. Damon) Runyon, in whose name the filly had been purchased for $700 from W.B. Miller's Saratoga yearling consignment the previous August.

Prior to her stakes wins Angelic had survived a starting gate incident in an early juvenile race at Hialeah. As reported by the *Miami Daily News*, she "fell with her feet in the air," and for "three minutes was wedged in her stall." Her trainer, Jacobs, was quoted that the incident caused Damon Runyon to "go through the agony of hell." Perhaps it reflects a more casual attitude about such matters than exists today, but once Angelic was righted, she was returned to her task and proceeded to win by a nose!

When Angelic won the Youthful, she defeated promising and well-bred juveniles from such fashionable stables as Greentree, Brookmeade, and Wheatley. Such wins were a step beyond the "claiming trainer" image for Hirsch Jacobs.

Nevertheless, it was accurate for the press to stress the claiming acumen of the man. Certainly, the claiming aspect of the game was uppermost on Jacobs' mind on June 25, 1937. When he arrived at the races that day at Aqueduct, he learned that Sahri II had won earlier on the card, with a $2,000 claiming price. Sahri II's stablemate, Caballero II, was in for $4,000 later on the program, and Jacobs' glib calculation was that the horse therefore must be twice as good. Jacobs reported forthwith to the racing secretary's office to enter a claim. As a result, in 1937 and 1938 Caballero II won the Aqueduct and Excelsior handicaps for Bieber and Jacobs.

Also in 1938, Sweet Patrice (Halcyon—My Tide, by My Play) won an early season juvenile stakes, the Fashion, as well as one of the claiming stakes. Sweet Patrice was bred by Silas B. Mason and had been purchased in the name of Mrs. Jacobs for $3,200 in the summer of 1937, indicating that the stable was becoming more confident at higher levels of investment. Patrice was also the name of Mrs. Runyon, and the Jacobses in later years would name their daughter Patrice in Mrs. Runyon's honor. (Ethel and Hirsch Jacobs also were to name horses after their own children, and Our Patrice and Our John William gained above-average distinction.)

In those days Maryland was virtually an adjunct to the New York season, on roughly the same status plane. In 1940 Jacobs saddled Conde Rico to win the Bowie Handicap in a dead heat with Aethelwold.

That same year, Jacobs won his richest race to that time, the $10,000 Rhode Island Handicap at Narragansett Park, with Bieber's Confiado. This race name had a nice ring to it, for two great horses from high-status stables, Alfred Vanderbilt's Discovery and Samuel D. Riddle's War Admiral, had won 1930s runnings of the event. In Confiado's running, the field included Widener Handicap winner Many Stings. Confiado also won two $5,000-added handicaps, the Brandywine and Portsmouth, that year.

Jacobs had developed a keen interest in pedigrees and often spent time at the races discussing breeding with the noted breeder-owner Colonel E.R. Bradley. Jacobs came to believe in the concept of nicks, in the quality of the Teddy and Man o' War sire lines, and in the Bradley bloodstock in general, particularly the mare La Troienne.

As his first winner, by Fair Play, indicated, pedigree does not equal class in every case, but Jacobs had some opportunity to deal with well-bred horses, even if they were not expensive. One example was Bright Gallant, with whom he won the 1942 Exterminator Handicap. Bright Gallant was by Sir Gallahad III, who had been renowned since 1930, when his son Gallant Fox won the Triple Crown. Bright Gallant had been bred by A.B. Hancock Sr., at whose Claiborne Farm Sir Gallahad III held court, and had been purchased privately by Leigh Taliaferro. Bieber-Jacobs claimed Bright Gallant for $3,000 less than three months before he won the Exterminator.

The following year, 1943, brought the development that would allow the sea change in the operation of Bieber-Jacobs Stable. This was the famous claim of Stymie, but it would take two years before this would begin to be recognized for the bellwether event it was. Stymie did not win his first stakes until 1945.

In the meantime, Jacobs won stakes with Flaught and Haile in 1943 and with Bertie S. and Ahmisk in 1944. Flaught's wins came in a pair of claiming stakes, but Bertie S. won the Fashion and the Viscaya stakes. Bertie S. had been bred by Mrs. Parker Corning, and Bieber bought her as a yearling, along with the dam, Fib, for only $600 from the sale of Mrs. Corning's estate.

The victories of Ahmisk demonstrated Jacobs' versatility. Jacobs won four rich stakes of 1944 with the well-bred gelding by Blenheim II—Little Muff, by Sardanapale. All four were steeplechases, and each carried at least $5,000 in added money.

The image of the steeplechase set generally focuses on lifelong horsemen and women from Virginia, Maryland, and Pennsylvania, people who ride as well as manage horses. Here, however, was a guy from Brooklyn, whose horsemanship was demonstrated with his own feet on the ground, excelling in this difficult pursuit.

American Race Horses of 1944 noted in its review of prominent trainers of jumpers: "And among the leading steeplechase trainers, who should show up but Hirsch Jacobs, who saddled eleven winners of $43,825." (James E. Ryan led the division in earnings with $65,295, and John T. Skinner led in wins, with nineteen.)

Otherwise, Ahmisk fit the frequent Bieber-Jacobs profile of an acquisition, i.e, a horse bred by a prominent breeder that had not panned out for the original owner. Ahmisk had been bred by Mrs. Marion du Pont Scott. After being acquired to race in Bieber's name, Ahmisk won the Harbor Hill, Battleship, Chevy Chase, and Glendale steeplechases and picked up a win over the year's jumping champion, Rouge Dragon. Ahmisk added the International Steeplechase the following year.

While Stymie was far and away his chief resource in 1945, Jacobs added a victory that otherwise would have been his richest to that time. He sent out the seven-year-old Moon Maiden to win the $20,000 Comely Handicap. The Comely was having its inaugural running, at a mile and one-sixteenth for fillies and mares at the Empire City meeting at Jamaica in New York. Finishing third was Elpis, who won the Coaching Club American Oaks that year and eventually had nine stakes victories.

THE HIGH-HEADED CHAMPION

So, Stymie's emergence was not Hirsch Jacobs' introduction to high-class stakes. He was, however, over and above anything the trainer had dealt with before.

Jacobs claimed Stymie from the colt's third race, on June 2, 1943, for $1,500 at Belmont Park. Stymie had been beaten by eight and sixteen lengths in two earlier starts and was seventh, beaten four and a half lengths, in the race from which he was haltered. Stymie was claimed from King Ranch and trainer Max Hirsch. As pointed out in the chapter in this volume on Hirsch, the ways the story has been told include one that seems to minimize Jacobs' role in the decision. More commonly accepted in the lore of the Turf, however, is that Jacobs saw something in the colt that prompted the claim. Many years later Mrs. Jacobs summarized this as, "He claimed Stymie on his looks. There was something about the way he carried his head."

Officially, Max Hirsch bred Stymie, but Robert J. Kleberg of King Ranch organized the mating that produced him. The colt offered Jacobs a cross of the Man o' War blood he liked, for both mares in the second generation were by the great stallion. Stymie's sire, Equestrian, was by Equipoise—Frilette, by Man o' War; and his dam, Stop Watch, was by On Watch—Sunset Gun, by Man o' War.

Stymie did not come to hand quickly. By the end of his two-year-old season, he had run twenty-eight times. This was a bit under Seabiscuit's now-famous thirty-five races as a juvenile but was a vigorous, active season indicative of Jacobs' preference for racing horses often rather than working them often. Stymie broke his maiden in his fourteenth start and could have been claimed for $3,300, but was not. Jacobs ran him for a price ten times, the tags ranging from $2,000 to $5,000.

At three Stymie won only three of twenty-nine races and did not break through as a stakes winner, but he placed fifteen times and was able to avoid disgrace when exposed to top-level company. For example, he was third in the Flamingo Stakes and second in a division of the Wood Memorial. His step into classic waters found him sixth in the Preakness. All told, Stymie placed in seven stakes that year.

By the end of his three-year-old season, Stymie had run fifty-seven times, had won seven races, and had placed twenty-seven times. Jacobs gave him some time off, and Stymie did not have a start from late November 1944 until late May 1945. Coming back at four, he won his first stakes in his third outing, taking the mile and one-eighth Grey Lag Handicap by a half-length over Alex Barth, with Belmont Stakes winner Bounding Home in third.

Stymie now had proven that he fit in among the best company. He next was second in the Suburban and Queens County handicaps before closing from ninth and last to defeat the champion Devil Diver in the Brooklyn Handicap. New York racegoers had been forewarned that their hearts were being seduced by a high-headed, middle-sized colt with a flashy chestnut coat who would hold them spellbound as he charged from behind, doing his best weekend after weekend.

Before the year was out, the Butler Handicap, Saratoga Cup, Continental Handicap, Westchester Handicap, Riggs Handicap, and Pimlico Cup also would fall to Stymie. The last-named race was run at two and a half miles, and Stymie won by eight lengths from Calumet Farm's major winner Pot o' Luck.

Stymie, who raced for Bieber-Jacobs but in Mrs. Jacobs' colors, had won nine of nineteen races that year, placed in eight others, and earned $225,375. To put that into perspective for the stable at the time, the highest earnings for Jacobs as trainer for a given year had come in 1944, when Stymie's paltry three victories were absorbed into a total of 117 wins and earnings of $306,821. Now, Stymie had danced through a campaign in which he alone accounted for 74 percent of that sum. He also was voted champion handicap male, the first championship for Bieber-Jacobs.

At five Stymie won eight of twenty races and placed in eleven of the twelve others. To win or place in nineteen of twenty races is admirable for any horse. For one whose style generally was to lag far behind and come on with a swooshing run, this was an even more remarkable display of consistency, for such strategy often can be confounded by a slow pace.

In his third race of 1946, Stymie won his second Grey Lag Handicap, on May 4. He was not to win again until August, but in his intervening seven races, Jacobs kept him sharp enough to place in the Dixie, Suburban, Sussex, Brooklyn, Butler, and Monmouth handicaps. He broke the losing streak in high, and unusual, style, taking command well before the stretch of the muddy Whitney and winning by two lengths at a mile and a quarter.

The Whitney was run on August 10, and the next big target was the Saratoga Handicap on August 24. Jacobs' style of training this particular horse called for a prep in between. Stymie won neither the prep nor the stakes, but on August 31, the mile and three-quarters of the Saratoga Cup seemed to set up so well for him that no one entered to test him. Stymie won in a walkover.

This launched a flurry of victories. From his next five races, Stymie won the Edgemere, Manhattan, New York, and Gallant Fox handicaps, losing only the Jockey Club Gold Cup. The longest of those victories came in the two and a quarter-mile New York Handicap.

Stymie then lost the Pimlico Special to the Triple Crown winner Assault, who was named Horse of the Year. Armed topped Stymie in voting for handicap champion.

Joining Stymie as a stakes winner for Jacobs in 1946 was Mahmoudess. An example of increasing fashion in the stable's holdings, Mahmoudess was by Epsom Derby winner Mahmoud and out of Forever Yours, by Toro. She was bred by Mrs. Ethel V. Mars and purchased off the racetrack. She won but a single stakes, the Molly Pitcher, racing in the name of Jacobs' father-in-law, Joseph G. Dushock.

The day of the Molly Pitcher, Jacobs was preoccupied in saddling Stymie for the Brooklyn Handicap, which the horse lost by a neck to Gallorette. Trainer Happy Buxton saddled Mahmoudess for Jacobs down at Monmouth and gave a leg up to his son, jockey Merritt Buxton. Mahmoudess cut up at the gate but ran professionally, defeating a good field that included Rampart and Elpis.

Mahmoudess was a study in soundness, if not consistency, for she made 117 starts. She won seventeen races and earned $95,312.

At six in 1947, Stymie won seven races and placed in seven others, from nineteen starts. His earnings total that year, $299,775, was his best for any year, thanks in part to his triumph over champions Assault and Phalanx, plus other important winners, in the $100,000 International Gold Cup at a mile and five-eighths. Author, editor, and historian Kent Hollingsworth declared this "his greatest race. Natchez went to the lead, and nothing much happened for one and one-quarter miles. Then Eddie Arcaro sent Assault after the leader when the South Americans [Endeavour, Talon, Ensueno] made their moves; but Assault could not take Natchez and faded with the South Americans. Then came Stymie, hard on the outside, [jockey] Conn McCreary with a mouthful of mane, and he was not to be denied. He caught Natchez, won by a neck," and regained the leading-earner status he had been fussing over with Assault.

Stymie's other wins that year came in the Metropolitan, Questionnaire, Sussex, Massachusetts, Aqueduct, and Gallant Fox handicaps. That a stretch runner par excellence would win the Metropolitan Handicap indicates Stymie's tremendous ability under the demands of a race of one mile, wherein sprinters are often strained beyond their capacities while stretch runners have to be sharp to get up in time.

A milestone for Stymie was the Aqueduct Handicap victory, for his weight that day, 132, was the most he ever carried to victory. He defeated the great mare Gallorette (122).

Nonetheless, Armed prevailed as older male champion and Horse of the Year.

Stymie was back at seven to win four of eleven races. Remarkably, one of these was his second Metropolitan. He also won another Aqueduct and another Sussex. This robust paragon of soundness finally had a mishap, for he came out of the July 24 Monmouth Handicap lame. Mrs. Jacobs was in the hospital in New York, and Jacobs only reluctantly had decided to go down to Monmouth for the race. It was a fortuitous decision.

The young veterinarian William O. Reed, only four years out of Ohio State University's veterinary school, was on the scene and, as Jacobs recalled years later, "had X-ray equipment in his car. I told the blacksmith to cut part of the [right front] hoof away and Reed took X-rays there and also farther up." A fractured sesamoid was discovered. Jacobs said Stymie was walking soundly within a few days and was turned out on Jack Skinner's farm in Maryland "with the cast still on." Dr. Reed, who for many years was to be one of the most renowned backstretch practitioners in New York and Florida, as well as a farm owner, looked back on the situation as creating publicity that boosted his own career. More importantly, Stymie proved sound enough to return at eight, after serving a small book of mares.

Stymie failed to win in five races at eight, but that is deceptive if taken to mean he was no longer effective. He was good enough to run second in the marathon New York Handicap and undoubtedly could have won a number of lesser races. He was retired permanently with thirty-five wins and sixty-one placings, from 131 starts. His earnings record had been bumped up to $918,485. That figure stood as a record until Citation topped the million-dollar mark two years later. Stymie was elected to the Hall of Fame in 1975.

Stymie's regularity as a stakes competitor, his flashy stretch runs, and his honesty — win or lose — endeared him to race fans, especially in his home base of New York. Although his comeback was not a gratifying success, he was saluted in a special ceremony at the Jamaica racetrack before returning to stud. On that day he posed as he had run — alert, head high, adulation his for the asking.

WHAT STYMIE HAD WROUGHT

Stymie's success gave Bieber-Jacobs the financial wherewithal to make some major moves. Jacobs purchased a Maryland farm, which he named Stymie Manor, although Stymie himself was sent to stand at Hagyard Farm in Kentucky. More important than the purchase of property, perhaps, was the ability to be selective in adding fillies to the nascent Bieber-Jacobs broodmare band.

Stymie was five when the first stakes winner bred in the name of Bieber-Jacobs was foaled. This was Palestinian, a 1946 colt by Sun Again—Dolly Whisk, by Whiskaway. The dam, Dolly Whisk, was bred by George V. Barnes and was sold for only $185 to Scoggan Jones. She was destined to change hands several times. Dolly Whisk raced in the name of E.A. Carney when she won the 1938 Debutante Stakes. She won three races the following year and did not race in 1940. When she reappeared in the entries in 1941, the owner was listed as J. Fendrick, with Hirsch Jacobs the trainer. She won two races for Fendrick, but from the beginning of her produce record, Dolly Whisk's foals were bred by Bieber-Jacobs.

Dolly Whisk's foals created an example of the divergent naming preferences of Isidor Bieber and the Hirsch Jacobs family. Bieber was prone to give foals names that reflected world events and, especially, the thought that the two world wars constituted sufficient evidence that Germany should not be armed again. Examples of Bieber names were Nothirdchance and Remember History. Dolly Whisk's 1946 foal took up another cause. He was named Palestinian and years later sired Promised Land.

Ethel and Hirsch Jacobs, on the other hand, tended more toward the sentimental when it was their turn to name foals. As we have seen, Patrice Runyon had been honored in the naming of a filly years earlier, and two of the Jacobses' children were honored in the names of Dolly Whisk's foals, i.e., Our John William and Our Patrice.

Palestinian won the Endurance Stakes at two and the next year was to be the vehicle for one of Hirsch Jacobs' most remarkable illustrations of horsemanship. That year, Palestinian won the Jersey Stakes and Empire City Handicap, but what was most remarkable about his 1949 season was that he placed in each of the Triple Crown races — on a bowed tendon.

"Yes, he's bowed," Jacobs responded to tentative comments at the time. "No, it isn't some other injury that looks like a bow. It's just a bowed tendon. Always when a horse bows, you stop on him. So, you never know what he would do if you went on. Judging by Palestinian, he might do all right."

In 2006 Jacobs' son, John (i.e., "Our John William"), a classics-winning trainer in his own right, recalled Palestinian's bowed tendon and added that there was an oddity of the situation. "It was a floating bow," the son recalled. "It started high, then dropped down to the middle of the tendon. It was something my father had rarely seen."

John Jacobs has vivid memories of being a fifteen-year-old flying from New York to Louisville with Hedley Woodhouse, who was to ride Palestinian. Young John and his father stayed at the Brown Hotel, and one night when they went down to dinner, Calumet Farm's famous trainer Ben Jones was waiting for a table. Jacobs and Jones were friendly, and the three had dinner together. Jones had finished second in the Derby Trial on Tuesday of Derby Week with Ponder, and although that night he described Ponder as not a really top-class colt, he wound up winning the Derby.

"My father told me he had made a mistake," John Jacobs told us, thinking back some fifty-seven years. "He would say that to me, although not publicize it. He said, 'Ben Jones uses the Derby Trial for a reason. He gets a race over the track. If I had run Palestinian in the Derby Trial, he would have had a better chance in the Derby. Palestinian had run second [to Olympia, winner of the Derby Trial] in the Wood Memorial, which was then two weeks before the Derby."

Palestinian was third in the Kentucky Derby and Belmont Stakes and second in the Preakness, surely a triple crown of sorts for three-year-olds with bowed tendons. He finally needed a rest but came back to win the Westchester Handicap at four in 1950. Also in 1950, Bieber-Jacobs showed another aspect of adventurous nature, sending Palestinian across the country to the Hollywood Gold Cup in California. The colt finished second.

The following year, at five, Palestinian again had a coast-to-coast campaign, and he won the historic Brooklyn Handicap in the East and the Golden Gate Handicap in California. Palestinian had a career record of fourteen wins in forty-five starts and earnings of $296,525.

Nothirdchance, a name with a message, was by Blue Swords—Galla Colors, by Sir Gallahad III. While Bieber came up with the politically aggressive name, it was Hirsch Jacobs who had come up with the purchase of the dam years before. Galla Colors was a daughter of Sir Gallahad III (by Teddy) and, according to Mrs. Jacobs, that was a key reason for her purchase. Galla Colors was unraced, but in addition to her exalted sire line, the pedigree showed Coaching Club American Oaks winner Creole Maid on the bottom side. Jacobs paid $12,000 for Galla Colors, who had been bred by Circle M Ranch.

Galla Colors passed along a rugged constitution to Nothirdchance, whose sire, Blue Swords, had chased Count Fleet during his Triple Crown spring of 1943. Nothirdchance ran ninety-three times in six years and won eleven races, earning $112,660. Like Mahmoudess, Nothirdchance won only a single stakes, but it was important, the triumph coming in a division of the Acorn Stakes. A mare generally has no third chance at immortality, for her career is divided into two aspects, racing and producing. Nothirdchance hit in the second phase of her career, for she became the dam of Hail to Reason. "My father never trained horses hard, but he raced them hard," recalled daughter Patrice many years later. "He proved that racing a mare had no relationship to whether she was a good producer or not."

Another of Jacobs' significant broodmare prospects acquired during the transition aided by Stymie was No Fiddling. This was an example of seeking the Bradley bloodstock Jacobs had learned to respect. No Fiddling was by King Cole and from Big Hurry, a daughter of La Troienne. La Troienne was destined to earn pride of place among American-based broodmares. Ogden Phipps had purchased No Fiddling from Bradley, but her form justified racing her in claiming company. Jacobs claimed her for $7,500.

The years 1952–59 illustrated the new dimension of Bieber-Jacobs Stable. Nine horses won stakes for Jacobs during those years, and all but one, Searching, was a Bieber-Jacobs homebred.

In 1952 Bieber-Jacobs won the Jersey Stakes with 1949 homebred King Jolie, whom Bieber had named in honor of a friend, the singer Al Jolson. King Jolie was by Platter—Jaconda, by Belfonds.

From 1953 through 1956, the stable's stalwarts included Joe Jones, who had been sired by Stymie during his first stint at stud in the spring of 1949. Joe Jones was out of the Challenger II mare Moon Maiden, who had won stakes for the stable some years before. Joe Jones was a horse in the mold of his sire and his trainer, for he won thirty-four races from 175 starts and earned $423,567, tops for a son or daughter of Stymie. Joe Jones' ten stakes wins included the John B. Campbell Handicap, Vosburgh, Bowie, and Lincoln Special.

Paper Tiger was another son of Stymie who won stakes for four consecutive years. A 1951 colt from Ally Bal, by Challenger II, Paper Tiger ran in 114 races, winning nineteen, of which his four stakes victories included the Saratoga Handicap and Lincoln Special.

Searching, the lone stakes winner of the era who was not a homebred, was acquired from Ogden Phipps. She was out of Big Hurry, a daughter of La Troienne.

Years prior to his participation in a tripartite division of the bulk of the stock from Bradley's estate, Phipps had purchased Big Hurry individually. By 1954 he had considerable holdings of Bradley bloodstock, and while recognizing the quality of the La Troienne brood, Phipps knew he could not keep everything, even from that family. Searching was by Triple Crown winner War Admiral, and both Bradley and Phipps recognized the combination of War Admiral and La Troienne as highly potent. Nevertheless, Searching had not accomplished enough for Phipps to be determined to keep her. Jacobs purchased the filly for the Bieber-Jacobs Stable for $16,000 (some published reports said $15,000). In 1954 this was not a casual deal.

"I remember when my husband came home and told me he had purchased Searching," Mrs. Jacobs said years later. "He said he bought her for $16,000. That was a lot of money in those days, and I think he was a little apprehensive."

When Jacobs had Searching's shoes pulled, he observed that the walls of her hooves were thin. He figured her poor form might have been the result of the nails causing slight discomfort. John Jacobs recalled that "we tubbed her and when we put the shoes back on, my father used felt [between hoof and shoe]." For Jacobs, Searching underwent a typically rigorous campaign of racing but only light training between races. She won a dozen stakes, including two runnings each of the Gallorette, Correction, and Diana handicaps. Her other stakes wins included the Vagrancy, Molly Pitcher, and Top Flight. She was retired with twenty-five wins from eighty-nine races and earnings of $327,381. Searching was elected to the National Museum of Racing's Hall of Fame in 1978, perhaps reflecting the fact that the Hall of Fame had not yet articulated that its criteria for horses involved racing only, rather than incorporating breeding prowess. As we shall see, Searching was a significant broodmare and was pivotal to the heights to which Bieber-Jacobs rose in the realm of fashionable breeding.

John Jacobs thought back to Searching as an illustration of two aspects of his father's career that are prominent in his memories. One was the tendency to want to race horses rather than work them, and the other was attention to detail.

"He said to me, 'They don't pay you to work them and keep them in a stall,' " John recalled. "He liked to train them lightly, blow them out on Friday, and run on Saturday. All this working is harder on a lot of horses than racing. They keep fit racing. Of course, if any went wrong and they weren't right, he would turn them out." Another example was running the filly Dashing By three times in five days. Dashing By won all three races.

As for attention to detail, Hirsch Jacobs "liked to stand and watch the blacksmith. Then he would pick up the foot to see if it was level and tell the blacksmith if there was anything else he wanted done to the foot."

If a horse did not seem to be doing as well as it should for no apparent explanation, Jacobs sometimes would change its groom. He realized, his son said, that some grooms are just kinder and easier with horses than others. So small a difference as how hard a horse is brushed, when it might prefer a light touch, was worth consideration, especially with fillies.

Searching's career overlapped Bieber-Jacobs' homebred Promised Land. A son of the classics-placed Palestinian, Promised Land was foaled from the stakes winner Mahmoudess. The dam had won her only stakes in the name of owner Joseph G. Dushock but was in the fold of Bieber-Jacobs as breeder of record of her son. Promised Land won stakes for three seasons, from 1957 to 1959, and while he never was a champion, he toiled not far from the rungs of divisional leadership.

The gray colt came to hand at three in 1957, when he won a half-dozen stakes. Given that the season in question was that of three-year-olds Bold

Ruler, Round Table, Gallant Man, and Gen. Duke, it was difficult for any other three-year-old to attain much renown. However, Promised Land broke into the sport's consciousness when he put together four Saturday stakes wins from the five available weekends of November.

Typical of Jacobs' training, Promised Land had been risked for $10,000 claiming when that level made sense to the horseman, but later he had been tested in the Preakness when such a race seemed logical. Promised Land finished fourth in the classic.

Progress continued, and Promised Land won the Lawrence Realization before his November-fest brought victories in the Knickerbocker, Roamer, and Idlewild handicaps, and the Pimlico Special. The first Saturday of November had not been so friendly, for he was beaten that day in the Gallant Fox Handicap. During his November streak, Promised Land defeated an impressive array of high-class runners, among them Swoon's Son, Third Brother, Vertex, Oh Johnny, and Eddie Schmidt.

At four in 1958, Promised Land was all over the map. He won the Campbell on dirt in Maryland eighteen days after winning the mile and three-quarters San Juan Capistrano on grass in California. He also added the Massachusetts Handicap in a season in which he took on Bold Ruler, Round Table, and Gallant Man with verve but no success. Such a campaign was a tribute to the sportsmanship, imagination, and sheer horse savvy of his trainer. Promised Land added the Bay Meadows Handicap at five and concluded his career with twenty-one wins from seventy-seven starts and earnings of $541,707. John Jacobs recalled Promised Land as "the most versatile horse I was ever around. Track surface, conditions, distance did not matter to him. He just ran."

By that time, Hirsch Jacobs perhaps could be styled as much a breeder as a trainer. He still was the meticulous man of the stable, famed for poking a penknife into the racetrack in the morning to test the going, but he was living an aspect that had been merely academic before.

Jacobs had always been interested in pedigree. In addition to his afternoon sessions with Bradley, he had jawed on the subject of breeding horses with his friend Damon Runyon. Mrs. Jacobs recalled that the playwright and journalist Runyon "enjoyed questioning my husband about this sire or that dam. He would ask him about the pedigrees of horses that raced before my husband ever started training."

Jacobs' daughter, Patrice, pointed out that during her father's career, stallion registers and broodmare records were not as readily available as they are today. At that time, knowing pedigrees required more research and memory.

Once finances allowed Hirsch Jacobs to do the matings that produced the Bieber-Jacobs runners, his wife recalled, "He trained horses and planned matings in his head. He would scribble a mating on the back of an overnight [sheet of race entries]. He had it all figured out in his head."

A footnote to the record of Hirsch Jacobs as the 1950s waned was the victory of Basil Bee in the 1959 International Steeplechase. The victory harked back to Ahmisk's 1940s prowess in the jumping ranks and reminded that the old maestro still could tune a variety of instruments.

REASON AND AFFECTION

The dawn of the 1960s completed a transformation. The outfit that was not quite accurately styled "a claiming stable" in the 1930s could now be openly described as "upscale," or "high class," or "fashionable," depending on the verbal preference of the commentator.

During the winter of 1960, Jacobs was stabled on the West Coast, and he had under his shed row a growthy homebred by Cain Hoy Stable's Garden State Stakes and Flamingo Stakes winner, Turn-to. The dam was none other than Nothirdchance, a homebred stakes winner. When Nothirdchance was carrying the Turn-to colt, Jacobs responded to a potential buyer's inquiry by pricing her at $30,000. Luckily for Bieber-Jacobs, the buyer turned down the opportunity.

The Turn-to—Nothirdchance colt was named Hail to Reason. Although he bore a decidedly blunt Bieber/World Events name, he was selected to race in the colors and name of the Jacobs' teenage daughter, Patrice.

It took some time for Hail to Reason to get his legs under him, and Jacobs employed the time-honored technique of racing him into his skin, skeleton, and confidence. Hail to Reason ran twelfth, thirteenth, and sixth, in his first three races. He then finished second twice before breaking his maiden in an Aqueduct dash, which he won by nine lengths. The date of his first victory was April 4, and it came some two and a half months after his debut in a three-furlong sprint at Santa Anita.

This was a step, but Hail to Reason had not yet put his strength, stride, and stature into a cohesive unit. Jacobs continued to employ competition and experience as the best teachers. Hail to Reason was third in his next race, then won an allowance race and the Youthful Stakes, all this by the first of May. However, he then finished third in the Juvenile and fifth in the Tyro Stakes.

From then on, Hail to Reason was a man among boys. With jockey Bob Ussery on board for the rest of the season, Hail to Reason began racing to his image of long-limbed superiority.

At Aqueduct, Hail to Reason won the Tremont by three lengths and the Great American by two. At Saratoga he added the Sanford by six lengths and then, in New Jersey, he took Monmouth Park's Sapling Stakes, although having to work to get home a half-length before 40-1 He's a Pistol.

(Carry Back, destined to many major wins in Hail to Reason's absence, was third.)

The four-race winning streak ended stunningly when Hail to Reason went wide on the turn of the Saratoga Special and struggled home sixth behind Bronzerullah.

Patrice Jacobs had become thoroughly smitten by the big colt that raced in her name. She would visit him in the barn and sit outside his stall feeding him carrots. Faced with this stunning defeat, she recalled, "The tears just flowed." The moment found Hirsch Jacobs combining roles as horseman and father. "He said to get over that [crying] quickly and to realize we would always have disappointments along the way. The Hopeful was just ten days away, but he said, 'I bet he bucked his shins. I think I have time,' and he went to work with mud and all the old remedies."

Jacobs verfied the diagnosis of sore shins. The treatments included white iodine. Ten days after the Special, Hail to Reason demolished his field to win the Hopeful Stakes by ten lengths. His time of 1:16 for six and a half furlongs set a record for a track that had seen many a brilliant two-year-old compete at the distance.

The World's Playground Stakes at Atlantic City offered a rich first prize of $81,792, some $5,000 more than the traditional Hopeful had tendered. Bieber-Jacobs put up $6,000 to supplement the colt, this figuring at about 13-1, whereas backers of Hail to Reason at the windows that day had to settle for 9-10.

In *American Race Horses of 1960*, Joseph A. Estes commented that "running in what had come to be his favorite style, Hail to Reason got away well, took the outside path on the turn, and went to the front at the top of the stretch. He won by four and a half lengths from the second-choice Itsa Great Day, which got the nose-nose-neck decision for second over Ross Sea, Carry Back, and Beau Prince." Those who have followed such matters in sufficient detail over the past few decades will recognize that the description would fit some of the tales of dominance from Secretariat's juvenile campaign of twelve years later.

Hail to Reason had clinched the juvenile colt title and with such rich events as the Futurity, Champagne, and Garden State stakes still in the offing.

Then misfortune struck. On a Sunday morning at Aqueduct, on the weekend following the September 10 World's Playground, Hail to Reason (apparently) smashed down on a horseshoe that some other animal had thrown and lurched just enough to cause a grave injury. Both sesamoids of the left front fetlock were fractured.

"Diabolical fate," Hirsch Jacobs was said to mutter at least once during that dark morning, but he would not accede to comments that the injury was too severe for the horse to be saved.

Sunday racing in North America was still a few years in the distance, and the veterinary corps of the backstretch did not routinely go to the track on Sundays. Jacobs' son and assistant, John W. Jacobs, later provided a succinct, dramatic account, crediting his father for saving Hail to Reason: "There were no veterinarians around that early. I grabbed his leg. Father had me hold it up so he wouldn't step down on his ankle."

The injured colt was hauled back to his stall in a horse ambulance, manned by an African-American whom the backstretch knew as Old Blue. John Jacobs has a searing memory that when "Old Blue came up he said to my father, 'Mr. Jacobs, are you going to destroy him here or after we get him back to the barn?' My father said, 'If I have to put that leg back on myself I'm not going to destroy him.'"

In those days, with no veterinarian present, "we had no tranquilizers," John Jacobs recalled. "When we got him back to the stall, Father rolled a plaster of Paris cast on the leg."

Mrs. Jacobs' memory fused that of horsewoman, wife, and mother. She recalled that Hirsch Jacobs "stayed with him all night. He broke through the cast once, and my husband put another one on him. I was worried about Patrice. We went to the barn, and the horse was laying down in the stall, and she held his head in her lap."

John Jacobs takes up the drama again: "It was life and death for two months, and it was a miracle Father pulled him through." He credited Hail to Reason's intelligence as well as his father's acumen: "He was a very smart horse. He would lie down and just lay there. When they brought him his feed, he would get up carefully to eat and then lie down again. He knew how badly he was hurt. He kept the weight off."

The farm where Bieber-Jacobs mares were often boarded, and where Hail to Reason would stand, was Hagyard Farm, owned by a distinguished Bluegrass veterinarian, Charles Hagyard. He, too, gave tribute to Hirsch Jacobs as "a damned good horseman ... [the horse] was still in a cast and couldn't put any weight on the injured hoof [when he arrived at the Kentucky farm]. I called in a blacksmith and elevated the shoe about an inch or an inch and a half, and he immediately commenced bearing weight on it. He wasn't a sound horse by any means for a couple of years, but he had no real problem covering mares."

Hail to Reason prevailed as the champion two-year-old in balloting in 1960. He had won nine of eighteen races, and, more importantly, six of his last seven, and earned $328,434.

The year Hail to Reason starred at two, Bieber-Jacobs won the Gallorette Stakes with Sister Antoine. This was a Royal Serenade filly from the sentimentally named Our Patrice, by Bull Lea. The following year Sister

Antoine won a more important race, the Santa Margarita.

Hail to Reason was both a product and harbinger of the Bieber-Jacobs Stable's prowess as a breeder to match its status as a racing stable. The spring the colt was a gawky two-year-old taking time to become a champion, the Bieber-Jacobs foal crop included a lovely daughter of Searching. The filly was by the 1956 Horse of the Year Swaps, again illustrating the luxury that Hirsch Jacobs had earned in being able to reach out to top-class stallions. The man who had won stakes with the offspring of such pedestrian sires as Basileus II and Agitator now could write down the most exclusive names in his scribblings on overnights when he so chose.

If left to Bieber, a foal by Swaps—Searching might have been named something like No Hostage Deals, Notonyourlife, or Hunt for Victims. Left to more gentle touches, the filly lucked out with the graceful name Affectionately, and she was assigned to race in the name of Mrs. Ethel D. Jacobs. (We run the risk of overstating the dichotomy of naming patterns. After all, Bieber once raced a filly named Petticoat. Turf writers longed for her to finish third, creating the opportunity to note that "Isidor Bieber's Petticoat showed.")

Jacobs had the special filly honed and ready for action on January 17 of her two-year-old season, 1962. Affectionately dashed three furlongs in :33 1/5 at Santa Anita and was a maiden no more. Those early maiden races provided opportunities for plenty of experience only if a horse did not win, so with her eligibility for maiden races foreclosed, Affectionately did not race again for more than three months. At Aqueduct she picked up with two overnight wins before graduating to stakes prominence with victories in the Fashion, Polly Drummond, and National Stallion stakes.

Affectionately suffered a setback in Monmouth Park's Colleen Stakes but got revenge on winner No Resisting in the Astoria Stakes. Back at Monmouth, she further erased the image of her earlier defeat by whipping Fashion Verdict by five lengths in the Sorority Stakes. Nalee was third. (Fashion Verdict and No Resisting were among the last stakes winners trained by Sunny Jim Fitzsimmons, who retired the following year.)

At Saratoga, Affectionately defeated Nalee in the Spinaway, running her record to nine wins from ten starts. It proved her last win of the year, however. Next, in the Matron, Affectionately met her counterpart from the Midwest, Smart Deb, and after dueling a quarter-mile in a 2006-like time of :21 3/5 and a half-mile in :44 2/5, she retreated. Smart Deb won and also prevailed in the Thoroughbred Racing Associations and *Daily Racing Form* ballots for the two-year-old filly championship.

Another stakes winner for the stable in 1962 was Art Market (To Market—Drakensburg, by Admiral Drake), who won the Arcadia and San Gabriel handicaps at four at Santa Anita.

At three Affectionately had a disappointing season, failing to win a stakes race until she took the Interborough Handicap in November. At four and five, however, she rebounded to win a variety of races and solidified her status for the Hall of Fame, to which she was elected in 1989. Her four-year-old season ended with a winning streak that reached five races before she dead heated with Chop House in the Las Flores Handicap in California. The streak included a win over males in the seven-furlong Vosburgh Handicap.

Hirsch Jacobs and Isidor Bieber always knew they were running a business as well as a sporting enterprise. During part of Affectionately's career, the stable endured a mediocre period. In such a situation Jacobs would not necessarily refuse to sell some horses. The former secretary of the treasury and major Thoroughbred breeder, George W. Humphrey, approached Jacobs about buying Affectionately. Jacobs replied he would rather not sell Affectionately, but suggested Humphrey think about the dam, Searching. Nevertheless, Humphrey secured permission to send trainer Sherrill Ward to inspect Affectionately and said he would have someone go inspect Searching at the farm in Kentucky.

John Jacobs recalled that, at that time, Affectionately was not at her best: "She had been hitting the inside of an ankle, and there was a healed-up gash that did not look so good. Sherrill Ward turned her down."

Humphrey purchased Searching for $150,000. He had a broodmare from the La Troienne line he admired, and Bieber-Jacobs still had her daughter.

Only one championship came Affectionately's way, that being the sprinter title in 1965. While the majority of her races were sprints, she also raced to an eight-length victory at nine furlongs in the Top Flight Handicap in the spring of her five-year-old season. She left the highly accomplished Steeple Jill and the champion Old Hat in her wake. John Jacobs recalled that his father stipulated he would not have run Affectionately in the Top Flight had it been at Belmont instead of Aqueduct. On the larger Belmont oval, the distance is run around one turn. Contrary to popular notion, Jacobs thought a one-turn race of a mile and one-eighth was tougher than the same distance around two turns, believing that turns provide a sort of breather.

The Top Flight performance emboldened Jacobs to enter Affectionately for the one-mile Metropolitan Handicap. In the days of Stymie, one of his rivals had been the gallant distaffer Gallorette. Now the gender challenge emanated from Jacobs' camp.

Affectionately faced the brilliant runner Gun Bow and was getting nine pounds of actual weight from him. She led for a long way, with blazing fractions, but after six furlongs in 1:08 1/5, Gun Bow had her number and began to draw away. Affectionately wound up third, as Chieftain came along to pass her, too, and she was beaten about four lengths. She was giving four pounds in actual weight to Chieftain.

Any fear that such a grinding race would put a chink in her spirit proved unfounded when Affectionately came back nine days later to win the six-furlong Liberty Belle against other fillies and mares. She carried 132 pounds and won by six lengths in 1:09 2/5.

The weight went up to an unusually high 137 for the seven-furlong Vagrancy, but Jacobs did not blink. Walter Blum, Affectionately's regular rider that year, put her on the lead, and she sped a half-mile in :44 3/5 and six furlongs in 1:09 1/5. She had a six-length lead at that point, when reality set in. Sought After (111) was closing strongly, but Affectionately gamed it out to win by a head.

This effort earned her a try at something for which she really was not particularly suited, but she deserved the opportunity. Stretched to one and a quarter miles for the historic Suburban Handicap, she carried 119 pounds, giving weight by scale to winner Pia Star. Affectionately raced along in the middle of the back early, but fell back. She drifted out in the stretch and was beaten twenty-five lengths.

After a rest of two and a half months, Jacobs produced Affectionately, without a prep, for a major challenge — the one-mile Maskette. She was sharp enough to engage in a splendid battle with the champion filly Tosmah. Each carried 128 pounds, and they raced head and head through fractions of :44 4/5 and 1:08 4/5. Neither wilted, and Tosmah's margin of victory was only a nose. The final time was 1:35 1/5. Third was Bieber-Jacobs' Straight Deal, a developing three-year-old headed for her own championship status.

Affectionately was retired at the end of that year with a career record of twenty-eight wins from fifty-two starts and earnings of $546,660.

The years 1959–67 saw a flurry of Kentucky Derby entries for Bieber-Jacobs. Two fourth-place finishes were the best results. Jacobs had made his first Derby bid when Palestinian was third in 1949. He returned to Churchill Downs ten years later with Our Dad but got nothing, as the horse finished fifteenth. John Jacobs was trainer of record when Dr. Miller ran in the Derby in Mrs. Jacobs' colors in 1961. Dr. Miller finished fourth behind Carry Back. Hirsch Jacobs was back in 1963, when Bonjour was sixth in Patrice's colors. In 1965 Bieber-Jacobs' Flag Raiser earned a trip to the Derby when he defeated champion and winter-book Derby favorite Bold Lad in the Wood Memorial, but he finished only eighth behind Lucky Debonair. The next year saw Exhibitionist ninth behind Kauai King, and then in 1967 Hirsch Jacobs had his best Derby finish since Palestinian when Reason to Hail ran fourth behind Proud Clarion.

Aside from Flag Raiser, these horses had not been highly promoted in the pre-classics considerations, but they were not forlorn hopes entered for the Derby just for the sake of running. How antithetical that would have been to Jacobs' philosophy of horsemanship.

Bonjour (Prince Khaled—Muriel W., by Stymie) won the Derby Trial, then run on Tuesday of Derby Week, Jacobs recalling the lesson of Ben Jones and Ponder. Bonjour had won the Tremont Stakes at two, and he also won the Governor's Gold Cup and Roseben Handicap during his career, in which he captured nine of sixty-two races and earned $252,162.

Flag Raiser (Rough'n Tumble—Larks War, by War Relic) had an exceptional three-year-old campaign in 1965. In addition to the Wood Memorial, he won the Gotham, Bay Shore, and Withers stakes as well as the Stuyvesant and Princeton handicaps. At five he added the Atlantic City Handicap. Flag Raiser won twenty-one of seventy-five races and earned $391,915.

Exhibitionist (Promised Land—Michaels Angel, by Goya II) also won the Derby Trial, and he won the Woodlawn Stakes after his failure in the Derby. He won a total of four stakes at three and had a record of eight wins in forty-nine starts and earnings of $166,824.

Reason to Hail (Hail to Reason—Drakensberg, by Admiral Drake) had won the Tyro Stakes at two and the California Derby at three among four wins in thirty-seven career starts. He earned $191,382.

ALL HAIL

The era of Hail to Reason as an important stallion began in 1964. Admiring, from his first crop, became his first stakes winner when she won the Arlington-Washington Lassie for Bieber-Jacobs. The Lassie was Admiring's only stakes victory in a career of seven wins from forty-three starts and earnings of $184,581. That 1964 season marked an incredible milestone, for Bieber-Jacobs prevailed as the leading breeder in earnings in North America for the first time, with $1,301,677. Triangle Publications, then the record keeper for the industry, recognized Bieber, Mrs. Jacobs, and Patrice Jacobs as separate individual owners, working against the likelihood of any of them ever leading the owners' list. Wheatley Stable was the leading owner of 1964, and W.C. Winfrey, with the powerful duo of Wheatley Stable and Ogden Phipps, prevailed as leading trainer.

Admiring was the first of a pair of major winners resulting from Searching being bred to Hail to Reason. The next one was better, for she was Priceless Gem, famed for her defeat of the champion colt Buckpasser in the Futurity of 1965. Priceless Gem really came to hand for Jacobs that fall, for she also won the one-mile Frizette Stakes. Following Affectionately and Admiring, Priceless Gem was the third major winner foaled from Searching.

In Priceless Gem's year, as had been the case when Affectionately was two, a campaign that generally would have secured the two-year-old filly championship fell short. Moccasin went through the season unbeaten. She and Priceless Gem never met, and Moccasin prevailed in balloting in the division and was even named Horse of the Year by one poll.

Bieber-Jacobs repeated as leading breeder in 1965, with $1,994,649. The total was the second highest ever to that time, exceeded only by Calumet Farm's $2 million-plus as breeder in 1952. Also in 1965, Hirsch Jacobs led the trainers' list in earnings for the only time, with $1,331,628.

In addition to Affectionately, Priceless Gem, and Flag Raiser, the stable that year won stakes with Straight Deal, Turn to Reason, Hospitality, Isle of Greece, and Power of Destiny. Hospitality (Hail to Reason—Our Patrice, by Bull Lea) gained a unique distinction at two that year when he dead-heated with rising champion Buckpasser in the National Stallion Stakes. It was a hint of exalted status that was not to be duplicated. Isle of Greece (Porterhouse—Lysistrata, by Palestinian) contributed a rich score in winning the $75,000 Governor's Gold Cup at Bowie.

Straight Deal was another by Hail to Reason, and her emergence rescued No Fiddling's career as a broodmare from stark disappointment. The dam, a King Cole mare from Big Hurry, was seventeen years old when she foaled Straight Deal, her only stakes winner.

Despite the two-year-old form of Priceless Gem and some of the others, the expectation that the Hail to Reasons might come along late was fulfilled in Straight Deal. At three she won the Hollywood Oaks and then defeated Steeple Jill and other older fillies and mares in the mile and a quarter Ladies Handicap in the fall. The Ladies had been shortened from a mile and a half that year, but at the time was still one of the most important distaff races in New York.

In 1966 Bieber-Jacobs led the breeders' list for a third time with $1,575,027, but the year was one of alarm and sadness. That summer Jacobs suffered a stroke. Although he recovered, the crisis set into his mind the need to reduce the size of the stable to simplify the family's handling of whatever might come next. Bieber agreed to the plan. While still hospitalized, Jacobs began organizing a reduction consignment. Within a few months Bieber-Jacobs Stable sold thirty-five horses of racing age and eighteen yearlings at Saratoga. The older horses brought $1,370,300, an average of $39,151, and the yearlings brought $157,400, an average of $8,744. To place these figures into a perspective within the Thoroughbred markets at the time, the Keeneland summer yearling sale that year averaged $18,206 and the broodmares sold in the Keeneland November mixed sale averaged $6,035.

The ultimate seal of approval on the fashion of Bieber-Jacobs came within the auction when two of the highest-profile buyers of the day, Charles W. Engelhard and Paul Mellon, put together an impromptu partnership to bid on Admiring as a broodmare. The potent Engelhard-Mellon combine bought Admiring for a record $310,000. This was $75,000 more than the previous broodmare record of $235,000, paid for Berlo at the William du Pont Jr. estate dispersal earlier in the same year.

In addition to the horses in the dispersal, two shares in Hail to Reason brought top bids of $162,000 and $161,000. (John Jacobs recalled that his father was among horsemen of the day who were careful about how many mares a horse covered. He said his father had it written into the syndicate agreement that Hail to Reason would cover thirty-two mares a year: "There were thirty shares, and nobody got an extra season. There were two breeding rights, one for Dr. Hagyard and another [providing a season] to be sold every year to cover the horse's maintenance.")

Bieber-Jacobs continued dispersing horses at major sales across the country that year, ending with Keeneland in November. The average for the 153 horses sold was $20,095.

With John Jacobs assuming day-to-day training duties, the stable raced ahead despite the reduction. Regal Gleam had won the Blue Hen Stakes that summer, and in the fall she put together two major wins, in the Frizette Stakes and Selima Stakes, to secure the juvenile filly championship. Regal Gleam represented a confluence of many Bieber-Jacobs elements. She was another sired by Hail to Reason, and her dam, Miz Carol, was a Stymie mare out of the resurgent influence No Fiddling. Miz Carol had brought $139,000 at Keeneland. Regal Gleam won only three allowance races from nineteen starts the following year and was retired with eight victories from thirty-two races and earnings of $246,793.

Straight Deal came back at four to increase her status but could not quite wrest the older distaff championship that was shared by Open Fire and Summer Scandal. Straight Deal made twenty starts that year, from January at Santa Anita through November at Aqueduct. She won five important races, the Santa Barbara, Santa Margarita, Bed o' Roses, Sheepshead Bay, and Firenze handicaps. She was second to Summer Scandal in the Maskette and Beldame during the autumn.

Other stakes winners for Bieber-Jacobs in 1966 were Turn to Reason, Be Suspicious, Understanding, and Isle of Greece. Be Suspicious was an arch example of the Bieber naming scheme, for she was out of Nothirdchance. Turn to Reason (Hail to Reason—Insolence, by Mahmoud) won the $50,000 Tropical Park Handicap, having won the Christmas Handicap and a division of the Illinois Derby the previous year.

By the following year, 1967, Hirsch Jacobs had returned to work, but continued to rely heavily on his son for assistance. That season, Straight Deal broke through as a champion, with another January–November campaign. This one comprised twenty-two starts. "Straight Deal was hickory," wrote William H. Rudy in *Racing in America (1960–79)*. "This 16 hands, 2 1/4-inch daughter of Hail to Reason went about her business without flair; lost a lot of races, won a lot of big ones."

That year she began in Florida, where she won a division of the Orchid Handicap and lost the Black Helen Handicap by a nose to Mac's Sparkler. In New York, Straight Deal won the Top Flight and Bed o' Roses handicaps. In Delaware she won the $100,000 Delaware Handicap. In New Jersey she took the Vineland Handicap. Finally, in Kentucky she survived a ragged start in which jockey Howard Grant lost a stirrup iron and came home on top in the Spinster Stakes. Along the way Straight Deal defeated Gamely, Politely, Mac's Sparkler, and other contenders of the day. In two of her three ventures against males that season, she was third behind Stupendous and Ring Twice in the Whitney and third behind champion Damascus and Ring Twice in the Aqueduct Handicap. She won older female honors on both major polls then extant.

Bieber-Jacobs rode the prowess of Straight Deal to its fourth consecutive term as leading breeder, with $1,515,414. With so much of its treasure having been dispersed in 1966, Bieber-Jacobs would not lead the list again. Aside from Calumet Farm, which once led the breeders' list eleven times consecutively, only Harry Payne Whitney (nine years) had equaled the Bieber-Jacobs reign of four seasons. (In later years, E.P. Taylor led the list for seven consecutive years, and Allen Paulson and Harry Mangurian each led for four years.)

Supporting Straight Deal in 1967 were additional stakes winners Reflected Glory, Flag Raiser, Wise Exchange, and Reason to Hail. Reflected Glory (Jester—Lysistrata, by Palestinian) excited Kentucky Derby hopes during the winter when he won the progression of Hialeah's best three-year-old stakes, the Bahamas, Everglades, and Flamingo. However, he hurt a knee and did not make it to the Derby. As noted above, the stable did have a Derby starter that year, in fourth-placed Reason to Hail.

The following year, 1968, brought another Flamingo Stakes victory, with Wise Exchange (Promised Land—Coastal Trade, by Coastal Traffic). Wise Exchange added the Fountain of Youth Stakes at Gulfstream Park but got hurt just before the Florida Derby and also dropped off the Triple Crown trail.

In 1969 the stable landed its second Futurity Stakes in five seasons. High Echelon (Native Charger—Luquillo, by Princequillo) had a splendid autumn. In addition to the Futurity he stretched out to a mile and one-sixteenth and added the Pimlico-Laurel Futurity.

DEATH, AND ITS EPILOGUE

Hirsch Jacobs was hospitalized during the winter of 1969–70, diagnosed with an arterial blockage that hampered blood flow to the brain. Prior to that time one particular colt had held the family's attention. This was a handsome fellow by Hail to Reason and the first foal out of champion Affectionately. Jacobs had been known to show Turf writers a photo of the colt as a youngster, a bit of promotion that was so unlike Jacobs that it underscored just how excited he was about the prospect. The colt was christened Personality, after the name of a popular song that Mrs. Jacobs and Patrice recalled hearing over and over while staying in a Louisville hotel on one of their Derby trips.

In 1970, gravely ill and having trouble talking, Hirsch Jacobs gazed at another picture of the colt. It was the win photo from Personality's sprint victory the previous week, and son John had brought it to the hospital room in the Miami Heart Institute.

"He took the picture and held it for the longest time. He kept looking at it and studying it," John Jacobs later recalled, "and I remember thinking, 'What is he looking for?' He was having trouble talking then, and finally, he sort of pointed toward his eyes, and said, 'No blinkers?' I said there were no blinkers, and Dad studied it a little longer and then sort of whispered, 'Do better — blinkers.' "

His last jewel of racetrack savvy thus safely delivered, Hirsch Jacobs lapsed into a coma four days later and soon passed away. He was sixty-five.

A Hollywood version would have had John Jacobs fitting Personality with blinkers and saddling him to win the Kentucky Derby. This did not happen, but reality in its own way was prepared to outdo romantic fiction. Personality failed in the Derby, with blinkers, but he won the Wood Memorial and Preakness with them. Hirsch Jacobs had won 3,596 races, the all-time record at the time, and had won stakes with fifty-one horses but had never won a classic race. Now, his son John had achieved this distinction, and with a sentimentally special colt who carried Mrs. Jacobs' silks.

More astonishing was the next chapter. Personality won the Jersey Derby after the Preakness but then caught a cold and was forced out of the Belmont Stakes. Jacobs had also run High Echelon in the Kentucky Derby, where he finished third, and in the Jersey Derby, when he was fourth, and substituted him in the Belmont. It was an archetypal case of Jacobs wisdom, of either generation. High Echelon was a difficult horse and did not like to train. Jacobs believes his race in the Jersey Derby kept him fit enough that he was able to score his subsequent victory in the Belmont Stakes. John W. Jacobs thus had won two classic races the same spring with different horses.

Personality came back in the fall and won the Woodward Stakes to secure the three-year-old championship, as well as, on the TRA poll, Horse of the Year honors — Bieber-Jacobs' first such title.

Such a flurry of wins, however, was a short-lived phenomenon in the aftermath of Hirsch Jacobs' death. Jacobs had an agreement with Bieber that upon the trainer's death the horses would be dispersed. He apparently felt he would thereby protect his widow from the complications of dealing with the financial aspects of keeping the stable and breeding operation going.

In the four years since the reduction, the numbers of horses had been built back up, and in the summer and fall of 1970, at Saratoga in August and Keeneland in November, Bieber-Jacobs sold thirty-six horses for $1,844,400, an average of $51,233. Priceless Gem topped the sale at $395,000, setting a new record for a broodmare at auction.

Sold privately as a weanling was Priceless Gem's Sea-Bird II filly, who would carry the name Allez France and the Daniel Wildenstein colors. Extending the Bieber-Jacobs influence abroad, Allez France became an idol of the French racing fans, and her many victories included the 1974 Prix de l'Arc de Triomphe. Also sold privately was Regal Gleam, who was purchased by Claiborne Farm and produced major winner Royal Glint. Regal Gleam also became the second dam of European classic winner and international stallion Caerleon.

Hail to Reason's stallion career coincided with the long reign of Bold Ruler, but the Bieber-Jacobs horse did manage to lead the sire list on one occasion, in 1970. He had the distinction of siring a winner of each of the American Triple Crown races: Kentucky Derby (Proud Clarion, 1967), Preakness (Personality, 1970), and Belmont Stakes (Hail to All, 1965). Hail to Reason also sired the English Derby winner Roberto, identified as a key influence of soundness and stamina in a sire line that flourishes today. The sire line is that of 2006 Kentucky Derby winner Barbaro and other contemporary group/grade winners.

Isidor Bieber died in 1974. The Jacobs family had not totally abandoned racing and breeding. With the assistance and encouragement of family friend Louis Wolfson, they saved out a few favorites, including Straight Deal and Affectionately, and enjoyed a continuity of stakes winners through Mrs. Jacobs' death in 2001. Son John Jacobs segued from training into a successful bloodstock advisory business. As a young man, the Jacobses' other son, Tom, worked for his father briefly and then moved on to a career in promotion. This proved helpful in promoting the Bieber-Jacobs reduction and dispersal sales.

Wolfson had been an admirer of Hirsch Jacobs and had befriended the family. Wolfson once had a good stakes-winning filly named Royal Patrice. He and Patrice Jacobs were married in 1972, and some of the Bieber-Jacobs stock was melded into Wolfson's own Harbor View Farm operation. The Wolfsons were to enjoy the thrills of Affirmed's Triple Crown and his epic duels with Alydar and later the championships of the Affirmed mare Flawlessly.

So much success, thus, was founded and nurtured for many years by the keen insights of Hirsch Jacobs.

"He was elected to the Hall of Fame in 1958, along with Ben Jones and Sunny Jim Fitzsimmons," daughter Patrice recalled. "They were the first living trainers inducted. He was elected as a trainer, but his real achievement was breeding and also training those horses of the 1960s.

"My father was the complete horseman, probably the Federico Tesio of American racing."

Photo credits

Cover photo: (Keeneland-Cook)

Page 1: James Rowe Sr. (Keeneland-Cook), Rowe with H.P. Whitney and Regret (National Museum of Racing), Colin (Keeneland-Cook)

Page 2: Sam Hildreth portrait (Keeneland-Cook); Zev (Blood-Horse Library); Hildreth in paddock (Keeneland-Cook)

Page 3: H. Guy Bedwell and J.K.L. Ross (Keeneland-Cook); Bedwell with group (Hugh Miller); Bedwell and Sir Barton (R.L. McClure)

Pages 4-5: John E. Madden and Max Hirsch (Keeneland-Cook); Hamburg (Blood-Horse Library); Madden head shot (Keeneland-Cook); Madden and Hildreth (Keeneland-Cook)

Pages 6-7: Max Hirsch and Robert Kleberg (Blood-Horse Library); Hirsch with Assault (Bert Morgan); Hirsch head shot (Paul Schafer/NYRA)

Pages 8-9: Sunny Jim Fitzsimmons (Bert Clark Thayer); Fitzsimmons with Bold Ruler (Baltimore Sun); Fitzsimmons with trophies (Bert and Richard Morgan)

Pages 10-11: H.J. Thompson (Brownie Leach); Thompson and Fitzsimmons (Blood-Horse Library); Burgoo King (Kinetic Corp.)

Pages 12-13: Preston and Elliott Burch (Bert and Richard Morgan); Preston and W.P. Burch (Keeneland-Cook); Bold (Maryland Jockey Club); Burch with Isabel Dodge Sloane and Leslie Combs II (Skeets Meadors)

Pages 14-15: Ben and Jimmy Jones with trophy (Hialeah Photo); With Citation in Derby winner's circle (Churchill Downs); With Warren Wright, et al. (Arlington Park); Ben Jones (Stan Taylor)

Page 16: Hirsch Jacobs (Bert and Richard Morgan); Jacobs leading horse (Blood-Horse Library); Stymie (NYRA)

ABOUT THE
AUTHOR

Edward L. Bowen is considered one of Thoroughbred racing's most insightful and erudite writers. A native of West Virginia, Bowen grew up in South Florida, where he became enamored of racing while watching televised stakes from Hialeah.

Bowen entered journalism school at the University of Florida in 1960, then transferred to the University of Kentucky in 1963 so he could work as a writer for *The Blood-Horse*, the leading weekly Thoroughbred magazine. From 1968 to 1970, he served as editor of The *Canadian Horse*, then returned to *The Blood-Horse* as managing editor. He rose to the position of editor-in-chief before leaving the publication in 1993.

Bowen is president of the Grayson-Jockey Club Research Foundation, which raises funds for equine research. In addition to *Masters of the Turf*, Bowen is the author of seventeen other books, including *Belmont Park: A Century of Champions, Man o' War, At the Wire: Horse Racing's Greatest Moments*, and the two-volume set, *Legacies of the Turf*. Bowen has won the Eclipse Award for magazine writing, as well as other writing awards. He lives in Versailles, Kentucky, with his wife, Ruthie, and son, George. Bowen has two grown daughters, Tracy Bowen and Jennifer Schafhauser, and two grandchildren.